HOLLYWOOD IN CRISIS

October 1929 saw the Wall Street Crash, heralding the Great Depression and the descent of American society into a decade of political, social and economic turmoil. How did the cinema industry respond to this period of uncertainty and social upheaval? What links can be traced between the movies and the real threat of an American revolution?

Hollywood in Crisis is a detailed study of the workings of the American film industry during the 1930s. Colin Shindler looks at Hollywood as an agent of Roosevelt's New Deal and the attempts film moguls and movie-makers made to withstand the political turmoil that threatened to engulf America. Shindler illustrates how the studios and their product, from the glamour of MGM stars and escapist musicals to gangster movies and Westerns, even to the 'radical' films of the Warner studios, helped foster ideas of social unity and patriotism.

Hollywood in Crisis makes considerable use of original studio archives and the recently released files from the Hays Office, and draws on interviews recorded over twenty years with industry figures from Henry Fonda, Frank Capra and Robert Lord to the leader of the Hollywood Communist Party, John Howard Lawson. Colin Shindler's study redefines the way in which the golden years of Hollywood will be understood.

Colin Shindler was born in Lancashire and educated at Bury Grammar School and Caius College, Cambridge. He is a television producer and has worked on many dramas from *A Little Princess* to *Lovejoy*, and wrote the screenplay for *Buster*. He is the author of *Hollywood goes to War* (1980). Colin lives in London with his American wife, two children and the neurosis which comes from supporting Manchester City.

CINEMA AND SOCIETY
General Editor: Jeffrey Richards
Department of History, University of Lancaster

Also available in this series:

HOLLYWOOD IN CRISIS

Cinema and American society 1929–1939

Colin Shindler

London and New York

First published 1996
by Routledge
11 New Fetter Lane, London EC4P 4EE

Simultaneously published in the USA and Canada
by Routledge
29 West 35th Street, New York, NY 10001

Routledge is an International Thomson Publishing company I(T)P

© 1996 Colin Shindler

Typeset in Times by Routledge
Printed and bound in Great Britain by Clays Ltd, St. Ives PLC

British Library Cataloguing in Publication Data
A catalogue record for this book is available from the British Library

Library of Congress Cataloguing in Publication Data
A catalogue record for this book has been requested

ISBN 0–415–10313–4 (hbk)
ISBN 0–415–10314–2 (pbk)

To Steve and Freda
For a lifetime of every kind of nourishment

CONTENTS

GENERAL EDITOR'S PREFACE

The pre-eminent popular art form of the first half of the twentieth century has been the cinema. Both in Europe and America from the turn of the century to the 1950s cinema-going has been a regular habit and film-making a major industry. The cinema combined all the other art forms – painting, sculpture, music, the word, the dance – and added a new dimension – and illusion of life. Living, breathing people enacted dramas before the gaze of the audience and not, as in the theatre, bounded by the stage, but with the world as their back drop. Success at the box office was to be obtained by giving the people something to which they could relate and which therefore reflected themselves. Like the other popular art form, the cinema has much to tell us about people and their beliefs, their assumptions and their attitudes, their hopes and their fears and dreams.

This series of books will examine the connection between films and the societies which produced them. Film as straight historical evidence; film as an unconscious reflection of national preoccupations; film as escapist entertainment; film as a weapon of propaganda – these are aspects of the question that will concern us. We shall seek to examine and delineate individual film *genres*, the cinematic images of particular nations and the work of key directors who have mirrored national concerns and ideals. For we believe that the rich and multifarious products of the cinema constitute a still largely untapped source of knowledge about the ways in which our world and the people in it have changed since the first flickering images were projected on to the silver screen.

Jeffrey Richards

PREFACE

This book is an examination of the relationship between American history and the American film industry in the ten years before the outbreak of the Second World War in Europe. It is not a history of Hollywood during those years, nor does it pretend to be a revolutionary approach to the study of American history during the 1930s.

Instead, the book throws a sharp spotlight on an area of American history which has not previously proved of much interest. The films which interest me, as a historian, are not necessarily those which have previously captivated film historians who have written about this decade. Although they both emerged from MGM in 1933, Gregory La Cava's *Gabriel Over the White House* is more significant for me than Cukor's all-star version of *Dinner at Eight*.

There are plenty of histories of Hollywood in the 1930s. Libraries can scarcely make shelf space for all the biographies of the stars of the period. The use of the recently opened studio files, together with the oral testimony placed in historical context of those who lived and worked in Hollywood in the 1930s, I hope makes for a different view.

My own subjective view of movie-making is that it represents the triumph of hope over the combined forces of ill-tempered Nature, unwanted executive interference and directorial urges which ought to be suppressed. Film historians and critics have rarely sat on a dining bus and watched the rain cancel shooting for the day, sending the budget into overspend. They have never sat and watched their own rushes, bemused by the director's inspired touches which have transformed a carefully written scene into one of total incomprehension.

The man who first taught me what to expect as a working writer–producer was Robert Lord, a much respected practitioner of this hyphenated art whom Hal Wallis regarded as his most reliable colleague at Warner Brothers during these years. His name and his influence are to be found with some regularity on the following pages. He survived the Hollywood factory system to emerge with credits ranging from *Little Caesar* and *Gold Diggers of 1933* to *The Private Lives of Elizabeth and Essex* and *The Letter*. He knew that the movies of his era did not spring fully formed from the creative loins of the studio's directors. It is his philosophy which has shaped the nature of the history to be found in this book.

ACKNOWLEDGEMENTS

The basic research for this book was originally conducted as part of a doctoral thesis awarded by the University of Cambridge in 1974. Recently many of the studio archives, unavailable in the 1970s, have been deposited for scholarly inspection in the libraries of American universities. I am hopeful that the book benefits from the recollections of the original participants as well as the insights derived from the new primary material.

I am grateful, therefore, at last to be able to acknowledge the vital contribution made to this study by Neil McKendrick and Gonville & Caius College, Cambridge, whose timely financial intervention permitted the thesis to be written and a long-standing marriage to take place.

Many of the films discussed in this book were first seen during an invaluable year spent as Research Fellow at the American Film Institute's Center for Advanced Film Studies in Beverly Hills. I am happy to record the thanks I owe to the staff and facilities of the Margaret Herrick Library of the Academy of Motion Picture Arts and Sciences and to the British Film Institute in London. At the Doheny Library of the University of Southern California I greatly appreciated the help given by Ned Comstock and Stuart Ng of the Warner Brothers Special Collections. Acknowledgement is made to The Samuel Goldwyn Company for permission to reproduce lyrics from *Roman Scandals* (1993).

Apart from Robert Lord, who, sadly, died in 1976, a number of people have provided the professional or personal help to enable me to write this book. The editor of this series, Professor Jeffrey Richards, has been a source of constant support and personal encouragement on both this book and its predecessor, *Hollywood Goes to War*. Professor Jack Pole has guided me with deft skill throughout my years of study under him. In more recent times my wife Lynn, whom I met in an otherwise empty movie theatre during a screening of *Boys Town*, has provided me with the comfort and inspiration without which no writer can exist. My children, Amy and David, have grown up with a love of classic Hollywood musicals from a precociously early age, which has been a source of great comfort to their father if a source of bewilderment to their friends.

1

SNAPSHOT

Hollywood and the nation, September 1929

Go to a motion picture ... and let yourself go. Before you know it, you are living the story – laughing, hating, struggling, winning! All the adventure, all the romance, all the excitement you lack in your daily life are in Pictures. They take you completely out of yourself into a wonderful new world ... out of the cage of everyday existence! If only for an afternoon or evening – escape!

Robert S. Lynd and Helen Merrell Lynd, *Middletown*

On 3 September 1929 the Dow Jones average of stock market prices reached its peak before the Crash which was to begin seven weeks later. On 3 September 1939 Great Britain declared war on Germany. Between these two events lay a decade of political, economic and social turmoil from which the American film industry, despite its apparent rude health, was not immune. Indeed one of the purposes of this book is to evaluate to what extent the changes of the decade were reflected in its motion pictures and conversely to question whether some of those changes were positively caused or at least influenced by the movies. To chart the progress of this decade of change it is necessary to begin by examining the state of the American film industry and the condition of the United States in 1929.

Appropriately enough Hollywood was built on a dream. It wasn't the dream of the Jews who started and operated the major film studios. That came later. The original Hollywood dream was that of Horace Henderson Wilcox and his wife, Daeida. In 1883 they moved from Kansas where they had grown rich in real estate development to Los Angeles where they bought a ranch of 120 acres in the flat waterless country, eight miles north-west of the city centre at the foot of a range of hills. Their dream was to build a Christian Utopia.

In 1887 the Wilcoxes began to subdivide the ranch into small parcels of land which they offered free to any denomination that would erect a house of worship. The Wilcoxes were unreconstructed Methodists, passionate campaigners for Prohibition. All purveyors of alcoholic beverages were strictly forbidden from this spiritually uplifting environment. Daeida called the ranch

Hollywood after the country estate of some friends who lived in her home state of Ohio. The Christian Utopia never materialised but the name stuck.[1]

What lingered after this first dream died was the sensation that Hollywood still offered a geophysical paradise. In the very first days of the pioneers the air was attractively temperate, fragrant with orange blossom, jasmine and eucalyptus. Even in 1929 it was still possible to be astonished by the bunches of red berries on the ubiquitous pepper trees which lined the major roads. The writer and producer Robert Lord who arrived in Hollywood in 1925 recalled vividly nearly fifty years later, 'Los Angeles at that time was a charming place. You had a feeling of the Old West. There were beautiful trees. Hollywood Boulevard was lined with pepper trees, beautiful pepper trees.'[2]

Los Angeles was a veritable cornucopia of flora and fauna which survived the first onrush of the movie pioneers. In 1929 it was still possible to notice the orange pansies and clusters of mariposa dotting the sides of the Hollywood Hills, the geraniums, bougainvillaea, roses and poinsettias growing wild. From the top of the Hills away to the east the snow-capped San Gabriel mountains towered over the desert. Looking westward there was an unobstructed vista for miles all the way to the Pacific Ocean.[3]

Certainly southern California attracted early film-makers because of the variety of its locations and the availability of land, not to mention local wage levels which were half those in New York or San Francisco.[4] It was aided too by its proximity to the Mexico border in the event of financial or legal complications but the effect of working in such an attractive environment is too frequently overlooked entirely. The way in which movie personnel behaved and thought and hence the style and content of their work were to a considerable degree affected by this environment. In 1929 it was still possible to be aware of Hollywood's physical origins.

In 1915 when Rabbi Edgar Magnin arrived in Los Angeles he had found it to be 'a rustic patch of rose-covered bungalows, sighing palms, dirt roads that got impossibly rutted when it rained, an ostrich farm and 400,000 residents'.[5] Those who profited early in the successful westward transplant of the film industry had the pick of the countryside in which to settle. West of Hollywood, Pickfair, the house built by Douglas Fairbanks and Mary Pickford, arose on the ridge between Benedict and Coldwater Canyons, close to Chaplin's stately home on Summit Drive. To the east of the studios on the hills overlooking the Cahuenga Pass were built a rival series of grand houses. Cecil B. DeMille lived in Los Feliz on the eponymous DeMille Drive. In some areas of the San Fernando Valley an acre of land reportedly sold for a nickel. It was in referring to these relatively placid early days that an actor could recall,

> There was nobody out here. Hollywood was a beautiful, sleepy town. At night there was nothing. It was very quiet. The Security Bank at Hollywood and Cahuenga, that was the skyscraper – it must have been

all of four stories – and that intersection was the hub of activity such as it was.[6]

Such tranquillity was destined to be short-lived. Between 1910 and 1920 the population of metropolitan Los Angeles rose from 325,000 to 576,673 but in the next ten years it increased to 1,238,048. In the wake of this population boom facilities were constructed to meet the soaring demand. In 1927 the neo-Gothic fantasy hotel, the Chateau Marmont, opened its doors within weeks of the transformation of Nazimova's home, directly across Sunset Boulevard, into the legendary series of twenty-five separate villas known as the Garden of Allah. The following year saw the completion of the Beverly Wilshire to compete with the long-established Beverly Hills Hotel.[7]

Cultural life in the city struggled to keep pace. In 1916 the Hollywood Bowl was constructed and in 1919 the Los Angeles Philharmonic Orchestra was founded. Already Pasadena had an Academy of Fine Arts, Los Angeles a well-established School of Art and the architects Frank Lloyd Wright and Rudolph Schindler were building some of their most innovative houses in the new city.[8]

Between 1924 and 1927 eight new theatres were built so that by 1929 Los Angeles had a fair representation of cultural organisations and artistic activities. What the city did lack, however, was an intelligentsia, any sense of an intellectual ferment from which movements might be born. This was a deficiency that was to be remedied in the following decade as the power of the movies strengthened and the predominantly Jewish intellectual exiles of central Europe gravitated towards Hollywood.

In the popular imagination the 1920s were a decade of uniform economic growth but such prosperity was really built on construction and the automobile industry – two key trigger industries. It certainly bypassed the farmers and the coal industry altogether. However, the postwar boom released a flood of consumer spending and encouraged the growth of conspicuous consumption, from both of which trends the American film industry benefited enormously.

The superficial results of prosperity in Hollywood were very apparent. On 27 September 1929 Richard Barthelmess signed a new contract with First National which Warner Brothers (who were in the process of negotiating the purchase of First National) were legally obliged to honour. Under the terms of the agreement Barthelmess, whose faltering career had recently been revived by the success of the now-forgotten *The Patent Leather Kid*, was to be paid $187,000 per picture or $7,000 a week. He was able to command such figures because he was one of the few silent movie stars whose first sound film had succeeded.[9]

The effects of the sound revolution were still reverberating through Hollywood in 1929. It was the coming of sound which provided a dramatic climax to the years of studio consolidation. Following the lead of Warner Brothers and the Fox Film Corporation the rest of the studios recognised that sound was not a temporary fad and they began their conversion in 1928. By September 1929 the dominance of talkies was complete in the major urban areas and only small towns were still showing silent pictures with piano accompaniment.

The transformation wrought by the arrival of sound was total. A myriad of technical problems was created whose solution demanded the soundproofing of studios, the wiring of cinemas and the employment of a whole new range of technicians whose services had never previously been necessary. Title writers were supplanted by playwrights, and silent film actors, particularly those of European extraction, were replaced by Broadway actors. MGM were probably the most suspicious of the major studios but once Thalberg saw that the profits from *The Broadway Melody* approached $1.5 million his personal conversion was absolute. In a typical Thalberg manoeuvre MGM raided Broadway and quickly signed Robert Montgomery, Ruth Chatterton, Leslie Howard and John Barrymore. The growl of Wallace Beery and the foghorn of Marie Dressler turned them into stars but John Gilbert's light tenor voice, Mae Murray's squeak, the thick Mexican and French accents of Ramon Novarro and Renee Adoree soon terminated their careers.[10]

It was the biggest revolution to date in the fledgeling film industry but it appeared to have no adverse effect whatsoever on its profitability. None of the companies collapsed, a new one – RKO – was founded and major studios enjoyed a new surge of profits that allowed them to ride out the first years of the imminent Depression.

Between 1926 and 1930 weekly attendance at the movies in America rose by 45 per cent to ninety million paid admissions. In those years the assets of the industry tripled to reach $1 billion.[11] Another source puts the total investment in exhibition real estate at closer to $1,250 million.[12] Certainly, Warner Brothers' assets rose from $5 million in 1925 to $230 million in 1930. They and the Fox Film Corporation owned five hundred cinemas while Paramount, the most acquisitive of the studios, owned over 1,400. In fact the five major studios (Paramount, Warners, Fox, RKO and Loews, the parent company of MGM) owned the crucial 2,600 first-run theatres. They might have been only 16 per cent of the total number of cinemas in the United States but they delivered three-quarters of the total revenues.[13] Each studio owned theatres in the big cities but they carved up the country between them into areas of influence like Great Powers subdividing the African continent for imperial ends. Fox controlled the West Coast as Warner Brothers dominated in Pennsylvania and New Jersey and Paramount in Canada, New England and the South.

The reason for the massive expansion in studio profits in the 1920s lay in the ability of their theatre chains to model themselves on the retailing of major American corporations like Sears, Roebuck and F. W. Woolworth & Co. They regularised costs, booked from a central office and exploited the advantage that came from operating nationally.[14] Additionally, the parent companies divorced the manufacturing process (Hollywood) from the financial decision-making (New York) and employed unit managers (producers) to supervise the production of six to eight films a year within previously agreed budget limits.

They all had substantial production facilities in southern California, a worldwide distribution network and a sizeable chain of cinemas. It might have been the dominance of the companies as distributor-exhibitors rather than the existence of the studios as production centres which was the true source of their economic power but it was the success of this vertically integrated system of operation which gave them the means effectively to exclude other companies. By any other name the major studios operated as a cartel and colluded to keep out competition as far as it was possible.

All parent companies played rival studios' product when it was in both their interests to do so. A successful Warner Brothers film might be good news for Loews Inc. if it played in their cinemas in towns in which Warners didn't own a theatre, although Louis B. Mayer might not have seen it that way. There was considerably more competition between the rival studio heads than there was between the chairmen in New York who shared a common interest in reducing risk and maximising profits. The risk element was thus left to Mayer, Jack Warner, Darryl F. Zanuck and so on in Hollywood at whom the finger of blame could be pointed if their choice of pictures was unsuccessful. It accounts for the deep and abiding hatred within the production chiefs for their nominal employers on the East Coast.

The sound revolution was no doubt an inevitable outcome of the many experiments in research and development which Sam Warner and William Fox in particular had financed in the 1920s. The immediate increase in profits certainly justified the outlay in capital expenditure required by the sound conversion which was estimated at anything up to $500 million. Production budgets virtually doubled as production schedules expanded to incorporate the extra time necessitated by the use of the new cumbersome technical equipment.

Such major financial restructuring exacted its own price. It came in the form of alliances with the Eastern investment banks. The chaotic slapdash Hollywood of the early years with dozens of independent production companies fighting for survival had become by 1929 a tight core of eight powerful studios subdivided into the Big Five (Loews, Warner Brothers, Paramount, Fox and RKO) and the Little Three (Columbia, United Artists and Universal).[15]

Warner Brothers moved into the ranks of the major powers as the result of an alliance with Goldman, Sachs. Waddill Catchings, the head of its investment division, was impressed by the prospects of future growth through strict cost accounting, tight budget control and managerial talent. He agreed to accept a seat on the board as Chairman of the Finance Committee in which capacity he persuaded New York's National Bank of Commerce to lend money. This was followed by four other significant banks and Warners soon had the money in place to purchase Vitagraph Corporation and aggressively pursue the sound revolution. In April 1926 Warner Brothers and General Electric formed Vitaphone.

Other alliances soon followed. Loews Inc. approached Lehman Bros and Paramount joined forces with Kuhn Loeb & Co. The very existence of RKO was the result of this revolution. It had been formed in October 1928 by a merger of RCA and its sound process known as Photophone, with the FBO studios and its limited distribution network and the hundred theatres of the Keith Orpheum vaudeville circuit. RCA, the prime financial mover, failed to sell its Photophone process to Loews or Paramount as it had hoped. On 11 May 1928 United Artists, Paramount and Loews instead signed an agreement with Western Electric. RCA moved quickly to include under its umbrella the NBC radio network, RCA Victor records and music publishing.[16] It was a trend that was to continue in the 1960s with the swallowing of studios like Paramount into the conglomorate Gulf & Western and United Artists into the TransAmerica Corporation. It reached its most recent apogee with the purchase of Columbia by the multinational Sony Corporation.

Other mergers were also proposed at this time. Warner Brothers held talks on a merger with United Artists but Charlie Chaplin swiftly vetoed the move. Instead a new company, United Artists Consolidated, was capitalised at $15 million in January 1929.[17] More significant was the threatened merger of Fox with Loews. In 1927 with the death of its founder, Marcus Loew, the company was ripe for a hostile takeover. The new Chairman, Nicholas Schenck, entered discussions with Harry Warner and Adolph Zukor but the real interest was exhibited by the voracious William Fox.

Fox proposed to buy out MGM and merge it with his own holdings, financing the $50 million deal with a combination of loans from New York investment houses, chief among them Halsey, Stuart and Company, and by the sale of shares in Fox Film Corporation and Fox Theaters. Schenck would emerge from the deal with a commission of $10 million and Fox would control the richest and most powerful studio complex in the world. The deal was signed on 24 February 1929.

It was killed in short time by a combination of events. Although Fox had received a provisional approval from the antitrust division of the Justice Department, Nicholas Schenck was unable to prevent Louis B. Mayer, who deeply resented the manner in which his studio was being carved up without due consultation, referring it to his political friends in the newly installed Hoover administration. Evidence has recently emerged that Mayer was ready to accept a payoff of $2 million to approve the deal but before it could be consumated Fox was badly injured in a car crash and out of action for three critical months.[18]

By the time he had recovered his health the momentum had been lost. Before he could recover the momentum the Stock Market had crashed. Loew's shares lost half their value and Fox was forced by his brokers to cover the margins on which he had bought the stock. He spent $4 million of his own money in a single day rather than sell the stock on a plunging market and compromise his objective of total control. It was a vain bid. Hounded by creditors and lawsuits Fox lost control of his own company and was unable to prevent its merger with the nascent Twentieth Century of Joseph Schenck and Darryl Zanuck. In September 1935 the government issued a demand for $3.5 million in back taxes and forced Fox into bankruptcy. Meanwhile Loews went on to a decade of profits totalling over a hundred million dollars with assets increasing from $128.6 million in 1930 to $161 million in 1940.[19]

Loews was the only company to survive the Depression without sliding into loss at any point, principally because it had acquired so few movie theatres. The combination of the Wall Street Crash and the capital investment demanded by the sound revolution led Fox, Paramount and RKO into receivership. The film industry lost its soul to Wall Street in the years 1928 and 1929 and it was to be thereafter attached irretrievably to the bastions of American capitalism. This underlying economic condition was to assume even greater significance as the film industry and the country at large struggled with the onset of the greatest crisis ever to beset the United States.

Although in many ways Hollywood was uniquely insulated from the rest of the world, partly by its geographical location but mostly by its psychological introspection, the American film industry and its personnel could not avoid being subjected to the wider pressures of life in America in 1929. If we are to understand the Depression of the 1930s and Hollywood's place in it, it is vital to start by understanding the nature of the prosperity of the previous decade.

In the late nineteenth and early twentieth century the productive capacity of the American economy increased at a rate greater than that of the Industrial Revolution. After the First World War the United States, benefiting from its delayed arrival into the Great War (no industry more so than the movies), achieved the highest standard of living any people had ever known. National income soared from $480 per capita in 1900 to $681 in 1929. Real wages rose at an astonishing rate in the decade after the Armistice and at the same time the hours of work were frequently cut. In 1923 US Steel abandoned the conventional twelve-hour day and put its Gary, Indiana plant on an eight-hour shift. In 1926 Henry Ford instituted the five-day week and the famous five dollars a day incentive for workers at his Dearborn factory. A complete automobile rolled off his production line every five seconds of the working day.

With more efficient management, greater mechanisation, intensive research and ingenious sales methods, industrial production almost doubled during the 1920s. Using the years 1933–9 as the 100 base, it was estimated that if the index was at 58 in 1921 it had reached 110 by 1929. While workers' income rose 11 per cent from 1923 to 1929, corporate profits rocketed 62 per cent and dividends 65 per cent over the same period. Such massive growth, particularly in the newer industries like synthetics, chemicals, petroleum-based products, consumer durables and of course the movies, was the direct and indirect result of rapid expansion of the construction and automobile industries.[20]

In 1929 4,800,000 cars were manufactured and there were more than twenty-six million cars and trucks on the road. In the United States there was a ratio of one car to every five persons compared to the ratio in Britain of 1:43, 1:325 in Italy and 1:7,000 in Russia.[21] There were many people in blighted industrial areas of Europe who would have been puzzled to see the supposedly impoverished Joad family travelling from the Oklahoma dust bowl to the promised land of California in their own car no matter how delapidated. In America the possession of an automobile was not the privilege of class as it was in Europe but a statement of consumer confidence.

The motor industry was the most important purchaser of rubber, plate glass, nickel and lead; it bought 15 per cent of the nation's steel output and was the direct cause of the rapid expansion of the petroleum industry. The ever-increasing number of cars demanded public spending on the creation of new roads and the maintenance of old ones. Just as industry expanded on the back of the growth of the railways in the second half of the nineteenth century so national life was significantly altered by the widespread use of the motor car in the 1920s. People could now live further away from their workplaces in the city and a suburban housing boom grew to accommodate their wishes.

Detroit became the Mecca of the modern world and Henry Ford its prophet. Unfortunately the prophet's words included a deep-rooted belief in reincarnation and a virulent hatred of Jews, Catholics, bankers and tobacco, all of which were to be found in his widely disseminated newspaper *The Dearborn Independent*.

Nevertheless, Ford's pronouncements were accorded solemn consideration because his rise from farmboy-mechanic to the self-appointed post of High Priest of mass production fulfilled the dreams of the acquisitive society in which he lived. He was the new Lincoln, a twentieth-century variation on the theme of Log Cabin to White House. He ran a family firm which steered well clear of Wall Street; he believed in low prices and high wages and as a single human being he had apparently come as close as it was possible to do to wiping the curse of poverty from the face of the earth. A group of college students voted Henry Ford the third greatest figure of all time, surpassed only by Napoleon Bonaparte and Jesus Christ. Many of his supporters wondered whether this was a strictly fair order of merit.

'Just as in Rome one goes to the Vatican and endeavours to get audience of the Pope,' wrote one British traveller, 'so in Detroit one goes to the Ford Works and endeavours to see Henry Ford.' 'As I caught my first glimpse of Detroit,' recorded another, 'I felt as I imagine a Seventeenth Century traveller must have felt when he approached Versailles.'

By 1929, stimulated by the soaring Stock Market, business and religion were inextricably merged in the popular imagination. Religion became more secular as business turned into a religion. It was a uniquely American, twentieth-century slant on the previously held connection between religion and the rise of capitalism. Religion repaid devotion in purely financial terms.

The Dean of the University of Chicago Divinity School told a reporter that a businessman could make more money if he prayed about his business. 'The man who builds a factory builds a temple,' observed President Calvin Coolidge. 'The man who works there, worships there.'[22]

In 1925 Bruce Barton wrote a best-selling book about Christ called *The Man Nobody Knows*. Jesus was portrayed as 'a topnotch businessman.... He picked up twelve men from the bottom ranks of business and forged them into an organization that conquered the world.' The parables were categorised as 'the most powerful advertisements of all time'. It was a language which everyone understood. More to the point when the Stock Market crash precipitated the Depression, Americans were not only traumatised by financial hardship but also betrayed by the religion they had believed in so fervently.

The result of this new wealth was a diversification into leisure activities. Organised sports turned into mass spectator sports because people now had the money, the time and the means of transportation to attend baseball and football games instead of just reading or hearing about them. As a consequence, sports stars like Babe Ruth, Jack Dempsey, Red Grange, Bill Tilden and Bobby Jones joined the pantheon of radio and movie stars as subjects of endless public speculation.

The American film industry was a major beneficiary of the changes in national character, morals and manners in the 1920s. Previous eras had emphasised the virtue of saving and investment. The economic boom and the prospect of unlimited widely disseminated prosperity encouraged the belief that thrift could be socially and economically harmful and that spending was a virtue. Spending money not only satisfied acquisitive desire but in itself created wealth in a self-accelerating spiral. In 1900 there were four million owners of stocks; in 1929 there were twenty million. There seemed to be no logical reason why the spiral should not continue indefinitely.

The effect of this national increase in wealth was by no means restricted to consumer consumption. By 1929 the country spent twice as much on libraries as it had in 1914 and three times as much as it had on hospitals. In 1928 the United States paid out more to educate its children than the rest of the world combined. Increased wealth financed research, improved sanitation and provided better nutrition. As a result life expectancy rose from forty-nine years at the turn of the century to nearly fifty-nine years by 1929. Infant mortality was cut by two-thirds and the rate of death from typhoid fell from 36 to 2 per 100,000 of population. Deaths from diphtheria fell even more dramatically.[23]

The critics of contemporary values had been silenced. The sceptical columnist Walter Lippmann noted that 'the more or less unconscious and unplanned activities of businessmen are for once more novel, more daring and more revolutionary than the theories of the progressives'. Scott Fitzgerald portrayed Jay Gatsby as the businessman as gangster but it made no real impact. The best that novelists could do was the cultural poverty, vulgarity and insularity of the Sinclair Lewis *Babbitt* books. The haven of disaffected radicals in the 1920s was Montparnasse not Moscow. Their heroes were not radical economists or proletarian novelists as they were to be in the next decade but Cézanne and T. S. Eliot, Jung and H. L. Mencken.

The signs of impending disaster were certainly visible during the decade but it was assumed that they were aberrations rather than harbingers of doom. The collapse of agricultural prices in 1921 had led to years of depression on the farmlands of America and accelerated the drift of the population towards urban centres. The textile towns of New England and the coal towns of Pennsylvania were similarly afflicted by privation leading to bitter industrial disputes which were to feature so widely in the following decade. The rapid increase of mechanisation which had made possible some of the economic achievements also brought in its wake unemployment and the creation of a proletarian underclass which would later be known as the structural unemployed.

However, with selective vision, it was possible for President Coolidge to declare in 1928: 'No Congress of the United States ever assembled, on surveying the state of the Union, has met with a more pleasing prospect than that which appears at the present time.' Within a few weeks he was to hand over office to Herbert Hoover who had similarly pronounced:

> We in America today are nearer to the final triumph over poverty than ever before in the history of any land. The poorhouse is vanishing from among us. We have not reached the goal but ... we shall soon with the help of God be in sight of the day when poverty will be banished from this nation.

Lincoln Steffens, who had been one of the original Muckrakers, a writer who specialised in exposing the evils of American capitalism, was moved to predict: 'Big Business in America is producing what the Socialists held up as their goal – food, shelter and clothing for all. You will see it during the Hoover Administration.[24]

It was in this atmosphere of prosperity and harmony, sharing a belief that everyone was meant to get rich and that everything that happens, happens for the best in the best of all possible worlds, that Americans approached the fateful last two months of 1929.

2

TROUBLE IN PARADISE
October 1929 to February 1933

What if our bread line should be
The long slow match of destiny? ...
Creep, my ember! Blaze my brand!
The end of all things is at hand.
Idlers in the market place
Make an end to your disgrace.
Here's a fair day's work for you
To build a world all over new.

'Breadline', *Atlantic Monthly*, January 1932

From the vantage point of the Depression, the days before October 1929 began
to assume for Americans an image similar to that which the Edwardian
summers before August 1914 had become for the British. Just as the long
Edwardian summers and the previous hundred years of general peace in
Europe had disguised the fundamental problems of social and political unrest
with which Britain was in reality struggling, so the American economy in
September 1929 was not the ever-booming phenomenon the prices on the New
York Stock Exchange suggested. Such grossly inflated prices bore little
relation to the real economic status of the firms involved. When the Crash
came it was made even more spectacular by the unreal heights from which the
stocks had fallen. 'My uncle died in September,' said Eddie Cantor. 'Poor
fellow. He had diabetes at 45. That's nothing. I had Chrysler at 110.'

People who had seen their own invisible investments double themselves on
paper many times over were tempted to plunge more heavily into the market by
borrowing on margin, and their friends followed suit. When the index levels
began to turn rapidly downwards at the end of October, the biggest of the Wall
Street bankers formed a pool to support prices.

Richard Whitney, the pool's accredited representative, marched on to the
floor of the Exchange and offered to buy 10,000 shares of US Steel at 205, but
found only 200 for sale. The very news that the bankers had met with the
intention of steadying the market had apparently stopped the rot. Unfortunately this halt in selling flattered only to deceive.

11

Between September and December 1929 Americans lost $30 billion on the Stock Market. Morrie Ryskind, a playwright and later a Hollywood screenwriter, remembered the night of 24 October as an occasion when he was working on a screen version of the Marx Brothers' stage hit *Animal Crackers*: 'I was sat in Groucho's house the night the market had just gone to hell and Groucho sat there and said, "I think I'm all right. I think I've still got the house." '[1] Many Americans were not so fortunate. Altogether, they lost assets which totalled the amount that had been spent on the First World War and which in 1930 represented a figure more than twice the National Debt.

President Herbert Hoover proved singularly unable to cope with the problems which had sprung from the collapse. We may assume here for the sake of argument that the Depression and the Stock Market Crash are causally connected although some historians maintain that there is no such relationship between the two events. The consensus of historical opinion certainly believes that what happened on Wall Street triggered declines in other securities markets and led bankers to make borrowing more difficult, which in turn caused a further decline of already depressed commodity prices.

In the 150 years since the Declaration of Independence the American nation had survived any number of economic recessions. The Civil War had slashed overseas trade and the junketings of international high finance had caused chaos between 1905 and 1907. In common with much of Europe, there had been a lasting depression in the final quarter of the nineteenth century and it has already been noted how the prosperity of the 1920s managed to evade the clutches of the South, the farming states of the Mid-West and the textile and bituminous coal industries.

Throughout all these reverses the Great American Dream remained intact. 'All the conditions of American life', Herbert Croly had written in 1909, 'have tended to encourage an easy, generous and irresponsible optimism.' Somehow it was still believed that natural and human obstacles to the pursuit of happiness could be defeated. By 1920 the frontier was closed, railroads ran from the Atlantic coast to the Pacific and bridges spanned what were once feared to be impassable rivers. The course of American history seemed to lead automatically to a nationally held philosophy that elevated the happy ending long before motion picture producers took it over as a staple of their products.

The Depression of 1929–33 succeeded in destroying the self-confidence that had been the hallmark of the country. First to feel the pinch, almost inevitably, were the farmers. Wheat, which had sold in Chicago during July 1929 for $1.25 a bushel, sold one year later for 76 cents. The 1929 harvest produced 200 million surplus bushels of wheat. A witness before the Congressional Subcommittee on Labor reported,

> The last thing I saw on the night I left Seattle was numbers of women searching for scraps of food in the refuse piles of that city. A number of Montana citizens told me of thousands of bushels of wheat left in the

fields uncut on account of its low price that hardly paid for the harvesting.[2]

It frustrated and angered farmers that they could not sell their produce for a price that would enable them to live decently. It frustrated and angered hungry, desperate people in the cities to hear of fruit rotting on trees and milk cans overturned on highways. It was frightening and incomprehensible that there should be so much want in a land that was capable of producing so much.

Hoover's public pronouncements were limited to sporadic declarations on the lines of 'Prosperity is just around the corner' and he quickly became the focus for the widespread and deep-seated discontent. In October 1930 he declared that the major cause of the American Depression came from Europe. Overproduction of raw materials from abroad led to a decrease of foreign purchasing power. He persistently overruled suggestions of federal aid to the distressed. In a radio talk in February 1931 he stated, 'If America means anything it means the principles of individual and local responsibility and mutual self help. If we break down the principles, we have struck at the roots of self-government . . . . I have faith in the American people that such a day [of federal aid] shall not come.'[3]

He constantly emphasised that his lack of action was born of a deep desire to help, and to avoid subjecting local communities to 'a remote bureaucracy with its minimum of understanding and sympathy'. He concluded his address by reminding his listeners that the old values he was defending were 'not the easy way, but [they represented] the American way. And it was Lincoln's way.' (It was later also Bush's way because what Hoover was describing as his ideal was the 'trickle down economics' for which Bill Clinton so roundly castigated George Bush.)

It wasn't that Hoover was either an unsympathetic man or an incompetent politician. His earlier career had caught attention in the First World War when he was a Food Administrator and the man in charge of Belgian relief. John Maynard Keynes observed that he was 'the only man who emerged from the ordeal of Paris with an enhanced reputation' and Justice Louis D. Brandeis remarked that he was 'the biggest figure injected into Washington life by the war'. It was simply that he proved incapable of responding to the major dislocation caused by the Depression because nothing in his previous experience had prepared him for a disaster in American life on this scale. The Depression flew in the face of everything people believed that the previous 150 years of American history had taught them.

It was the sheer magnitude of the distress which exposed the inadequacy of the private relief in which Hoover maintained his unswerving belief. The family, the neighbour, the landlord and the employer were incapable of grappling with unemployment relief on this scale. The burden then fell upon the cities and their private and public welfare agencies which, not surprisingly, proved incapable of carrying it. A wry story of Babe Ruth's contract negotiations with the New York Yankees was told at this time. He held out for a rise to $80,000 for the summer and was informed by the management that such a figure was more than President Hoover made. To which he replied, 'So what? I had a better season than he did.'[4]

Hoover argued for high wages, high production and high consumption to be made possible by increased mechanisation and he begged firms not to lower wages; but as the deadly downward spiral cut away at consumer spending and purchasing power, sales dropped, production decreased and firms found no alternative to cutting wages other than slashing payrolls. Between 1929 and 1932 factory wages fell from a total of $12 billion to $7 billion. After declaring that they would co-operate with the President and freeze wages, US Steel cut them by ten per cent. General Motors and Bethlehem Steel followed suit. In 1929 US Steel had 225,000 workers on its books; three years later there were only 110,000 and many of them worked only part-time. A man who worked forty-eight hours a week in 1929 would work only thirty-one hours a week in 1931. During the short-lived depression of 1921 Ohio manufacturers had paid out a yearly average wage of $1,252; ten years later it was down to $960. Average weekly earnings fell from $28.50 in 1929 to $22.64 in 1931. High wages alone of course could not guarantee prosperity but they were an integral factor.[5]

Wage cuts cannot give an overall picture of America during the Depression. The unemployment figures were the statistical companion of the 1930s man as the baseball batting averages had been of the 1920s man. In March 1930 the figures suggested three-and-half million unemployed. A year later it was eight million and when Roosevelt took office in March 1933 there were anything between twelve and sixteen million people without jobs.[6]

Perhaps more important, although less tangible than these figures, was the imprint made on the psyche of working men. An executive without a job would scramble for a labouring job before applying for relief (itself no easy matter). Frances Perkins, who became Roosevelt's Secretary of Labor, recalls reading in the *New York Times* in January 1930 a story put out by President Hoover proclaiming a large reduction in unemployment. The story, she knew, was based on inaccurate statistics.

> I knew the story was going to hurt and grieve the people being laid off in great numbers. They would not understand, they would feel betrayed, they would feel there was something wrong with them personally. A great despair would enter their hearts and they would say, 'Why don't I get a job if things are getting better?' I knew that wives would read the story and reproach their husbands. I knew that young people would read the story and say, 'Why doesn't Papa work?'[7]

The work ethic had been part of the fabric of American society. The successive waves of immigrants who had arrived in the nineteenth century had always been attracted by the prospect of 'bettering' themselves irrespective of other basic desires such as political or religious toleration. The dream of the Golden Land was the dream of a society in which if a man were prepared to work hard he could provide a decent standard of living for his family, and his children would be able to enjoy an even higher one.

The Puritan ethic, which had long equated unemployment and poverty with wilful laziness and moral laxity, did not die overnight. Even at the height of the Depression there remained fifty million people who were employed, a fact which served only to increase the bitterness of the jobless. Until 1930 economists believed that unemployment was a cyclical event; in the Depression they realised it was structural. Relief would, therefore, have to be a permanent measure. Harry Hopkins, one of Roosevelt's closest advisers, admitted that even in prosperous times there would remain a hard core of four or five million men for whom jobs would never be available.

In January 1931 New York City had eighty-two breadlines serving 85,000 meals a day. All the major cities experienced the problems associated with massive unemployment. In the autumn of 1931 the ever-growing band of jobless people rose to over 624,000 and the cities' private and public resources ran out. Detroit reported six hundred relief applications a day in the wake of the crisis at Ford. In March 1929 the payroll contained over 128,000 names. Two years later it was down to 37,000. Oakland, California, devised a 'sewer pipe city' at the foot of 15th Avenue; Oklahoma City permitted the growth of a 'town' for vagrants who lived at the bottom of the (presumably dry) river bed. In the spring of 1931 the population of the Cameroons contributed over $377, which was sent to New York City for the relief of the starving.[8]

The social symptoms of these statistics were only too familiar. Street corners were occupied by men with faded suits selling apples; the harsh signs, NO HELP WANTED and NO MEN REQUIRED were ubiquitous. On the banks of rivers and beyond the cities' limits were the drab, disconsolate Hoovervilles, where hungry, tired and homeless people gathered to warm themselves beside a dying brazier flame as they waited for the soup kitchen to open.

By 1931, the third hard winter of the Depression, it was obvious to everyone except President Hoover, his Cabinet and his economic advisers that this was no ordinary financial recession, no traditional downswing of the conventional trade cycle. Murray Kempton wrote of capitalists in general:

> The year 1931 was not a time when the American business man held his head high. All the ancient values he represented seemed to wither around him. The early Thirties tried bankers and found them guilty as steadily as the Fifties were to try Communists. The image of the American Dream was flawed and cracked; its critics had never sounded more persuasive.[9]

Widespread economic distress, combined with federal inactivity, revelations of conspiracy and fraud on the part of prominent businessmen all helped to create an atmosphere of violence. It seemed as if the classic Marxist prophecy was coming true, as the response of Hoover's government to the

15

gravity of the situation called into the question the ability of the capitalist system to solve its own problems. The journalist W. A. White pleaded for relief since it now appeared to be 'the only way to keep down barricades in the streets this winter and the use of force which will brutalize labor and impregnate it with revolution in America for a generation'.[10]

In the spring of 1932 the Senate Subcommittee on Labor was warned that 'if something is not done and starvation is going to continue, the doors of revolt in this country are going to be thrown open'. As if to prove the point, in Minneapolis, several hundred men and women stormed a grocery store, smashing windows and beating up the owners in order to help themselves to food. Testimony before that committee showed that one Mid-Western farmer wanted to capture a local fort with four hundred machine guns, artillery, tractors, munitions and rifles and then march East, whence the trouble had stemmed. The evidence continued:

> That man may be very foolish and I think he is, but he is in dead earnest; he is a hard shelled Baptist and a hard shelled Democrat, not a Socialist or a Communist but just a plain American cattleman .... I have heard much of this talk from serious minded prosperous men of other days.

Even if there were no revolution, the sullen indifference of the unemployed to the fate of parliamentary democracy might lead to a fascist dictatorship.

> What if day after day the newspapers brought word of further disaster; the stalling of utilities, the stoppage of trains, the crippling of communication until, at last, the Federal government suspended the writ of habeas corpus, proclaimed martial law throughout the land and established a dictatorship? And what if despite all this the function of government was powerless? What then? What should I do? To which question the answer is: We don't know.[11]

In 1932 the mutual hostility with which government and the growing numbers of unemployed faced each other was vividly illustrated by the fate of the Bonus Army. Between fifteen and twenty thousand veterans of the Great War moved into Washington to press for immediate payment in full of the bonuses owed to them for military service. The House quickly passed the Bill, but the Senate rejected it by a large majority. Half the men left quietly but the remainder, destitute and homeless, decided to set up residence in huts on the muddy Anacostia flats on the edge of the city.

After some weeks of quiet life the government decided it wanted to evict a group of bonus marchers from government buildings on Pennsylvania Avenue. A scuffle followed in which two veterans were killed and a dozen police injured. Hoover panicked and summoned the Army. Waving machine guns and bayonets, they rolled in tanks towards the hapless bonus marchers. Led by General MacArthur (and including junior officers Patton and Eisenhower), the soldiers dispersed the marchers and set fire to the billets. The Attorney

General prepared a report, which was released by the President, in which it was alleged that the Bonus Army was composed almost exclusively of Communists and criminals. MacArthur agreed and declared that, had the government tolerated the situation for as much as another week, the institutions of government would have been greatly endangered. It was an ignoble incident in American history.

There undoubtedly were some Communist agitators in the Bonus Army, as there were Communists in most cities during the depths of the Depression. On 6 March 1930 the Communists had arranged demonstrations in New York and Washington, to mark International Unemployment Day. New York's turnout was a respectable thirty-five thousand people. In December 1931 they organised a national Hunger March on Washington, carrying banners which proclaimed, 'IN THE LAST WAR WE FOUGHT FOR THE BOSSES; IN THE NEXT WAR WE'LL FIGHT FOR THE WORKERS.'[12]

Lincoln Steffens's influential autobiography, published in 1931, revealed the former muckraker to be a convinced Communist. It was the end of the era of American reform, he proclaimed, 'All roads in our day lead to Moscow'. During that same year 350 American citizens applied each day for jobs in Russia. John Strachey's classic book *The Coming Struggle for Power*, published in 1933, included the remark that 'to travel from the capitalist world into Soviet territory is to pass from death to birth'. He was not alone in his view. Famously, George Bernard Shaw and the Webbs were of a similar opinion. Among the impressive list of Communist voters in the 1932 election were Theodore Dreiser, Sherwood Anderson, John Dos Passos, Edmund Wilson, Granville Hicks and Sidney Hook.[13]

It was in this bleak and ever-darkening atmosphere that Hollywood was having to make films which its patrons wanted to see. For as long as the industry had been in existence its basic philosophy had been firmly rooted in the optimism engendered by the national self-confidence. In the early 1930s, in its attempts to give the customers what they seemed now to want, Hollywood started to make movies which portrayed American society in flux. The cycle lasted no more than a couple of years but during that time Hollywood made more bleaker, darker pictures than at any other time during its so-called Golden Age.

Arguably the bleakest and darkest of them all was the Warner Brothers film *I Am a Fugitive from a Chain Gang* directed by Mervyn LeRoy and released in the black days of 1932. Paul Muni plays James Allen, a First World War veteran, who finds it impossible to return to his former desk-bound existence because of his newly acquired 'wanderlust'. Tramping the country in search of occupational stimulation, he is invited by a dosshouse colleague to a hamburger stand, and finds himself, unwittingly, an accomplice at a robbery where he is arrested. Sentenced to ten years' hard labour, Allen contrives to escape from the hideous chain gang and makes his way to Chicago, where he registers under the name of Allen James as a manual labourer at a wage of $4 a week. Through the classic American virtues of diligence and thrift he rises to the post of General Field Superintendent, with a commensurate increase in salary.

However, his scheming landlady (played by Glenda Farrell) discovers his real identity and his guilty secret. She blackmails him into marriage but when Allen falls in love with another woman she informs on him to the appropriate state authority. Yielding to public pressure the State offers Allen a nominal ninety-day sentence, to be served as a clerk, if he will return voluntarily. He does so only to discover that he has been tricked; he is transferred to a hard labour chain gang and his request for remission is rejected.

Even a second escape proves to be no solution. Allen manages to see his girlfriend again after a year on the run. He describes how he hides by day and travels by night. 'I keep running. That's all that's left for me.' The girl cries, 'But it was all going to be so different.' 'It is different', replies Allen bitterly, 'They made it different.' Allen hears a noise and prepares to leave. The girl panics. 'Can't you tell me where you're going? Do you need any money? Will you write?' to all of which Allen shakes his head, his eyes wide and staring. 'But you must, Jim. How do you live?' screams the girl hysterically. Through the murk comes Allen's urgent whisper, 'I steal'.

The film is a crushing indictment of American society. Muni tries to pawn his *croix de guerre* in a seedy shop, whose proprietor grimly opens a large box full of similar items. In the camp the camera pans symbolically from the chained mule team to the chained convicts. Allen Jenkins plays one prisoner who, on his release, is unable to avoid walking with the shuffle bred by years of walking with the shackles round his ankles. The pinched, hard, hostile faces of the prison officials and Allen's own Southern lawyer represent a cynical, ruthless and totally inhumane authority, which condemns an innocent man to a subhuman existence.

The story of the film was taken from the autobiography of Robert E. Burns, *I Am a Fugitive from a Georgia Chain Gang*. The Hays Office was, unsurprisingly, disturbed by the proposed production of this 'inflammatory' document. Colonel Joy, Joseph Breen's predecessor in Hollywood, wrote to Will Hays while the book was under consideration for purchase by both Warners and MGM,

> While it may be true that the systems are wrong, I very much doubt that it is our business as an entertainment force to clear it up, and thereby possibly get into trouble with the Southern states who, as our Southern representative puts it, 'can stand any criticism so long as it isn't directed at themselves'.[14]

Joy wrote identical letters to both Irving Thalberg at MGM and Darryl Zanuck at Warner Brothers, warning them that any proposed film must studiously ignore the details of the cruelty and any condemnation of Georgia and/or the South.

Darryl Zanuck wrote back in high dudgeon:

I am not interested in having a meeting with the other producers who are making chain gang stories. I purchased the only legitimate chain gang story on the market and, incidentally, the property that started the interest.

I have instructions from our New York office not to discuss the matter further with anyone except of course yourself later in the matter of censorship.[15]

In the end the only compromise that the Hays Office was able to force on Warners was the omission in the film of any mention of the name of the state in which Burns had been victimised. Ironically, the substitution of a pronoun for 'Georgia' has an extremely sinister and unsettling effect on the viewer. Perhaps even more ironically LeRoy's bleak but memorable ending stands as a contrast to the fate which eventually befell Burns. He was awarded a full pardon outside of the state of Georgia but his real-life 'happy' ending has failed to dim the shocking power of Hollywood's fictional one.

Mervyn LeRoy had made his mark on the film industry two years previously when he directed *Little Caesar*, the first of the classic gangster movies. The success of this film and William Wellman's *The Public Enemy* (1931) made movie stars out of previously little-known Broadway actors Edward G. Robinson and James Cagney. It was a time when gangsters were raised to heroic stature. We shall examine the genre in greater depth elsewhere but at this point it is relevant to note that the first spurt of popularity for it coincided precisely with the years 1930–2. If justification for illegality were needed, the crumbling nature of the economic, moral and institutional framework of the country appeared to provide it.

To those people who had suffered from bank collapses and closures and whose minds were unable to fathom the ways of high finance, it simply appeared as though the money they had deposited had been stolen by the banks. Not surprisingly in these years there was a widespread, if grudging, admiration for the gangsters who carved fortunes out of the fortresses of power and wealth with their tommy guns. They at least were doing something besides worrying how to pay the grocery bills, how to find another job, how to keep up payments on the mortgage.

It was *Little Caesar*, along with *The Public Enemy* (1931), *Quick Millions* (1931) and *Scarface* (1932), which defined the prototype of the gangster film. Rico and his friend Joe (Douglas Fairbanks Jr) leave the small town where they have been living off the proceeds of filling station robberies and travel to Chicago (referred to in the film as 'the City'), where Rico joins a gang and Joe becomes a professional dancer. Rico takes over the gang having proved his bravery and ingenuity, while Joe tries to detach himself from his former friend. Rico drives one rival gang leader out of town and is promoted by the 'Big Boy' over the head of another. There is no question but that we are expected to admire Rico's ruthless climb to power.

Similarly, *The Public Enemy* glorifies Cagney's rise from small-time hoodlum to full-time racketeer. At no time do the police even appear in the film and Cagney is eventually murdered by a rival gang. Nobody in the film can offer anything to match Cagney's exuberant enjoyment of the life of a gangster. His brother Mike (Donald Cook) berates him for moral laxity but Cagney replies by accusing Mike of stealing small change from the bus company for which he works and scornfully derides Mike's example of 'going to school to learn how to be poor'. Cagney's next movie, *Blonde Crazy*, depicts an America entirely populated by confidence tricksters and their dupes – a disconcerting world in which ostensible pillars of society are more likely to be revealed as liars and crooks. Even Joan Blondell's love is not suffiecient to compensate for Cagney's inevitable prison sentence.

Quick Millions is full of references to the imperfections of law and justice. An underworld 'trial' is proved to be $75,000 cheaper than a state trial and one of the characters indicates the general moral apathy of the world when he exclaims, 'What difference does it make? – a law made by lawyers for lawyers to break or a law made by hoodlums for hoodlums to break?' When MGM, that model studio of moral rectitude, also released two pictures about gangsters and criminals in 1930 and 1931 (*The Big House* and *The Secret Six*) it was apparent that the gangster film fashion had been awarded a medal of some distinction.

After *Little Caesar* Mervyn LeRoy continued his successful partnership with Edward G. Robinson on a different kind of bleak story of corrupted innocence. *Two Seconds* stars Robinson as a murderer who dies in the electric chair at the opening of the film. A college student, who is present at the execution to gather information for a term paper, asks a hardened crime reporter how long it takes for a man to die in the chair, and is told that the current takes two seconds to pass through a man's body from the moment the switch is pulled. The student murmurs, 'I'll bet those are the longest two seconds of his life', and Robinson, lip curled in defiance to the assembled reporters, proves it by remembering his life in flashback, while sitting in the chair.

The transition is made by a jump cut from the switch being thrown to an electric drill being used by Robinson in his work as a steeplejack. Robinson plays John Allen, who, as he proudly declares, earns $62.50 a week – 'more than most college professors'. Allen has some intellectual curiosity, and is reluctant to ape his room-mate's addiction to cheap women and gambling, so he wanders away from a possible date and into a dance hall, where he is confronted by a revolting line of gum-chewing hostesses, waiting to be pawed. The girl whom he chooses is surprised at Allen's studied politeness and spins him a tale of her parents back on the farm in Idaho. (It transpires that they live in a speakeasy on Tenth Avenue.)

The girl, Shirley, sees in Allen a likely complaisant husband and hastens the wedding by getting the man drunk on bootleg gin, served in a tea cup, and then rapidly hauling him in front of a judge. The ceremony is conducted with a cigarette dangling from the bridegroom's lips and the tea cup still stuck on his little finger. The judge pronounces them man and wife before Allen can say 'I do', pausing only to snatch his ten dollar fee as the answer.

Shirley proceeds to destroy the marriage almost before it has started, by keeping up her former relationship with her 'manager'. Allen accidentally kills his best friend in a fight over his marriage, pushing him from the top of the skyscraper on which they had both been working. As a result Allen loses his nerve as a steeplejack and is unable to work. The only money coming into the household is that which is earned by Shirley in her dubious extra-marital activities.

A win on the horses enables Allen to pay back the money that made him feel unclean and, to round things off neatly, he shoots his wife. In the courtroom he is duly sentenced to death. He cannot believe that the judge, as the representative of the society by whose mores he has tried so hard to live, could pronounce such a sentence. Bewildered, he cries, 'I sunk as low as anyone could get – that's when you should have burned me. It ain't fair to let a rat live and kill a man.' But the law is not concerned with the finer point of ethics or even natural justice. Allen dies and the audience is left without catharsis.

Despite this most atypically bleak view of the world for a Hollywood picture, Warner Brothers' faith in the film was more than justified by its performance at the box office. The basic cost of production was $310,000; domestic receipts amounted to $665,000 and foreign grosses amounted to $157,000 making a book total of $822,000.[16]

Shirley's portrayal of the wife as whore was a reflection of a whole new sub-genre of pictures which made their appearance in the years 1931 and 1932. Greta Garbo starred in *Susan Lenox: Her Fall and Rise* in which she joined the well populated ranks of women who sold their affections to relieve economic pressure. In the movie Garbo takes up with a circus owner and a politician before falling for Clark Gable. His response to the discovery that she has followed him round the country is a blunt 'Same old trade?' *Motion Picture Herald* commented disdainfully,

> Having sent Miss [Norma] Shearer to Europe on a well-earned or much-needed vacation following her appearance as a gorgeous lady of dubious morals in *Divorcee*, *Strangers May Kiss* and *A Free Soul*, MGM seems to have continued its 'sin and succeed' series with Greta Garbo.[17]

When the picture was released, it quickly became apparent that the popularity of the star was in no way diminished by the new morality and the same trade paper commented,

Her Fall and Rise having much to do with Susan Lenox, we must admit that she is doing much more falling than rising. This is 'b.o.' most anywhere except where the long-nosed, straight-laced, keeper-of-the-public-morals are concerned.[18]

Marlene Dietrich's contribution to this new genre was *Blonde Venus* (1932) directed by Josef von Sternberg, in which a separation from her husband (Herbert Marshall) seemingly leaves her no alternative means of feeding herself and her young son than by appearing in a cabaret that might have stepped from Weimar Germany. One of her classic numbers proclaims:

> Things look bad – stocks are low
> So today, my best beau
> Went back again to live with his wife
> Why should I care a lot?
> So he's gone – well, so what?
> It doesn't mean a thing in my life.

Almost every female star appeared in one or more of these popular vehicles in 1931 and 1932. Joan Crawford in *Possessed* plays a small-town factory girl who becomes the mistress of a rich New York lawyer (Clark Gable). Constance Bennett in *The Easiest Way* climbs out of poverty by going to bed with her boss (Adolphe Menjou). Claudette Colbert is eventually reformed by Gary Cooper in *His Woman*, Ruth Chatterton sacrifices her reputation in *Unfaithful* in order to shield her brother's wife, while Tallulah Bankhead was imported from Broadway to play the *Tarnished Lady*. In 1932 Bankhead cuckolded Robert Montgomery in *Faithless*, while in *The Crash* Ruth Chatterton deserted her husband, impoverished by the collapse of the stock market, to live with a rich Australian in Bermuda.

Variety, in its annual review of the year's films, noticed the trend in an article headlined 'SINFUL GIRLS LEAD IN 1931'.

> The Easiest Way was the easiest way to b.o. success in 1931. Important ladies of the screen, those whose names mean drawing power, found smash films the wages of cinematic sin. The Great God Public, formerly considered as a Puritan censor, voiced its approval with admission fees that fully endorsed the heroines of easy virtue.... Public taste switched to glamorous shameful ladies, coddled by limousines, clothed in couturier smartness.[19]

The appeal of the fallen woman and the gangster as hero certainly gives a clear indication that the crisis in national life brought on by the onset of the Depression was overturning conventional attitudes. It is perhaps under-standable therefore that films which continued to show figures of authority in an attractive light would probably perform poorly at the box office.

MGM, the studio with the strongest links to the political establishment, tried a compromise when, in 1932, the studio purchased the film rights to Henri Bernstein's play *The Claw* which was to be renamed *Washington Masquerade*. The screen treatment was a collaboration between MGM staff writer John Meehan and Samuel Blythe, who was regarded as 'the best informed of all the older generation Washington commentators and perhaps the wisest and most sophisticated'. The final script, one must conclude, owes more to Meehan than to Blythe and shows that this most conservative of studios found it difficult even at this time to rid itself of its reverence for its political masters despite the popular climate.

Lionel Barrymore plays Jefferson Keane, Man of the People, lawyer and eventually Senator after having defeated a megalomaniac, crooked opponent. Keane wants to introduce a Bill into the Senate which will advance the public ownership of the power and light utilities. Before he can complete his task he is seduced by a woman played by Karen Morley who is promised $100,000 by vested interests if she can divert Keane from his purpose. Not only is he thus diverted but he marries Miss Morley and accepts a half a million dollars bribe to retire from politics and return to private practice.

Fortunately he is tormented by guilt, part of which probably originates from the fact that his new law offices are startlingly overlooked by a positively anthropomorphic Capitol building, which casts a baleful eye on his new prosperity. Keane decides to reveal the history of his corruption to a Senate investigation committee. Keane's confession includes references to Valley Forge and concludes, 'Right here in Washington now, there's a man whose heart is breaking because some of us are traitors'. One assumes that this must be a reference to Louis B. Mayer's friend and hero, Herbert Hoover, but the reference is so vague it could apply to anyone in Washington with cardiovascular problems.

The reviews in the trade press did not take too kindly to the inclusion of certain 'non box office' elements. *Variety* stated baldly,

> The people – the theater-goers for this discussion – are at the moment pretty thoroughly impatient with politicians and a story that undertakes to glorify the Washington salon isn't going to win any popular acclaim.[20]

Also in 1932 Columbia acquired the rights to the Maxwell Anderson play *Washington Merry Go-Round*. Eight months prior to its release it was announced quite bluntly,

> *Washington Merry Go-Round* and all stories of that ilk will be purchased strictly for title value. Stories in each instance will be completely rewritten.... After several trips to the Capitol to fully discuss governmental factors concerning *Merry Go-Round*, such pictures will reach the screen with the approval of all political parties say Columbians.[21]

Even after the script had been carefully checked for evidence of political extremism, Columbia executives insisted on certain changes after seeing an answer print. 'Scene causing the most concern', reported *Variety* laconically, 'is where the body of a lynched politician is thrown on the Capitol steps'. The film eventually appeared, to be greeted by a blistering attack from the metropolitan critics.

> The whole picture is ... apparently dedicated to the principle that all politicians are noble statesmen and their only fault is that they are just a leedle [*sic*] feeble-minded and let themselves be hoodwinked by sinister master-mind crooks bent on sending the country to the dogs for their own fell purposes.[22]

The story of this film was similar in outline to Capra's *Mr Smith Goes to Washington* but 1932 audiences were understandably unsympathetic to films which portrayed politicians as crusading heroes.

The sort of politicians audiences wanted to see at that time were those shown in Paramount's comedy *Million Dollar Legs* which was released in the autumn of 1932 with the intention of exploiting the interest in the Los Angeles Olympic Games taking place at that time. Jack Oakie plays an American brush salesman on business in Klopstockia, a remote republic, whose chief exports are goats and nuts. The chief imports, indeed the chief inhabitants, of the country are also goats and nuts. All the boys in this strange country are named 'George' and all the girls 'Angela'.

The President is played by W. C. Fields who announces his arrival in any room by performing on a one-man band. He keeps his position of authority over a sullen and mutinous cabinet by beating each member at arm wrestling, but, just to make sure, he conducts all cabinet business clutching a revolver. The plot, such as it is, concerns the $8 million needed to save the country from bankruptcy. The money is eventually awarded by a sponsor after he sees Fields fling a thousand-pound weight at Jack Oakie for having stepped on his foot. Fields's athletic feat wins him the Olympic weight-lifting and shot-putting gold medals simultaneously. If it is not itself a political satire, *Million Dollar Legs* has many relevant things to say as to how politicians were seen by the American public in 1932.

The dismal early years of the Depression also created the cycle of movies which concerned the unscrupulous dealings of shady lawyers and cynical newspaper editors, both of them anxious to increase their profits at the expense of the human beings they are supposedly serving. The stock theme of the lawyer films portrayed a basically good man who, for a combination of economic and sexual reasons, renounces the ethical basis of his vocation to work for the underworld.

For The Defense (1930), made by Paramount, contained a central performance from William Powell as a lawyer who specialises in springing his clients from prison. In 1932 Powell appeared in the Warner Brothers film *Lawyer Man*, in which he leaves his humble practice on the Lower East side to go uptown, where he is promptly seduced and framed by Clare Dodd and indicted by a Grand Jury. Bitter, because of the plot which has deprived him of his partnership, Powell stares out of the window at a teeming Manhattan scene and comments acidly, 'Every guy, pushing, trampling, selling each other short. When they kick you, you kick back – only harder. They made me a shyster. Well, I'll be the biggest shyster of them all.' Having achieved the satisfaction of revenge, Powell returns to his 'own' people and to being poor but honest in the company of his faithful secretary, Joan Blondell.

A few months later Warners released *The Mouthpiece*, based on the flamboyant career of the criminal lawyer William J. Fallon. The film stars Warren William, who defends criminals by a series of sensational tricks, in order to demonstrate the fallibility of the law. His partnership with mobsters and scheming local politicians ends when he experiences a change of heart and decides to betray his crooked friends and opt out of his unethical if lucrative practice. 'I've decided to go back to civil practise. I want to breathe. I'm tired of crooked streets and crooked people.' At this point William is shot by one of his erstwhile criminal clients and he dies in a taxi in the arms of his faithful secretary, played this time by Aline McMahon. Such films obviously struck a responsive chord with the public because lightly disguised imitations, such as *Public Defender* (1931), *Attorney for the State* (1932), *State's Attorney* (1932) and *Counsellor at Law* (1933)[23] followed each other in rapid succession.

The disreputable side of newspaper life was exposed in a series of films made in the early 1930s. The biggest single influence on these movies was the 1928 Broadway comedy *The Front Page*, written by Ben Hecht and Charles MacArthur, almost as a documentary record of their days as journalists in Chicago. The play's thesis is that all newspapermen are totally devoid of human decency and their only concern is to make the next edition of their paper with a sensational scoop. The jounalists in *The Front Page* keep requesting the Sheriff to bring forward the time of the execution of a condemned man which they are gathered to watch so that they can file in time for the last morning edition, and they remain unsurprised at the successive revelations of human perfidy and incompetence. The main reporter, Hildy Johnson (played in the 1931 Howard Hawks version by Pat O'Brien), and his unscrupulous editor, Walter Burns (Adolphe Menjou), hide the 'murderer' in a rolltop desk while they write their exclusive story.

Plainly, such situations are open to melodramatic as well as comic treatment, and the newspaper movies which followed the success of *The Front Page* exposed the ruthlessness of 'yellow' journalism. *Five Star Final*[24] (1931) showed Edward G. Robinson as the editor of an evening tabloid who, under pressure from his publisher to increase circulation, devotes more space to items of a sensational nature. 'We're not selling newspapers on Park Avenue.... We've got to print stories about shop girls and murderers – something that our readers know.'[25] Robinson, with misgivings, digs up the story of Nancy Voorheis, who had shot her husband twenty years ago. The ensuing scandal drives the woman and her second husband to suicide and almost destroys her daughter's wedding. At the end, the daughter is dissuaded from shooting Robinson and the publisher only by her fiancé and she is led from the room screaming, 'You grow rich on filth'. The incident convinces Robinson that 'There are things in life that transcend dollar grabbing' and, in a truly biblical gesture, he washes his hands for the last time and leaves the newspaper business accompanied by his faithful secretary, played by Aline MacMahon.

The film's treatment of mankind's finer sensibilities is described in the script in a montage of people who form a representative section of the five-star final's readers.

A pasty-faced, shuffling dope fiend buys a paper, reading it eagerly as he exits. The next customer is an over-dressed street-walker. There follows, a vicious-looking Negro, a witch-like unkempt scrub woman ... a loud dressed gold toothed pimp... all the licentious, illiterate scum of a city, feeding their insatiable greed for filth upon a filthy tabloid's latest sensation.

Among *Five Star Final*'s successors were *Scandal Sheet* (1931), *Final Edition* (1932) and *Scandal for Sale* (1932), the first of which starred George Bancroft as a newspaper editor who at the conclusion of the film shoots his wife and then writes up the story for his paper before surrendering to the police.

One film in particular from 1932 appears to sum up the mood of America better than any other. At Paramount seven directors were each assigned to direct a short sequence, concerned with the reactions of people who are unexpectedly left a million dollars by a crusty old millionaire. The man no longer has any use for the money, as he is about to die, but he despises his family sufficiently to deprive them of it. *If I Had a Million* is remarkable for the violence in which many of the beneficiaries indulge.

Charlie Ruggles as a hen-pecked husband smashes everything in the china shop in which he works, on learning of his new-found wealth, while W. C. Fields and Alison Skipworth destroy car after car, driving after and wrecking the automobiles of those people they consider to be irresponsible drivers and hence, if only indirectly, resposnsible for the destruction of Fields's first cherished car. The section starring Gene Raymond is in effect an apologia for the gangster, as he points out in justification of his criminal activity, 'You don't think when you're hungry'. It is tacitly acknowledged that, if the money had come sooner, a smart lawyer could have saved him from conviction.

Justifiably the most famous (and shortest) sequence, directed by Ernst Lubitsch, features Charles Laughton as a downtrodden clerk who shows no emotion on learning of his legacy. Slowly, he walks out of the room, up a flight of stairs, through interminable outer offices, until he opens the final door. 'Mr. Brown?' he enquires politely. The man, who is obviously the President of the company, looks up expectantly, a little puzzled by the appearance of one of his anonymous workers. 'Yes?' he replies. Laughton screws up his mouth, blows an enormous raspberry and the scene dissolves. The film reflects a nation, where the old values of thrift and industry have decayed. The expression of individualism, violent and otherwise, is only consequent upon the god-like intervention of the unexpected inheritance.

Hollywood had survived the initial onset of the Depression. *Variety* reported in early 1931:

> Despite general depression, the film industry's leaders will pass the fiscal period of 1930 to their biggest net profit in history ... the belief is expressed that next year's profits will probably equal those of 1930 or nearly so.[26]

It was not to be. On 23 June 1931 the trade paper admitted: 'For the fourth successive month, the box office decline in monthly receipts for the big centers amounts to a 14% drop. That's from February to May inclusive as compared to the same period 1930.[27]

In 1930 Paramount and Loews both cut admissions in half. Fox Theaters admitted two people on each ticket and Warner Brothers slashed admission prices from forty cents to a dime. It was enough to delay the dramatic decline for a few months. Among the many incentives offered by the cinemas as free gifts during 1931 were pillows, china, bicycles, silk stockings, lamps and watches but now such practices were insufficient to lure back the big audiences of previous years.[28] At the end of the year *Variety* stated, 'Filmdom is left awaiting the birth of 1932 dizzy from its first real churning in the economic maelstrom.'[29]

Of all the studios Paramount was the worst affected. It had voraciously acquired theatres in the previous decade and was now suffering from the vast debts it had accumulated on the way. John Hertz of Lehman Bros was appointed Chairman of Paramount's Finance Committee in November 1931. His first decision was to cut all film budgets by a third and institute a reduction in salaries for all studio personnel. He sold the studio's shareholding in the CBS radio network for a capital gain of $41.2 million and removed the management team of Jesse Lasky, Sydney Kent and Sam Katz in a series of boardroom reshuffles. Founder Adolph Zukor became a figurehead as power remorselessly shifted from the West Coast to the East. The result was that gross receipts in 1932 dropped by $25 million. A profit of $8.7 million in 1931 became a loss of over $20 million in 1933. Before the end of the year John Hertz had resigned and Paramount was in receivership.[30]

RKO had called in the receivers in January 1933 after following a similar corporate path. Saddled with debts because of the large mortgage payments with which the studio had been greeted at birth, it tried to defy economic gravity in 1931 by acquiring the assets of Pathe Exchange Inc. Like Paramount, the studio devalued the deals of its contracted employees and searched fervently for a production chief who had the magic touch. In 1932 Schnitzer and William Le Baron were replaced by David O. Selznick, who signed John Barrymore, Leslie Howard and Katharine Hepburn. Selznick lasted barely more than a year before moving to MGM and leaving RKO to Merian C. Cooper. Meanwhile profits of $3.4 million in 1931 declined to losses of $5.7 million and $11.2 million in the next two years.[31] Universal lost money in the early 1930s but never more than $2 million; Columbia maintained profitability, albeit small, throughout the decade because like United Artists, the other member of the so-called Little Three, they were not encumbered by the mortgage bills attached to the movie theatres. For the same reason, of the Big Five only Loews Inc. continued to produce healthy surpluses. Nevertheless, profits of $10 million in 1930 had declined to $1.3 million three years later. Assets over the same period declined from $128.6 million to $123.7 million.[32]

By the time Roosevelt assumed office the Fox Film Company had joined Paramount and RKO in the hands of the receivers, having recorded a deficit of $16,964,499 in 1932 after posting a $9 million profit in 1931. Warner Brothers survived but lost $8 million in 1931 and $14 million in 1932 after profits in 1929 and 1930 of $17 million and $7 million respectively.[33]

It is no wonder, therefore, that the movies of 1931 and 1932 should reflect this time of bitterness and unrest both in theme and tone. In addition they were aided by the still recent innnovation of sound on film. Many of the action films discussed in this chapter, the gangster movies, the newspaper melodramas, the stories about shady lawyers and shyster politicians and others on the fringes of crime in the big cities were considerably aided by sound, which lent a credible noise, pace and realism. The writers of such screenplays, too, tended to be recent imports from New York and Chicago where they had been playwrights or journalists. When sound made title writers redundant the clamour from the studios was for the writers of pacey dialogue. It was their experience in the Eastern cities which also influenced the nature of Hollywood's output in 1931 and 1932.

During these years America was wracked by an economic and moral crisis whose dimension it had previously never experienced. Automatically it exposed flaws in the fabric of society, which the motion picture industry, with its uncanny eye for the topical, not to say transitory, currents of life, exploited with customary zeal. A bewildered and hurt nation found some relief in the depiction of cynical charlatans, vicious gangsters and shyster, untrustworthy figures of authority. It wasn't difficult to believe that violence was a justified means of advancement in a corrupt society, populated at the top of the hierarchy by fools, incompetents and crooks. Audiences could understand more easily the simplistic plots of the Hollywood action film than they ever would the intricate workings of the economic system by which they lived.

For fifteen years Hollywood had been regarded as America's last frontier, the town where the rags-to-riches myth had been seen to work its magic many times, and its spiralling success in the 1920s had been a towering symbol of the decade's prevailing hedonism, materialism and general infallibility. When the country collapsed in 1929 Hollywood, because of the novelty of talking pictures, seemed to escape unscathed. By 1933, however, it was obvious that there was trouble, even in the paradise of southern California.

It was in this atmosphere of distrust and disaster that the Presidential election campaign of 1932 began. Although popular belief has now raised Roosevelt to mythic status it must be stated that in November 1932 Roosevelt had no more idea how to solve the Depression than his Republican opponent. It is true that Roosevelt presented a considerably more attractive façade than the mournful Hoover. The Democratic candidate smiled in public a lot and, in 'Happy Days Are Here Again', he chose one of the great campaign songs in political history and one which has survived the past sixty years to remain the theme song of the Democratic Party. With his invention of the Fireside Chats on the radio and the carefully controlled photo opportunities to ensure that his physical handicaps were minimised, Roosevelt started the creation of a Presidential 'image'.

It was nothing like as sophisticated as it became after 1960 when the impact of television crucially changed the nature of Presidential campaigning but it was, in its own way, a significant step away from the 'laissez faire' attitudes of Republican Presidents in the 1920s. A useful companion in Roosevelt's new image was the aid of Hollywood. Together they metaphorically sang and danced through the decade, echoing each other's ringing declarations of confidence and pointing to each other as inspiring symbols of recovery from past troubles and optimism for the future.

In the Second World War the alliance between the President and the film companies resulted in open propaganda harnessed to the wider war effort. In the previous decade the alliance was less formalised but no less important. Roosevelt had an instinctive liking for and understanding of the mass media which none of his predecessors in office (with the possible exception of his distant relative Theodore Roosevelt) could match. It is unlikely that Hollywood's contribution to the war effort between 1941 and 1945 would have been so immediate and so effective without the preparation of the relationship conducted in the previous decade.

Ironically, the key campaigning issue appeared to be Prohibition rather than the all-pervasive Depression. John Dewey wrote caustically, 'Here we are in the midst of the greatest crisis since the Civil War and the only thing the two major parties seem to want to discuss is booze'.[34] Perhaps it was because it was about the only major issue on which the two men fundamentally disagreed. Roosevelt promised to repeal the Eighteenth Amendment while Hoover stuck rigidly to his dream of a God-fearing, alcohol-loathing White Anglo-Saxon Protestant utopia. Although Roosevelt won forty-two states to Hoover's six the result was less a resounding endorsement of the new President than a heartfelt rejection of the old.

With the benefit of historical hindsight Franklin D. Roosevelt appears to tower over the history of America in the first half of the twentieth century. He was the central figure in the Depression and the Second World War, elected an unprecedented four times to the highest office and when he died in April 1945 the lives of all Americans had been significantly affected by his actions as President. Yet in November 1932, after his comprehensive Electoral College victory over Hoover, the President-elect, it must be admitted, inspired something less than total confidence. Walter Lippmann, the country's foremost political commentator, wrote at the time,

> Franklin D. Roosevelt is an amiable man with many philanthropic impulses, but he is not the dangerous enemy of anything. He is too eager to please ... Franklin D. Roosevelt is no crusader. He is no tribune of the people. He is no enemy of entrenched privilege. He is a pleasant man, who, without any important qualifications for the office, would very much like to be President.[35]

The ninety-two-year-old Justice Oliver Wendell Holmes made a more considered judgement when he said of the President-elect after a short meeting, 'A second class intellect – but a first class temperament'. A first-class temperament and an intellectual flexibility were ultimately to serve America better than any intellectual brilliance could have done.

Roosevelt came to office with no great blueprint for solving the problems of the Depression. Certainly the deficit spending which formed such an integral part of the New Deal was regarded with enormous suspicion by Roosevelt, who had always believed in the traditionally balanced budget. In February 1933 Roosevelt had received a desperate hand-written letter from the outgoing President urging him to announce 'that there will be no tampering or inflation of the currency [and] that the budget will be unquestionably balanced even if further taxation is necessary'. Roosevelt needed, at this stage, little urging. 'Any Government, like any family, can for a year spend a little more than it earns', he said. 'But you and I know that a continuation of that habit means the poorhouse.' One of his first acts as President was to urge Congress to reduce federal expenditures by $500 million, in order, he said, to save the country from bankruptcy.[36]

The ideal of the balanced budget was not the exclusive property of either American or necessarily conservative politicians. The British Labour Chancellor of the Exchequer in 1929, Philip Snowden, was just as convinced of its necessity as was Heinrich Bruning, Chancellor of Germany in 1932 and Mackenzie King, the Prime Minister of Canada. The economic orthodoxy, as exemplified in the desire for a balanced budget, produced a standard argument. If a government spent more money than it collected in taxes it would have either to borrow to bridge the gap or to inflate the currency. If it borrowed, its competition for investors' funds would force up interest rates, which would hinder recovery. The effects of inflation had been seen less than ten years ago in Germany when the chaos which destroyed the life savings of the middle classes nearly destroyed the country itself.[37]

The other argument in favour of inaction was related to a belief that the economies of all countries moved in cyclical formations. The depression, it therefore followed, was merely a typical crisis of overproduction. It had happened before and it would happen again. It was the conventional downward phase of the business cycle. It followed a period of growth and the consequent crisis (seen in the events of 1929–30) would, in its turn, be succeeded by a period of recovery.

There wasn't a great deal a government could do to help the process. Production would simply have to slow down or cease altogether while surplus stocks were sold. Wages would fall so that goods could be sold profitably at lower prices. Inefficient firms would go out of business or reduce their workforces and organise more efficiently. Wage cuts, unemployment and their attendant miseries were the natural concomitants of this depressed phase of the cycle. The worst thing a government could do was to incur a deficit that would hinder the arrival of the recovery phase of the cycle. On 4 March 1933, as Roosevelt succeeded Hoover, this fiscal orthodoxy still held sway.

3

THE BLUE EAGLE
March 1933 to November 1936

> Plodding feet
> Tramp, tramp,
> The Grand Old Party's breaking camp.
> Blare of bugles,
> Din, din
> The New Deal's Moving In
> > Robert E. Sherwood, 3 March 1933

On 4 March 1933, when Franklin D. Roosevelt took the Presidential Oath, the Republic faced its gravest crisis since 1776. Already, however, the fiscally conservative pronouncements of his days as the Democratic Party nominee and as President-elect were starting to change. Roosevelt the pragmatist soon realised that the calamitous series of bank failures which terrified the nation on the day of his inaugural required an entirely new government response. In the previous two weeks the trickle of bank failures swelled into a torrent. 'We are at the end of our string,' muttered Hoover, 'there is nothing more we can do.'[1]

On 1 March 1933 the Governors of Kentucky, Tennessee, California, Alabama, Louisiana and Oklahoma proclaimed bank holidays as people stood in long queues outside the bank doors with satchels and paper bags to withdraw their savings and place them, for safety's sake, in a shoe box under the bed. By 4 March thirty-eight states had closed their banks. Richard Whitney returned to the Stock Exchange but this time to close it down. On the same day, for the first time since 1848, the Chicago Board of Trade shut its doors. This was no short-term collapse of one or two unsound financial institutions. The country itself appeared on the verge of collapse. Eyes were cast in the direction of the Fascists in Italy, the Nazis in Germany, the Communists in Russia. During the night of 3 March two young men were arrested in New York for daubing 'CLOSED! SOCIALISM WILL KEEP THEM OPEN' across the doors of a bank.[2] Was America heading for a similar political revolution?

On the journey to the Capitol from the White House Roosevelt tried in vain to make conversation with a taciturn and guardedly hostile Hoover. The crowds along Pennsylvania Avenue cheered, perhaps more in hope than expectation. The new President waved and doffed his silk hat. The old President sat stony-faced and unresponsive. It was a useful symbol of the nature of their respective presidencies.

As if the general outlook were not gloomy enough the weather in Washington on Inaugural Day was cold, bleak and cheerless, seemingly making its own apt comment on the state of the union. Roosevelt took the oath and turned to the densely packed crowd in the Capitol plaza and to the radio microphones which would transmit his speech all over the country.

Stylistically it didn't compare to any of Lincoln's public pronouncements and its rhetoric was less impressive than John F. Kennedy's twenty-eight years later, but it was nevertheless a masterly speech for it caught the mood of the nation perfectly. One hundred and twenty million people who felt themselves to be rudderless were captivated by the fifth sentence which set the tone of the day, the man and the Administration.

> First of all, let me assert my firm belief that the only thing we have to fear is fear itself – nameless, unreasoning, unjustified terror which paralyses needed efforts to convert retreat into advance.

The rest of the speech mixed the conventional appeal to honest government ('The money changers have fled from their high seats in the temple of our civilisation') with a request for a mandate for immediate action. Action was the *mot juste*. It was action that defined the difference in philosophy between Hoover and the New Deal. It was action, above all, which people wanted. 'You felt that they would do anything – if only someone would tell them what to do,' said Eleanor Roosevelt later.

Washington was galvanised into action and in the first hundred days of Roosevelt's administration passed enough legislation to alter fundamentally the public's perception of its government's philosophy. Emergency banking legislation was rushed through both Houses of Congress so quickly that even the Proposers hardly had time to read it, let alone the Congressmen and Senators who blindly voted for it.

On Sunday 5 March, the day after the inauguration, Roosevelt approved a presidential edict proclaiming a national bank 'holiday'. Every bank in the country closed down for four days. The American film industry let it be known that in the national absence of liquid money their box offices would accept both personal notes which could be redeemed when the banks opened again and payment in kind. It was like another Nativity. Sheepishly at first, gathering confidence as they saw their neighbours doing likewise, people bore their offerings to the local cinemas. Chickens, fruit, anything in the house that was edible, was carried to the box office and exchanged for tickets to see *She Done Him Wrong*, *State Fair* and *King Kong*, the top grossing movies of that first week in March 1933. [3]

Nevertheless, the movies had hit rock bottom. The industry depended on the rapid release of a film so that it could earn its production costs back as quickly as possible, and the studios could avoid the payment of high interest loans. The Bank Holiday lasted only a few days but the studio chiefs reckoned it had cost them a million dollars a day in lost revenue.

The film industry was and is unlike most other businesses. Industrialists believe that if their business is soundly based it will take a major economic catastrophe to destroy it. Men and women who have succeeded in show business know that life is a rollercoaster and a huge downward spiral is inevitable at some point. The pants-pressers, the glove-makers and furriers who became movie moguls and rich beyond their wildest dreams took one look at the Crash, the Depression and the Bank Holidays and saw the Cossacks who had chased them out of Russia.

These men were, almost without exception, Jewish immigrants. In addition they dealt in a commodity that obeyed no known law of business. A pair of trousers, a pair of gloves, a fur coat were tangible assets. They might be affected by predictable effects of a change of style but they remained tangible assets. Eight and a half thousand feet of 35mm film offered no such assurance. Stars, good directors and writers could sometimes mitigate the bewildering effects of the public's rapidly changing tastes but in essence every movie was, and still is, an expensive gamble. In a climate of national financial uncertainty the movie moguls knew that desperate measures of their own were also demanded.

When the Bank Holiday was announced, the Academy of Motion Picture Arts & Sciences (set up to honour its distinguished members by awarding its Oscars but, in effect, at this time operating as an organisation for the studio bosses) sanctioned a move by the studios to slash the wages of their employees by fifty per cent. Louis B. Mayer addressed his beloved 'family' at MGM with the tears rolling down his cheeks, begging his 'children' to accept the salary reduction in the selfless spirit that the troubled times required. Lionel Barrymore, deeply affected by this moving spectacle, endorsed Mayer's sentiments and the motion was carried. [4]

However, if the artists were swayed by the passion and drama of the moment, the lower-paid, more level-headed and significantly better-organised technicians were not. They refused to accept the deal and their strike on 13 March 1933 effectively closed down all the studios for that day. The executives hastily met again and agreed to exempt from the cuts all workers who were receiving less than fifty dollars a week; all others would waive a percentage of their salaries on a sliding scale up to fifty per cent for a period of up to eight weeks.

In Washington legislative action continued to be the keynote of the new administration. On 20 March the Economy Act was passed and, before the end of that first month, the Civilian Conservation Corps had been established. In the first hundred days the New Deal placed on the statute books fourteen pieces of significant legislation.

Of the immediate relief projects the National Industrial Recovery Act (NIRA) and the Agricultural Adjustment Act (AAA) were eventually struck down by the Supreme Court but those designed as reform measures, like the

Tennessee Valley Authority (TVA), the Securities Act and the Glass-Steagall Banking Act, were eventually sustained. Robert Sherwood, whose grim prognostication is quoted at the head of this chapter, went on to become a committed New Dealer and a speech-writer of Roosevelt, while Walter Lippmann, who had written so slightingly of the prospective President, also had cause to revise his original estimation.

> At the beginning of March the country was in such a state of confused desperation that it would have followed almost any leader anywhere he chose to go .... In one week the nation which had lost confidence in everything and everybody, has regained confidence in the government and itself. [5]

The New Deal was, at heart, a contradiction, a series of political and economic compromises overlaid with Roosevelt's own strategic sleight of hand. At the time it was both lauded and criticised for pouring unheard-of sums from the federal coffers into a variety of programmes for work relief. At the same time $400 million owing to veterans and $100 million owing to federal employees were simply repudiated.

Lewis Douglas, Director of the Budget, who had been attracted to Roosevelt by his campaign utterances against the spending plans of the Hoover adminsitration, played an important part in the policies of the Hundred Days. The budget balancers, through the Economy Act of 20 March 1933, won a victory for orthodox finance that had been impossible under Hoover. Thus, at the same time that he was trying to draft the NIRA and the AAA to raise domestic commodity prices and thus force up wages, the President was also pursuing a deflationary policy by means of a retrenchment programme which cut purchasing power still further. Having defeated the conservative Democrats at the convention in Chicago, he then proceeded to translate their policies into executive action on reaching the White House.

Raymond Moley, one of Roosevelt's key radical advisers, wrote in his memoirs:

> To look upon those policies as a unified plan was to believe that the accumulation of stuffed snakes, baseball pictures, school flags, old tennis shoes, carpenters' tools, geometry books and chemistry sets in a boy's bedroom could have been put there by an interior decorator. [6]

A later commentator added that to condemn these policies for their inconsistency was to miss the point. From an economic standpoint condemnation might be appropriate because one line of action tended to cancel another so that little was accomplished. However, from a political standpoint this very inconsistency, so long as the dilemma persisted, was the safest method of retaining political power. His own mixed emotions so closely reflected the popular mind that they were an asset rather than a liability. [7]

The NIRA, which, along with the AAA, was the cornerstone of the early torrent of legislation, known collectively as the First New Deal, contained many of the conservative and radical elements which so infuriated entirely opposite spheres of interest.

Initially the NIRA gave jobs to two million workers and helped to stop the deflationary spiral of falling prices and falling wages causing further unemployment. It (supposedly) improved business ethics and encouraged a spirit of civilised competition in which the Federal Government would intervene only to stop business or labour from flagrant abuses. It was designed to get American industry moving again, not to increase the power of the government to interfere. The latter was the result of the legislation, not its purpose.

Most importantly, the NIRA established through its various codes a national pattern of maximum hours and minimum wages. The Act itself was in two titles. The first, the National Recovery Adminsitration symbolised by the ubiquitous Blue Eagle and headed by General Hugh Johnson, was to be responsible for the setting up and the working of the individual codes, while the second provided for the Public Works Administration under the direction of Harold Ickes, the Secretary of the Interior.

Unfortunately for Johnson, the clamour for the codes was largely raised by the smaller industries while the oil, steel and automobile industries, the real target of the Act in that they covered such a large proportion of the working population, all procrastinated. By the end of July 1933, however, most of the industries had agreed to co-operate. In the last two weeks of that month 144 draft codes arrived in Washington and in the following month 546, including codes from the bulk of the car industry. Henry Ford, predictably, remained obdurate to the last. [8]

The most controversial part of the NIRA was Clause 7(a), which dealt with the right of labour to organise and bargain collectively with management by representatives of its own choosing. Although it was included almost as an afterthought to satisfy William Green and his American Federation of Labor, this clause quickly became the flashpoint of renewed hostility between labour and management. The clause appeared to both sides to suggest that the Federal Government was lending its support for increased union activity.

Ironically the American Federation of Labor benefited only slightly from the passage of the Act. Between 1933 and 1935 membership of its craft unions increased by only 13 per cent. Over the same period industrial unions' membership rose 132 per cent, presaging the impetus that would lead to the formation of the Congress of Industrial Organizations. Certainly John L. Lewis went back to his Union of Mine Workers with the slogan 'The President Wants You to Join the Union'. The President himself stayed noticeably silent on the issue.

The rise in union militancy led to a rash of strikes as the unions tested the limits of their power. In the spring and summer of 1934 the number of strikes was the highest since 1922. In nineteen states the militia had to be called out, clashes were numerous and forty-six workers were killed. In 1932 union recognition was the cause of less than a fifth of official strikes but in 1934 it was the overriding concern in half the quarrels. On 9 May 1934 the San Francisco dockers (longshoremen) struck and as the dispute spread further north the whole coastline to Seattle ground to a halt. Union recognition was eventually granted but only after two strikers were killed and scores of others and police injured. The National Guard was summoned to restore order.[9]

Unions came to Hollywood almost as a direct result of the last triumph of the studios' old-fashioned paternalism. Hollywood's own emergency legislation produced not so much a renewal of confidence in the benevolent despotism of the studios' administration as a deeply rooted belief that in future the workers needed their own unions to fight their battles. At the end of the eight weeks which had been reluctantly agreed as the duration of the fifty per cent pay cuts, Warner Brothers refused to restore the wages of their employees to their former level. Darryl Zanuck, their head of production, resigned (supposedly as a protest but in reality it offered a good pretext for a tactical move to join Joseph Schenck in the formation of Twentieth Century Pictures) and Warners relented only after considerable pressure was exerted on them. Sullenly, Harry Warner issued a statement that no Warner Brothers picture would in future be granted a shooting schedule of longer than eighteen days. A ninety-minute feature film, therefore, had to produce five minutes of cut film a day. Even in the controlled conditions of the studios' own sound stages this was a tall order, particularly for musicals and period dramas which both needed more time for preparation.

Producers liked to have the first set-up completed before 9 am. Actors and actresses required for the first few shots would have to be in make-up by 7 am. Frequently (notoriously on the Busby Berkeley musical numbers) shooting didn't finish until after midnight. It was such flagrant exploitation of the workforce which eventually led to the studios facing the demands of guilds and labour unions for recognition of maximum-length shooting days.

Although there were political extremists in union politics at this time, their power was the result of the moderates offering them support in the wake of their employers' intransigence. When steel owners walked into the office of Frances Perkins, the Secretary of Labor, and found William Green already seated there waiting for a discussion on the steel National Recovery Administration (NRA) code, they shuffled around in embarrassment and refused to talk either to Green or to Perkins in Green's presence. Perkins wrote later that their behaviour remainded her of naughty boys at a birthday party.[10]

Employers' suspicions of the NRA were increased by their workers' whole-hearted acceptance of it. Sidney Hillman, the influential head of the Amalgamated Clothing Workers of America, conceded before a Senate Finance Committee that the NRA had been instrumental in affording some protection against starvation wages.[11] One worker felt that there was something even more important than the minimum wage and maximum hour provisions: 'There is knowing that the working man doesn't stand alone against the bosses and their smart lawyers and all their smart tricks. There is a government now that cares whether things is fair for us.' [12]

The irony is that in historical hindsight the actual legislation and the way in which it operated was much more in favour of the employers and business in general than either side was prepared to admit. Section 7(a) soon proved to be grossly inadequate for the unions, as all it did was to stimulate an increase in company unions. In 1934 Senator Robert Wagner introduced a Labor Disputes Bill in which he tried to put teeth into 7(a) but his appeals to the White House were greeted with a deafening silence. Wagner's Bill was heavily defeated.

The NRA worked best in those industries where there was already a history of, or at least a potential for, co-operation between labour and management. With the defeat of the Wagner Bill the NRA was left only one power of punishment and that was by the withdrawal of the Blue Eagle. This never proved to be a sufficiently great threat.

The NRA's biggest failing was that under Johnson, who transformed this new government agency into a quasi-religious experience, it led people to believe that it would achieve more than it possibly ever could. Workers believed that if management signed the NRA Code it would solve all their problems instantly. This was not the case and finally Johnson disappeared for days on end while he tried to drink himself into a solution. In September 1934 he resigned and his position was never filled before the Supreme Court struck down the Act. However, Johnson had been personally responsible for the NRA's early triumphs as much as he was for its subsequent failures. Frances Perkins concluded:

> It was dynamic. It was as though the community arose from the dead: despair was replaced by hope. Certainly, an enormous number of good enterprises grew out of the NRA whether or not it was itself successful. [13]

Predictably, the Blue Eagle was a great success in Hollywood, where it threatened for a time to replace Mickey Mouse and Rin-Tin-Tin as the town's most successful non-human star. There were two distinct reactions to it. First, there was general delight that consumer purchasing power was recovering to the extent that movies started to be profitable again and, second, there was the wary caution with which movie executives approached anyone sent out from the East Coast with orders to pry into the functioning of Hollywood business.

On the first note *Variety* was persuaded to report information which, unusually, made sense outside theatrical circles.

> With NRA, the flag business commercially and patriotically has been given its biggest boost since the World War.
> If it isn't the NRA banner that's being rapidly hoisted atop flag posts

all over the country it's the Stars and Stripes or both. Looks almost like the discovery of a new country. [14]

MGM, that bastion of Republicanism, even incorporated in its advertising copy a comparison between the NRA's Blue Eagle and its own Leo the Lion with the conclusion that MGM star pictures led to prosperity. Paramount announced its own 'recovery program' in the shape of its 1933–4 releases. Warner Brothers took a similar line. In its advertising copy the picture of an exhibitor with his hand raised as if taking an oath was covered by the words

I SOLEMNLY SWEAR that in 1933–34 I will serve the best interests of my theater and patrons by doing business with [Warner Brothers] .... And so I now whole-heartedly resolve to subscribe to every one of the 60 pictures of Warner Brothers RECOVERY PROGRAM for 1933–34.

Variety reported that George M. Cohan was writing an official NRA song. It was to be called 'Over Here'. It owed perhaps a little to his famous marching song of 1917, 'Over There'. This time it ended 'And we won't lay down till it's over over here'. More typical was the reaction of *Variety*'s man in St Louis who, recording the box office news for the last week in August 1933, speculated, 'Maybe the Blue Eagle has something to do with it. Business around here in the local cinemas certainly continues to leave no cause for complaint.'

An economic interpretation of Hollywood is illuminating because of the volume at which money has always spoken in the film community. Thus, a graph of almost direct proportion could be drawn between Hollywood economics and the national economy and the current attitude towards the government in film circles.

The short four-month boom of March to July 1933, the period covered by the Hundred Days, coincided directly with a huge uplift in picture morale. The Warner Brothers movie *Breadline*, a contemporary account of a war veteran's struggle to survive in the Depression, was renamed initially *The Forgotten Man* and eventually, after Roosevelt's inauguration, *Heroes for Sale*, a considerably more upbeat title. On 27 January Darryl Zanuck, the Executive Producer, sent a new page of dialogue to Robert Lord, the Associate Producer. The film was to finish over a shot of the dead Richard Barthelmess as follows:

BOY

He was a wonderful man, wasn't he?

GIRL

He loved everybody but himself.

BOY

Was there anybody else like him?

GIRL

Yes, another man – a man who died on the cross at Calvary 1900 years ago.

On 8 March Zanuck rewrote the ending again, jettisoning the religious overtones.

Page 135 – I want the action and dialogue changed as following:

TOM

It's not optimism – just common horse sense. Did you read President Roosevelt's inaugural address?

ROGER

He's right. You know it takes more than one sock in the jaw to lick a hundred million people.

The reason I use the Inaugural speech at the finish is that everyone throughout the world is talking about FDR's speech. It was a bombshell and is being compared to great speeches like Lincoln's Gettysburg Address and it seems to me much more constructive for Tom to be talking about what somebody else said than to be talking about what he thinks.

The director, William Wellman, must have objected to the overt propaganda because ten days later Zanuck wrote him a stiff note:

When you shoot the episode at the end of the picture, where I rewrote the scene and I want a Roosevelt speech – I want him to mention FDR's speech and take out the paper and read it to him. Shoot it the way I wrote you in the last note with the FDR speech in the newspaper. [15]

On the other hand, for all the personwal acclaim for Roosevelt and the relief that the banks had reopened and audiences were returning to the movie theatres, Hollywood retained a fundamental suspicion of any threat of federal interest in the workings of the film industry. The question of a code of business practice to be included within the constraints of the NRA, and which would be the result of negotiations between Washington and labour unions as well as the film companies themselves, immediately rang warning bells on the sound stages. Sol Rosenblatt, a bright young Jewish New Deal lawyer, was the man appointed to help Hollywood draft its NRA code. He was received as only the film capital receives an honoured guest. Music greeted him as he stepped off the train on to the platform of a station which was decorated with banners. Celebrities (unspecified) waited to meet him and a parade escorted him to his hotel.

By day he interviewed executives, talent groups and labour leaders, and the meetings were reported in the news sections of the following day's trade papers. By night he visited all the smart night clubs and restaurants Hollywood had to offer in the company of attractive young actresses cast by their studios for the role. His social engagements featured heavily in the gossip columns. Rosenblatt fell into the trap baited for him with obliging neatness. By the time he was finished, the Independent Exhibitors had to hire Clarence Darrow to prepare a report on their behalf because the eventual NRA code favoured the big studios so overwhelmingly.[16] In fairness it wasn't entirely Rosenblatt's fault. His gregariousness, wit and charm made him an instant hit in a town which has long known how to evaluate and manipulate such assets. A hard-bitten experienced lawyer without a trace of stardust might have accomplished more.

To ensure their 'triumph' the Hollywood establishment concentrated their fire on Rosenblatt with devastating accuracy. *The Hollywood Reporter* issued a blistering attack on the prospective code and urged Rosenblatt to return to Washington on the next stagecoach. Stars and their agents protested vehemently at the Communist-inspired suggestion that nobody could earn more than $5,000 a week. On the other hand the lower-paid workers, technicians and stenographers welcomed the NRA as a guarantee of a $40 weekly wage. *Variety* reported

> The NRA Blue Eagle is being hung next to 'God Bless Our Home'.
>
> Young wives who had to go out to work on overtime etc. are now back home to greet and cook for their husbands. They can indulge in the cook-your-own racket because they knock off work at five o'clock under the NRA code.[17]

The NRA code was eventually drawn up and signed by the President on 27 November 1933 and was announced to Congress on 6 December. It banned company unions, set minimum rates of pay and allowed labour to organise and bargain collectively. The code was signed by 140 different labour unions. If they thought it was a triumph, they were soon disillusioned. The movie moguls used the code to impose the ceiling on salaries their stars had dreaded. The actors telegrammed Washington without success. The studios also successfully resisted attempts to have the Production Code (administered by the Hays Office) incorporated into the NRA Code which effectively legalised their restrictive monopolies.

Hollywood's attitude to the NRA was one of wary acceptance provided federal interference was a matter of temporary political expediency only. Hollywood appreciated that the Blue Eagle commanded respect as a crowd-puller. The big companies ended all their movies with a shot of the Blue Eagle after the final credits and the slogan 'We Do Our Part'.

The most famous example was the sudden inclusion of the Eagle in *Footlight Parade*, during Busby Berkeley's 'Shanghai Lil' number. James Cagney plays a deserting American sailor on the search for Shanghai Lil, a Chinese lady of dubious morals. When he finds her he is so happy that he steals a fellow sailor's uniform so that he can return to his ship. The company parades, shouldering arms, and at the appropriate time flicks up cards which form a mosaic picture of the Stars and Stripes. The cards are then reversed to reveal a picture of Franklin D. Roosevelt while, for the grand finale and to the accompaniment of a medley of patriotic songs, the sailors position themselves in such a way as to shape the outline of the Blue Eagle. At an appropriate musical juncture each of the protruding angles unleashes a ceremonial volley of blank cartridges.

This was the Blue Eagle which Hollywood appreciated, just as it was prepared to acknowledge the aid of the NRA in stimulating the box office recovery during the spring of 1933. It was only when federal intervention threatened to upset existing trade practices, in particular allowing the various crafts in the industry the opportunity to seize a little more power, that the studios reacted with their time-honoured show of injured innocence.

On 27 May 1935 the NRA was invalidated by a decision of the Supreme Court. Two years before Jack Warner had been appointed an NRA official for California as part of his plan to gain the ear of the President. After the Supreme Court's decision Warner Brothers was stuck with the Blue Eagle on all its letterheads, stationery and memo pads. The symbol of hope reborn was neatly chopped off and the pads were reversed and then reused with true Warner Brothers parsimony. [18] It was an inglorious end to a glorious crusade.

The belief of the picture business was similar to any other American business. The business of the government was to create a favourable economic climate in which it could operate, not to poke its nose into the inner recesses of an industry it didn't understand. It therefore approved wholeheartedly of the economic nationalism underpinning other New Deal measures. Roosevelt's ideological pragmatism enabled him efffectively to devalue the dollar so that American goods became cheaper to export, a major factor in the success of the American film industry which had already penetrated most world markets.

Roosevelt demonstrated his strength by threatening to sink the London Conference of 1933 which had been arranged to bring about an international agreement on tariffs and trade. He sent a 'bombshell' telegram which clearly indicated that America had no intention of jeopardising its early gains in the economic field by a commitment to internationalism which might leave the recent rise in domestic prices unprotected against foreign 'dumping'.

The film industry also approved of the changing pattern of relief under New Deal legislation. It had been a fundamental tenet of Hoover's response to the Depression that it was wrong to give money directly to the unemployed and impoverished because it was bad for morale and would create a nation of work-shy shirkers. Roosevelt was not hidebound by such thinking. The money doled out by the Federal Emergency Relief Administration, and other government bodies, went directly to meet the needs of the most badly affected people. The largely Republican movie moguls might have disapproved in principle but they certainly approved in practice when it became clear that some of that money was behind the recovery in ticket sales.

The relative and limited prosperity which followed the massive pump-priming of the Second New Deal found an immediate echo in the fortunes of the major film companies. In the weeks leading up to the 1936 election pro-Roosevelt feelings were running at their highest levels in Hollywood since the heady days of March 1933. *Business Week* commented:

Though attendance in 1936 will not pop to an alltime high, it ought to average not less than 88 million persons weekly, which would be 10% higher than 1935 and not far removed from 1930's record 110 million.

Warner Brothers fiscal year gain of 345% over 1935 demonstrates what the leverage of more movie goers can do . . . .

Looking ahead the movie magnates can see nothing but champagne and nesselrode pudding. Though not all of them favored the re-election of Roosevelt, his social program, so they say, plays right into their pockets. The President seeks higher wages, shorter hours, unemployment insurance and old age pensions. Wrap that into one small capsule and it means to the motion picture mentality more money to spend on movies and more leisure in which to spend the money. [19]

As the national income rose from $34.6 billion in 1933 to $64.7 billion in 1936, so the motion picture income rose in proportion. At the time of Roosevelt's overwhelming Presidential victory over Governor Alf Landon, *The Hollywood Reporter* referred to it as a time 'when even good pictures made money'. [20]

In a poll conducted at all the studios four weeks before the election *The Hollywood Reporter* discovered that support for Roosevelt over Landon was predictably lowest at MGM where only 76 per cent preferred the Democratic President but rose to 92 per cent at Warner Brothers and averaged a healthy 84 per cent. [21] Apart from the fact that Roosevelt was a great film fan (it was solemnly recorded that between March 1933 and March 1934 he watched 1,327 reels of film) his first bid for re-election came at a time when nearly every Hollywood studio had climbed out of receivership and heavy financial deficits and was once more making those huge corporate profits it had regarded as its due. A week after the election *Variety* reported:

The re-election of President Roosevelt was particularly pleasing to the amusement business as a whole, and particularly motion pictures . . . . Business at the b.o. is estimated as being up about 50% over four years ago when an all-time low per theater was reached . . . Consequently, it is logical for the industry as a whole to be satisfied with an administration that is credited with making the recovery possible. [22]

Whatever its deficiencies, and however self-interested might have been the stimulus to action, the Second New Deal solidified in people's minds the assumptions aroused by the First New Deal, to the effect that the Federal government cared about conditions on the farms, and in industry, and was prepared to enact federal legislation to ensure a minimum standard of living for all Americans.

The series of decisions by the Supreme Court, which declared many of the key Acts in the First New Deal unconstitutional, aroused a need 'to make America over'. Having found big business to be an uneasy bedfellow, and ever mindful of the growing popularity of the respective Utopias of a number of demagogues, principally Father Coughlin, Dr Townsend and Huey Long, the Governor of Louisiana, Roosevelt found himself being pushed ever further to the left. The attitude of the President to the Wagner Labor Relations Bill is a classic illustration of his great flexibility or, from another perspective, his total lack of principles. By his refusal to act on behalf of labour in 1934 he had given tacit support to the company unions and killed off Wagner's first attempt at birth. When the new Wagner Bill came before the House in 1935 it received the Presidential signature within a week of obtaining final Congressional approval. Frances Perkins wrote: 'It ought to be on record that the President did not take part in developing N.L.R.A. and, in fact, was hardly consulted about it. It did not particularly appeal to him. All the credit for it belongs to Wagner.' [23]

Yet the new Act helped to increase trade union membership from three and a half million in 1935 to eight million by 1940, and thereafter labour was Roosevelt's most consistent electoral supporter. When in 1938 industrial disputes fell by a half, and after the National Labor Relations Board had announced that by early 1940 over twenty-five thousand complaints had been filed with it, *The New Republic* commented approvingly that 'the workers have seemingly discovered that they can safely turn from naked economic warfare to the processes of government'. [24]

Apart from the Wagner Act, the legislation usually referred to collectively as the Second New Deal included the Social Security Act, the Holding Companies Act, the Wealth Tax Act (which prompted Hearst to instruct all his employees to refer to the New Deal at all times as 'the Raw Deal'), [25] a relief law, which included the establishment of the Works Progress Administration (WPA), the NYA and the various offshoots such as the short-lived Federal Theater project.

Much has been made of the new influences on Roosevelt in the 1935–6 era. Men like Frankfurter, Corcoran, Cohen and Landis were supposed to replace Tugwell, Moley, Berle, Richberg and Johnson in the President's esteem as if that explained the sudden lurch to the left. Yet Moley was still writing speeches until late in 1936 and both Berle and Tugwell had been considered practically Communists at various points of the First New Deal. This view also overlooks the continuity of Roosevelt's Cabinet members in the shape of Hopkins, Ickes, Hull and Perkins. More to the point, all the legislation throughout the Roosevelt era was shaped to a greater or lesser extent by the philosophy of the President himself.

The Second New Deal, although it aroused violent passions on both sides, was neither as horrifying as the Right exclaimed nor as radical as the Left wanted to claim. Roosevelt's broad human objectives remained consistent even if his strategy was subject to a moment's change. He judged to a nicety just how radical he had to be in order to ward off the electoral threat posed by the Coughlin–Townsend–Long–Smith coalition. The result was that Roosevelt swept the country and denied what had looked in 1935 to have been a formidable third party the satisfaction of achieving even a million popular votes.

An example of the continuity Roosevelt liked is afforded by his economic policy in the eighteen months following his second Inaugural Address in which he complained of 'one third of a nation ill-housed, ill-clad, ill-nourished'. Despite increasing federal spending by the WPA and associated agencies Roosevelt had, at heart, always been a budget balancer. At the same time he had always, at heart, been in favour of using federal funds to alleviate the poverty caused by unemployment. Somehow he managed to reconcile the two beliefs in his own mind in much the same way as he had urged Moley to write a speech which 'wove together' Tugwell's ideas on economic nationalism and Hull's belief in the destruction of all trade barriers. [26]

After the injections of federal relief allocations had given an urgently needed boost to the economy, Roosevelt proceded in 1937 to cut back government spending as a sop to his conservative alter ego. If the radical Corcoran and Cohen really had influenced Roosevelt greatly, their influence was destined to be short-lived. In the fiscal year of 1931–2, the Hoover government had spent sufficiently liberally as to achieve a deficit of $2,942,051,000. In the election year of 1935–6, at the height of the recovery, government spending reached a deficit of $4,952,928,000. Two years later the deficit had been cut to $1,449,625,000. In other words, Roosevelt spent in the fiscal year 1937–8 much less than an administration which he and his supporters had criticised as a 'do nothing' government. In the following year expenditure rose from $7.5 billion to well over $9 billion and the government deficit climbed again to over $3.5 billion.

The years 1937–8 were known colloquially as the Roosevelt Recession. In the twelve months following May 1937 the index of industrial production fell from 118 to 76, wholesale prices dropped from 88 to 78.1, farm prices fell by over forty points to 92 and payrolls in the manufacturing industries fell back from 110.1 to 71.1, so that there was only a two point difference over the index in July 1935, before the big spendings of the Second Hundred Days. Above all, the unemployment level rose to a disastrous ten million and recalled the horrors of the winter of 1932–3. At this point Roosevelt withdrew his objections to 'pump-priming' and the WPA rolls were restored to just short of their original length. [27]

At various times, Roosevelt and the New Deal were attacked from the Left for being fascist and from the Right as being Communist. *The New Republic* was constantly probing the New Deal for Fascist intentions, and in a carefully argued essay published in the *American Mercury* George Skolsky pointed out that, to all intents and purposes, America was in the summer of 1934 a Fascist country. [28]

The slanders of the extreme Right were perhaps the more venemous of the two. Commentators of this persuasion seemed to develop an intense personal hatred of Roosevelt to whom was attributed a plethora of moral and political depravities. Roosevelt was a patrician from Dutchess County, New York, where he lived on his Hyde Park estate in comfort. He was an unlikely American version of Lenin but his flirtation with radical solutions to the seemingly intractable economic problems of the Depression smacked of 'betrayal' to his enemies. The Hearst press, during the 1936 election, delivered itself of the conviction that the New Deal was:

> The Red New Deal with a Soviet seal,
> Endorsed by a Moscow hand
> The strange result of an alien cult
> In a liberty loving land.

A typical anti-Roosevelt salvo was fired by P. Crosby in his book *Three Cheers for the Red, Red and Red*: 'I think it is unfair to call Roosevelt a Socialist. He is an agitator of the worst type . . . . A vote for Roosevelt in 1936 is a vote for bloodshed in 1937.' The book was published by The Freedom Press. Similar books also published in 1936 were *America Swings to the Left*, *America Faces the Barricades* and *Roosevelt versus Recovery*.

In the late 1960s historians, possibly disaffected with the Welfare State the 1930s had bequeathed and with the current Democratic President's seeming obsession with the morass of South-East Asia, began to criticise what they now perceived as the shortcomings of the New Deal. They reiterated that Roosevelt had been inconsistent, that his programmes were inadequately financed and that real recovery did not begin until after Pearl Harbor. It is certainly true that in 1939 there were still nine million people unemployed and in 1941 ten per cent of the working population were unable to find a job. [29]

The battle between Right and Left continued to rage in the pages of New Deal historiography. In 1983 W. E. Leuchtenburg noted that writers on the Left still believed the New Deal to be worthless or pernicious. Contemporary Right-wingers saw in the New Deal the origins of the centralised state they sought to dismantle and Ronald Reagan himself insisted that the New Deal had derived from Italian Fascism. [30]

The New Deal can best be understood by constant reference to the conditions prevailing in March 1933 when Roosevelt took the oath of office. The country had never been as close to social revolution as it was in that week. In a recent televison documentary on America in the 1930s, Gore Vidal referred to Roosevelt and his New Deal with the simple statement 'He saved capitalism'. Certainly he understood the need for the government to be seen to be doing something. For all the bitterness of his opponents Roosevelt instigated a change in the mood of deep despair which had seemingly gripped the country and paralysed its political institutions. Within weeks he restored people's faith that the country was going to climb out of the Depression, that not all politicians were cynical or incompetent.

In 1932 the movie theatres were filled with portrayals of such characters. In November 1933 Paramount released the Marx Brothers' *Duck Soup*, which attacks anything and everything to do with the established practice of government. Groucho, playing President Rufus T. Firefly, keeps the Cabinet waiting while he attempts to scoop up some pins as he bounces a rubber ball, writes notes to himself about getting the plumbing fixed and plays games with a minister who wants to get a tariff discussed by persistently ruling him out of order. Firefly plunges his country into war after having been called 'an upstart' by the neighbouring country's evil ambassador and then rejects an offer of mediation because 'I've already paid a month's rent on the battlefield'.

Chico, after two unsuccessful attempts, manages to arrange a children's choosing rhyme, so that Harpo becomes the one who has 'the rare privilege of sacrificing his life for his country'. Groucho congratulates him warmly, reminding him that 'While you're out there risking life and limb through shot and shell we'll be in here thinking what a sucker you are'. At the end Margaret Dumont tries to inject some heroic patriotism into the proceedings by singing the Freedonia National Anthem, but her action merely encourages the Brothers to shower her with cooking apples.

Duck Soup opened to poor notices and dreadful business. It is true that the Marx Brothers' earlier screen originals *Monkey Business* (1931) and *Horse-feathers* (1932) had done less well than *Animal Crackers* (1930) and *The Coconuts* (1929), which had had the benefit of considerable runs on Broadway, so it is possible that the Brothers' humour was diminishing in popular appeal. *Duck Soup* was also, arguably, a less approachable movie than their previous two films which had been set in the recognisably contemporary world of colleges, football games and gangsters, with songs to keep audiences constantly entertained. In addition the very factors which the purists admire about *Duck Soup* may also be factors in the film's initial rejection. Certainly when the Brothers moved to MGM in 1935, Irving Thalberg immediately returned Chico and Harpo to their musical instruments and reintroduced the songs and the lovers' subplot. *A Night at the Opera* became their greatest hit.

Most significantly, *Duck Soup* suffered because of its unfortunate timing. William Troy, in his review in *The Nation*, felt that the antic fooling of the Brothers was 'a luxury in which we can no longer afford to indulge'.[31] In November 1933 Roosevelt's immense personal popularity deflated the humour in Firefly's wrapping his sandwiches in the indictment papers, and the spectre of European dictators did not yet loom sufficiently large for the film to be seen as biting anti-Fascist material. The mood of the nation swung dramatically after the first hundred days of the Roosevelt Administration. *Duck Soup* was left trailing in its wake.

The essence of the New Deal was contained in those bewildering first Hundred Days. A firm declaration of action by a strong new President and a torrent of impressive if sometimes contradictory legislation was sufficient to generate a renewal of national confidence which manifested itself in a short but decisive economic boom. It might have been rooted in nothing more than speculation based on cheap credit and the expectation of inflation and future profits but it was sufficient to fuel a rise in the production index from 56 to 101 between March and July, while farm prices rose from 55 to 83, retail stocks from 59.8 to 71 and the Wall Street industrial stocks average price from 63 to 109 during that same period. On 3 March 1933 motion picture stock averaged 16.17; on 22 April it had risen by 9 per cent to 17.61, and by 6 June it had reached 24.74. The Dow Jones industrial average rose on these dates from 53.84 to 72.24 until on 6 June it was at 90.90. *Motion Picture Herald* reported with satisfaction:

> Since March 3, the day before Mr Roosevelt was inaugurated, the market value of motion picture shares on the New York Stock Exchange alone has swelled some $130,000,000 in the liveliest trading since the boom – and crash – days of 1929 and 1930. [32]

The Hollywood Reporter also found a break in the clouds.

> The jump in the theater business, promised and expected every week during the past ten months has finally arrived, with the nation's box offices ... taking in more money during the past two weeks than during any similar period in the past eight months.

The top grossing movies in the first six months of 1933 were the film version of Noel Coward's patriotic play *Cavalcade* and the two Warner Brothers musicals *Forty Second Street* and *Gold Diggers of 1933* [33] whose heart-warming stories of backstage triumph were also clear morality tale parallels of the possibilities of individual victories over the indignities inflicted by the Depression.

This was why the New Deal was so apprreciated by Hollywood. It was cheerful, optimistic and financially rewarding. An editorial in *The Hollywood Reporter* on 12 May 1933 found that

> Business is getting better. Very much better. We have had quite a few letters in the last few days from exhibitor friends scattered throughout the country and every letter is filled with anticipation of better business for 1934. Each correspondent is 100% for the Roosevelt administration and believes that if the President is given the least bit of help, his new deal will turn into a GOOD DEAL and this country will jump back to its feet. [34]

A few days later Sol Rosenblatt arrived in Hollywood and the tone of the industry's response altered significantly.

The real conflict between Hollywood and the New Deal was invariably over what the former considered to be unwarranted interference by the latter in the legitimate business affairs of the former. Even a relatively harmless questionnaire sent to studio employees aroused the Editor of *The Hollywood Reporter* to a disproportionate fury.

> So Uncle Sam is going digging for dirt. He is sending a questionnaire out that is asking anything and everything of everybody connected with the motion picture industry except possibly the legitimacy of their birth. And why is Uncle Sam snooping? Because a goat is needed for the next six months or so.... Why, oh why, oh why? Has the picture business ever asked anything of the government – a nickel, a dime or even an inflated dollar?[35]

Understandably, therefore, Hollywood took great exception to the New Deal when it appeared to set itself up as a rival studio. The Resettlement Administration, one of the many federal agencies spawned by the New Deal, hired the film critic Pare Lorentz to make two documentaries, *The Plow that Broke the Plains* and *The River*, which have now become accepted as classics of their time. However, when the federal agency then tried to get the films distributed and seen by the public they met with a curt dismissal.

The two cameramen assigned to the project, Leo Hurwitz and Paul Strand, took advantage of Lorentz's comparative lack of technical knowledge to assume considerable responsibility for the writing as well as the photographing of the scripts. Both were enthusiastic supporters of the Russian style of film-making and their project, which was to make a film about the destruction of the top soil and the havoc wrought by the great dust storms of the 1930s, soon took on the overtones of class consciousness. Their script, Lorentz later told an interviewer from *Scribners*,

> Was all about human greed and how lousy our social system was .... For Pare Lorentz, in spite of the impact of his work, will get socking mad if you tag him as a 'Leftist'. He insists he's a 'realist' and that there is a big difference – that he's just a strong New Dealer and that he can't see all this uproar about Russian movies.[36]

Strand, Hurwitz and Ralph Steiner, the major figures on the production crew, were all Communists, but their influence was considerably lessened as Lorentz went through the film and carefully removed all traces of the infamous Russian style. *The Plow that Broke the Plains* was eventually written by Lorentz in the style of epic poetry. It achieved many of its best effects by means of short sentences juxtaposed with corresponding images.

> Great herds are driven on the range. Countless heads of cattle feed on the sea of grass. Steers grow fat. The cattlemen grow rich. The range is free. More ranchers drive in their herds. The herds increase. Scramble for

water rights and control of range .... More stock men. Each after what he can get. No responsibility to safeguard the great resource – the grass.

The film shows the beginnings of the great trek westward by sharecroppers, driven from their traditional homes in the Dust Bowl of Oklahoma: 'Blown out – baked out – and broke ... nothing to stay for ... nothing to hope for ... homeless, penniless and bewildered they joined the great army of the highways'.

Reaction to the film encapsulated the various responses from the political fringes to the New Deal itself. The Left- wing review *New Theatre* was not at all impressed.

> The film as put together in its present form by Mr Lorentz is a pale imitation of what it was intended to be .... The lack of a clear message or a decisive point of view weakens the structure of the film and makes it rhetorical and literary instead of dramatic. Evasion has never helped documentary.

Variety offered the predictable response of the Hollywood establishment.

> At the Rialto, the audience accepted it apathetically as something to be endured until the feature ran again. Several in the show caught went to sleep and the others just stared stolidly, evidencing neither interest nor disapproval. The picture may find more favor in the rural districts but it will not interest the city folk. It is not entertainment. [37]

Those last four damning words combined with a horror of the very idea of government-financed film-making were sufficient to deny the picture a distribution through orthodox channels. The Resettlement Administration booked it into independent cinemas with the aid of its regional offices in Lincoln, Nebraska but major exhibitors would have nothing to do with it. *The Motion Picture Herald*, the exhibitors' trade magazine, edited by the Right-wing Catholic Martin Quigley, seized on an ominous report of *The Plow* which was discovered to be playing in the Cameo, a New York City cinema, on a bill that also included the Russian movies *The Life of Maxim Gorky, May Day Parade 1936*, and *Fifteen Years of Soviet Cinema*. The demonology of the New Deal was in full swing.

> The Soviet Government's controlled and operated cinema has long been the most conspicuous supply of b.o. material for the Cameo. Now, however, there is a promising rival in the field, none other than the cinema of the U.S. Government's Administration WPA [sic], which has made its debut in the Red Sector on the screen of the Cameo with *The Plow That Broke the Plains*.

The same journal noted a few weeks later:

> To Texas legislator Eugene Worley was imputed one threat to demand of

the D.N.C. that the film be suppressed and another to give Rexford Tugwell a 'punch in the nose' if it is not. Mr Tugwell caused *The Plow* to be produced in his official capacity as Resettlement Administrator. [38]

Direct conflict between the Roosevelt administration and the American film industry was relatively rare because the basic ingredients of the New Deal were also the staple diet of Hollywood movies. The New Deal was a patchwork of political tradition and experiment. The resulting compromise, which held out some comfort for nearly every section of society, accounts for much of the New Deal's legislative ambiguity and is surprisingly akin to Hollywood's unshakeable belief in the harmonious (if mythical) society. If the New Deal was conceived by Roosevelt as a means of experimenting with the content of politics to preserve its traditional institutional form, so the American film industry, in its fevered searchings for the largest possible audiences, unconsciously or not, also dedicated itself to the preservation of the country's social and institutional framework.

The essence of Roosevelt's rhetoric was an irrepressible and disarming optimism. The President's own triumph over his physical disability, his firm decisive speaking voice (which had such a stirring effect when broadcast in a radio fireside chat), and his high-flown phrases both symbolised and inspired hope for the future of America. The New Deal as a series of legislative measures was a mass of philosophical contradictions. The New Deal as an extension of the Presidential personality carried all the optimistic charisma of a Warner Brothers musical.

4

THE SWIMMING POOL REDS

Shirley Temple, Clark Gable, Robert Taylor and James Cagney sent greetings to the Paris newspaper *Ce Soir* owned outright by Reds, while Bette Davis and Miriam Hopkins have let their names be used by the League of Women Shoppers, an organisation which has a Red hook-up.
                                          Statement issued by the Dies Committee, 1938

The political paranoia of the late 1940s and 1950s, the time of rampant McCarthyism, fed on the idealism of the 1930s. Just as it is impossible fully to understand the Alger Hiss trial without acknowledging Hiss's work as a New Dealer in the Department of Agriculture under Rexford Tugwell, so it is equally difficult to appreciate the Red baiting of Hollywood after 1947 without recognising that its origins lay in the Depression.

In 1934 Elizabeth Dilling published a booklet called *The Red Network* in which she implicated as Communists Clarence Darrow, Eleanor Roosevelt and the YMCA. Although it made little impact on the national consciousness, it was endorsed by the press baron William Randolph Hearst.[1] Fifteen years later such ritual denunciations were common and taken extremely seriously. Men like Hiss whose political opinions were formed by the scars of the Depression were later to be judged by the standards of the Cold War.

The Depression was a massive blow to America's economic and moral strength. Since the day of the capitalist reckoning seemed to be at hand it was reasonable for many thinking people in the 1930s to assume that some form of socialist government was a feasible alternative. Robert Warshow observed that 'For most American intellectuals, the socialist movement of the 1930s was a crucial experience'.[2]

Socialism in the cities, particularly in New York, where *New Masses, Masses and Mainstream* and *New Republic* preached to healthy circulations, was a commmon experience in various degrees of intensity. The writer Alfred Kazin, who was the product of a typically Jewish working-class background of the time wrote:

I felt moral compulsions to be a Socialist since the society in which sixteen million people were jobless that summer [1934] and one million on strike, did not seem to admit of saving except by a socialist government .... Socialism was a way of life since everyone I knew in New York was a Socialist, more or less.[3]

Milton Sperling, who arrived in Hollywood as a writer early in the Depression, recalled his own background as also typical of many of his kind:

My father read the [*Jewish Daily*] *Forward* [a Socialist newspaper]. He was a member of a union. And my grandfather was a member of a union. The Jews in New York were socialists. They were old-country Socialists ... and unions and left-wing thinking of that simple sort that was so Jewish was translated to their children.[4]

This heritage of political conscience gained impetus both from the human wreckage of the Depression and the feeling that they were in the vanguard of a new society. They believed that one of the most devastating of Trotsky's actions had been to consign some of his 'revisionist' supporters to the dustbin of history. They had no intention of being so categorised. Murray Kempton wrote later:

The dustbin of history was, to the revolutionary of the Thirties, what Hell was to the Maine farmer. To fall out of history, to lose your grip upon its express train, to be buried in its graveyard – the conflicting metaphors descriptive of that immolation recurred again and again.[5]

The economic, social and consequent spiritual collapse of the early 1930s accounts for much of the initial vigour but the great moral issues of the latter part of the decade were provided by the rise of Fascism in Europe and the outbreak of the Spanish Civil War. Alfred Kazin was again in the ranks.

History was going our way and in our need was the lifeblood of history. Everything in the outside world seemed to be moving toward some final decision, for, by now, the Spanish Civil War had begun and every day felt choked with struggle. It was as if the planets had locked in combat .... Unrest and unemployment, the struggles within the New Deal, suddenly became part of the single pattern of struggle in Europe against Franco and his allies, Hitler and Mussolini.[6]

The majority of Left-wing activists in Hollywood in the 1930s were writers from this background. Clifford Odets, John Howard Lawson, Lester Cole, John Wexley and Albert Maltz had all been involved in radical theatre in New York. They were later to feature prominently in the large wave of investigations into the extent of Communism in the film industry conducted by the House UnAmerican Activities Committee in 1947. The leading members of the Hollywood Anti-Nazi League were the same people who fought for union recognition, sent money to the Loyalists in Spain and campaigned for intervention after Hitler's invasion of Poland and before Pearl Harbor. They were mostly writers.

Writers in Hollywood have traditionally suffered from a unique set of afflictions but in the 1930s, with the experience of silent pictures less than ten years distant, they were undergoing them for the first time. Title writers and scenarists in the days of silent film had grown up with the industry. The latter worked closely with or simply regarded themselves as servants of the director who was fleshing out a storyline rather than interpreting a script. Title writers appeared at the end of the post-production stage. They both had a sound grasp of their humble place in the social hierarchy of Hollywood.

New York playwrights, eagerly sought in the early days of sound movies because they held the secret to writing dialogue, came out to Hollywood because their achievements on the East Coast had preceded them. On Broadway people like George S. Kaufman, Edna Ferber, Moss Hart, Marc Connelly, Sidney Howard, and Lillian Hellman were arguably as valuable as the Lunts or Helen Hayes. Producers needed them and directors remained faithful to the text. New York Jewish intellectual socialist writers came out to Hollywood to change the medium if not the world. Both held a higher appreciation of their importance in the business than the old scenarists or title writers.

Unfortunately Hollywood society, both in and out of the studios, took no account of such artists when it created its own formal structure. The elite of Hollywood was composed of the executives and the producers (and to a lesser extent the stars) who had lavish offices and their own private dining rooms. The writers ate in the commissary with the technicians.

MGM, under the leadership of Irving Thalberg whose stock has always remained bewilderingly high[7] even amongst those writers who felt most betrayed by his behaviour, pioneered the system of teams of writers working sequentially on each other's scripts. The better the writer (F. Scott Fitzgerald is an example), the less likely he was to make a good screenwriter. The art of screenwriting was prized but the office of the screenwriter wasn't. This was something that most playwrights and novelists took an agonisingly long time to comprehend. The best Hollywood writers were those like the prolific Ben Hecht who never denied that he worked mostly for the money. Distinguished writers, as Neal Gabler has pointed out, were hired for the distinction they brought to the men who hired them. Jack Warner boasted on signing William Faulkner, 'I've got America's best writer for $300 a week'.[8] Two writers were working on a script for the producer David Susskind when the door to their poky office opened and a couple of B'nai B'rith ladies peered in, shepherded by Mrs Susskind who said, 'And this is where my son David the Producer keeps his writers'.[9]

Lack of status manifested itself in conditions of service. Like other employees, writers found that they had to punch a time clock on arrival at the studio and that their contracts worked almost exclusively in favour of their employers, since they could be laid off for short periods, without pay, under the form of contracts which guaranteed only a maximum of forty weeks' employment a year. Writers worked a five-and-a-half-day week and, according to Billy Wilder, at Paramount they were expected to turn in about eleven pages of script every Thursday to the head of their department. At Columbia Harry Cohn was known to lean out of his office window and shout in the direction of the Writers' Building if he became aware that the volume of typing sound had started to diminish.

In return for such humiliating treatment writers were paid extremely well. It was not necessarily an arrangement that they welcomed. Clifford Odets went to Hollywood in the mid-1930s after the Broadway success of his two radical plays *Awake and Sing* and *Waiting for Lefty*. Albert Maltz's bitter drama *Black Pit* (an examination of the effects of a coal strike) and John Wexley's *They Shall Not Die* (a dramatic treatment of the notoriously racially motivated Scottsboro Boys' case) earned them both lucrative contracts at Warner Brothers. Neither wrote anything quite as good again. Maltz went to prison as one of the Hollywood Ten. Odets became a 'Friendly' witness before HUAC.

Once these radical writers arrived in Hollywood their effectiveness as political dramatists was eroded. Living in the sunshine in large houses with the ubiquitous swimming pool, their priorities drastically changed. The capricious awarding of screen credit, the need to ensure that the option on the lucrative contract was taken up by the studio became overwhelmingly important.

Their sincerity was not in doubt in that they remained genuinely concerned to harness the vast potiential of talking pictures to the wider desire of raising the political consciousness of the proletariat. However, they no longer controlled the means of production and were unable to achieve it. In New York at the premiere of Clifford Odets's first film, *The General Died at Dawn* (1936), many people in the audience, Odets's home town supporters, frantically cheered each vaguely heroic speech delivered by the leading character, played by Gary Cooper, but as the plot progressed it became apparent that it was simply a standard Hollywood melodrama. As the disappointed radicals slowly filed out of the theatre, one of them was heard to remark, 'Odets, where is thy sting?'

Embarrassed by the ease and standard of living in southern California and frustrated by successive professional humiliations, these men had only one weapon to fight the deadly onset of self-loathing. Politics, Left-wing, radical politics within the bastion of entrenched privilege, was their escape hatch. They fought the studio bosses and the Republicans with the same passion that they raised money to send ambulances to Spain and to bring Jews out of Germany. There were estimated to be around three hundred members of the Hollywood branch of the Communist Party during the decade 1936–46. At least half of them were writers.[10]

The first attempt to form a union of screenwriters took place in 1931 under the aegis of John Howard Lawson and Dudley Nicholls. It was firmly

55

squashed by the studios. Two years later, after the great betrayal of the wage cuts in the spring of 1933 and in the wake of the arrival of more writers from the East Coast, a more successful movement started. In the summer of that year the nucleus of the Screen Writers' Guild split from the Academy, to which it automatically belonged, because it regarded the Academy as little short of an appendage of the producers against whom most of their attacks were directed.[11]

For the next three years producers waged a constant war against the Guild, hoping, as in 1931, to strangle it at birth. For some time the writers believed they would be protected under Section 7(a) of the NIRA, but when this did not prove forthcoming they turned for protection to their fellow writers in the Authors League of America. Despite warnings from the producers, the writers voted overwhelmingly in favour of amalgamation and all contracts with the studios were to be deemed null and void from 2 May 1938.[12]

The producers regarded this as an act of war, and the thirty-two who had voted against amalgamation, fearing just such an outbreak of hostilities, quickly resigned from the Guild. Irving Thalberg at MGM and Darryl Zanuck at Twentieth Century Fox invited top writers to join a company union to be known as Screen Playwrights and offered long-term contracts as an incentives. The Guild retaliated with the call for a strike, which brought Thalberg to an unaccustomed fury as he announced that he would close down MGM and trigger large-scale unemployment if the Screen Writers' Guild carried out its threat.[13]

The remaining members of the Guild were now faced with the prospect of either joining the company union or being unofficially, but no less effectively, blacklisted. At this stage, in mid-1936, the situation was further complicated by the fact that the Wagner Act of 1935 could now be seen to apply to screenwriters, therefore offering the representative body the chance of government support for their claims for collective bargaining.

Eventually, in the summer of 1938, the National Labor Relations Board met to decide whether the Screen Playwrights' or the Screen Writers' Guild was to be the official voice of the Hollywood scriptwriters. The producers tried to intimidate the Board by claiming that motion pictures were not engaged in inter-state commerce and therefore were not governed by the provisions of the Wagner Act. When that was summarily rejected they tried to prove that, since screenwriters were artists rather than workers (an ironic twist), they were not covered by the collective bargaining clauses of the Wagner Act either. These legal antics failed to make any headway and the Board duly recognised the Screen Writers' Guild at the end of June 1938. The studio heads were furious and initially reacted to the final decision by sulking. A trade paper reported: 'It is expected that the producers will refuse to negotiate with the Guild ... the producers have indicated they will carry the fight to the Supreme Court if necessary'.[14]

Despite the eventual recognition of the official status of the Screen Writers'

Guild by the producers in 1939, and despite the government support indicated by the NLRB decision, Leo Rosten's examination of Hollywood writers in 1940 revealed the strength of grievances that had been supposedly redressed. The writers claimed that there was still no equity or collective bargaining rights, no minimum wages or minimum employment periods, no notice given prior to dismissal and no assurances on the tricky subject of screen credit. There still remained the unpaid twelve-week lay-off periods and there was no way of protecting the theft of ideas submitted to a producer in treatment form.[15]

Just before its case for representation went before the NLRB, the Screen Writers' Guild was fortified by messages of solidarity from Rouben Mamoulian, President of the Screen Directors' Guild and Franchot Tone on behalf of the Screen Actors' Guild, for during the years that the writers were unionising a parallel struggle was going on in the ranks of the players and the directors.

In May 1937 ninety-two stars and feature players announced that, despite the fact that they were under contract to the studios and that their weekly combined salaries came to over $200,000, they would willingly ignore their contracts and forgo their salaries in support of a strike by the Screen Actors' Guild should such industrial action become necessary.[16]

The directors, under the command of Frank Capra, who had latterly championed the Academy against the disruption of the Screen Writers Guild, fought bitterly with the producers for similar artistic freedom. Capra wrote an article for the *New York Times* in which he claimed:

There are only half a dozen directors in Hollywood who are allowed to shoot as they please and who have any supervision over their editing.

We have only asked [the producers] that the director be allowed to read the script he is going to do and to assemble the film in its first rough form for presentation to the head of the studio ....

I would say that 80% of the directors today shoot scenes exactly as they are told to shoot them without any changes whatsoever and that 90% of them have no voice in the story or in the editing.[17]

Pandro Berman, who sat as one of the producers' representatives on the committee bargaining with Capra, John Ford and Leo McCarey later remembered a slightly different but equally partisan scenario:

When the Directors Guild was formed, the directors tried to take advantage of the opportunity to take over all the authority. They wanted autonomy. They would have liked to have gotten rid of the producers entirely ... but we did successfully keep them in check for maybe twenty years after that.[18]

The leading directors like Capra, Ford, McCarey and DeMille were politically conservative and with the exception of Rouben Mamoulian did not conform to the ideological make-up of the activists in the Writers' Guild and Actors' Guild. The directors' demands really were solely about creative power. The others had a different supporting agenda. The relative triumph of their Guilds in the late 1930s was certainly due, at least in part, to the fact that their leading members were linked by their common anti-Fascist beliefs. John Howard Lawson and other Communist writers were on the best of terms at this time with Melvyn Douglas, Fredric March and other liberals. The announcement of the Nazi–Soviet Pact on 23 August 1939 caused a deep split in this Popular Front and resulted in much personal acrimony. Thereafter the Communists ignored the liberals for two years until Hitler's attack on Russia and the entry of America into the war produced a further four years of uneasy co-operation.

Joseph Freeman, editor of the Communist periodical *New Masses*, expressed a desire on a visit to Hollywood to attend a meeting of the Anti Nazi League, only to be told by his host that the meeting was open only to those earning at least $1,500 a week and he himself earned only $1,000. Appalled at such snobbery, Freeman went to the party anyway and began to harangue the servants who comprised two bemused Germans and two Blacks. A crowd soon gathered to hear Freeman's fiery speech, which drew an instant contribution of $20,000 and the fulsome congratulations of Freeman's Hollywood colleagues on a brilliant piece of stage management.

The effectiveness of the Hollywood Communist Party was frequently blunted by the incompatability of the needs of party unity and the desire for social prestige. Murray Kempton wrote bitterly:

> The Hollywood Communists had not so much violated their essence as found their proper level. The slogans, the sweeping formulae, the superficial clangor of Communist culture had a certain fashion in Hollywood precisely because they were two dimensional appeals to a two dimensional community.[19]

After the war, during which most of the writers produced their best work in political conditions which positively encouraged it, not only were the Communists attacked from outside in the general wave of anti-Soviet feeling but the Hollywood branch underwent a bloody civil war out of which there emerged a patchy unity to face the common enemy of the HUAC trials. It is illuminating to recall that the two questions which the so-called Unfriendly Ten always refused to answer were, 'Are you a member of the Screen Writers' Guild?' and 'Are you now or have you ever been a member of the Communist Party?' The leading members of the Communist Party also proved to be strong unionists, anti-Nazis and supporters of the Spanish Loyalists.

It should not, however, be supposed that even in the 1930s the Hollywood branch of the Communist Party was not riven by dissent, which was frequently discovered in the oddest places. Budd Schulberg, who joined the Party in 1937 after several years of youthful idealism, decided to turn one of his short stories into a full-length novel. First published by *Liberty* magazine, *What Makes*

Sammy Run? was the story of a working-class Jewish kid and his struggle to claw his way to the top in Hollywood. The Party advised him not to proceed on the grounds that the story was too 'individualistic' and 'insufficiently progressive'. Schulberg left Hollywood and wrote the novel in Vermont. Its publication aroused screams of outrage both from the Party, who castigated its erstwhile member for not obeying Party discipline, and from the Jews in Hollywood, who feared that such an unflattering portrait of a Jew would arouse the latent wrath of America's many anti-Semites.[20] Schulberg eventually became a Friendly witness, transmuting his experience into the screenplay for *On the Waterfront*.

The movie moguls, the heads of the big studios, shared a common Jewish immigrant working-class background. Their outrage at Schulberg's novel was partly instinctive; they knew there was a deep, not so latent anti-Semitism in America, and memories of the pogroms they had experienced in Eastern Europe had never disappeared. However, there was also a sense that Budd Schulberg, the son of Ben Schulberg, hitherto an executive at Paramount with Jesse Lasky and Adolph Zukor, had betrayed his own kind by his portrait of an insatiably ambitious, myopic, unsympathetic Jewish anti-hero.

The Jews who 'invented' Hollywood were living embodiments of the success of the American Dream and they had no intention of allowing their Left-wing employees, Jewish or not, to call that Dream into question. Carl Laemmle, the founder of Universal, and William Fox, who started the original Fox Film Corporation (merged with Twentieth Century Pictures in 1935), both came from families of twelve children. Adolph Zukor, the leading figure in the development of Paramount, immigrated from Hungary with a few dollars sewn into his waistcoat. Louis B. Mayer was born in Minsk and started life as a rag picker in New Brunswick; Sam Goldwyn arrived in the film industry via Poland, Birmingham and glove-making. The Warner Brothers were the sons of a Youngstown immigrant cobbler.

These men shared a common background as short, aggressive kids from very poor homes and large families, with weak fathers, strong mothers and little formal education. They had all known great poverty before they enjoyed their enormous wealth. Having sampled both they decided that they preferred the wealth and were accordingly dedicated to the preservation of their own fortunes. They were businessmen and showmen who were attracted to motion pictures because they were the quickest and easiest way to make money. Ben Hecht described the typical movie magnate as 'a man who has no taste to be violated or distorted. He admires with his whole soul the drivel his underlings produce in his factory.' S. J. Perelman, on a visit to the Chamber of Horrors, found 'a frieze of wax facial sculptures of criminals who had been executed at Newgate, many of them evocative of the movie magnates ... I had hobnobbed with in Hollywood in the 1930s'. S. N. Behrman maintained that the emblem of the movie mogul ought to be 'A mailed fist in an ersatz Renaissance glove, fashioned in a British factory'.[21]

In the tradition of the successful immigrant, the movie magnates soon became more American than the native-born Americans. Adolph Zukor wrote that 'No sooner did I put my foot on American soil than I was a newborn person'.[22] When it transpired that Louis B. Mayer's naturalisation papers had been lost and the man was short of an official date of birth, Mayer was allowed to choose a date for his birthday. Predictably he chose to have been born on the Fourth of July. When Zukor opened the palatial Paramount Theater in New York in 1926 he proclaimed: 'I do not think this is a monument to me ... but rather a monument dedicated to America. To think that a country could give a chance to a boy like me to be connected with an institution like this!'[23]

These Jews worked on Saturdays and ate shellfish and pork. Budd Schulberg described the religious fathers of the moguls as

> aged anachronisms in their dark suits and long beards with Yiddish as their daily speech and Hebrew for their daily prayers. All of them mystified that from their loins had sprung such unlikely offsprings as a loud, wise-cracking sports-jacketed Jack Warner: a profane, irreverent mob-oriented strongman like Harry Cohn .... Somehow the seed of the Old World had produced these brash, amoral, on-the-make Americans. The sons with their bankrolls and their girlfriends and their *fuck you*'s would tolerate and humor these old men as relics of the past.[24]

Mayer was the most politically conscious of his breed and served actively in the Republican Party. In 1924, during the successful campaign to elect Calvin Coolidge, Mayer hired as his personal secretary Ida Koverman, who had held a similar position with Herbert Hoover and who proved instrumental in cementing a deep mutual respect between the two men. Mayer was a California delegate at the 1928 Republican convention and was largely responsible for persuading W. R. Hearst to transfer the votes of the California, Texas and Illinois delegates (which the newspaper owner effectively controlled) from Andrew Mellon to Hoover. Shortly after the election Koverman wrote to Lawrence Rigby, an aide to the President-elect:

> Re Louis B Mayer, do you remember our talk about making a gesture? Why could we not include a trip to Florida [where Hoover was vacationing] for a couple of days? This is another small boy – new at the game and used to a great deal of attention. I know he would strut around like a proud pigeon.[25]

After Hoover's Inauguration Mayer was his first guest to stay overnight at the White House. *Fortune* magazine pointed out that this connection made it easy for MGM to borrow a battleship for *Armored Cruiser* or a fleet of planes for *Hell's Divers*.[26] More importantly, Hearst had to ask Mayer to plead with Hoover so that Hearst could obtain the wavelength he wanted for a new radio station. Thus Hearst was in Mayer's debt. This was the way power operated.

Mixing at the highest levels of politics gave the Jews of Hollywood a fragile foothold on the slopes of real power. As Jews the movie moguls were barred from the best country clubs as their children were from the best private schools. Their response was to found the Hillcrest Country Club for their own leisure, but in their movies they took enormous pains to downplay their Jewishness. With all the wealth and glamour at their command there remained in front of them a long climb to acceptance as part of the American elite.

Despite the Warner Brothers' pragmatic flirtation with Roosevelt and the New Deal, the political instincts of the moguls were unswervingly Right-wing. As early as 1920, after a conference between representatives of the Harding Administration and top film producers, it was announced that

> The movies will be used to combat Bolshevist propaganda .... Mr. Lane [Secretary of the Interior] emphasised in his address the necessity of showing films depicting the great opportunities which industrious immigrants may find in this country and of stories of poor men who have risen high.[27]

In the aftermath of the Palmer Raids of 1919 and the general social unrest after the First World War, the Hollywood contribution to law and order was a number of anti-Bolshevik and anti-labour movies such as *Bolshevism on Trial*, *The Right to Happiness* and *Democracy, the Vision Restored*. Fox led an industry campaign against Bolshevism by preparing a film in which members of America's 'Four Hundred' appeared, demonstrating their happy, quiet family lives. *Variety* reported that the idea was 'to sell the Ruskys the comfortable notion that J. P. Morgan and his coterie were "just folks" and should be spared liquidation'.[28] The first real attempts at a sympathetic portrayal of Soviet Russia did not arrive until the opening of the second front against Nazi Germany. The films produced in that brief period such as *Mission to Moscow* (1942), *The North Star* (1943) and *Song of Russia* (1943) were to return to haunt the film industry during the HUAC hearings.

The extraordinary number of Jews at the top of the American film industry made them all feel that they had to demonstrate 'sound' American conservative principles lest the hordes of anti-Semites be unleashed against them. As early as 1920 one broadside directed against the movie industry proclaimed:

> The lobby of the International Reform Bureau, Dr. Wilbur Crafts presiding, voted tonight to rescue the motion pictures from the hands of the Devil and five hundred un-Christian Jews.[29]

Two years later in the book *The Sins of Hollywood* an anonymous author wrote of 'a leering foreigner with a large nose and small ratty eyes trying to seduce any attractive applicant who knocked on his door'.[30]

Ten years or so later a campaign was started by the Anti Communist Federation of America calling upon Christian vigilantes to arise and boycott the movies. Hollywood was proclaimed 'the Sodom and Gomorrha where

International Jewry controls Vice, Dope and Gambling'. It was also apparently where 'young Gentile girls are raped by Jewish producers, directors and casting directors who go unpunished'. The portrait of the Jew on the poster was of a hook-nosed caricature which would not have been out of place in a publication operated by Julius Streicher.

In September 1941 Charles Lindbergh, in one of his speeches on behalf of the America First movement, remarked:

> The three most important groups who have been pressing this country toward war are the British, the Jewish and the Roosevelt administration ... their [the Jews'] greatest danger to this country lies in their large ownership and influence in our motion pictures, our press, our radio and our government.

The movies, depending as they do on the frequently unpredictable response of the paying customers, have always been a precarious way to make a living. Add to this insecurity the separate insecurities of the Jews in Hollywood and the result is paranoia. Lester Roth, a vice-president at Columbia at the time of the 1947 HUAC hearings, voiced the general fear.

> Every executive in the business knew that it was just a question of time before a drive would be made to take it away from them. There's always the complexion that, 'Hell we're the Jews and we built this thing up. They wouldn't let us get into the banks. They won't let us get into the insurance companies. They wouldn't let us get into any of the nationally wealthy hard industries. Now we've built up this one and they want to take it away.'[31]

William Fox, founder of the Fox Film Company, told Upton Sinclair a similar story in the latter's classic biography *Upton Sinclair presents William Fox*. Sinclair concluded:

> It was too rich a plot to be left in the hands of one man, a Jewish boy who had been born in a village in Hungary and raised in a slum tenement on the East Side of New York. There gathered around him the elegant and cultured gentlemen of Wall Street with the carnations in their buttonholes and they put a whole battery of machine guns against his head and held him up and took away from him the control of that business.[32]

Fortune magazine ran an article in February 1936 detailing the precise holdings of the Jews in Hollywood. Henry Ford's *Dearborn Independent* complained bitterly that the movies were

> Jew controlled, not in spots only, not 50% merely, but entirely .... As soon as the Jews gained control of the movies we had a movie problem. It is the genius of that race to create problems of a moral character in whatever business they achieve a majority.[33]

The film critic of *The Spectator* reported with evident satisfaction: 'How the financial crisis has improved English films! They have lost their tasteless Semitic opulence and are becoming English.' The critic was Graham Greene.

In general the Jews who produced the movies were reluctant to make films about politics of any persuasion because they were commonly held to be box office poison. The public did not flock to the movie theatres to see thinly disguised polemical pieces of any political hue. The fierce anti-unionism of the studio heads was a result of the combination of the desire for profits and for political quiescence. They saw the rise of the Guilds as a threat to their internal power rather than as the first blow in a revolution that would deliver the country into the hands of the Soviet Praesidium.

The internal political battles between the studio heads were much exaggerated by the dramatic circumstances in which they lived their lives. As Gabler points out, despite their heated rivalry the Hollywood Jews knew that their real enemies were not each other but the New York boardrooms and the *goyim* of Wall Street who were constantly plotting to take over their studios. After the Depression tore Paramount apart Harry Warner helped Jesse Lasky, and Louis B. Mayer offered similar aid to Adolph Zukor. Predictably Zukor spurned the offer, prompting a hysterical rage in Mayer.[34]

With the exception of Louis B. Mayer the moguls voted Republican, not, as he did, because they held deeply Republican convictions but because they were rich and most apolitical rich Americans voted Republican.[35] If status could be acquired by voting for the Democrats, as was the case with the Warner brothers, they were quite prepared to vote Democrat. In the end, like most of the electorate, their politics were circumscribed entirely by self-interest.

A classic example of the moguls' politics, showing how deeply involved they were with the fortunes of their studios, was seen in their conduct during the 1934 gubernatorial election campaign in California. The Warner brothers, already loud in their praise of the New Deal, joined with the Republican Mayer and the politically indifferent trade press to defeat Democratic candidate Upton Sinclair's bid for election as governor. Not only did they endorse the Republican incumbent but they consented to allow registrars to invade the Burbank lot to persuade their employees to register so that they could vote.

In the summer of 1934 Sinclair launched his campaign, which he termed End Poverty In California (known by the acronym EPIC), to such an effect that by the end of August he had won the Democratic primary, polling 436,000 votes against his Wilsonite opponent's 288,000. In early September *The Hollywood Reporter* scoffed:

> It really is a lovely dream. No more want, no more poverty, no more gaunt, haggard men walking Hollywood Boulevard. And who is going to pay for the fruition of Mr. Sinclair's vision? The taxpayers!! ... And this man Sinclair wants to be Governor so he can do all these things. Sorry,

Mr Sinclair, but the days of miracles are popularly believed to have passed.[36]

As the weeks progressed and Sinclair's support seemed to be growing, the trade papers gave up precious front-page column inches every morning to cry terrible warnings of what would happen were Sinclair to be elected. Sinclair was going to institute massive relief, put idle men to work in re-opened factories and, above all, sit very heavily on the motion picture industry.

Joseph Schenck, then the Chairman of Twentieth Century Pictures, cried out that 'Republicans and Democrats must unite to save the state' and he threatened that if Sinclair were elected the picture industry would pack its bags and move to Florida. *The Hollywood Reporter* commented that this was no idle threat.

> While conditions for picture making in the East are not so ideal as here, the picture men feel that the saving in money would more than atone for the less advantageous conditions.[37]

Florida legislature responded by passing a Bill which would exempt the film industry from all taxes if it did choose to flee there.

A month before the election Billy Wilkerson, the influential owner and editor of *The Hollywood Reporter*, continued to echo the moguls' warnings.

> Never in the history of the state has there been an election so fraught with the possibilities of danger to its citizens. Unless a lot of people wake up, Sinclair is going to be the next Governor of the state.

The paper also printed a patently fake letter from one set of writers to their colleagues who might have been thinking of voting Democratic.

> Upton Sinclair will do more than ruin the motion picture industry with one move and we mean RUIN than all the activity, phoney and false, that has been heaped on the industry in its 30 or 40 years of existence. The job of every man, woman and child in the picture business is at stake if Sinclair gets in.[38]

Big business in general, as well as the motion picture industry in particular, was appalled at the prospect of Sinclair's election. Wall Street investment houses in October 1934 reported that capital was taking flight from California. California municipal bonds, corporation bonds and preferred common stocks of state organisations took a drastic fall in the financial markets. When election betting reached even money on Sinclair the stocks of six leading California enterprises fell by $60 million in a day.[39]

Louis B. Mayer ordered all MGM employees earning over $100 a week to contribute to the incumbent Governor Merriam's campaign. The film industry thus mobilised a war chest of half a million dollars. At RKO the free-spirited Katharine Hepburn was threatened with dismissal if she continued to support

Sinclair while, at Warners, James Cagney led an actors' rebellion against the Merriam tax. Gene Fowler and Morrie Ryskind, the latter still in his salad Liberal days, helped to organise an Upton Sinclair committee. Responding to this assistance, Sinclair announced

> that unemployed actors, artists, musicians and other film workers will find a place in his program of self-help. Idea is to put jobless film employees to work in state managed studios, producing films of various sorts for distribution, probably by unemployment colonies and for showing to other jobless.[40]

Variety reported one of the plans to help Merriam devised by the movie industry: 'Idea is to illustrate through radio playlets and stage presentations, the hypothetical effects of Sinclair's "epic" movement on the people of California one year hence.'[41] By far the most potent weapon was the pseudo newsreel, *The Inquiring Reporter*, produced by MGM under Irving Thalberg's direct supervision. 'Housewives' were interviewed and revealed how they feared the loss of their homes if Sinclair were elected. Dirty, bearded hoboes, with bad East European accents, were shown to be heading towards California in order to take advantage of the Sinclair relief bonanza which they expected to find. 'Vell', opined one of them, 'his system vorked vell in Russia.' Prints of the film were quickly run off and distributed to California cinemas free of charge. Central Casting even ran a special section to provide appropriate-looking vagrants. When photographs of these migrant hoboes were in short supply, Warner Brothers publicity department helpfully dug up some stills from the previous year's release *Wild Boys of the Road* and passed them off on the public as the real thing.[42]

On the day before voters went to the polls the trade papers, never the greatest exponents of subtlety, outdid themselves.

> If you are a registered voter in the state of California – be certain to cast your vote tomorrow.
>
> VOTE TOMORROW
>
> VOTE AGAINST UPTON SINCLAIR
>
> CAST A VOTE TO SAVE YOUR JOB
>
> VOTE TO SAVE THE MOTION PICTURE INDUSTRY

In the end it all proved worthwhile. The power of Hollywood and the power of the press (Hearst had hurried home from Bad Nauheim to supervise the press campaign) carried too many guns for Sinclair and he received only 880,000 votes against the anonymous Merriam's 1,139,000. Significantly, President Roosevelt's endorsement of his Democratic colleague, already promised privately in a White House conversation, failed to arrive. Is it too fanciful to suppose that the shrewd Roosevelt saw the continued support of

Hollywood for his national policies a reasonable price to pay for a local Democratic defeat? Certainly Merriam sent a gushing letter of thanks to his many supporters in Hollywood with a particular word of appreciation for that 'splendid hard worker, Louis B. Mayer'.[43] Ironically, Merriam's administration actually imposed certain new taxes on the film industry after all but they were insignificant compared to the potential wreckage threatened by Sinclair.

The results of the 1936 landslide election illustrate just how personal was the campaign waged by Hollywood against Sinclair and his EPIC plans. The significance of this campaign was pointed out by Leo Rosten in his classic 1941 publication *Hollywood: The Movie Colony, the Movie Makers*. It was the first political occasion in which Hollywood demonstrably took sides. Prior to this actors were permitted to love but not to think, so that their declared political affiliations were entirely irrelevant. By speaking out on public issues they violated the pretty role to which they had been assigned in a million fantasies. They were breaking a spell, betraying a public faith, destroying a cherished dream. Congressmen and editors expressed their dismay at Hollywood's perfidy and eventually made eagerly sought headlines by 'smearing red herrings across the gossamer gowns of Hollywood'.[44]

In spite of concerted attempts on a number of fronts, radical Left-wing activists in Hollywood during the 1930s failed to make much significant headway except in the matter of the formation of the Guilds in which they were joined by their apolitical colleagues. Nevertheless, despite their lack of success and Dorothy Parker's much-repeated remark that the only 'ism' Hollywood believed in was plagiarism, the American film industry still found itself subject to periodic Congressional investigation.

In 1938 the House Un-American Activties Committee began its first probe into Hollywood affairs and made a considerable impact for a short time by brandishing the Communist sobriquet at certain screen stars. Franchot Tone, a former member of the Group Theatre in New York and later the second husband of Joan Crawford, had to fly to Washington to plead his case in order to assure the committee's Chairman, Martin Dies, of his unswerving loyalty to his country. Clark Gable, Robert Taylor, James Cagney, Bette Davis and Miriam Hopkins all suffered similar attacks but the more indiscriminate Dies became in his denunciations, the less effective he became in the eyes of the public he was seeking so hard to impress. When he accused ten-year-old Shirley Temple, appearances notwithstanding, of being a Communist dupe he lost all credibility.[45] Hollywood was safe from further federal investigation until after the war although in 1944 a California state HUAC investigation, chaired by Jack Tenny (formerly a songwriter and President of the Hollywood Musicians' Union), sat in session, but it never found anything worth sensationalising and soon dissolved.

The behaviour and treatment of Left-wing activists, especially writers, in Hollywood in the 1930s gives a particularly valuable insight into the mores of the town during that decade. The basic rule was that they would be tolerated as long as they contributed to the commercial good health of their studios and they kept their political views under control if outsiders came enquiring. In 1935 an article appeared in *The Hollywood Reporter* which warned gravely of the spread of Communism.

> Major studios are gravely perturbed over the asserted growth of Communistic activities in the studios, which, investigators have reported, are not wholly confined to workers in the laboring or artisan classes but have also been found to exist among writers .... Executives have been asked to watch closely for any significant signs of Red proselytising in order that drastic action can be taken to offset a more dangerous growth of the radicalism.[46]

Yet 1935 was the year that Clifford Odets was first invited to Hollywood after the triumphant New York opening of his play *Awake and Sing*. The following four or five years saw, arguably, the greatest concentration of Communists that there had ever been in Hollywood. Major studios fell over themselves to sign successful writers; their politics were considered largely immaterial. Even the Red-baiting Mayer was reluctant to start witch-hunting if it meant reducing the number of good writers at MGM. At a luncheon in 1936 he spoke on his traditional theme of making 'the parlor pinks pack their bags and start back to Moscow'. He continued:

> We've got Communists in Hollywood drawing down $2,500 a week. Some of them are great writers, who are demanding 'free expression' in their work for pictures. The industry knows who they are and knows too that they are financed and supported by the Third International .... All we have to do is to take a lesson from Spain and the rest of Europe to realise what we must fight against.[47]

Eleven years later, just after he had been subpoenaed to appear as a witness before HUAC in Washington, Lester Cole was summoned to Mayer's office and offered a lucrative producer's job if he would simply go through a formal renunciation of his political beliefs.[48] Cole refused and was one of the Hollywood Ten who went to jail. Donald Ogden Stewart remained one of the most highly paid writers at MGM for twenty years despite the fact that Mayer had already denounced him as a Communist before the HUAC. The screenwriter of *The Philadelphia Story* and *The Prisoner of Zenda* was simply too valuable a writer to be sacrificed at the first exchange of fire.[49]

If Communists were tolerated because they helped to make good commercial pictures, King Vidor's occasional forays into the world of social 'realism' were tolerated because he was an excellent film-maker with such solid hits behind him as *The Big Parade* (1925), *Street Scene* (1931) and *The Champ* (1931). *Our Daily Bread* (1934) was adapted by Vidor from a short story published in *Reader's Digest* dealing with the 'back to the earth' philosophy which was in fashion at the time of the production.

John and Mary (the names of the characters are carried over from Vidor's previous film about Everyman in the City, *The Crowd* (1928)) are persuaded by John's uncle to take over the running of a farm 'near a town called "Arcadia"', since the couple are unable to secure employment or pay the rent on their city apartment. The farm is in a dreadful state but the couple set to their task with a will. After a dispossessed farmer, whose truck breaks down outside his gate, helps John with the planting, the whole idea of collectivisation instantly materialises.

Signs are erected welcoming volunteers and, suddenly, the world is full of budding collectivised farmers. Round the camp fire they talk of John Smith and the Pilgrim Fathers ('Did they beef about the unemployment situation?'). John walks over to the sprouting crop and, in a gesture more typically found in a John Ford film, he scoops up a handful of earth and murmurs, 'There's nothing for people to be worried about – not when they've got the earth'. At this point the sexual imperative intrudes and John is lured away from the commune by Sally, an attractive young blonde woman. A sorrowing con-science and a brainwave combine to arrest his flight and John returns to the farm to put into operation his strategy for saving the precious crop which is threatened by a drought.

During his defection John is struck by the blinding idea that water can be channelled from a nearby river into the field two miles away in order to irrigate the crop. Feverishly he returns to the commune, convinces the other men to help him and together they construct the appropriate makeshift aquaduct. The final sequence of the water on its way to the crop owes much to the Russian school of film-making; peasant faces shot against the sky in dramatic close up, rapid cutting between the rushing water and the mounting excitement of the workers and the ecstasy of the successful climax. Additionally, the editing is strongly influenced by the cream separator sequence in Eisenstein's *The General Line* (1929), while the documentary style of shooting (anathema to Hollywood) and the lingering shots of the restorative powers of Nature are reminiscent of Dovzhenko's *Earth* (1930).

Our Daily Bread, however, is a very American, New Deal version of the new agrarian revolution. The Left-wing periodical *New Theatre* thought that it moved 'in an unmistakable fascist direction'[50] on the grounds that the commune chose a leader rather than having its actions certified by constant elections in which the democratic majority vote would always prevail. John, the hero, is indeed happy to abide by the majority vote but the co-op demands a strong leader. Left-wingers therefore felt *Our Daily Bread* to be a flawed film, unable to resolve its own internal compromises – which was not dissimilar to their attitude to Roosevelt and the New Deal.

An early draft of the script reached a different conclusion.[51] After the irrigation canal is dug the water source runs dry and the power plant is closed down. The fate of the commune is then saved by the personal order of President Roosevelt. The final draft of the script backs away from any direct government interference, although in October 1934 at the time of the film's release Vidor wrote to Steve Early, Roosevelt's Press Secretary, that he felt that the sprit of the picture was in line with the philosophy underpinning the New Deal. Early wrote back that the President had seen the film and enjoyed it greatly.

Our Daily Bread certainly makes plain its condemnation of the behaviour of big business. It advocates a populism which champions the individualism of the little man, the farmers and other artisans against the tentacles of the banks and industrialists. It suggests the inherent goodness of country ways against the evils generated by the city through the character of Sally, the blonde urbanite who leads John astray. She is seen listening to jazz on her phonograph, a furtive, solitary, sedentary vice as opposed to the lively community dancing and the simple pleasures of listening in a group to the violinist on the hill. For all the New Deal, or even the Soviet, overtones, such grass-roots conservatism has a pedigree stretching back to the Jeffersonian Democracy which similarly distrusted East Coast mercantilism and placed its faith in America's yeoman farmers.

The Hollywood studios, however, saw the script in its simplest terms as pure Communist propaganda, which is why Vidor experienced such difficulty in acquiring financial backing for the film. After rejection by every major studio he eventually secured a distribution deal with United Artists through the good offices of Chaplin and Joseph Schenck (somewhat ironically in view of the latter's involvement in the campaign against Upton Sinclair).

The greater part of the film's cost was borne by Vidor himself, to the extent of mortgaging his own house. The film drew some excellent notices but meagre audiences in America, although it performed well in Europe. Andre Sennwald wrote in *The New York Times*:

> To describe King Vidor's *Our Daily Bread* as the most significant cinema event of the year is to state a plain fact plainly ... an adult interest in the cinema and its artistic possibilities can [not] afford to miss this powerful and invigorating drama of a subsistence homestead. Based on the return to the soil motif which President Roosevelt recommended in his inaugural address as a partial solution for the unemployment crisis, it is an infinitely touching song of faith in the eternal fruitfulness of the land and an inspring chant of hope for the future.[52]

William Troy, the film critic of *The Nation*, however, savagely exposed every flaw, calling it

> a travesty of the kind of collectivist film that the U.S.S.R. produced several years ago. Once again King Vidor reveals the sort of fundamental confusion which has prevented him from becoming a truly fine director. The confusion here, of course, consists in the familiar enough attempt of the liberal mind to reconcile the hope of a small collectivist unit with an

acceptance of the larger pattern of capitalist society .... The film is nothing if not propaganda and as propaganda it has not even the virtue of being clear headed as to its object.[53]

Troy's judgement is harsh and unforgiving but not without substance. *Our Daily Bread* was a well-intentioned, supposedly radical film which failed to be radical enough. The compromises imposed on Vidor by the need to secure a wide release for the film fatally flawed it. To be fair to the limitations within which the director was working, had it been any more radical it would have been unlikely to have found any support within the industry at all and the director would have been homeless. His chances of finding a helpful commune in Beverly Hills would have been remote.

One reason for Chaplin's support, apart from a philosophical sympathy, was that he too was testing the radical waters at much the same time. *Modern Times* (1936), which contained even less ideological material likely to jeopardise democracy in America, found itself nevertheless instantly imbued by critics with political overtones. In one sequence the Tramp picks up a red flag which has fallen off a lorry and waves it to attract the attention of the driver, only to find himself, coincidentally, at the head of a marching demonstration of strikers. He is seized by police and thrown into jail. The sequence appears to be comic with little basis in ideology but *Motion Picture Herald* reported,

> *Production No.5* by, with and of Charles Chaplin, just now called *Modern Times*, is, as it nears completion, by way of becoming a subject of international discussion, by reason of the zeal of reds and the red and pink press, which would have us believe that the picture has, by Russian influence, been converted into a document for their cause.[54]

There are elements in the film, such as the shooting of the heroine's father by the riot police, which could be construed as sympathetic to the oppressed proletariat but Chaplin was no revolutionary. *Modern Times* is a logical continuation of Chaplin's constant reworkings of his own poverty-sticken upbringing in Victorian London and, like most of his other films, rarely moves from the setting of dark Dickensian streets and its atmosphere of heavy melodrama, tinged with original comedy and pathos. As Otis Ferguson wrote, 'Modern Times is about the last thing they should have called the ... picture .... Its times were modern when the movies were young and screen motion was a little faster and more jerky than life.'[55]

The film, effectively his last to be made as a silent movie because Chaplin never wanted the Tramp to speak, is a piece of typical Chaplin comic fantasy. The Tramp imagines himself living with the pretty orphaned girl (played by Paulette Godard) in a neat detached cottage, dressed in working overalls and idly plucking fruit from a tree which grows conveniently outside the living room window. When he learns there are jobs available the Tramp speeds off to

70

the factory, fights through the crowd, secures employment, only to be informed by a fellow worker that he is now on strike.

Far from elevating the idea of collectivism, *Modern Times* is a plea for individualism. The famous sequence of the Tramp going crazy on the fast-moving production line suggests that he is the sane individual in an insanely conformist world. The foreword to the picture states categorically, 'A story of industry, of individual enterprise ... humanity crusading in the pursuit of happiness'. Chaplin's solution to the various problems confronting him is a deliberate retreat to prison, and at the end of the film we are faced once again with the traditional soft-focus long shot of the Tramp and the Girl walking down the lonely road, facing the new dawn together. 'Buck up', says the Tramp, 'Never say die. We'll get along.' Thus the great supposedly radical statement.

On a larger scale, the big studios were also making compromises. In their case it was between what they wanted to sell to foreign countries and what those countries would buy. Hollywood films tried to earn back their gross costs in the domestic market, leaving foreign sales, minus the charges incurred for prints and advertising, as pure profit. Accordingly, producers learned to delete various scenes, words or themes that would be considered objectionable in specific countries. Japan slashed every scene in which there was kissing and once removed a shot of a policeman eating a banana on the grounds that it might generate a lack of respect for the police force. Egypt excised a sequence showing an escape from an orphanage for fear that it might start an unhealthy trend. A scene depicting a drunken officer of the Royal Spanish Guard in von Sternberg's *The Devil Is a Woman* (1935) created such a fuss in Spain that the Spanish authorities demanded its withdrawal not only from Spanish cinemas but from worldwide circulation; in addition, the negative was to be destroyed. The Hays Office tried to intervene on behalf of Paramount, the production company, but the Spaniards bluntly refused to discuss the matter except with official representatives of the US State Department.[56] *The Hollywood Reporter* was sufficiently moved by the incident to warn that

> More and more the American film industry is becoming the political football of foreign governments. Films now figure almost as importantly in trade and political agreements as do oil concessions, mainly because of the propaganda possibilities in films and the desire on the part of some governments to hamper films as a means of promoting their own national film industries .... The recent trouble between Spain and Paramount ... is indicative of the importance the State Department will play hereafter in matters where American films are involved in foreign squabbles.[57]

The politics of Hollywood in general and its foreign sales in particular were always dictated less by ideology than by finance. While executives might accept the fact that *Duck Soup* with its merciless lampooning of dictators would be unlikely to find favour in a number of European countries, they were unhappy at the prospect of writing off a wholesale loss of foreign revenue. In the early part of 1936 MGM toyed with the idea of filming Sinclair Lewis's controversial book *It Can't Happen Here*. By the middle of February, the project had been 'indefinitely postponed' because of the studio's fear that the anti-Fascist elements in the story would prohibit a profitable release.[58]

The 1930s were a time of confusion for the radicals in Hollywood. They faced not only ideological incoherence but also the idiosyncratic workings of the motion picture industry and its unique mixture of art and commerce. The studios were in business to make money, and politics were thought to be an obstacle to the pursuit of profits. In the light of this and the studios' fear of a drop in overseas sales, it was hardly surprising that Hollywood's political films lacked ideological clarity and power.

The Hollywood Communists in the 1930s, never powerful at the best of times (except, perhaps, in their own minds and those of the extreme Right wing), found themselves a comfortable niche in Hollywood society, higher in prestige than cameramen but lower than directors. Despite their best endeavours, the complexities of motion pictures as international products and the contortions of inter-studio and intra-studio personal politics frequently meant that radicalism in Hollywood, before Pearl Harbor, was hopelessly compromised.

5

FANFARE FOR THE COMMON MAN

He's Joe Doakes - the world's greatest stooge and the world's greatest
strength. We always bounce back, because we're the people and we're
tough .... Listen to me, you John Does, you're the hope of the world.
    Spoken by Gary Cooper in Frank Capra's *Meet John Doe* (1941)

However much Hollywood might have wanted to disown the Depression, to
have pretended that it never existed or, that if it did, it should not be allowed to
affect the film industry, it was not possible to do so. The economic debilitation,
the social, physical and psychological suffering were too pervasive. The
Depression scarred America, and the wounds could not be ignored. Hollywood was too conscious of its awesome responsibilities to do more than flirt
with radical ideas. It sympathised with 'the little man' only to the extent that
the industry depended on his and his family's cash admissions.

The American film industry was a significant building block in the
American economy. It was also the most influential medium of communication and, dominated as it was by the studio executives whose political
sympathies ran no farther Left than Jack Warner's personal admiration for
President Roosevelt, the motion picture business was never likely to sanction
any revolutionary solutions to the Depression.

The Hollywood response to the Depression and the prospect of social
revolution, particularly after 1933 when Roosevelt had restored some measure
of economic and moral confidence, was basically twofold. On the one hand it
emphasised the durability of certain American institutional and mythological
traditions. On the other it suggested that the Depression was akin to a bout of
influenza, something to be endured with good humour until it went away as
swiftly and mysteriously as it had arrived. In President Hoover's unfortunate
phrase, 'Prosperity is just around the corner'.

The American worship of the cult of individualism, the belief that anyone
through honesty, perseverance and faith can achieve anything, is employed in
both these remedies for the Depression as a means of defusing a potentially
revolutionary situation.

One illustration of this 'influenza syndrome' is the series of wide-eyed films

73

made by the major studios'[1] which concerned the 'little man' buffeted by the Depression. In Columbia's *Man's Castle* (1933) Loretta Young plays the part of a girl who has been without food for two days when she meets Spencer Tracy, dressed in top hat and tails, on a New York street. The distressed girl compares herself unfavourably to the pigeons to whom people scatter crusts. Tracy is unimpressed. 'No female has to starve in a town like this,' he declares, scoffing at her protestations with the line 'Oh I suppose the river would be better'. Eventually he leads the girl into a smart restaurant, where he orders an expensive meal for her. At its conclusion he reveals that he is as impoverished as she, but he successfully gambles on the manager's preferring to hustle them out of the restaurant without paying rather risk the indignity of a public argument.

His philosophy, 'when people have nothing they behave like human beings', strikes a happy note with Young, who latches onto Tracy with a determination which he finds disconcerting. The two go swimming in the Hudson River and Tracy finds that his former freedom to do as he pleased is gradually being eroded by his protective feelings for his new friend. He serves process papers on Glenda Farrell to earn the five dollars' down-payment on a stove on which Young has set her heart. She looks at Tracy, then at their little shack on the banks of the East River and exclaims with deep conviction, 'There can't be any heaven nicer than this'.

On learning of the girl's pregnancy Tracy tries to leave her but finds he is morally incapable of doing so. Instead, he marries her but without renouncing his desire to recapture his former freedom. The director, Frank Borzage, constantly shoots Tracy lying on his bed, under an open skylight, listening longingly to the whistles of the roaring trains.

At this point a crude and heavy-handed melodrama impinges on the tender love story. Tracy tries to steal $5,000 so that he can leave his wife and impending child with a substantial parting gift, but the robbery proves successful only in raising the police, whose proximity forces both man and pregnant wife into precipitate flight. The girl remarks that she will miss the little stove but she has him and that is all that really matters. The final shot of the film is of the two of them lying contentedly on a bed of straw in a box-car heading out west.

The implications of such a picture are clear enough. No real attempt is made to deal with the problems of poverty or unemployment. The solution to all ills – economic or spiritual, national or personal – is romance. Nevertheless the film is undeniably moving, and its denouement leaves the audience with a hopeful glow. There is more than a suggestion to the film that, if the characters in the movie can solve their problems, there is no reason why the audience should not find equally simple solutions.

This cavalier attitude towards the Depression was standard for the time. In the Fox picture *One More Spring* (1935) a failed musician (Walter Woolf King) and a failed antiques dealer (Warner Baxter) go to live in Central Park where a

Park Ranger offers them accommodation in a toolhouse in return for violin lessons from the musician. Warner Baxter picks up another despairing character in the elfin shape of Janet Gaynor who plays the part of a recently fired chorus girl. A banker (played by Grant Mitchell) joins the unlikely trio when he abandons his attempt to commit suicide in the lake because the water is too cold.

The Hollywood Reporter saw great possibilities for the film.

> Fox certainly hit the nail on the head when it made *One More Spring*. A more timely picture it would be hard to imagine – or one more naturally designed for the box office mood .... It is clean without being insipid, optimistic without being Pollyannaish; it hints cleverly at a nice, cheerful moral without preaching.[2]

Variety on the other hand summed up the ending of the picture with more cynical relevance: 'Spring comes, King gets a job, the banker backs Baxter in a new venture and Baxter proposes to the girl. Everyone's happy along with the bluebirds.'[3]

Fox would have done better to have taken notice of the financial disaster that had befallen an earlier movie set in Central Park. *Hallelujah I'm a Bum* (1933), with a script by S. N. Behrman from a story by Ben Hecht, also dealt with the unemployed who, this time, form an entire community, of which Al Jolson plays the part of the singing mayor. Among his acquaintances Jolson counts the Park cleaner (Harry Langdon), who is a Communist, and the Mayor of New York City (Frank Morgan), who is in love with Madge Evans.

Jolson finds the latter's handbag with a thousand-dollar note in it but the discovery prompts only an unlikely Lorenz Hart lyric, which suggests that money is irrelevant to their life. (The other tramps prove less impressed with this economic logic.) Jolson falls in love with the amnesiac Miss Evans and, just as Tracy went to work to acquire Loretta Young's stove, so Jolson agrees to work in a bank to provide his new love with the material necessities of life. When she recovers her memory she also recovers her wits and retreats to her former life with the Mayor. Jolson returns wistfully, though not unhappily, to Central Park.

Both *One More Spring* and *Hallelujah I'm a Bum* were financial failures. The latter was entirely written in stilted rhymed dialogue and both were poorly produced. The philosophy underlying them, however, remained popular when contained in a more attractive vehicle. In the financially successful *Roman Scandals* (produced by Samuel Goldwyn in 1933) Eddie Cantor is thrown out of his job as a curator in a museum of Roman history in the town of West Rome and finds himself evicted in the company of similarly unfortunate tenants of an unscrupulous local politician. With commendable lack of distress, Cantor sings:

With a million little stars
We can decorate the ceiling
With an optimistic feeling
We can build our little home.

Cantor's vision of life under the stars is so seductive that it inspires the other evicted citizens to join in the song and start a series of dances, much to the surprise and anger of the evil politician who arrives hoping to find everyone suitably cowed. Poverty, in Hollywood's eyes, not only was not a moral crime but it could be made into a source of carefree pleasure.

On a more sober note, at the very end of the decade came the most famous of such 'little men' films. John Ford's *The Grapes of Wrath* (1940), adapted from the previous year's best-selling novel by John Steinbeck, detailed the experiences of the Joad family, dispossessed sharecroppers from Oklahoma. Darryl Zanuck bought the book as soon as it was published and presented it to his favourite screenwriter, Nunnally Johnson, to prepare a script which was then handed over to the reliable Ford.[4]

Rumours in Hollywood suggested that Zanuck had bought the book in order to suppress it. *The Hollywood Reporter* noted:

> Rarely has so much heat been poured on a studio and its affiliates to stop the production of a picture, as is the case with Twentieth Century Fox's announced production of *The Grapes of Wrath*. All the heat is from organised groups, mostly the farm element which see ... a terrific slap at the functions of their organisation.[5]

Even when the picture was finished there was still considerable fear in 'important circles': 'They regard the very excellence of the workmanship which distinguishes the picture as the lure which might spread the spirit of unrest throughout the country.'[6] Martin Quigley, the publisher of *The Motion Picture Herald*, wrote heatedly:

> If the conditions which the picture tends to present as typical are proportionately true, then the revolution has been too long delayed. If ... the picture depicts an extra-ordinary, isolated and non-typical condition and tends to persuade an audience that it is typical then no small libel has been committed against the good name of the Republic.[7]

Critical praise from the trade press was almost unanimous, and the combination of political pressure with financial and artistic success has been the reason for the long-standing Hollywood conviction that *The Grapes of Wrath* is a faithful reflection of the anger and documentary style of the Steinbeck novel.[8]

The film is nothing of the sort. It is, on its own terms, a cinematic masterpiece and fit to rank with any of Ford's better pictures. It is not, however, a great radical statement or even a film of radical intentions. The bleak realism of the book is replaced by a sympathetic look at the plight of a poverty-stricken farming family, forced off the land that has been their home and means of subsistence for seventy years. Ford makes constant reference to this fact, so that it becomes a motif of the film, linking it more to *Drums Along the Mohawk* (1939) or *My Darling Clementine* (1946) than to the original novel.

Grampa, rebelling against the prospect of a journey to California, bends down and scoops up a handful of dirt. 'This is my country. I b'long here. It ain't no good but it's mine.' His last gesture before dying is to pick at the earth and sprinkle it over his body as if in a religious ritual. Muley makes much the same gesture as he too faces forcible eviction from his farm.

I'm right here to tell you, Mister, ain't nobody goin' to push me off *my* land. Grampa took up this land seventy years ago. My Pa was born here. We was *all* born on it, and some of us got killed on it and some died on it. And that's what makes it ourn – bein' born on it, and workin' it and dyin' on it – and not no piece of paper with writin' on it.

The ending of the film, as conceived by Ford, is similarly religious in feeling. Seated together on an empty bandstand, Tom Joad (Henry Fonda) tells his mother (Jane Darwell) that he has learned from the death of Casey, the preacher, that he must exchange his natural family for a greater family – the American people. 'Maybe it's like Casey says, a fella ain't got a soul of his own, but only a piece of a big soul - the one big soul that belongs to everybody.' Ma wants to know what conclusions to draw. 'Then it don't matter ... I'll be everywhere – wherever you look. Wherever there's a fight so hungry people can eat, I'll be there. Wherever there's a cop beatin' up a guy, I'll be there too. He turns and walks away across the empty dance floor and up over the hill, forming an obvious parallel to the end of *Young Mr Lincoln* (1939), in which Fonda walks over the hill outside Springfield, Illinois, to save the country.

Steinbeck's novel ended with Rose of Sharon suckling a starving man to the breast that should have fed her stillborn baby. Ford softened his ending into a spirit of religious acceptance.[9] Darryl Zanuck, however, decided that such an ending was too ambiguous and retained too many traces of the book's corrupting pessimism. Zanuck himself wrote the uplifting coda to the film,[10] which, however much it has since displeased Ford's legion of critical admirers, elicited no public condemnation from the director himself. The family leaves the sanctuary of the Government camp and sets off for Fresno and the promise of twenty days of cotton picking. Ma declaims with conviction:

Rich fellas come up an' they die, an' their kids ain't no good, an' they die out. But we keep a-comin'. We're the people that live. Can't nobody wipe us out. Can't nobody lick us. We'll go on for ever, Pa. We're the people.

This Zanuck-inspired ending is an excellent indication of the way in which

Hollywood considered it was necessary to act in order to provide an optimistic ending for those pictures which dealt with dangerous political or social issues. It wasn't so much that producers were frightened of addressing political issues as such as much as the fact that they made for poor movies. Zanuck saw in *The Grapes of Wrath* not a story that stripped bare America's social conscience but a heart-warming, life-affirming story about a particular family – in modern parlance a 'feel-good movie'. Zanuck performed a similar operation on Ford's next movie for him, *How Green Was My Valley* (1941), in which the labour-versus-capital struggle was excised in favour of a movie about a particular mining family. However inconsistent with Steinbeck's original idea it might have been, the new denouement was sufficient to turn a risky commercial proposition into a financial success. Although the review of the film in the *Los Angeles Evening Herald* might today be regarded as negative, in 1940 it was seen as high praise.

> While Steinbeck's book was vicious, often false and contained parlor-pink communistic leanings, the motion picture has eliminated the cheap sensationalism, along with the other 'isms', and centers upon the tragic, befuddled Joad family, a composite of thousands of sharecroppers and migrant farmers.[11]

The difference between Ford's ending and Zanuck's is a significant one in that it illustrates why Ford made so many films which fared poorly at the box office. Zanuck was interested in the triumph of the common man because it was his patronage on which Twentieth Century's prosperity was founded. Ford was interested in the struggle of the common man (for whom he poured out an affection on the screen he was incapable of transferring to his sets)[12] for different reasons. Physical triumph for Ford was less important than physical strife and spiritual satisfaction.

While one of Ford's early triumphs, *The Iron Horse* (1924), was a celebration of the railroad pioneers, his other famous silent film, *Three Bad Men* (1928), ends on quite a different note. The three heroes sacrifice themselves to protect the girl and her lover and, in killing the evil pursuers, they ensure (in Ford's vision) the birth of a perfect small society. After their mortal deaths the ghosts of the three men ride towards the sunset in silhouette, stretching out their arms in a stylised representation of the crucifixion. Such a gesture is echoed time and again in Ford's later work, for the three bad men form a religious image which can be equated with Tom Joad's walk over the hill to protect the world from its oppressors, or Young Mr Lincoln's similar departure.[13]

Ford's individuals tend to find their deepest spiritual satisfaction in small communities. All of Ford's many Westerns deal in some form or other with the relationship of man to the soil, although, as *The Grapes of Wrath* has demonstrated, the motif is not restricted to the Western. In *Stagecoach* (1939) the evil Gatewood declares to general dissatisfaction:

What's good business for the banks is good for the country. Money makes the world go round, my friend .... We're cut off from the world in this slow-poke town. The place to make the big money is in the East – in the big cities .... What the country needs is a businessman for President.[14]

Gatewood (Berton Churchill) speaks this, clutching a black bag in which is contained $50,000 he has just stolen from his small-town depositors. At the end Ringo (John Wayne) and Dallas (Claire Trevor) ride off to Ringo's ranch to live, presumably, happily ever after. They are accompanied by the words of one of the other stagecoach passengers, Doc Boone (Thomas Mitchell), 'They're saved from the blessings of civilisation'.

In *Drums Along the Mohawk* Ford's insistence on the equation of agrarianism with happiness is made even more explicit. Lana (Claudette Colbert) marries Gil (Henry Fonda) and leaves the comfort of her affluent Colonial home to live with her husband in a log cabin in the Mohawk Valley. However the local Indians, spurred on by impossible Tory promises, invade the little community and drive them off their land.

As in most Ford films the family divisions are traditional and perfectly understood. Lana watches with resignation as Gil goes off to war to defend his community and his country. The local society lady, who has seen it all before, comforts her with memories of her own bitter experiences. As the Indians gather for another attack, the local militia rounds up the community of settlers and ushers them inside the fort. Gil, in a slightly improbable forty-mile sprint, outpaces three pursuing Indians to summon aid for the beleaguered garrison. The picture concludes with the Stars and Stripes raised aloft and the national anthem sounding stirringly as Ford's camera strays from one proud yeoman farmer's face to the next. Jeffersonian democracy is the basis of Ford's ideal world.

Young Mr Lincoln concentrates on the unknown side of the President's early life in Springfield, although even here the characterisation of Lincoln is treated with due reverence.[15] Lincoln, as portrayed by Henry Fonda, is a gauche, awkward-looking country boy with a loping walk and a very slow, deliberate way of speaking. He indulges with great delight in the Veterans Day contests, although he is not above tying his end of the rope in a tug-of-war contest to a cart, thus proving the supremacy of brain over brawn.

Having decided to become a lawyer, he rides slowly into town on the back of a mule, his formal dress-coat and stove-pipe hat proving a striking contrast to his form of transport. An old acquaintance asks what he is doing. 'Figurin' to set myself up as a lawyer.' 'What do you know about the law, Abe?' 'Not enough to hurt me', comes the considered reply.

Lincoln practises law with common sense. He solves one dispute between two dogged farmers like Solomon dealing with the two mothers and reveals the true murderer of a local boy with remorseless logic in the face of an emotional lynching atmosphere in the courtroom. As with the other Ford films it is the end of the movie which most clearly shows Ford's own feelings. Lincoln muses, 'I think I might go on a piece. Maybe to the top of that hill', and as he walks into silhouette, the 'Battle Hymn of the Republic' swells on the music track and the image dissolves to that of the Lincoln Memorial.

In the last scene of *The Grapes of Wrath* Pa Joad concedes that it is his wife who keeps the family going now. 'Seems like I spen' all my time a-thinkin' how it use' ta be.' Ironically, as we have seen, Ford was not responsible for shooting this scene but it is, nevertheless, an excellent comment on Ford himself and on his relationship to American history. His films are exercises in a wistful nostalgia, executed with brilliant technical skill. His themes, the relationship of man to the soil, the importance of the family as a bastion of love in a hostile world, and the action of those individuals who are forced by age, temperamental instability or economic vicissitude to fight a hopeless battle, are those of a man with a definite historical perspective.

Ford was as adept at making modern pictures as he was at filming Westerns. *The Whole Town's Talking* (1935) or *They Were Expendable* (1945) are perfect illustrations of his ability to transfer to other genres with dexterity. He wrote his own epitaph, however, as 'He made Westerns',[16] presumably because in his Westerns all his feelings about the perfect society, a rural community of individuals, tied to each other and to the soil but doomed to oppression by the rising tide of history, come to the fore.

Ford's early pictures with Will Rogers (a possible model for his young Lincoln?) such as *Judge Priest* (1934) or *Steamboat Round the Bend* (1935), the later return to Billy Priest in *The Sun Shines Bright* (1953), can now be seen to link him to his other portraits of history's individual losers like *Mary of Scotland* (1936), Nathan Brittles in *She Wore a Yellow Ribbon* (1949), Frank Skeffington in *The Last Hurrah* (1958) and more collectively the Joad family and the Native Americans in *Cheyenne Autumn* (1964). Ford exalts the individual in defeat as well as in victory. His patchy commercial record as a film-maker indicates that he was frequently guilty of the ultimate Hollywood sin of pessimism in his poetic examinations of the common man.

The Western (along with the gangster film) was the genre in which the individual was afforded the greatest scope for heroic activities. This was principally the result of the growth of an instant mythology surrounding the westward expansion of the nineteenth century but it also owed something to an even earlier popular perception. The individual self-sufficient farmer beholden to no one but loyal to his country and his local community was the ideal citizen of Jefferson's utopian democracy. Jefferson's vision of how the United States should develop was at the very least pastoral if not Arcadian.

> Cultivators of the earth are most valuable citizens. They are the most vigorous, most independent, the most virtuous and they are tied to their country and wedded to its liberty and interests by the most lasting bonds.

As the frontier expanded westward the mythology developed to include the freelance cowboy as well as the settlers who cultivated the land, or, as a later commentator phrased it so memorably, 'The farmer and the cowman should be friends'.

In 1893 the historian Frederick Jackson Turner presented his paper on the significance of the frontier in American history, in which he pointed out how frontier life had shaped a character that was uniquely American, individualistic and democratic.

> The existence of an area of free land, its continuous recession and the advance of American settlement westward explain American development .... The frontier is productive of individualism and the frontier individualism has, from the beginning, promoted democracy.[17]

In the second half of the nineteenth century, to the west of the Alleghenies was a huge expanse of land, sparsely populated by Native Americans and scattered white settlers. Elsewhere in the country, especially along the eastern seaboard, lay cities with all the technological sophistication of the time. This weird mixture of unchartered prairies and rapid urbanisation and industrialisation laid the foundations for the growth of the mythology of the Wild West.

An interweaving of historical fact and romantic fiction, disseminated by popular literature, art and stage presentations, soon enshrined the myths of the noble pioneer and the lone frontiersman. Jesse James, Wild Bill Hickcock and Wyatt Earp were transformed into absurdly romanticised versions of their real selves, but they proved in this new light to be extremely attractive to a public longing for heroes. That Buffalo Bill's fame was probably a greater tribute to the power of his press agent than to his six-shooter serves only to demonstrate the desire of Americans to believe in the mystique of the frontier.

The expansion of the narrative cinema, with its own need for impressive individual heroes, solidified the Western mythology. In 1900 a Union Pacific Railroad train was held up and robbed by Butch Cassidy, Harvey Logan, Bill Carver and Deaf Charlie, near Tipton, Wyoming. In 1903 Edwin S. Porter filmed *The Great Train Robbery*, the first great narrative success of the American film industry. The interaction between the closing of the frontier, the formulation and popularisation of the Turner thesis and the birth of the Western makes it extremely difficult to untwine specific cause and effect. Just as Charles Russell's paintings, such as 'Smoke of a 45' and Cody's 'Fight With Yellowhand', were inspired by myth and, in turn, influenced that myth's development, so the movie Western was involved in a similar interaction.

The essence of the 1930s Western, in so far as 'A' pictures were concerned, proved to be an epic heroic quality which captured and glorified all the classic myths of frontier life. During the early years of the decade a combination of the technical difficulties associated with filming on location and a perceived public indifference to Westerns resulted in an almost complete abandonment of the genre by the Hollywood studios. A trade paper noted:

Doffing its hat to a dying market for outdoor Western pictures, Paramount has decided to abandon making any more pictures of that type this season .... Fox, it is authoritatively stated will duplicate Paramount's move, throwing up the sponge on the action pictures.[18]

One of the few exceptions to the rule was RKO's successful production of *Cimarron*, directed by Wesley Ruggles from Edna Ferber's novel. Made in 1930, it told the story of the fortunes of one particular family during the growth of the Cimarron territory in Oklahoma. Sabra (Irene Dunne) and Yancey (Richard Dix) find their first real home together on the frontier and in the small town of Osage. Sabra attempts to convince Yancey that he should help to organise some classes in American history, to which Yancey replies, 'Early American history? Don't you know you're making it?'

Yancey's big problem is that he is essentially a lone frontiersman and not a domesticated settler, so that, as soon as the Cherokee strip is opened by President Cleveland, Yancey is off, heading westward with a turf for a pillow. At the conclusion of the film Yancey reappears as an old oil worker, to die in the arms of Sabra who, as a Congresswoman, has just unveiled a statue to commemorate the Oklahoma pioneer. *Cimarron* was an artistic as well as a financial triumph (the land rush sequence directed by the famous Second Unit/ Stunt director, B. Reaves Eason was particularly noted) but, in true Hollywood style, the sequel was but a pale imitation of the original.

The Conquerors (1932) tried a similarly episodic approach to American history in order to prove that the panics of 1870, 1902 and 1913 were endured with greater prosperity resulting from them but, in the depths of the Depression, nobody was very interested, or in the slightest way convinced. It was later described by its screenwriter, Robert Lord: 'It wasn't very good, it wasn't very bad. There was a lot of running around, a lot of horses, a lot of cowboys and that was all there was to it.' Interviewed about it at the same time, the director, William Wellman, couldn't remember anything about it at all, even denying initially that he had made it although his name remains on the credits.[19]

By mid-1936, however, the revival of national confidence, brought on largely by the pump-priming of the New Deal, had created an atmosphere in which the old myths could work their spells again. *The Texas Rangers* (1936), one of King Vidor's lesser works, showed the conversion of two outlaws into law-abiding Rangers. The picture's closing eulogy is devoted to the transformation of the lawless frontier into the settled civilised state.

A few months later Paramount also released one of Cecil B. De Mille's lavish re-interpretations of American history, *The Plainsman*, starring Gary Cooper as Wild Bill Hickock and Jean Arthur as Calamity Jane. The film opens with the declaration that 'Kansas, Illinois and the West must be made safe for the plow', a statement that is fully endorsed by Abraham Lincoln, during his brief albeit obligatory appearance. Lincoln constantly appears in character and portrait throughout this genre as a sort of cinematic equivalent of the Good Housekeeping Seal of Approval.

The villains of *The Plainsman* (played by Charles Bickford and Porter Hall) are engaged in the underhand practice of selling guns to the Indians, well aware of the dangers of their being used against the settlers. Captured by the Indians, Hickok is tortured for information about an army patrol, by being stretched out on a cross-shaped bar and dangled over a roaring fire. The image is clearly a parallel to the crucifixion. Calamity Jane, who is in love with Hickcok, releases the information in return for the sparing of his life. Hickok scurries off to help the patrol stave off the ambush and then pursues three deserters, who have also been involved in the illicit gun-running. Having killed them, he prepares to hand himself over to the ministrations of justice (in the shape of his very good friend, Buffalo Bill) when he is shot down from behind (in other words martyred) by Porter Hall.

This highly entertaining film has as much historical credibility as the musical film *Calamity Jane* (1953), starring Doris Day and Howard Keel in the roles of Jane and Hickok. In January 1937 *The Plainsman* proved to be the second-biggest-grossing picture for the month in the North American market. Predictably it drew enormous support from the states of the Mid-West. A British reviewer was moved to write, 'The period in general is presented very much as it must have appeared to those who lived through it. It is this which gives to a mixture of fact and fiction the atmosphere of authenticity.' Graham Greene called it 'certainly the finest Western since *The Virginian*, perhaps it is the finest Western in the history of film'.[20]

The Virginian (1929), along with *Cimarron*, had been the only Western film to cope successfully with the introduction of sound. It was also, however, notable for making a star out of Gary Cooper, even though the actor had appeared in a number of features previously. *The Virginian* helped to shape the image of the shrewd, slow-talking, immensely courageous and implacably honest frontiersman.

In 1940 Cooper appeared in much the same role in William Wyler's *The Westerner*, in which he finds himself working for the settlers of a valley against unscrupulous cattlemen. The film takes place around the West Texan hamlet of Langtry, where Judge Roy Bean[21] (Walter Brennan) dispenses elementary justice at his bar-cum-courtroom. His high-handed methods inflame the local farmers, particularly the heroine, Jane-Ellen, who storms into the saloon to scream at Bean, 'There will always be more coming and more and more, and we'll stay on the land despite you and your courtroom and your killers'.

Gary Cooper, the eponymous hero, after a skirmish with Bean from whom he escapes only by a false confession of admiration for Bean's idol, Lily Langtry, arrives at the farm of the heroine. He is on his way to California, but succumbs to the charms of Jane-Ellen and agrees to stay to help with the harvest. At this point Bean and his cattlemen break down the fences of the homesteaders, so that the cattle can roam freely, but Cooper promises Bean a locket of Lily Langtry's hair (which he cuts from Jane-Ellen's head) if Bean will remove the cattle from the valley.

The harvest is gathered and dedicated, but during the celebrations a fire (started by Bean) destroys the crop and kills Jane-Ellen's father. Cooper, accused by the girl of forcing the cattle out of the valley in order to save them from the fire of which he had prior knowledge, settles the matter himself by shooting the Judge in an otherwise entirely empty theatre, where Bean is bizarrely seated, waiting to see Lily Langtry. The Westerner ends up back on the homestead with Jane-Ellen, and, looking at a wall map of Texas and then out of the window, he declares, 'They're coming back. Wagonloads by the score. It's going to be the promised land.'

The last years of the 1930s were marked by a proliferation of Westerns, dealing with most aspects of the pioneers, the settlers and the frontiersmen. *Variety* noted:

> The big crops are booming the market for Westerns. Bountiful yields and comparatively high prices spell prosperity and increased buying power for farmers, and they and their families and farm-hands are starting to flock to the theaters and the small towns, but they demand Westerns or action pictures.
>
> Society and sex dramas, in particular, are nix with this element. The farmers give the musicals a slight tumble, but even the girl shows don't begin to supplant their first love – the cowboy drama. As a result, local film exchanges are selling all the westerns they can get their hands on and report the demand for this type of picture is the biggest in history.[22]

These pictures starred romantic leading men, reinforcing the romanticism surrounding the Western hero. Gary Cooper was one of the most frequent artists to appear on horseback, but the list includes Joel McCrea, Randolph Scott and, on one occasion, Errol Flynn, who in *Dodge City* (1938) plays a largely Westernised version of Captain Blood and Robin Hood (two of his previous successes in the partnership with Olivia De Havilland and the director Michael Curtiz).

Errol Flynn successfully cleans up the Kansas town, destroying the power of the evil Surrett, who had made Dodge City into a place 'that knew no ethics but cash and killing'. After the death of a young boy to whom Flynn had taken a particular liking, the latter becomes the Mayor of Dodge City and imposes the strict observance of the rule of law. The outcome of his final confrontation with Surrett means that the town is assured of the peace in which it can thrive and fulfil its original premise, stated by Colonel Dodge, to be a tribute to 'honesty, courage, morality and culture – all that the West stands for'. Flynn's individual heroics have preserved the purity of the small Western community.

It was not always possible (or, in Hollywood terms, desirable) to keep the hero strictly within the letter of the law. Henry King's *Jesse James* (1939) raised the murdering bank robber to mythic status. The film opens with Mrs James refusing to sign over her farm to a railroad official, whereupon he returns shortly afterwards as a Deputy and sets fire to the farm house, killing the woman in the process. Jesse shoots the official in defence of two of America's most revered institutions – home and mother. The merciless railroad company threatens the whole community, who 'built our homes, plowed the fields, planted crops and raised our kids', and so justifies Jesse's act of violence.

Jesse and his girl, Zee, are married by a preacher, who reveals that he too was evicted from his farm. Zee persuades Jesse to give himself up and serve a nominal prison sentence, but is dismayed to discover that the local judge is replaced for Jesse's trial by one from the city (St Louis), who is ordered by the railroad company executive to hang Jesse. The town engineers the latter's escape, however, when the posse stops to collect the dollar bills flung high into the air by the fleeing outlaws. Jesse, hounded into a life of crime by the persecution of a vengeful authority, temporarily forgets himself so far as to start enjoying his robbing and killing. This, in turn, reflects poorly on the rest of the gang, who take offence at such indiscriminate violence, and his wife and child are disgusted by such behaviour. Zee returns to live with her uncle, the editor of a small town newspaper, who has a running gag in which he dictates an angry editorial beginning, 'If ever we are to have law and order in the West, the first thing we have to do is to take out all the lawyers/governors/railroad company directors[23] and shoot them down like dogs'.

Jesse snaps out of his sullenness and returns to his wife, with the promise of taking his family out to California to live. On the day of their intended departure, however, he is shot in the back by a treacherous friend, who has decided to betray him for the promise of a state reward. Dying, Jesse clutches at the wall plaque 'God Bless Our Home'. As the Judas slinks off to collect his reward, the final line is an unambiguous 'I don't think even America is ashamed of Jesse James'. The casting of Tyrone Power as Jesse James ensured that the romantic legend of the outlaw would be accepted unquestioningly. The glowing colour photography and Henry King's careful, sensitive direction served only to enhance the legend.

Henry King, a long-time contract director, first with the Fox Company and then with Twentieth Century Fox, was particularly adept with stories of a rural nature. His first film of major interest was *Tol'able David* (1921), a rural melodrama, starring Richard Barthelmess. In 1933, he was assigned to a Will Rogers vehicle called *State Fair*, a film which revolved around the lives of Rogers, his wife and two children and their activities at the highlight of their existence – the state fair. The introduction to the first scene of Sonya Levien's[24] script gives an excellent indication of the tone of the whole. 'A field of growing corn, swaying in the breeze. A meadow by a brook with a dozen or more horses, mares and colts standing in the knee deep grass, swishing their tails.'

The usual blunt review in *Variety* was replaced by one extolling the picture's ingenuousness. It had

> the charm of naturalness and the virtue of sincerity. No villain, little suspense but a straight-forward story of a rural family who find their great moment at the state fair .... Those who know their rural America will find it ringing true.[25]

One exhibitor agreed enthusiastically, 'A picture fit for the gods. It has everything for the small town. Just a downright good old hokum plain-folk picture', while a trade paper reported the film's commercial performance.

> The top-ranking picture for the sticks is Fox's *State Fair*. Exhibitors in these parts are yelling for more *State Fair*s. Every time a salesman calls on an exhibitor, the salesman hears that story. 'After all, the sticks don't want sophistication. The Garbos and the Dietrichs are so much baloney to the small towns. They always will be,' an exhibitor said.[26]

Only Dwight Macdonald dared to attack the film as outdated, sentimental nonsense.

> There is a limit to the detachment of art from present-day realities. At a time when the American farmer is faced with ruin, when the whole Midwest is seething with bitterness and economic discontent, a movie like *State Fair* is an insulting 'let them eat cake' gesture. The vaudeville rusticity of Will Rogers, the 'cute' little-doll face of Janet Gaynor – thus Hollywood embodies the farmer![27]

Quite obviously, however, Hollywood was giving the rural communities what they wanted to see. When the Resettlement Administration produced *The Plow that Broke the Plains*, it elicited more favourable reaction from New York intellectuals than from audiences in the Mid-West at whom the picture was really directed and who, if they ever saw it at all, were noticeably apathetic in their response. *The Plow* depicted the broad sweep of history and failed to get a full release in the neighbourhood cinemas. *State Fair*, with all its 'vaudeville rusticity', starred Will Rogers and was a huge commercial success.

Plainly, audiences felt more comfortable with the old legends about rural life and the West. It could be argued that there was nothing dreadfully wrong with America, if the old cowboy heroes were still triumphant and still attractive. Perhaps most pertinently, the harsh reality of contemporary existence could be momentarily assuaged by wallowing in myth. *State Fair* was a rural equivalent of the common metropolitan man, whom we examined at the start of the chapter. Just as Jolson and Cantor sing happy songs and wash away their tears with a bright smile, so the cavortings of Will Rogers and Janet Gaynor somehow reassured the farmers that there was still hope for the individual on the soil.

At the height of the dustbowl disasters *Variety* reported,

A dozen or so pix are getting ready for release, or are in production, that have farm life as their story theme. Studios feel that the farmer should be edified and glorified .... One producer ... said that such pictures were demanded by the public who feel that small-town atmosphere is much more wholesome than that of the metropolitan area.[28]

The apogee of the small-town stories was reached at the end of the decade when MGM's *Andy Hardy* series, dealing as it did with an idealised small-town America, suddenly swept to triumphant public acclaim.

The films of Frank Capra raised 'the little man' to the status of a national hero. Other countries have resorted to similar celebrations of small-scale enterprise, most notably the Ealing comedies in the late 1940s and early 1950s nostalgically yearning for an England fast disappearing under relentless postwar urbanisation. Capra, however, had the rare gift of capturing on film the mood of his country at the time. Although his movies, like the Western, fed on myth, they also conveyed the contemporary mood with the technical assurance of a brilliant film-maker.

The people of the time interested me. They were my times and I knew them. I have never made a picture overseas, because I like to know what I'm talking about. If I'm making a film, it's my own film. I couldn't see myself making a picture about Frenchmen because I don't know Frenchmen. I would be ill at ease with Frenchmen. I wouldn't know the little mannerisms .... I was entirely engrossed with my own surroundings – American surroundings, Americans as people – in my own time. Even with historical American novels – I'd work at them, but at the last minute I'd pull back.[29]

The movies of Capra's maturity aroused remarkable popular enthusiasm in the 1930s and 1940s, because he found and developed a hero who represented the wishes of the mass public. In Capra's films the individual as an honest, practical, sensitive man overcomes the forces of cynicism, selfishness and economic disaster by the sensible application of his homely virtues. During his rebirth of popularity in the early 1970s following the publication of his successful autobiography, the director remarked,

I had always been a rebel against conformity; for the individual, against mass conformity .... I'd rather see some individuals. That was the common man idea. I didn't think he was common, I thought he was a hell of a guy. I thought he was the hope of the world ... I think that the individual is the way we have leaped forward, the way we have progressed.[30]

The triumph of the Capra hero was to be seen as the triumph of the underprivileged and disadvantaged of the Depression. As Richard Griffith pointed out, this was 'the fantasy of goodwill'.[31]

The first film to reveal hints of Capra's later thematic preoccupations was *Platinum Blonde* (1931), in which the plot hinges on a poor journalist, who marries a rich society girl only to find that money and society life are not worth the loss of his self-respect. In *American Madness* (1932) Capra dealt with a phenomenon of its time, the bank run. Between 1929 and 1932 over 3,600 banks had failed, creating an atmosphere in which Americans were reported to be hoarding more than a hundred million dollars because they were afraid to trust the banks.

Capra's hero, Dickson, the Bank Manager (played by Walter Huston) is seen to stand firmly opposed to the conservative policies of the Wall Street interests. Consequently he is criticised by his board of directors for making loans to small businessmen, who have only their good character to deposit as collateral. He defends his decision with passion. 'Jones is no risk. Nor are the thousands of other Joneses throughout the country. It's they who have built up this nation to be the richest in the world and it's up to the banks to give them a break.'

However, an inside bank robbery starts a rumour, which ends in a stampede to withdraw funds. Just as all seems lost, one of the men whom Huston has trusted calls all the small businessmen, who immediately rush to the bank with their spare cash and, in a triumphant vindication of lending on character, inspire the directors to raise enough money to save the bank from total collapse. At this time Capra, in an interview with a reporter from *Variety*, indicated his desire to use film comedy as a means of combating the despair of the Depression.

> Satirical treatment of a plutocrat, insanely trying to conserve wealth and finding happiness only when he is reduced to the breadline, will strike a responsive note in the mass mind. The man in the street has had so many dogmas crammed down his throat that he is prepared to revolt against current underestimation of his intelligence. He's fed up: politics, prohibition, . . . big business, high powered advertising are ripe subjects for ridicule.[32]

In 1934 Capra and his regular screenwriter, Robert Riskin, adapted the short story *Night Bus* for the screen and called it *It Happened One Night*. *Night Bus* was written by Samuel Hopkins Adams and appeared initially as a serial in *Cosmopolitan* magazine. It concerns a bus journey across America and the fortunes on it of a young male itinerant and the daughter of a millionaire, who is running away to marry a playboy of whom her father disapproves. Capra, attracted by the story outline, added a number of significant details. The hero, Peter Warne (Clark Gable), becomes a reporter and the girl, Ellie (Claudette Colbert), much more of a wealthy prig, so that the audience can identify more easily with Peter and his values. Once more Abraham Lincoln is called upon, this time to endorse Peter's ideas of humanity, as he chides Ellie for her inability to distinguish between a piggyback and a fireman's lift.

PETER

To be a piggybacker requires complete relaxation – a warm heart and a loving nature.

ELLIE

And rich people have none of these qualifications I suppose?

PETER

Not one.

ELLIE

You're prejudiced.

PETER

Show me a good piggybacker and I'll show you somebody who's a real human. Take Abraham Lincoln for instance – a natural piggybacker.

The resolution of their affection for each other is provided by Peter's lack of concern for money. Ellie assumes that Peter wants the $10,000 offered for information leading to her capture, whereas he really only intends to make sure that Ellie's father reimburses his $38.90 expenses. Peter states the general Capra philosophy of good will and slow-paced content:

Life's swell if you don't try too hard. Most people want to get a stranglehold on it. They're not living. They're just feverish. If they didn't get themselves all filled up with a lot of manufactured values they'd find out what they want. Peace and calm. When you get right down to it what's the shouting for? After all, you can only eat three meals a day, only sleep in one bed.

It Happened One Night proved to be the film that made the reputations of all who worked on it; it won the five major Oscars and was the only film in the history of the awards to have been so honoured until *One Flew Over the Cuckoo's Nest* achieved the same triumph in 1975. *Broadway Bill* (1934) followed much the same path as its predecessors, but it lacked the divine spark of inspiration in showing how Warner Baxter leaves a comfortable job with his father-in-law (Walter Connolly) in order to train and race his horse, Broadway Bill. At the film's conclusion Baxter swaps the socialite daughter for the simple, unaffected one (Myrna Loy) and Connolly renounces his snobbish, sycophantic family to join the two youngsters, giving his corporate holdings back to the companies which he had individually absorbed.

With *Mr Deeds Goes to Town* (1936) Capra scaled the heights of excellence, and began a run of masterpieces that still looks daunting today. He wrote that the pictures he wanted to make were films about America and its people; films that would be my way of saying, 'Thanks, America'. I would sing the songs of working stiffs, of the short-changed Joes, the born poor, the afflicted .... I thought I could understand his problem. That was the kind of film material I looked for.[33]

Longfellow Deeds, Jefferson Smith (*Mr Smith Goes to Washington*), George Bailey (*It's a Wonderful Life*) and, to a lesser extent, John Doe (*Meet John Doe*) are the classic Capra heroes – small-town, shrewd, lovable and triumphant by virtue of their honesty and sincerity. In James Stewart and Gary Cooper, Capra found actors of perfect empathy for these roles. Cooper, he wrote, was

Tall, gaunt as Lincoln, cast in the frontier mold of Daniel Boone, Sam Houston, Kit Carson, this silent Montana cowpuncher embodied the true blue virtues that won the West – durability, honesty and native intelligence.[34]

Neither Smith nor Deeds is impressed by social prententiousness. Deeds throws a crowd of opera 'lovers' out of his house, leaves a committee meeting to watch a fire engine as it races past and warns his valet never to kneel, while helping him on with his shoes. Jefferson Smith, as a junior Senator, stays in a Washington boarding house and brings a crate of carrier pigeons to send messages to his mother in the Mid-West. Ingenuous and naive, Deeds and Smith give vent to their emotions on their discovery of the duplicity of big city ways. Smith attacks the Washington Press Corps single-handed, while Deeds wades into Poets Corner and has to be restrained from punching the editor of the New York scandal sheet which is vilifying him.

Both Deeds and Smith have simple economic plans, which arouse the ire of self-interested opponents. Deeds wants to give away his inheritance of $20 million in a way that recalls very strongly the terms of the original Homestead Act.

I was going to give each farmer who needed help 10 acres of land, a horse, a cow and some seed. And if they work it for three years it's theirs. Now if that's crazy maybe I *ought* to be sent to an institution. But I don't think it is.[35]

Smith wants to build a boys' camp in his home state by borrowing the necessary funds from the government and providing for repayment by the boys themselves in 'pennies, nickels, nothing more than a dime'. Above all, Deeds and Smith are reverential in their devotion to the heroic figures and ideas of American history. Deeds justifies his move from Mandrake Falls, Vermont, to New York City by commenting that he had always wanted to visit Grant's Tomb. Outside the monument Deeds's girlfriend, Babe Bennett (Jean Arthur), asks him what he sees in it.

I see a small Ohio farm boy becoming a great soldier. I see thousands of marching men surrendering. I see the beginning of a new nation – like

Abraham Lincoln said. And I can see that little Ohio boy being inaugurated as President. Things like that can only happen in a country like America.

Smith is lost in wonder as he arrives in Washington and abandons his companions to take a bus tour of the sights. He points out the Capitol to people who work there and pauses in reverence beside the Lincoln Memorial as a small boy reads to his blind grandfather the inscribed words of the Gettysburg Address. Smith is referred to as 'Daniel Boone' by Saunders and as 'Honest Abe' by the tycoon, James Taylor, but, as the senior Senator points out, Smith is indeed honest, not stupid, 'a rare man these days'. His idea of the boys' camp is motivated by more than a simple desire to keep the boys occupied during the summer months.

Boys forget what their country means – just reading 'land of the free' in history books. And they get to be men and they forget even more. Liberty is too precious to be buried in books, Miss Saunders. Men ought to hold it up in front of them every day of their lives and say 'I am free – to think – to speak. My ancestors couldn't. I can. My children will.'

Deeds, Smith and George Bailey are all shaped by their backgrounds in the American small town atmosphere with its sense of community and mutual aid. As Deeds leaves Mandrake Falls ('Where the scenery enthralls / And no hardship e'er befalls'), forty of his friends press baskets of flowers and fruit upon him and he mutters that he never knew he had so many friends. His comments on the city are disarming in their simplicity. 'People here are funny. They work so hard at living they forget how to live .... They're always hurting each other. Why don't they try liking each other for a change?'

His affection for Babe is increased, when she reveals that she, too, comes from a small town, 'so clean and fresh – it always smells as if it had just had a bath'. Smith cannot leave Washington to tell his Boy Rangers in the small town that everything he had taught them about American history had been 'a lot of hooey', while the greatest compliment he can bestow on his secretary, Saunders (Jean Arthur), is to tell his mother to send her some of her preserves. Bailey's dismay at never being able to get out of Bedford Falls is soon dispelled when he sees how the small town would have been destroyed by the vulgarities of big business, had his Building and Loan firm never existed.

As Deeds and Smith temper their naivety with resolution, so their girlfriends soften their cynicism and help the fight. Saunders remarks in *Mr Smith*, 'When I first came to Washington, my eyes were big blue question marks – now they're green dollar marks'. In *Mr Deeds*, Babe muses, after her 'Cinderella Man' press exploitation of Deeds has taken its effect, 'Because he's sincere, he looks like a freak to us ... we're too busy being smart alecks'. Saunders reflects, 'Diz, maybe this Don Quixote's got the jump on all of us. I've wondered, maybe it's a curse to go through life all wised up like you and me.' It is Saunders who persuades Smith not to leave Washington but to stand and filibuster, until his case can be made known to the people.

> Remember that day you got here? What you said about Mr. Lincoln? That he was waiting for someone to come along? Well, that was you. Someone with a little rightness to root out the Taylors – yeah and really light up that dome for once.

Smith's fight is conducted against Capra's omnipresent bogeyman, the inhuman forces of big business. James Taylor (Edward Arnold) runs his political machine in Smith's state so effectively that he appoints governors and senators in addition to controlling business and the media. The governor complains that Taylor's high-handed methods might ruin his political future. 'Your political future?' snaps Taylor. 'I bought it for you and made you a present. And I can grab it back so fast it'll make your head spin.'

From his Washington hotel suite Taylor talks to Jackson City and plans the final solution of Jefferson Smith. 'I'll make public opinion out there in five hours,' he claims, 'I've been doing it all my life.' A neat piece of parallel editing demonstrates the fight of the Boy Ranger newspaper, *Boy Stuff*, and its attempts to defeat the dissemination of lies by the Taylor machine papers. The kids slowly set the type as they race against the Jackson City linotypists; they use a hand apparatus paper cutter against a huge roll set in a giant press; the composition and locking of type in little flats is set against the moulds put into place on the rollers; the press painfully produces one little circular, as the giant press whirls out at triple-hammer speed; finally Taylor thugs are shown beating up the scouts on their delivery calls and destroying their papers.

Edward Arnold represents the unacceptable face of big business in two other Capra pictures; as the semi-Fascist D. B. Norton, rendered helpless at the end of *Meet John Doe* (1941) by the steadfastness of ordinary people, and as the munitions manufacturer in *You Can't Take It With You* (1938). Capra turned the successful Broadway play by Kaufman and Hart into his individual movie by the incorporation of certain ideas basic to his own philosophy. The character of Anthony P. Kirby Sr (Arnold) is expanded from the tight-lipped businessman of the play to a munitions tycoon, who has put profits before people. Grandpa Vanderhof (Lionel Barrymore) is not so much a rather fuzzy but kindly old man (as Henry Travers had played him on stage) as an evangelist of basic human values. In the play Vanderhof refuses to pay the government twenty-two years' back taxes, because he doesn't believe in income tax, and the tax inspector retires in confusion. In the film Vanderhof adds in extenuation, with a little smile, 'I don't owe the government a penny.' Capra and Riskin wrote in another character by the name of Mr Poppins (Donald Meek), who, unhappy in his job at a real estate firm, gratefully accepts Vanderhof's invitation to come and live in the crazy household, and carry on with his experiments and inventions.

They also opened up the play by including a courtroom sequence which follows the arrest of the Kirbys and Vanderhofs on a charge of manufacturing fireworks without a permit. Grandpa and his family accept the situation calmly, but Kirby is prompted to a furious outburst, drawing from old Vanderhof the remark, 'The only thing you can take with you is the love of your friends. You may be a high mogul but you're a failure to me – as a human being and as a father.'

In the courtroom, the Judge deals with the case before the Vanderhofs by suspending sentence on a young man, on the condition that he return to his family in Kansas. Kirby offers to pay the $100 fine imposed on Vanderhof, but the latter refuses, to the delight of all his friends in the audience who quickly raise the money in small change themselves. The judge, with a wise smile, drops in the final nickel. At the end of the film, Kirby Sr has sufficiently mellowed as to renounce his intentions of crushing all his business competitors. He goes to see Grandpa Vanderhof, who persuades him to join in a harmonica duet of 'Pollywolly-doodle', and, sure enough, the difficulties of the family and the neighbourhood, if not the nation, are quickly resolved.

The key speech, as far as Capra is concerned, is probably that delivered by Grandpa in his dismissal of fashionable political causes.

> Communism, fascism, voodooism, everybody's got an 'ism' these days ... John Paul Jones, Patrick Henry, Samuel Adams, Washington, Jefferson, Monroe, Lincoln, Grant, Lee, Edison, Mark Twain .... When things got tough for these boys they didn't run around looking for 'isms'.

The final link between all the major Capra films is what the director himself calls 'Christian humanism'. He wrote of his decision to buy *You Can't Take It With You* that 'hidden in the play was a golden opportunity to dramatize Love Thy Neighbor in living drama'.[36] In *Lost Horizon* (1937), his previous film, the High Lama (Sam Jaffe) tells the lost English diplomat Robert Conway (Ronald Colman), 'We have one simple rule – be kind. The brotherly love of Shangri-La will spread throughout the world; the Christian ethic will at last come true and the meek shall inherit the earth'.

In *Mr Smith* the hero desperately appeals to Senator Paine (Claude Rains) to remember the lost causes he had championed as a young lawyer.

> He said once they were the only causes worth fighting for and he fought for them once for the only reason that any man fights for them. Because of one plain, simple rule – love thy neighbor. And in this world of today, so full of hatred, a man who knows that one rule has a great trust.

At the conclusion of *Meet John Doe*, Anne (Barbara Stanwyck) dissuades John (Gary Cooper) from leaping off the roof of City Hall to fulfil a fake promise to protest against social injustice by telling him, 'You don't have to die to keep the John Doe idea alive. Someone already died for that once. The first John Doe. And he's kept that idea alive for nearly 2,000 years'.[37]

Although it is a limiting, and somewhat vague, term, Capra's films may be described as 'populist' in feeling and content. He championed the individual against the Organisation, the small businessman against the tycoon, the small town against the big city and the community against the amorphous mass of city dwellers. *It's a Wonderful Life* (1946), Capra's personal favourite among his pictures, is, in a way, a summary of his philosophy. There is a run on the bank, as seen in *American Madness*; the financial co-operation of Bailey's friends to make up the missing $8,000, which had threatened him with imprisonment, is a repetition of the courtroom sequence in *You Can't Take It With You*.[38] In a world buffeted by economic misfortune and political incompetence, the Capra hero was a reaffirmation of the power and potential of the honest individual. Time and again the films suggested that innate honesty and virtue would triumph over all obstacles. As Richard Griffith has observed,

> What need for the social reorganisation proposed by the New Deal, if prosperity and peace could be recovered by the redemption of the individual? This idea, absolving the middle classes from realistic thinking about the forces which governed their lives, has proved perennially popular.

In a recent revisionist biography[39] Joseph McBride has argued that Capra's political beliefs were confused. It is true that Capra appears to reconcile the traditional populist idealisation of small-town America and suspicion of the cynical city with a promotion of the self-made man. At various points in his films Capra seems to espouse Communism, Fascism, Marxism, populism, conservatism, McCarthyism, New Dealism, jingoism, socialism and capitalism. McBride suggests that the confusion stems from the clash between Capra's own innate conservatism and the liberal, possibly Left-wing views of his main screenwriters, Riskin, Jo Swerling and Sidney Buchman.[40]

As a ghetto kid ashamed of his Old-World, ignorant, poverty-stricken family, Capra was eager to succeed as an American. In an industry run by immigrant Jews from equally impoverished backgrounds he felt a natural affinity for the traditions of populism - isolationism, resentment of big business and trade unions, Wall Street, the cities along the eastern seaboard - in other words almost everything articulated by Longfellow Deeds and Jefferson Smith. Just as Louis B. Mayer's proudest boast was his production of the *Andy Hardy* series and the other moguls strove manfully to eradicate nearly all elements of Jewishness or other divisive ethnic matter from Hollywood films which promoted a strictly Aryan all-American wholesomeness, so Capra latched on quickly to the benefits imparted by his small-town heroes. McBride details Capra's notorious reluctance to share his glory with Riskin (or any other writer) although why Capra's fragile ego should be more reprehensible than any other director's in a town fuelled by such fears is not made clear. What is incontrovertible is that Capra's films still have a distinctive philosophy, however confused later commentators may think that philosophy is.

In the films of Frank Capra the two great fantasies of 1930s individualism are given their most impressive treatment. First, they exhalted the dignity of the individual by emphasising his uniqueness as a person, the value of his friends and the rewards of his steadfastness. Capra himself wrote:

> When I see a crowd, I see a collection of free individuals; each a unique person; each a king or queen .... Let others make films about the grand sweeps of history, I'd make mine about the bloke that pushes the broom.[41]

Second, they restored a sense of patriotism that the nation as a whole had left in abeyance in 1929. The Capra films were hardly alone in this, but they added a powerful voice. The ten or so million unemployed individuals, and their companions similarly afflicted by the Depression who had secured a job of some description, might have been attacked by the most unpleasant of capricious economic and social forces, but their resistance was well buttressed by the moral support of some of Hollywood's finest artists.

6

THE HAYS OFFICE

If it is felt that a motion picture is offering affront, it is very easy ... to begin thinking of a tax or censorship bill against the industry.
Will H. Hays, internal memorandum, 14 February 1933

The overriding purpose of the Hays Office was to stave off state or federal control by forces unsympathetic to the wishes of the movie moguls. The Hays Office acted as a thermostat, by which the American film industry could broach such political, social or sexual themes as would prove commercially successful but which stopped short of provoking punitive reaction by offended external pressure groups.

The beginnings of the Hays Office were significantly political in character. During the 1920 Presidential election campaign, Will Hays, as Chairman of the Republican Party Committee, made representations to the film industry with a view to obtaining maximum favourable newsreel exposure of the Republican candidate, Warren G. Harding. After Harding's electoral triumph it was appreciated in Hollywood that the industry had a sympathetic ear in the federal administration, and two movie moguls, Nicholas and Joseph Schenck, secured the immigration of a Russian friend by the use of a judiciously placed telephone call to Will Hays in Washington. At the same time the startling growth of the film industry into a big business aroused hostility with which its loosely organised, chaotic nature was ill-equipped to deal.

Just as baseball had responded to outraged claims that the 1919 World Series had been fixed by gambling interests by appointing the conservative Judge Kenesaw Mountain Landis as its 'Czar', so the film industrialists offered Will Hays a similar supervisory position. The Mid Western Presbyterian Elder, at that time Postmaster General in Harding's Cabinet, accepted the $100,000 a year job (later increased to $150,000) and neatly ducked the Teapot Dome and other scandals which were shortly to break over Washington. [1]

However, in his new job Hays was rapidly confronted with three scandals of a similarly unsavoury nature. First, the English director William Desmond Taylor was murdered in an affair that implicated two stars, Mary Miles Minter and Mabel Normand; second, the popular comedian 'Fatty' Arbuckle was tried for manslaughter after the death of a starlet called Virginia Rappe in a hotel bedroom during a wild party; third, the young matinée idol Wallace Reid died in a sanatorium after a vain attempt to cure him of drug addiction. Reid lost his life and Minter, Normand and Arbuckle their careers, driven out of the industry by an outraged public. It was a painful indication to Hays and the moguls of the bitterness of the opposition that awaited similar errors of judgement.

One of the efforts of the new organisation was to introduce a form of self-censorship, soon boosted by the adoption of an informal code of 'Don'ts' and 'Be Carefuls', which laid down general guidelines for acceptable film material.[2] The introduction of sound enormously increased the possible range of profanity and demanded a much more comprehensive code, which was intended to maintain the high moral tone of Hollywood pictures.

Unfortunately, this new code was approved by the producers in February 1930, at a time when social standards made its observance extremely difficult. Among the changes wrought by the First World War and intensified by the Depression was the new social freedom enjoyed by women. During the war women had been drafted in to fill labour gaps created by mobilisation, and after 1919 showed no inclination to abandon their new professions.

In the 1920s women became trappers, cab drivers, pilots and steeplejacks as well as secretaries and waitresses. Much the most sensational aspect of this change was the increase in sexual experience of unmarried women. New forms of processed food, the appearance of domestic labour-saving devices and the rise in telephone and mail order shopping all helped to release women from their traditional house-bound drudgery. By 1930 over ten million women were in full-time employment. Although the Nineteenth Amendment had recognised the claims of female suffrage, the nineteenth-century Suffragette ideal of female emancipation from the dependence on man was replaced by a new freedom to go to bed with him.[3]

The movies, of course, were only too happy to exploit fashionable interest in the amatory experiences of the flapper, in such films as *Passion Flame* and *Bedroom and Bath*. MGM persuaded a sweaty Joan Crawford to drop her skirt for a hot Charleston number in *Our Dancing Daughters* (1928), while First National set a theatre on fire in *Paris* so that the chorus girls would have to evacuate the building in a state of undress. In *Mating Call* Renee Adoree swam nude before donning a sheer wet chemise.

Perhaps not surprisingly, by February 1929 W. R. Hearst was leading a popular campaign for federal censorship. The following month the Senator from Iowa, Smith W. Brookhart, introduced a Bill to place Hollywood under a Federal Trade Commission. The latter clearly had no time for the denizens of Hollywood, referring to the contemporary takeover battles between the major studios as 'a fight between two bunches of Jews'.[4] Fear of politicians like this had been the main reason behind the creation of the Hays Office. Reinforcement was clearly needed.

A code was devised by two prominent Catholics, Martin Quigley, publisher of *Motion Picture Herald*, and the Jesuit Father Daniel Lord, a professor at the University of St Louis. It was eagerly adopted by Hays and imposed on a dubious Hollywood after pressure from investment bankers on Wall Street who also feared federal interference for similar financial reasons. Maltby believes the coincidence of the Production Code's implementation shortly after most of the major companies were taken over by Wall Street interests to be highly significant. The Code's standardisation and neutralisation would be likely to appeal on both economic and ideological grounds to Morgan and the Rockefeller interests.[5]

More to the point was the fact that the Code was likely to ease the passage of films into states which maintained their own idiosyncratic censorship boards. Virginia censors hated sex, New York censors were quick to remove signs of political corruption, Maryland censors were wary of films depicting bad relations between capital and labour or anything to do with racial hatred, and Kansas censors were mostly upset by depictions of excessive drinking and the occasional thumbing of the nose. When the same print travelled from one state to the next, as from Pennsylvania to New Jersey, audiences in the latter state were forced to suffer from the tastes of the former state's censors.

The Code was approved in February 1930 but with the onset of the Depression, as we have seen earlier, the studios refused to accept it in its entirety and Hays was too weak to enforce it. Critically, the public proved responsive to what currently passed for risqué pictures, particularly since the traditional justifications of sex as the consequence of romance and personal gratification could now be supplemented by a new economic interpretation.[6]

The vogue for films sympathetically depicting women of easy virtue during the years 1931 to 1933 has already been partially examined in Chapter 2 from the political and economic standpoint. The triumph of the genre posed instant problems for the Hays Office which the studios, with their predictable preference for short-term gain over long-term defence, refused to solve. As long as sexually titillating films were successful at the box office, no amount of pressure from the Hays Office would cause them to be withdrawn.

Even MGM, the bastion of bourgeois respectability, was happy enough to join in the game. Greta Garbo began her Hollywood career as a sex siren with emotional problems. In *Susan Lenox: Her Fall and Rise* (1931), in which she appeared with Clark Gable, Garbo joined the ranks of those stars who sold their affections to relieve economic pressure. In this film Garbo takes up with a circus owner and a politician before the two lovers find an uneasy rapprochement. At the end she declares passionately, 'Since I last saw you, no man has had a minute from me – not even a second.' Gable continues to worry. 'Every time a man came along, I'd wonder', but Garbo kisses him firmly and declares, 'You wouldn't have to.' *Motion Picture Herald* commented disdainfully, 'MGM seems to have continued its "sin and succeed" series with Greta

Garbo. It is ... proof sufficient that in its present form, the Hays Code is nothing for producers to worry about.'[7]

In *Blonde Venus* (1932), directed by Josef von Sternberg, Marlene Dietrich separates from her husband (Herbert Marshall) and finds that the only way she can feed herself and her young son is by cabaret appearances and casual liaisons with men. In her last appearance in a night club, Dietrich, dressed in a white tuxedo and top hat, casually examines and dismisses a series of thinly veiled beautiful women. These lesbian overtones are constantly emphasised by von Sternberg's visual style, although Dietrich's songs are directed to members of both sexes with cheerful indiscrimination. 'You Little So-and-So' states baldly:

> It isn't often that I want a man
> But when I do it's just too bad.
> I know you're acting hard to get and yet
> I've got a feeling – you can be had.

For all this blatant sexuality, the Hays Office had considerably toned down the early scripts submitted to it. Sternberg wrote one script which B. P. Schulberg, head of production at Paramount, rewrote, to Sternberg's disgust. The director, with the backing of his star, left for a holiday in New York, while Paramount threatened him with a lawsuit. [8] Eventually Sternberg accepted the new version after some compromise on both sides, but the Hays Office was still unhappy. Lamar Trotti (a Hays official before joining Twentieth Century Fox as a screenwriter) wrote to Hays of the preparation of yet another script,

> The original version, which, I understand, is von Sternberg's appeared to Jason and me as utterly impossible. The second version, which is Schulberg's I suppose, is better, but it is still far off. A new script is being prepared ... however it still has grave worries in it and I secretly am reciting my prayers that the flight will result in a general agreement to forget the story altogether. [9]

The agreement between Sternberg and Schulberg ensured that Trotti's prayers went unanswered. He wrote again to Hays,

> There seems to be a very real and distressing tendency at Paramount to go for the sex-stuff on a heavy scale. One gets that feeling not only in the scripts but in the conversation with the studio where talk about pictures having to have 'guts' is ... frequently heard. [10]

Paramount was by no means the only offender against the Hays Code of 1930. MGM, with its roster of women stars (Garbo, Shearer, Crawford, Harlow), found it advisable to join the current movement of stories about women of dubious morality, many of them surprisingly similar in outline. Joan Crawford in *Possessed* (1931) plays a small town factory girl who becomes the mistress of a rich New York lawyer (played by Clark Gable). Constance Bennett in *The Easiest Way* (1931) climbs out of the poverty of her family by going to bed with her boss (Adolph Menjou) and Jean Harlow in *Redheaded Woman* (1932) attempts much the same thing, although here the acton is played for comedy rather than melodrama.

Barbara Stanwyck's appearance in *Illicit* (1931) drew the comment from one delighted exhibitor, 'She was a bad, bad girl, but oh, how GOOD at the box office.'[11] Some of the girls adapted to their changed circumstances with humour as well as fortitude. The popular series of Warner Brothers musicals raised to their ultimate expression that unique product of the Depression, the wise-cracking chorus girl, who sold her favours to producers with no moral doubts but simply as a form of unemployment insurance. In *Forty-Second Street* one of them remarks to another about a newcomer, 'The chorus'll be her *first* stop.' 'Yeah,' replies the other, 'and you don't have to be a mind reader to know her second.'

Juxtaposed against this unflappable cynicism is the naivety of the juvenile leads, played by Dick Powell and Ruby Keeler. Keeler, worried about a routine, is offered extra rehearsals by another dancer. The stage manager glances at them and remarks drily, 'Gluttons for punishment, aren't you?', to which she replies, 'This boy's showing me.' 'Yeah, I was just trying to make her ...' 'Trying to make her is right,' snaps the stage manager, to whom nothing is new in the theatre.

When Bebe Daniels, the star of the play-within-the-film, breaks her ankle on the day of the opening, the financial backer of the play, Abner (Guy Kibbee), brings to the theatre a chorus girl, Anytime Annie ('The only time she ever said "no" was when she didn't hear the question'). Annie, faced with the scepticism of the director, Marsh (Warner Baxter), rejects the opportunity of supporting Abner's claim. 'Let's quit kidding, Mr. Marsh. Abbie, all those promises sounded pretty swell at breakfast [Abner chokes] but I haven't got a chance of carryin' this show.'

Una Merkel, Ginger Rogers's cynical companion in the chorus, remarks sharply to her male partner during a lifting routine, 'My, you have the *busiest* hands' and to Ruby Keeler, who has completely misunderstood the nature of the relationship between Bebe Daniels, the star, and Guy Kibbee, who has invested $70,000 in a show for her, 'Say, you can't be only 18; a girl just couldn't get that dumb in only eighteen years.'

The same relationships are carried forward to the next film in the cycle, *Gold Diggers of 1933*. It is heard that the impresario, Barney Hopkins, is putting on a new show, for which the girls want to audition. Their problem is that they have only one decent dress between them and, 'If one doesn't look modish with Barney, it's thumbs down'. The girls rush to the window and choose a colour which has to correspond to the colour of the first taxi cab seen. Joan Blondell wins, to the dismay of Ginger Rogers, who has to remove the one presentable dress. 'Gee,' she remarks wistfully, 'I look much better in clothes than any of you. If Barney could see me in clothes ...' 'He wouldn't recognise you', finishes Aline MacMahon.

This cynical portrayal of backstage life was remarkably realistic, although it is unlikely that genuine chorus girls were capable of putting their feelings into quite such sparse epigrammatic dialogue as that written by James Seymour and Rian James. About the time of the release of *Gold Diggers of 1933*, *Variety* reported, 'Resumption of musicals has the town's chorus girls eating again – and on their own'. [12]

Two other major talents exploited the new sexuality and demonstrated the woefully inadequate nature of the Hays Code as a bulwark of traditional bourgeois morality. The first was Ernst Lubitsch, who had established a reputation for salaciousness with his silent pictures such as *Passion* (1919) and *Deception* (1920). After a successful apprenticeship in America, Lubitsch was one of the first directors to explore the possibilities of sound. Between 1929 (*The Love Parade*) and 1934 (*The Merry Widow*) Lubitsch made four other films, common to all of which was a sly acknowledgement of the importance of sex and the comic undercurrent that flows beneath all human relations.

In *The Love Parade* the seemingly statuesque courtiers have no moral compunctions about looking through the keyhole at what they suppose is a passionate love affair between the Queen (Jeanette MacDonald) and the disgraced diplomat (Maurice Chevalier). MacDonald, having been charmed by the commoner, spends much of her time trying to make the man who is now her husband act like a consort, while Chevalier, who insists on his primary role being that of the dominant male husband, eventually breaks down his wife's resistance by adopting the tactics of Lysistrata.

One Hour With You (1932), a re-make of his silent picture *The Marriage Circle* (1924), was partially directed by George Cukor, but it retains that deftness of touch normally associated with Lubitsch. In one song, which is comprised of asides sung to the audience by Chevalier and his wife (MacDonald again), they each sing of their attraction to other partners:

> If he were your husband/she were your wife,
> But you like him/You're crazy about her,
> Well, what would you do?
> That's what I'd do too.

Chevalier is, in fact, attracted to his wife's best friend, Mitzi, whose civilised husband (played by Roland Young) questions Chevalier about his actions the previous night when he had seen Mitzi home.

YOUNG

You stayed, let's see, until 2.45 a.m. – 1 hour and 25 minutes. Am I right?

CHEVALIER

Right.

101

YOUNG

You can't imagine how I feel.

CHEVALIER

I assure you, we simply had a friendly conversation.

YOUNG

I believe that – but unfortunately no one else will believe it.

Colonel Joy at the Hays Office wrote anxiously to Ben Schulberg, Executive Producer at Paramount: 'We ... frankly confess that were there any combination involved other than the particular director and cast of this picture, we would be inclined to believe that the story could not be handled on the screen.' [13]

In *Trouble in Paradise* (1932) Lubitsch is at the height of his powers. From the opening gag of a Venetian gondolier singing 'O Sole Mio', who turns out to be a garbage collector on the rounds, to the final exchange between Herbert Marshall and Miriam Hopkins as they pick each other's pockets, the film is one long paean in praise of dishonesty. Hopkins steals Marshall's wallet (containing 20,000 lire just stolen from Edward Everett Horton), he steals her pin, she lifts his watch and he removes her garter. Before returning each other's property, she has time to correct his watch, which is five minutes slow, and he has time to examine the quality of paste in the pin. There is also much more of the sardonic Lubitsch and his philosophy that everyone believes the next person's sex life is more interesting than his own: 'She says he's her secretary. He says he's her secretary. Maybe I'm wrong. Maybe he *is* her secretary.'

Much the most explosive single character introduced to movie audiences in this 'enlightened' climate was Mae West. She had already been a major figure on Broadway, but not until 1932 did Hollywood dare to invite the writer-star of *Sex* and other hit shows into its midst. She first appeared in an undistinguished Paramount picture called *Night After Night*, in which a woman was heard to remark with reference to a piece of Miss West's jewellery, 'Goodness, what beautiful diamonds', to which West replied, 'Goodness had nothing to do with it, dearie!'

Her first starring film, *She Done Him Wrong* (1933), was an enormous financial success and did much to relieve Paramount's ailing fortunes. It was adapted from her stage hit *Diamond Lil*, and was full of the usual Westian heavy breathings, lowered eyelids and sharp one-line retorts. The essential point about Mae West was that there was no deceit in what she offered and in what she expected. 'I like a man who takes his time,' she sang and instantly offended thousands of people, who should not really have known what she was implying.

West made no bones about her origins. In *She Done Him Wrong* a passer-by calls her a 'fine woman'. 'One of the finest that ever walked the streets,' she

102

mutters to herself. *I'm No Angel* proved that the former film had been no fluke, and it became the top-grossing production of 1933. [14] It deals with West's rise from a honky-tonk woman to a circus performer, who puts her head into lions' mouths and gets herself engaged to one of high society's most eligible bachelors (Cary Grant). She knows what it is about her that attracts men and shows no reluctance to admit it. 'When I'm good, I'm very, very good. But when I'm bad, I'm better.' An interesting light is thrown on the composition of the typical Mae West audience by an exhibitor in Louisiana, reporting on the huge box office take of *I'm No Angel*:

> Did the best business of the year on this one. Whether they like her or not, they all come out to see her. The church people clamor for clean pictures, but they all come out to see Mae West, and stay away from a clean sweet picture like *The Cradle Song*. [15]

Mae West's candour about the pleasures of sex was instrumental in stimulating a renewed and this time successful national campaign for the removal of smut from the screen. The volume of risqué film material had turned the spotlight from the private lives of the stars to the movies themselves.

As usual there was a financial reason behind the change. The box office receipts began to dip. In Philadelphia they plunged by forty per cent after Catholics were urged by their priests to boycott Hollywood movies. The Hays Office was subject to heavy pressure from the formation of the National Legion of Decency, a body of Roman Catholic film censors, who, with the Church's backing, graded all films from A-1 to C (for 'Condemned') for their moral content. Hays reacted by expanding the 1930 Code, making it mandatory and promoting the Catholic Joseph Breen to a position as head of the Hollywood Production Code Authority. All films had to obtain a Seal of Approval from the PCA, and a fine of $25,000 could be imposed on a studio that dared to release a picture without a certificate.

A further pressure on Hollywood was exerted by a tactical shift of the pressure groups. The Legion of Decency switched its negotiations to the East Coast, believing, rightly, that it would gain a more receptive ear in the boardrooms of New York, closer both physically and emotionally to the investment houses of Wall Street. The studio heads might not listen as attentively in the sunshine of Hollywood as the boards of directors in New York. *Variety* noted:

> Switch of all moral problems from the West to the East is revealed to have been motivated by an understanding that the crusaders have lost patience with studio heads but still believe in the judgement and good intentions of the Eastern executives. [16]

In the end all the studios submitted willingly to the new strictures. Such meekness on the part of powerful egomaniacs raises the question as to why

Hollywood positively welcomed this sharp turn to prudery, in view of the financial success of the films that had aroused the fierce outcry. Partly it was the result of the basic fear of the moguls at provoking the wrath of the mighty Catholic Church, who, along with the American Legion and the Daughters of the American Revolution, held a powerful sway over huge numbers of the movie-going public. A general boycott by these groups and their supporters could seriously harm the economic performance of any film, as *Blockade* was to demonstrate. [17]

Second, one must credit the moguls as showmen with the uncanny ability to sense the temper of their audiences. Many of them had started their careers as exhibitors and experienced audience antagonism to certain movies at first hand. The films dealing in overt sexuality had probably reached their high-water mark by 1933. They would never be as remunerative again, and it was thus unwise to risk reprisals by the Hays Office and external bodies. Had the studios blatantly ignored the Hays Code again, there was always the frightening possibility that the industry's self-regulation would be replaced by an insensitive federal control.

It was, above all, the worry about federal legislation which galvanised the Hays Office into action. When in 1933 Congress took the MGM political fantasy *Gabriel Over the White House* as a direct insult, Hays wrote a sharp letter to one of his employees:

> We must not lose sight of the fact that legislatures are meeting, that every possible source of revenue is being considered, and that if it is felt that a motion picture is offering affront, it is very easy ... to begin thinking of a tax or censorship bill against the industry. [18]

The Hays Office reacted to one such threat in a style appropriate to the guardian of Hollywood. When the Neely-Pettingell Bill, proposing certain changes in distribution practices, was being discussed in Congress, an anonymous pamphlet entitled *What Do You Know About Block-Booking?* was widely circulated in Washington. Its source was eventually traced to the Hays Office. [19]

The effect of the new powers invested in the Hays Office was significantly to modify the content of Hollywood films for thirty years. *Variety* reported:

> Stories which once seemed mild now bring criticism from producers. The agents no longer know just what to consider dirty any more ...
>
> All material goes to the Hays Office now before studio considers buying. Formerly, studios bought first and sought Hays morals visa later. [20]

When *The Greeks Had a Word For It*, *Hallelujah I'm a Bum* and *Tonight or Never*, which were produced in the early 1930s, were resubmitted to the Hays Office in 1937, they were refused the Seal of Approval, although on their initial release all three had been widely exhibited. [21] Mae West in *Klondike Annie*

(1936) or *Every Day's a Holiday* (1938) simply looked lost amidst her bowdlerised scripts. The Warner chorus girls disappeared, as the early musicals turned into a series of successively weaker pictures, culminating in the ghastly recruiting musical *Shipmates Forever* (1935) and the bastardised *Gold Diggers in Paris* (1938).

The years of the New Deal in politics coincided on the screen with an era of sweetness and light in Hollywood, typified by the Rogers and Astaire musicals and the astonishing triumphs of the young Shirley Temple. The sex stars of the early 1930s did a smart about-turn after 1934, or else suffered retribution in their careers.

Among those who made the transition were Norma Shearer, Ginger Rogers, Marlene Dietrich, Katharine Hepburn and Jeanette MacDonald. The late 1930s and early 1940s were the heyday of Irene Dunne's particular brand of antiseptic womanhood, while Jean Harlow died, Connie Bennett and Ruth Chatterton retired and Mae West appeared to be a declining power on the screen. Norma Shearer was fortunate in having a husband who was also the shrewdest and most powerful producer at MGM, so it was hardly surprising that in 1934 she was cast in the ideal role as Elizabeth Barrett in *The Barretts of Wimpole Street*. The film was a success and Shearer re-established her place as the First Lady of the Screen.

After the break-up of her volatile relationship with Josef von Sternberg, Marlene Dietrich made very few pictures of note, either artistically or commercially, until in 1939 she went to Universal, where she played the bar-room hostess, Frenchie, in George Marshall's famous *Destry Rides Again*. Katharine Hepburn, after a successful start in pictures with *A Bill of Divorcement* (1932) and *Little Women* (1933), went through a bad period when she appeared in one box office disaster after another (including Cukor's *Sylvia Scarlett* and Ford's *Mary of Scotland*); but in 1938 Howard Hawks gave her a change of character in the screwball comedy *Bringing Up Baby*.

Jeanette MacDonald's training as a singer offered MGM the opportunity to remove her from the association with risqué Lubitsch films by setting her opposite the heavy baritone Nelson Eddy. Together they made *Naughty Marietta* (1935), *Rose Marie* (1936), *Maytime* (1937) and *Sweethearts* (1938), all of them hugely successful, and McDonald thereafter rarely stepped outside the Goody-Two-Shoes characters, which represented a considerable loss to situation comedy.

As the stars changed their screen personalities to correspond to the new morality, so the nature of stardom (in this case it may be defined as the publicity put out by the studios and the stories written in the fan magazines) altered accordingly. In the 1920s, the image of the star had been that of a supernatural being who lived in a Moorish palace in the Hollywood Hills, someone to whom the usual laws of behaviour did not always apply.

What Valentino and Pola Negri were to the 1920s, Gable and Ginger Rogers (amongst others) were to the 1930s. Gable, earthy to Valentino's exotic, Negri dark and mysterious to Rogers's blonde 'girl next door', represented a marked change in the fantasies of the two decades. Where Theda Bara's publicity had persuaded her fans that she had been born of an Arabian sheik and an Egyptian pricesss, the editor of a popular fan magazine of the 1930s wrote,

I do want to assure you that we do try conscientiously and constantly to give you these gallant people as they really are – living, experiencing human beings who, underneath all their glitter and beauty, are very much like you and me. [22]

Helen Twelvetrees told an interviewer: 'Motherhood is of far greater importance than a career to me. Even if bearing a child means that I will have to retire definitely from the screen it will still be worthwhile.' Stars in the 1930s even admitted that they frequently had doubts as to whether they had really benefited from earning huge sums of money in their early twenties. One article was headlined, ' "Did I Really Get What I Wanted Out Of Life?" Asks Ginger Rogers'. [23]

Ginger Rogers indeed performed one of the most astute of lobotomies on herself, after the tightening of the Production Code Authority. In 1933 she was cast in the classic Warner Brothers musicals, where she revealed a fine comic delivery and a pleasant singing voice, but, for various reasons of a personal nature, her contract was not taken up by Warner Brothers and she went to RKO, where she appeared as fifth lead in a musical called *Flying Down to Rio* (1933). This was RKO's answer to the current musical craze, and, despite its somewhat laggardly appearance, it proved to be a resounding commercial success. More significantly it was a marked step in the early movie career of the fourth lead, Fred Astaire.

When RKO decided to consolidate their triumph by filming their new star's stage hit, *The Gay Divorce*, they cast Ginger Rogers as the female lead. *The Gay Divorcee* [24] (1934) was followed in its turn by *Roberta* and *Top Hat* (both 1935), *Follow the Fleet* and *Swing Time* (both 1936), *Shall We Dance?* (1937), *Carefree* (1938) and *The Story of Vernon and Irene Castle* (1939) before the team split up. Their formula of fragile plots, outstanding songs and innovative dances produced some of the most durable movies of the decade which flourished in the somewhat anodyne moral climate of the mid- to late 1930s.

The films were lavish in appearance but produced an excellent return on their investment. The budget for *Top Hat* was approved at $637,151.05, of which $40,000 went to Astaire while $7,172 was apportioned to Ginger Rogers. Gross receipts were almost $3 million. By *Swing Time* Rogers had renegotiated her contract as she received $60,000 but Astaire retained his differential with a salary of $85,000. All the Astaire–Rogers films until *Carefree* grossed in the region of two $2 million, leaving a clear profit of between $500,000 and $1 million after deduction of studio overheads, prints and advertising. [25]

In 1936 the team of Astaire and Rogers were ranked second to Shirley

Temple in the United States and Great Britain, while *The Hollywood Reporter*, working from another representative selection of figures, placed them ahead of the infant prodigy. [26] Plainly there was something about these films that made them very much a part of their time. Even if, as most commentators would say, they were nothing but pure escapism, that escapism was a particular kind of 1930s fantasy.

Initial viewers are invariably struck by the conventional morality which surrounds the couple. In the wake of the pictures of the early 1930s and the sly sexuality promoted by the early Warners musicals, the Astaire–Rogers films are the model of moral rectitude. The stars, indeed, only kiss once (at the end of a slow-motion dream sequence in *Carefree*). In *The Gay Divorcee* Mimi refuses to disclose her name or her address to the eager Guy, while in *Top Hat* Dale spends most of the film fleeing from Jerry because she supposes him to be already married. The relationship between Edward Everett Horton and Helen Broderick in *Top Hat* has much more sexual content than Astaire and Rogers ever arouse.

Another major ingredient of these 1930s successes was the nature of the hero and heroine. In *Swing Time* Astaire begins the picture on the run from a fiancée and arrives in New York with almost nothing except his God-given talents as a dancer. Ginger Rogers plays Penny, a dancing school instructress. By the end of the film the two are dancing in exclusive night clubs, at the summit of their professional careers, a distinction achieved purely by hard work and ability. In many of the movies they are surrounded by chic art direction (the work of the superb RKO art director, Van Nest Polglase), symbolic of the trappings of wealth, but there are reasons usually associated with stage success (rather than inherited wealth) to justify it.

In *Follow the Fleet* the general popularity of the series was in no way diminished by the fact that Astaire is a sailor in uniform and Ginger Rogers is a singer in a somewhat sleazy dance-hall. At the conclusion of the film is the number 'Let's Face the Music and Dance', in which the two are expensively dressed and each contemplating suicide, following an unsuccessful night at the Casino tables. The music in its dance development changes from introspection to exultation, and the film finishes on the vital upbeat.

The Rogers–Astaire pictures aroused fierce devotion in such diverse places as *The New York Times* and the New Jersey State Prison where, as the Recreational Director wrote, 'The dancing team of Astaire and Rogers took the place by storm'. Perhaps the classic testament to the entertainment provided by these films was that given by the man in New York City who, after having seen *Top Hat* a couple of times, went to the manager of the Radio City Music Hall and begged to be allowed to take out a charge account for the duration of the film's run there. [27]

Along with Astaire and Rogers, Shirley Temple was the perfect representation of the dominant asexual mood created by the Production Code Authority. Her first appearance was in a blatant piece of New Deal propaganda, called

Stand Up and Cheer (1934). It concerned the efforts of a Harry Hopkins figure called Laurence Cromwell (Warner Baxter) to do his job efficiently as Secretary of Amusement. The assignment is given to him by Roosevelt, who makes a short speech that was supposed to echo the First Inaugural Address. One of Baxter's tasks is to rifle through the talent available to him, and, sure enough, waiting in the anteroom is five-year-old Shirley Temple, who gives a remarkably assured rendering of the song 'Baby Take a Bow'. At the conclusion of this dreadful film, some people appear before the camera and shout, 'The Depression is over – men are going back to work. Fear is banished. Laughter is reborn.' It was an unfortunate choice of phrase.

The one success of the picture was Shirley Temple, who shortly afterwards was moved into starring feature roles. Reviews of *Little Miss Marker* (1934) were ecstatic. One exhibitor wrote that it was 'My first picture with this bundle of heaven', while another concluded,

> 99% of the people of the world will receive more moral uplift and helpful good influence from this picture than they will ever receive from any sermon preached at them from any pulpit. [28]

Her pictures were all designed as tear-jerkers, but like any true star she invested even the most insipid plots and dialogue with her effervescent personality. Frank Nugent in *The New York Times* ventured,

> When it comes to sheer histrionism we consider her greater than Garbo, Rainer, Hepburn, the Barrymore family, Ginger Rogers and Gipsy Rose – pardon us – Louise Hovick. And Shirley will get you too if you don't watch out. [29]

Shirley Temple, largely agreed upon as the top box office star from 1935 to 1939, was the most famous of a series of child actors who attained their greatest popularity in the late 1930s. Jane Withers, Freddie Bartholomew, Spanky MacFarland, Jackie Cooper, Judy Garland and Mickey Rooney all had a greater or lesser degree of success at this time. *Variety* noticed the trend in the early stages.

> Proof that the world is moppet-conscious lies in the present cycle of kid pictures which looks likely to click at the box office and has studio talent scouts and scenario writers haunting playgrounds for story material .... News that studios want kid talent has brought mobs to casting windows and agencies with proud parents as thick as grasshoppers in springtime. [30]

The charms of these child stars and the innocent musicals gave the Hays Office no trouble, but if Breen and his colleagues had calmed the sexual tempest they were still beset by certain difficulties in films of social and political intent. *Dead End*, Sidney Kingsley's Broadway play, was bought by Samuel Goldwyn in March 1936 for a record fee of $165,000 after stern competition from Warner Brothers. *Dead End* made a real effort to state explicitly the connection between slum housing and unemployment, and between slum housing and juvenile delinquency. It aroused considerable discussion when produced on Broadway, discussion that predictably worried the Hays Office into insisting on a number of crucial changes before they would sanction a film script.

In the play Francey, the former girlfriend of the gangster, Baby Face Martin, is suffering from acute syphilis as a result of being driven by economic adversity into a life of prostitution; in the film Francey appears to suffer only from a bad cough. Kay, who has risen from the slums to a life of relative luxury by sleeping with a rich businessman, is somewhat reformed by the Hays Office. Breen also made his usual demand for the removal of a scene showing a policeman who is shot by the escaping gangster. [31] The main change was the replacement of the play's hero, Gimpy, who is a cripple and on relief, by the more healthy Dave (played by Joel McCrea) who is a painter, decorating the outside of a small café in return for food. Perhaps the most significant of Breen's remarks to Goldwyn were that he wanted

> to recommend that ... you be less emphatic throughout in the photographing of this script, in showing the contrast between the conditions of the poor in the tenements and those of the rich in the apartment houses. Specifically, we recommend that you do not emphasise the presence of filth or smelly garbage cans or garbage floating in the river, into which the boys jump for a swim. [32]

The task of the Hays Office over *Dead End* was relatively simple in that Breen insisted politely but firmly on strict adherence to the Production Code, as he did with *Blockade* and other controversial movies of the late 1930s. During the turmoil of 1933, however, when the Production Code Authority was just in the process of being constituted, the Hays Office had to deal with one of the strangest, most provocative political films ever to be made in Hollywood.

It was called *Gabriel Over the White House* and it was produced by Walter Wanger at MGM. The picture opens with a conversation among party officials prior to the inauguration of a new President, Judd Hammond (Walter Huston). Hammond cynically reveals that he will break all his election promises and dismisses all thoughts of solving the problems created by the Depression. 'If you run the Senate like you ran for the White House, you'll make the best President the party ever had,' sniggers a party hack to Hammond. At a press conference Hammond categorises John Bronson, the leader of an army of the unemployed, as a 'dangerous anarchist' and the unemployment and racketeering situations as local problems. 'America will weather this through the spirit of Valley Forge and Gettysburg. Our party promises a return to Prosperity,' states Hammond platitudinously.

The President removes the only worthwhile politician on the scene by making him Ambassador to Greece, and spends much of his time reading detective stories or playing on the floor with his nephew, while, over the radio, Bronson's voice pleads earnestly for federal relief for the unemployed. Recklessly driving his own car, Hammond is involved in a road accident, as a result of which he hovers on the brink of death. At this dramatic juncture, the Archangel Gabriel infuses his spirit into the President, who awakes from his coma a spiritually cleansed man. He rejects the Cabinet's advice to turn the army against the marching unemployed and uses the constitutional power of the Executive to demand the resignations of the party hacks he had appointed to the Cabinet.

The President decides on immediate federal action. He sets the army to construction work, until the private building sector is strong enough to absorb its task. He secures the indefinite adjournment of Congress, prefacing this demand with references to Jefferson and Lincoln, while the image on the screen is that of the Lincoln Memorial and the background music, 'The Battle Hymn of the Republic'. [33]

Fortified with these powers, Hammond supervises the sale of illegal alcohol, thereby destroying the bootlegging industry run by the gangster, Diamond. The latter takes revenge by attempting to assassinate the President in the White House, but succeeds only in injuring Hammond's lady friend (played by Karen Morley). Diamond and his gang are eventually captured by the US Army using federal tanks. The criminals are swiftly tried, convicted, lined up against the Statue of Liberty and shot.

The scene changes to a conference on war debts, in which the President destroys the process of secret negotiation by denouncing it over the radio. Hammond abandons the naval holiday and cites the moral bankruptcy of Europe to renege on past promises. The decadent European countries have spent large amounts of money on defence, instead of repaying their war debts, so Hammond lines up all the European representatives to watch the US Air Force destroy its obsolete battleships and threatens to build the most powerful armed force in the world if there is any more quibbling about the signing of an international disarmament pact. The frightened emissaries quickly affix their names to the treaty and Hammond, dramatically clutching Lincoln's pen, is about to sign when he suffers a fatal heart attack. He dies, however, seconds after he has preserved the millennium of peace and prosperity.

Plainly, the story line was sufficiently controversial to cause immense problems for the Hays Office, as the exchange of correspondence with the studio proves. On 28 January James Wingate, Breen's predecessor as head of the Studio Relations Department in Hollywood, wrote to Hays in New York in evident alarm:

> I have learned indirectly that Fox is [also] contemplating the production
> of a picture portraying the plight of the farmers and their protest against

the national government, carrying it to the point of large bodies of them marching to the capital to make their protest felt.

As a matter of policy, I wonder if it would not be advisable for you to sound a note of warning to some of the responsible heads of the industry about making a type of picture portraying large groups of distressed, dissatisfied or unemployed people going en masse in an anti-government attitude of mind to the national capital to make their protest felt?

These are trying times. Industry, business and government are being keenly criticised and ... it is not beyond possibility that [such a] custom ... may lead to the radicals and communists ... doing the same thing, thus helping to lessen the confidence of people in their form of government and perhaps attempt to change the same through radical and unconstitutional methods. [34]

The same day Wingate wrote to Thalberg at MGM:

The preliminary portrayal of distressing conditions should be treated in such a way as not to over-emphasise organised discontent. We, of course, feel nobody engaged in the industry would want to do anything that might foment violence against the better elements of established governments, particularly in these times of stress and unrest. [35]

The following week Wingate received the comments of Mr Esmond, head of the New York censor board, which he immediately transferred to Louis B. Mayer.

The thing that producers should be careful about in my opinion, is these remarks about revolution. God knows there are enough people who are afraid of something of that sort without stirring it up on the screen. Even in the Jolson picture [*Hallelujah I'm a Bum*] there was a remark by one of the bums in the park somewhat as follows: 'When the revolution starts ...' meaning, if anything, that he expects a revolution to start here. [36]

On 6 February Wingate wrote to Thalberg, requesting changes in the first fifty-nine pages of the submitted script.

1. The occasional use of the word 'revolution' [must be avoided].
2. The action of the large group of organised, dissatisfied unemployed and distressed people, marching, some of them armed, to the national capitol, as a matter of protest [must be altered]. [37]

Two days later Thalberg received another letter from Wingate containing the latter's requests for cuts in the next twenty-seven pages. Wingate felt that he could not give the picture his approval, simply because the events of the day were so momentous that he was being forced to review his own policy on a daily basis. However, he stipulated,

Scene I-1: In the headlines stating that the President has assumed dictatorship, we think it might be well to follow this with some such statement as 'Country-Wide Constitutional Referendum Supports President In This Action' thereby indicating that this extraordinary situation has been reached through constitutional means. [38]

On 11 February a letter from Wingate to Hays indicated a new twist in the plot. *Gabriel*, it appeared, 'parallels very closely the program laid down in the Hearst press. Apparently Mr. Hearst is interested in the picture.' [39] Hearst was indeed so taken with the idea of *Gabriel* that he ordered his own company, Cosmopolitan Pictures, to take over production responsibilities. On 16 February Wingate reported further to Hays:

It is our understanding that while this picture is to be released through MGM it is a Cosmopolitan production and as such probably has the backing and financial support of Mr Hearst. [40]

It is believed that Hearst himself wrote some speeches for President Hammond. The rather pompous, verbose speech of the President, delivered before he signs the non-aggression pact, clearly betrays the leaden hand of Hearst.

The hysteria surrounding the production was dramatically increased when President-elect Roosevelt fortuitously survived an assassination attempt by an anarchist in Miami on 15 February. Roosevelt's companion, Mayor Cermak of Chicago, died in the hail of bullets. Wingate used the tragedy to apply increased pressure on Mayer.

Our concern is now increased by the attempted assassination of President elect Roosevelt yesterday .... If this picture had been in circulation now the effect might have been very detrimental to the industry. [41]

Meanwhile, the Hays Office was also worrying itself into a state of near-panic over the probability that Congressional revenge would follow.

The portrayal of a Congress so ineffective that it has to be dismissed by a President might possibly lead toward the enactment of legislation adversely affecting the motion picture industry. [42]

The following day Wingate reported triumphantly:

MGM have withdrawn the original script and will submit another. We hope that our correspondence has had the effect of lessening the danger. [43]

Apart from fomenting social revolution and federal legislation the third worry for the Hays Office posed by the movie was the danger of foreign repercussions. A letter to Wingate written on 28 February pointed out that the discussion of the sensitive foreign debt situation will stir up ill feeling in every European country .... God knows I agree ... that they owe us the money and they ought to pay us, but I don't think it is up to the motion picture industry to fight this battle for the United States .... We get a great deal of money from the foreign distribution of our pictures.

Every time irritants of this sort come out their answer is to pass more tax laws on our industry ....

Foreign producers ... see in all the anti-American feeling a splendid way to make more headway in legislating us out of their respective countries. The fact that this script is ... historically true does not excuse the fact that this material should not be used to make a picture. [44]

Walter Wanger and Gregory La Cava, the director of the picture, worked hard for the next three weeks to film a further revised script, while Louis Mayer and Hays Office officials conducted lengthy discussions to find out how to re-shoot it so that it offended nobody and suggested nothing controversial, but still intrigued the public. Wingate wrote encouragingly to Hays on 23 February after a meeting with Mayer:

I was also advised that when the picture was fully completed and finally edited and satisfactory to him and Mr Hearst he had no doubt it would have the full support of the Hearst as well as the Scripps-Howard papers. [45]

Wingate later confirmed to Hays:

Both of these gentlemen [Mayer and Wanger], but particularly Mr. Mayer, thoroughly understand the industry policy phase of the picture and are discussing changes which should mitigate the remaining danger points .... Our first reaction is one of relief at finding that the picture in its acting, direction and general treatment has been improved so much over the script. [46]

The following day a memo written by another Hays official, Geoffrey Shurlock, noted that after the preview Mayer had promised faithfully that he 'would do all he could to see that it was re-edited in such a way as to avoid giving offense'. The memo also emphasised 'the possibility of ending the picture on a hopeful note of confidence and trust in God', [47] while Wingate kept up his bombardment of Hays with a telegram to New York sent the next day, the fateful 3 March 1933: 'MAYER WAS EXCEPTIONALLY HELPFUL AND CON-STRUCTIVE STOP IF HIS IDEAS PREVAIL THE CONGRESSIONAL ANGLE WILL BE MATERIALLY HELPED AS WELL AS FOREIGN DEBT SITUATION STOP.' [48] In response Hays circulated, on 7 March, a confidential internal memorandum, reminding his colleagues that

It is imperative to remember that we are in an unprecedented situation. The whole country is prostrate and much of the country is literally on its knees .... A majority of the people are looking to Roosevelt and his associates as a drowning man looks at a life saver. The fact is hundreds of thousands of people have one eye on him and one eye on God and it is a temper and state of mind that in my opinion will resent seriously a reflection on the institutions and the factors in government that have to find the solution. [49]

The Hays Office anxiety was well founded. The very next day, 8 March 1933, *The New York Times* reported the introduction of yet another movie-related Bill into the State Legislature. 'Bills to ban movies picturing the life and working of politicians in a manner held to reflect on their standing in the community were introduced into the Legislature today.' [50] At this point, correspondence on the picture ceases and the only documented evidence that remains in the Hays Office file is a tantalising letter of congratulation from Wingate to Thalberg, written just before the film's release.

> Recalling the difficulties which presented themselves in the synopsis, the script and the first print which we reviewed, I am delighted that you have made it into such an excellent picture. I am particularly delighted with the changes made since the first preview. [51]

There exists no print of this first effort, and the best one can do is to surmise from the correspondence demanding changes. From the expressions of delight emanating from the Hays Office, one can only asssume that the initial print must have still contained a number of inflammatory statements. Even in its final form, the picture bears all the hallmarks of a Hearst editorial calling for a strong President, preferably himself, but at a pinch a man whom Hearst had helped to nominate. [52]

Reviews were mixed. The Hearst press was unanimous in declaring it one of the greatest pictures of all time, and certainly the best since the last Marion Davies film. 'It is your drama and mine and American. And it is tremendous. Perhaps the most tremendous the world has ever known. For upon its outcome depend civilisation and humanity itself.' [53] William Troy, in *The Nation*, felt that it might 'convert innocent American movie audiences to a policy of Fascist dictatorship in this country'. [54] *Variety* gave its opinion without political bias. 'A cleverly executed commercial release, it waves the flag frantically, preaches political clap-trap with ponderous solemnity, but it won't inspire a single intelligent reaction in a carload of admissions.' [55] Walter Lippmann pronounced his own epitaph on the film.

> The great lovers [of the screen] ... will not, I think, be pushed aside immediately by unattractive exponents of the gold standard and the regulation of public utilities. For now that I have seen some motion picture statesmen, the great lovers seem not only more enchanting than ever but astonishingly more efficient, learned and profound in their knowledge of what is common to the whole race of men. [56]

An interesting sidelight on *Gabriel* is provided by the fact that in 1934 the producer, Walter Wanger, and the screenwriter, Cary Wilson, made another picture dealing with super-Americanism. The film was called *The President Vanishes*,[57] and it died of asphyxiation at the box office, although it was seriously ill at birth. The plot revolved around a conspiracy of industrialists and bankers to force America into a European war by arousing public opinion to the defence of America's honour. The President, concerned to keep the country out of war and to protect freedom of speech, arranges his own kidnapping, in the wake of which the public forgets all about the possibility of war. The President also manages to plant the blame for the kidnapping on a gang of Fascist greyshirts, run by a crackpot called Lincoln Lee.

Notwithstanding the inanity of the plot, the film ran into trouble just before its release. Breen wrote to Wanger: 'The changed version should not portray the Vice President as a drunkard, a weakling, a fool, an excessively vain man, or as a man who is linked up with crooked politicians.'[58] The Hays Office also felt that the picture was 'dangerous' and might 'incite disrespect for law and order'. Among the changes demanded were a reference to 'capitalistic bloodsuckers', several speeches construed as 'communistic' and close-ups of street clashes between police and demonstrators. The solution to the problem of the capitalist villains was the traditional one. 'If you could group ... these men into a combination representing *international* munitions men with an *international* viewpoint you will escape much of the criticism.'[59]

Breen agreed orally to issue a certificate but wanted Hays himself to see it in New York. Hays categorically refused to issue the certificate, making Wanger so angry that he hired an attorney to sue the Motion Picture Producers and Distributors of America (MPPDA). Hays then wrote to Adolph Zukor, founder and presiding head of Paramount, the production company, to persuade Wanger to grow up.[60] If he agreed to a further three pages of cuts Hays would issue the Seal of Approval. It appears that Wanger must have still bitterly resisted because another note from Hays reminded Zukor pointedly that

> The industry has no right ... to present a distorted picture which condemns the banking industry, the oil industry, the steel industry and the newspaper industry per se as warmongers; which presents the Communist Party as the leading protagonist against these forces and which indicates such banality and corruption in our governmental and political machinery that even the Secret Service of the Nation cannot be trusted to protect the President of the United States.[61]

Paramount was forced to delay the release of the film from the last week in November 1934 until the new year.[62] Wanger had the last word. He deliberately sent the wrong print to Pennsylvania, whose State Censorship

Board refused the film a licence. The Hays Office was incensed. Paramount wrote back denying all responsibility and attributing the problem to human error. [63] Wanger must have smiled quietly – until he began work on the ill-fated *Blockade*.

The function of the Hays Office was to act as the agent of compromise, ensuring that the studios would not jeopardise their profits by the reckless treatment of sensitive subjects. It adapted conservatively to the conventional standards of sexual morality, never seeking to enlarge the areas of artistic freedom for film-makers, ensuring only that their efforts did not meet with a hostile response. Not until 1966, when *The Pawnbroker* obtained a Seal of Approval despite the inclusion of a shot of a black woman exposing her breasts to the camera, was the power of the Production Code Authority broken. Until that time American movies were forced either to ignore sex or to treat it with the symbolism and sniggering that did little to raise the public's moral or artistic standards.

Politically, the Hays Office adopted a similarly cautious tone. Whenever subjects arose that demanded realism in their portrayal, as in *Gabriel Over the White House* or, as we shall see later, in *Blockade* and Warner Brothers' *Black Fury*, the correspondence flew out of the Hays Office, advising, cajoling or threatening the studio, until the inevitable pale compromise resulted. The documents quoted, added to the knowledge of the artistic talent so plentifully in evidence in Hollywood in the 1930s, suggest only that the Hays Office was instrumental in ensuring that the decade was a period of missed opportunities. Many fine pictures were undoubtedly made at the time, but the restrictions imposed by the Hays Office compromised any really searching examinations of important social or political issues.

7

THE LEFT-HANDED ENDEAVOUR

Crime is only a left-handed form of human endeavour.

Louis Calhern, *The Asphalt Jungle*

Ray Mayer spent five years in Hollywood playing gangster character parts. Now, whenever he arrives at railway depots, police detectives who spot all incoming trains trail him. His face is familiar and they associate it with crime.

Variety, 3 May 1939

The problem confronting Mr Mayer attests to the popularity of the gangster, who, along with the cowboy, has perhaps been the American cinema's most enduring contribution to world folklore. The fascination with lawbreaking did not begin in the 1930s, but the harnessing of urban violence to the visual excitement of motion pictures, and the naturalism afforded by the coming of sound, made the first decade of the gangster film years of considerable interest for audiences, sociologists and reformers.

One of the reformers wrote in 1931,

One evening spent looking at a talking picture like *Underworld* gives these particular citizens more information about the ins and outs of crime than a week of patient study under Al Capone .... An underworld picture of a given event exerts perhaps 150 million times as strong an influence upon those who see it as the printed account of the very same event exerts upon those who read it.[1]

The writer's alarmist tendencies may have led him to exaggerate the danger to the population contained in the gangster movies, but he had quickly realised that this new genre had struck a responsive chord in American life. Robert Warshow wrote that the experience of the gangster as an experience of art is universal to Americans and plainly, despite the homage rendered to the gangster film by European movie-makers, the genre in its purest form has remained uniquely an American concept.[2]

Initially the gangster movie was written from the newspaper accounts of contemporary crime. *Little Caesar* and (more accurately) *Scarface* were based on the life of Capone, and the other classic gangster film, *The Public Enemy*, was a loose biography of Hymie Weiss. In 1929 a specially appointed action group of the Chicago Association of Commerce under the chairmanship of Colonel Robert Isham Randolph was set up to investigate the extent of racketeering in local business: it was called 'The Secret Six'. In 1931 a film of that name was produced by MGM. One of the wire services, AP, attributed the decline of organised crime in Chicago at the start of the 1930s to the effectiveness of the Secret Six.[3]

In *The Public Enemy* Cagney takes revenge on the horse that killed his boss, Nails Nathan, by tossing a bundle of notes to the owner and shooting the horse (off screen). In reality, the death of the stylish gangster Nails Morton occurred when he was thrown from a horse. The offending animal was dispatched by Two-gun Louis Alterie. One of the classic moments in film history, the deaths of Cagney and Bogart in a New Year's Eve incident at the end of *The Roaring Twenties*, was an echo of the death of Larry Fay, who was murdered on the eve of 1931, shot down in a New York night club by a disgruntled employee.[4]

There was more to the popularity of the gangster film than the mere apeing of sensational underworld events. The violence (in relative terms at least) of the gangsters was felt by many to be a healthy American trait, as if the lawlessness and rough personal justice of the days of the Western frontier were to be transplanted to the urban frontier of the twentieth century. The American nation was born in a bloody revolution and matured in a vicious civil war. The constitution had been amended to protect the right of the citizen to bear arms, but efforts to dispense with the amendment in times of peace met with no success.

The constant expansion of the country away from the areas where the writ of government ran, and into country fiercely defended by the original inhabitants, was an eloquent defence of the Second Amendment. Even in modern urban history violence has been a fairly constant feature of life. Few countries produced their labour unions without trouble, but in America labour–management relations were marked by frequent outbreaks of violence, some of them, as was the case at Republic Steel in 1937, reaching tragic proportions.

The proliferation of criminals, and the tendency for the law-abiding to maintain themselves in armed readiness against the approach of trouble, sprang in large measure from the general contempt in which the forces of law and order were held. In the 1890s the Rev. Dr Charles Parkhurst had been shocked that the New York police were affording protection to brothels, and demanded a state inquiry, in which the nefarious activities of 'Clubber' Williams, the First Inspector of Police, were exposed. Some sixty years later the Kefauver committee revealed that crime had benefited by the expansion of big business, so that the best criminals had applied the techniques of industrial management to the successful practice of illegal activities.

The election of Theodore Roosevelt as Police Commissioner, after the exposures begun by Dr Parkhurst, only made things worse for the police, since the mutual co-operation between police and criminals, which had existed for years, was ended. The success of the clean-up of the 1890s was reflected in the exposures of the muckrakers for the next decade.[5] But if the situation was bad at a time of federal concern for law and order, it deteriorated still further in the 1920s, a period of excessive federal laxity. William Hale Thompson, the Mayor of Chicago and an open supporter of Al Capone, seized every available opportunity to attack the federal encroachments on his territory. In a speech on the south side of the city, Thompson complained about the activities of US Senator Deneen and his attempts to enforce Prohibition.

> I will do all in my power to save Chicago citizens from any more suffering at the hands of the thugs and gunmen brought here by the Federal Government to further Deneen's political influence .... Vote for the flag, the Constitution, your freedom, your property, as Abraham Lincoln and William Hale Thompson would like to have you do.[6]

Thompson was the Mayor of Chicago for three terms between 1915 and 1931. When the Chicago Democratic party gave a testimonial dinner to the notorious Dion O'Bannion, the guests included O'Bannion, Gusenberg, Drucci, Moran, Weiss and Alterie (gangsters); W. S. Steward, Colonel A. A. Sprague and Robert M. Sweitzer (local public officials); Chief of Detectives Michael Hughes and Lieutenant Charles Egan (police).[7]

The police, in the eyes of the general public, were merely one gang in conflict with the others, and as deserving of moral support as Capone or O'Bannion. Coupled with this disgust of 'authority' was a grudging admiration for the 'success' and flair of the gangsters, who were only really another object of fascination in the Era of Wonderful Nonsense, more dangerous perhaps than the Charleston but more entertaining than flagpole sitting – provided one didn't live near them or have business interests which conflicted with theirs.

The heroic stature of the movie gangster was presaged by his real counter-part. Just as Tommy Connors on his way to Sing Sing[8] chats amiably, if conceitedly, to reporters and signs the autograph books of young girls, so Al Capone elicited on his infrequent public appearances mass demonstrations of affection. One biographer records his appearance at a Charlestown, Indiana racetrack, which caused thousands to stand and cheer while Capone waved his arms above his head like a prize fighter entering the ring. Pasley in his 1930 biography reported,

> 'There goes Al' would fly from lip to lip and pedestrians would crowd to sidewalk kerbs, craning necks as eagerly as for a circus parade. It was a civic spectacle to linger in the recollection of strangers during 1925, 1926, 1927 and 1928.[9]

Publicity made Capone into an international celebrity. His fan mail was as big as any film star's and most of it included a request for money. In a poll taken

119

in 1931 the American public was reported to be familiar with names in the following order of importance: first, film stars; second, gangsters; third, athletes and fourth, politicians. Capone was besieged by requests to appear in films for large sums of money, and at high society parties. One disappointed would-be hostess declared, 'Society would be a lot more fun if Al Capone would join in.'[10] Capone wanted to be regarded as equally American as the portraits of Washington and Lincoln which adorned his office walls. The most obvious way was to reveal himself as a supporter of the idea of conspicuous consumption. After the second Tunney–Dempsey fight Capone threw a three-day party which cost him $50,000. He generally tipped $5 to a newsboy, $10 to a hat-check girl and $100 to a waiter. A girl who came to plead for a place in one of his brothels, so that she could support her mother, was sent on her way with a $100 bill. During his residence in a Philadelphia jail he celebrated Christmas 1929 by buying $1,000 of the prisoners' goods for presents. His free Thanksgiving dinners were a regular feature and, in hard winters, the poor of Chicago could draw all the groceries, clothing and fuel they wanted and charge it to Capone's account.[11] It was decided that Matt, youngest of the Capone boys, was to be given an expensive education at the exclusive Villanova University in Philadelphia. Pasley grouped Capone with Will Rogers, Henry Ford, Rin Tin Tin, Babe Ruth, Charles Lindbergh, Tex Guinan and Al Smith as the quintessential Americans.[12]

Capone's place on such a roll of honour was not without merit. He was a pioneer in criminal territory and, in his own way, used his undoubted qualities of imagination, resourcefulness, ruthlessness and leadership to improve his business and, automatically, the trade he practised. Capone made the transition from small-time hoodlum to one of the most famous, wealthy and influential men in America and, in doing so, he altered the nature of American crime. He was a true professional, emphasising a dedication and a responsibility in his employees that would have been just as fitting in a top football coach.

Capone chose men who dressed well[13] and had a liking for diamonds and blondes. Just as top businessmen had season tickets to the major sporting events, so Capone made sure that he and his employees enjoyed that particular reward for their endeavours. The gangster was essentially conservative. He did not scorn property as much as covet it so intensely that he was compelled to acquire it in the easiest way – by violence. He indulged in conspicious consumption because he was proud (to the point of exhibitionism) of the fact that he had succeeded in the fiercely competitive world of American business. As Dion O'Bannion remarked of himself and his associates, 'We're big business without the top hats'.[14] Capone confirmed his status as a folk-hero by issuing periodic blasts against bankers after the Crash of 1929.

Why don't they go after all these bankers who took the savings of thousands of poor people and lost them in bank failures? Isn't it lots worse to take the last few dollars some small family has saved – perhaps to live on while the head of the family is out of a job – than to sell a little beer, a little alky?

Capone in his role of anxious parent pronounced adversely on the rise of the gangster film.

> They ought to take them and throw them in the lake. They're doing nothing but harm to the younger element of this country. I don't blame the censors for trying to ban them . . . . These gang movies are making a lot of kids want to be tough guys and they don't serve any useful purpose.[15]

It was no coincidence that Capone, and most of the other gangsters during the era of Prohibition, were second-generation Americans. The effects of slum backgrounds on aspiring youngsters with ambition may be a sociological cliché, but it certainly helps to explain the rise of the gangster in American society. *The Godfather II* (1975) is a compelling movie version of the growth of organised crime among Italian and Sicilian immigrants. On a wider scale Daniel Bell has pointed out that with each succeeding wave of immigrants the preceding arrivals found themselves moving up a rung on the ladder in the search for accommodation and employment.

The Irish, who immigrated in the 1840s, cornered the market in political jobs, and the Jews, who arrived in the second half of the century after the wave of pogroms in Central and Eastern Europe, gravitated towards positions of economic influence, so that the only course apparently left open to the avaricious Italians and Sicilians was to progress through the ranks of the underworld.[16] Of Chicago's three and a half million population in 1930, two and a half million were foreign-born or of foreign or mixed parentage. Forty per cent of female and fifty per cent of male delinquents were of foreign-born parentage. Exploited by rapacious landlords and unscrupulous bosses, the immigrants turned inwards for protection, to the family unit or block gang.[17] The two main gangs in Chicago were composed almost exclusively of Irish (led by O'Bannion) and Italians (under Capone), although men like Arnold Rothstein made sure that the Jews did not lack representation in the underworld.

In the short term two particular reasons were responsible for the popularity of the gangster film in the 1930s. The triumph of the organised advocates of the Eighteenth Amendment and the Volstead Act succeeded in making every American who wanted an alcoholic drink into a criminal. As a consequence gangs established themselves as big-time entrepreneurs of liquor, and such crime empires, founded on circumventing Prohibition, could expand with the accumulation of capital to become involved in the world of big business.

'The noble experiment' gave American crime the vital impulse to cartelisation. In 1925 General Lincoln C. Andrews, Assistant Secretary of the Treasury in charge of enforcement, suggested that agents intercepted about five per cent of the liquor traffic. In 1924 it was estimated that $40 million of illegal alcohol was smuggled into the country over the 18,000 miles of coastline. Chicago, in view of its proximity to Canada across the Great Lakes, was a particularly valuable strategic location for bootleggers. By 1927 Capone was running a business based on drink worth $60 million a year.[18]

In New York and San Francisco strangers could find speakeasies by asking policemen. Federal agents who destroyed barrels of beer, wantonly smashed bottles of whisky, raided speakeasies and waylaid rum runners at sea were hardly likely to be heroes to thirsty Americans, and the reverse of the coin was that the bootlegger was regarded as a courageous off-licence supplier. When Prohibition was repealed, in 1933, gangsters had stabilised their businesses to such an extent that they passed over relatively easily to prostitution, drugs and racketeering for their major sources of income.

The other spur to a favourable climate for the reception of the gangster film was, of course, the widespread effects of the Depression, which have been discussed in more detail elsewhere. If justification for illegality were needed, the crumbling nature of the economic, moral and institutional framework of the country provided it. To those people whose minds were unable to fathom the ways of high finance, it simply appeared that money which they had deposited had been stolen by the banks. Capone's tirades against bankers met an echoing roar of approval. Now, perhaps more than ever, there was a widespread genuine, if grudging, admiration for the gangsters who carved their own fortunes out of the fortresses of power and wealth with their tommy guns. They at least were doing something besides worrying how to pay the grocery bills, how to find another job, how to keep up payments on the mortage.

It is thus not surprising to discover that the most violent, 'purest', gangster films were made in the period 1930–2. Although Josef von Sternberg had made a number of silent pictures dealing with gangsters, the fully mature form of the genre appeared only in 1930, when a flood of gangster pictures emerged from Hollywood in response to public demand. One writer unsuccessfully hawked a gangster screenplay round the studios for months. Less than a week after *Little Caesar* opened in New York he got offers from four of the major studios who had already turned him down. It was *Little Caesar* which, along with *Doorway to Hell*, *The Public Enemy*, *Quick Millions* and *Scarface*, defined the prototype of the gangster film. Rico (Edward G. Robinson in his first important starring role) and his friend Joe Massara (Douglas Fairbanks Jr) leave a small town where they have been living off the proceeds from filling station robberies and travel to 'the city', where Rico takes over a gang, having proved in action his bravery and ingenuity. Rico's inability to dispose of Joe when his own personal safety dictates it, however, starts 'Little Caesar' on his rapid descent. His infamous final words, as he is mown down by police bullets, are 'Mother of Mercy, is this the end of Rico?', thus distancing himself, even at the moment of death, from the immortal creation of the gang world.

122

An advertisment for the film distributed by Warner Brothers emphasised what they thought to be the picture's main drawing power in their press release.

Little Caesar – King of the Underworld. He ruled supreme – a law unto himself, for in his racket he was court, judge and jury .... He runs the gamut of power – from gutter to gang ruler – to gutter again.

The basis of *Little Caesar*, as of the other gangster films of this period, was the deployment of power. In an early scene, as Rico thinks about the possibility of killing the garage attendant he has just robbed, he muses, 'Maybe I should o' done it too. That's all I got between me and them – between me and the whole world.' The film is symmetrically constructed. As soon as Rico makes the fatal mistake of deciding to spare Joe, his descent is as dramatic and rapid as was his climb to power. No doubt the makers of the picture were gratified to read in *The New York Times*,

Little Caesar becomes at Mr. Robinson's hands a figure out of a Greek epic tragedy; a cold, ignorant killer driven on and on by an insatiable lust for power, the plaything of a force greater than himself.[19]

A few weeks later Warners released *The Public Enemy*, in which Tom Powers (James Cagney) graduates from tripping up girls and stealing watches to full-time racketeering. Taken from an original story by John Bright and Kubec Glasmon called *Beer and Blood*, the film glorified the rise to power of Cagney. At no time do the police appear and Cagney is eventually murdered by a rival gang, justice generally being meted out in the roughest way.

Cagney demonstrated for the first time on screen his unique sexual aggression which complemented Robinson's professional dedication. In a scene which has now become a staple of tired documentaries on the golden years of Hollywood, Cagney objects to the questions of Mae Clark at breakfast and pushes a half grapefruit into her surprised face. Later on he is seduced while under the influence of alcohol but recovers the following morning to smack the offending woman across the mouth sufficiently hard as to make his point.

Quick Millions, released by Fox a few weeks later, forms the triangle of the year's classic gangster pictures. Bugs Raymond (Spencer Tracy) also starts in the humbler walks of life, by smashing cars parked inoffensively on the street so that they have to be towed into his garage. Raymond is completely at home in the world of sharp practice, so that, when he achieves his ambition of forcing his way on to the board of directors of a prosperous company, he feels happy to take the sister of one of the directors to the races and win large sums of money for her by acquainting her with the betting racket. The girl refuses to accept the money so easily won. 'Why not?' asks Raymond in surprise. 'It's something you wouldn't understand,' she replies, 'Ethics.'

One review complained that there was 'too much footage given to ... sneering at law and lawyers', but, in general, this was an auspicious directorial debut by Roland Brown, whose rendering of the underworld seemed so authentic that many people supposed it could have come only from personal involvement.[20]

Variety observed perceptively of this new genre:

> Treatment of crime as picture material has changed radically. Old criminal characters were instilled with a desire for coin and bloody spoils. The modern criminal as featured in films and public life thirsts primarily for power. It's bootlegging that gives him the momentum and there doesn't seem to be as much objection as there is admiration over boot-legging as a play plot. The chief murderer's power quest is what makes him so interesting.[21]

The film which effectively ended the first cycle of gangster films, and aroused widespread censorship, was Howard Hawks's *Scarface* (1932), starring Paul Muni and produced for United Artists by Howard Hughes. The final script combined the talents of Ben Hecht, Seton I. Miller, John Lee Mahin and W. R. Burnett. Muni plays Tony Camonte, a lightly disguised portrait of Al Capone. He appears initially as a menacing, whistling silhouette, about to commit a murder. His announced motto is 'Do it first, do it yourself and keep on doing it'. Many of the integral features of the gangster movie are in evidence. Camonte is released from prison by his shyster lawyer on a writ of habeas corpus, and illustrates his contempt for the law by deliberately striking a match on a policeman's badge and waving a mock salute.

He indulges in the traditional gangster's bad taste in the fine arts by decorating his apartment in loud colours. He brings the mistress of his boss, Poppy (played by Karen Morley), to admire it. 'How do you like it?' he asks, proudly. 'Kinda gaudy ain't it?' she replies. 'Glad you like it,' says Camonte without a hint of irony. He traces the usual path of ascendancy through violence, dispatching enemies and his former boss with admirable thoroughness. Hawks's predilection with the cross of doom furthers the intensity of Camonte's power. Boris Karloff as a rival thug is murdered in a bowling alley, where he has just made a strike, and puts the cross on the score sheet against his own name as the last remaining pin totters and falls. Camonte dies like the heroes of the other films, but the moral lesson which the film tries to point is entirely lost, since the audience has spent the previous ninety minutes admiring the forthright qualities of the man. The lack of moral competition also accounts for 'justice's' final pyrrhic victory.

The tendency of the audience to sympathise with these amoral gangsters was not a development exclusive to the new genre but a continuation of a particular form of literary and dramatic tradition. The gangster as hero was a very strong parallel to the heroic stature of many of the villains in Elizabethan and Jacobean tragedy. Shakespeare's Richard of Gloucester, although the instrument of death, is also the instrument of God, since most of those whom he dispatches – Clarence, Hastings and Buckingham among others – have committed some immoral act which justifies their deaths. The character of

Richard in *Richard III* is particularly attractive, since the characters opposed to him are either charlatans or ineffective politicians. Nobody can match Richard's wit, imagination and perverse charm, and Shakespeare, not surprisingly, delayed the entrance of the avenging Richmond until Act V, at which point the future Henry VII becomes not so much a character as a personal manifestation of future national glory.

The gangsters were clearly born and bred in the teeming slums of American cities in the early years of the twentieth century but their immediate appeal to the public through their representation in movies owed something to a longer-standing literary tradition in the portrayal of antiheroes. In an interview just before his death W. R. Burnett, the author of *Little Caesar*, claimed, 'I was reaching for a gutter Macbeth ... Rico is the picture of overriding ambition'.[22] Certainly the gangsters' insatiable desire for violence and the inevitability of their deaths echo Macbeth's

> I am in blood
> Stepp'd in so far that, should I wade no more,
> Returning were as tedious as go o'er.

Or as Richard muses fatalistically as he plans the murder of the Princes in the Tower: 'But I am in / So far in blood that sin will pluck on sin'.

Even closer to the tone of the gangster films were the dark revenge tragedies of Tourneur, Webster and Middleton. The villain-heroes, De Flores, Vendice, Bosola and Flamineo, move in a more artificially structured society than the gangsters but it is essentially their ambitition, desire for power and intellectual arrogance that impels them towards murder. Bosola, on learning of the ill-fated marriage between Antonio and the Duchess of Malfi, remarks in astonishment,

> Do I not dream? can this ambitious age
> Have so much goodness in't as to prefer
> A man merely for worth, without these shadows
> Of wealth and painted honours? possible?[23]

and Flamineo in *The White Devil* scoffs at Vittoria,

> Fool that thou art, to think that politicians
> Do use to kill the effects of injuries
> And let the cause live. Shall we groan in irons
> Or be a shameful and a weighty burthen
> To a public scaffold? This is my resolve:
> I would not live at any man's entreaty,
> Nor die at any's bidding.[24]

The same contempt for authority, the same despair for the world and the same refuge in cynicism is adopted by the gangsters. Bugs Raymond, Little Caesar, Tom Powers and Tony Camonte lie dead at the end of the films as

Vendice, Bosola, Flamineo, Richard and De Flores die at the end of the plays. But there is no purging of the emotion, except perhaps at the end of Richard, because the figures of authority who remain are once more intellectually inadequate. Similarly, the deaths of the gangsters hardly inspire an audience with the belief that the police now have matters well in hand.

It was this fear that prompted the widespread attempts to ban *Scarface* on its first release. Colonel Joy at the Hays Office wrote worriedly to United Artists,

> Murdering is more of a game than anything else, an outlet for his tremendous ability and energy. All of this is the more dangerous because of the resemblance to Capone, who so far has succeeded in defeating the law .... The action involving the State's attorney and the judges issuing habeas corpus ought to be eliminated as tending to show a breakdown in the forces of law as a connivance with criminals. Some people are almost fanatical, especially in places of authority, in their desire to stop the flow of these pictures.[25]

The Hays officials argued solidly with Howard Hughes for about nine months and even enlisted the help of the MGM executive, Irving Thalberg, to reach a satisfactory compromise.[26] Eventually, a lengthy foreword was written, urging the public to support federal laws for enabling the police to deprive criminals of their guns. It was discarded. A framing story was added opening with some juvenile delinquents in court being told a story by the judge, which constitutes the body of the film. At the conclusion of this the judge wags his finger at the boys and intones:

> That is the story that is certain to be repeated in the lives of many of you – if you persist in your folly. That is the inevitable fate that waits upon those who become drunk by the power of a pistol.

This too was discarded.

Hays himself, according to Robert E. Sherwood, demanded that Camonte be brought to trial, sentenced to death and hanged in the full view of the audience. Hughes, anxious to release the film, complied and brought the cast back to make the extensive and costly re-takes. When it was shown in this mutilated version to the New York Censorship Board, it was flatly rejected. Hughes decided that he could function without the official approval of the Hays Office, and released the film very much as it had been in the first finished cut.[27] Needless to say, the publicity campaign had been helped enormously by the fuss, and the film was a huge financial success. As for its excessive violence, one exhibitor in Lincoln, Nebraska, wrote, 'One of the year's best pictures. Gangster story that appeals even to the women. More than double the average gross.'[28]

In 1932 the torrent of gangster films slowed to a trickle and by 1933 it had almost dried up entirely. When the genre reappeared in 1935 it did so in a significantly different form. In other words, the 'pure' gangster film disappeared at precisely the same time as the disillusioned pictures of crooked politicians and shyster lawyers and the movies dealing with the relatively daring topic of women's sexual conduct. The Hays Office rearranged its personnel, the Production Code Authority tightened its control of film output, the new President followed his inauguration with an inspiring burst of legislative activity and the industrial production index began to move upwards once more.

Obviously all these occurrences were by no means directly related to each other; but equally obviously it was hardly coincidental that they all happened within weeks of each other. The gangster film changed for much the same reason that the female stars reformed their screen characters. Public taste, however nebulous and capricious a phenomenon, ruled the studios rather than vice versa. Innovative or desperate producers might be persuaded to gamble with a new theme, but none was prepared to persist in the face of public hostility, and the zeal of the reformers was slowly biting into gangster film audiences.

The genre between 1930 and 1932 was also something of a 'craze', which was burning itself out. Its demise, however, was additionally hastened by the changing political, economic and emotional climate of 1933. The New Deal restored hope, if it did nothing else. It restored faith in a society of which large numbers of Americans had previously sullenly despaired. In such an atmosphere the 'classic' gangster film was no longer welcome.

Another consequence of Hollywood's heroic treatment of the gangster was the emergence during 1933 and 1934 in the South and Mid-West of a series of petty criminals, such as John Dillinger, Baby Face Nelson, Bonnie Parker and Clyde Barrow. Philip French has noted[29] how these rural, Anglo-Saxon amateurs modelled themselves on the Hollywood image of the urban, immigrant gangster. Where Capone and his men had been successful professionals, Bonnie and Clyde, the Barkers, Machine Gun Kally, Pretty Boy Floyd, Dillinger and Nelson were loners, unprofessional and doomed to failure once they came up against an organisation that was at all united.

Although their incomes were tiny by comparison with Capone's and his associates', the audacity of their careers would no doubt have been much longer, but by 1934 the combination of public outrage and mockery persuaded Congress to make kidnapping (in the wake of the tragic murder of Charles Lindbergh's baby), robbing a national bank, flight across state lines to avoid arrest or giving testimony, and other offences into federal crimes. The FBI, under J. Edgar Hoover, interpreted this as an open invitation to make federal agents responsible for the destruction at all costs of the rural gangsters. He published a list of public enemies and was instrumental in promoting the transfer of public sympathy from the amateur hoodlum to the professional pursuer. The G-Men, as the FBI agents were known, made a series of spectacular, if bloody, arrests and they assumed the mantle of romance, hitherto the preserve of the gangsters and the Mounties. In July 1934 Dillinger was shot down by the G-Man Melvin Purvis outside a Chicago cinema, where he had been to see the MGM picture *Manhattan Melodrama*. It was a remarkable case of life imitating art.

The success of the G-Men provided Hollywood with the perfect formula for the revival of the gangster film. As the protectors of society, government employees and professional killers, the G-Men fulfilled every requirement for a Hollywood hero, circa 1935. Early in the year *Variety* reported,

GANGSTER CYCLE UP AGAIN

Using Moral Angle As Twist

Studios will try to take the curse off these yarns by weaving a 'crime doesn't pay' aura around the law breakers. This method was also used to taper off the previous gangster cycle.[30]

Just before the first of the new cycle appeared, the same newspaper differentiated between the new gangster pictures and the old ones.

Little Caesar, Scarface and The Public Enemy were more than portrayals of gangster tactics; they were biographies of curious mentalities. They were photographic and realistic analyses of mentality and character (or lack of it). But in the new idea of glorifying the government gunners who wipe out the killers, there is no chance for that kind of build-up.[31]

Predictably, first into the field were Warner Brothers, with a film unsurprisingly called *G-Men*. It instantly aroused the suspicions of the Hays Office. Hays wrote to Harry Warner warning him that the Attorney General, Homer Cummins, had been complaining that he had neither seen a script nor approved such a project. The letter continued that no such approval would be forthcoming

Unless the Department of Justice has had an opportunity to consider the matter, so that we may be assured that a dignified and technically accurate picture will be produced .... I will ask Mr Hoover to contact you for the purpose of bringing about a clearer understanding of our mutual problems.[32]

As the script progressed Breen wrote to Jack L. Warner: 'You will show policemen being hit by bullets or wounded *but will in no case ever show actual officers dying at the hands of gangsters.*'[33] Five days later he reiterated in another note to the same recipient: 'It is our belief that in pictures *we should avoid actually photographing illegal weapons in the hands of gangsters.*'[34] During shooting Harry Warner kept up the pressure on William Keighley, the director.

You are getting a little careless in the showing of guns. There's a big close up of Cagney laying his automatic down on the desk and while he is a government man, at the same time the censors object to these huge close ups showing guns .... Let's make these shots a little more clever so they won't be cut out on us.[35]

G-Men eventually starred erstwhile gangster James Cagney, whose stardom had been achieved through a rather mischievous violence. The scriptwriter, Seton I. Miller, cautiously opened the film by portraying Cagney as a lawyer who has been put through law school by a local racketeer. The combination of the death of a friend who was a G-Man and the failure of his practice sends Cagney to Washington to train for G-man duty. Mac, his racketeer mentor, supports the move and criticises Cagney for complaining about not getting ahead quickly enough as a lawyer: 'Nobody gets ahead fast when they're on the level. I've been in the rackets all my life and you don't get rich – 'cept in dough.' Midway through the film there is a strong plea for the arming of federal officials and the removal of the law requiring them always to obtain local warrants before making an arrest. Emergency legislation to that effect is immediately rushed through Congress.

Cagney's boss is a dislikable man with a very likable sister (Margaret Lindsay, with whom Cagney falls in love) but, unlike the gangsters, the two men try to work together for the good of the organisation. As one of them ungrammatically phrases it, 'We're gonna make the word "government" poison to them if it's the last thing I do.' Although the gangsters are surrounded in a hotel from which they shoot their way out (a depiction of numerous real events in the lives of Clyde Barrow and Bonnie Parker as well as most of the other recent criminals), Cagney evenually catches up with the Public Enemy number one, capturing him and the heart of Miss Lindsay at the same time.

Otis Ferguson called the film a 'rather flabby version of the rather cruel truth' and bemoaned the loss of 'the big time gangster ... a sort of inverted public hero (not enemy), a lonely, possessed and terrible figure, burning himself inevitably out at inhuman speeds'.[36] But Joseph Breen was delighted: 'It is very well done,' he wrote to Wingate in New York with some satisfaction and continued,

> The government men stand out as great heroes. There is, of course, considerable shooting but all of it is done according to our formula and it is not over-done. You ought to warn the censor Boards that there will be five or six of these pictures coming along during the next two months. We are giving them very considerable study in the hope of saving them from being mutilated. The result at Warner Brothers is most encouraging.[37]

Exhibitors and the general public shared this view. One of the former wrote: 'We honestly believe every theater should play this picture for the reason it leaves a lot of people thinking our government is Okay after all the filth we read in the paper'.[38] A journalist from the *Kansas City Star* cabled Jack Warner:

> WAS AT TRIAL OF ADAM RICHETTS TODAY DEFENSE ATTORNEY ASKED PROSPECTIVE JURORS IF THEY HAD SEEN G MEN AND IF THE PIC HAD CREATED A NEW RESPECT FOR FEDERAL AGENTS IN THEM. WHEN [THEY] SAID IT HAD DEFENSE ATTORNEYS SCRATCHED THEM FROM THE PANEL THOUGHT THIS MIGHT MAKE GREAT PUBLICITY FOR A GREAT PICTURE[39]

At the foot of the cable Jack Warner scribbled a note: 'Hal – Please read. Very funny.' What must have pleased Jack Warner even more was that *G-Men*, budgeted tightly at $260,000 ($40,000 of which was earmarked for Cagney), made a tidy profit.

The success of *G-Men* enabled producers to go ahead with the production of the inevitable imitations. Breen wrote to Will Hays with evident satisfaction:

> You will be pleased to know that the half dozen so-called G Men pictures which have given us some concern in recent months are coming through in grand style .... The two pictures we have seen and the three or four scripts we have read have the general thesis of glorifying the agents of the Department of Justice. The Government men are heroes and ... much footage is given over to ... the intelligence with which they proceed .... In all these pictures there is a fine uplift. It made you feel proud to be an American.[40]

Melvin Purvis, killer of Dillinger and Pretty Boy Floyd, was equally pleased. *The Hollywood Reporter* revealed that the 'former head of the Chicago office of the U.S. Bureau of Investigation is being offered to the studios as a writer and technical advisor on G-men pictures. Purvis ... wants to write the story of his experiences as a G-man.'[41]

MGM produced *Public Hero No. 1*, but it was Warners who churned out more (and better) pictures of this kind. *Bullets or Ballots* (1936), based on the true life exploits of Dutch Schulz and Johnny Broderick, again employed the talents of the director, Keighley, and the writer, Miller, but this time it starred Warners' other major crime figures – Edward G. Robinson and Humphrey Bogart. Here emphasis is placed on the diversification of gangs into business rackets. Robinson plays an honest policeman, who pretends to have left the force in disgrace so that he can join the big organisation from inside and find out how wide its range of interests is and who are the men behind the syndicate. Robinson discovers that the latter are a group of bankers working under the title of Oceanic Bank and Trust Co., and he succeeds in killing Bogart and incriminating them with his dying gasp. As he expires in the arms of Joan Blondell, he croaks, 'I like to think that when those mugs pass a policeman, they'll keep on tipping their hats.'

An alternative ending was written, in which Robinson recovers from the gunshot wound inflicted by Bogart and is visited in hospital by the Crime Commissioner and Joan Blondell, but it was presumably felt that Robinson's screen image was such that he could be killed off without destroying the potency of the picture's message. The film was well received by public and critics, although there was a definite fear that this was still the tip of the gangster film iceberg.

In the wilds of Washington an exhibitor pronounced his satisfaction: 'Good action picture with plenty of shooting and killings and that's what they like in this neck of the woods.'[42] *The New York Times* in effect said much the same thing: 'If this sounds like the old formula – and it is – still there is no disputing the picture's claim upon your attention ... [in] its fidelity to known criminal facts.'[43] *Variety* also emphasised the close relationship between the picture and recent news events and revealed the fact that Martin Mooney, the New York crime reporter, had been in Hollywood helping with the original story so that Miller's final screenplay reflected Mooney's experience of G-Man activities in New York.[44]

Public Enemy's Wife suggested that the Warner Brothers story department was running out of ideas, as this was a tedious and predictable story of a G-Man played by Pat O'Brien and his attempts to capture a vicious criminal. The criminal is evil and psychopathic, while the G-Man's only defect is a slight wariness at the charms of Margaret Lindsay. The resolution is unhappy only in its excessive delay.

The only possible excuse for such a film was that the G-Man cycle was so successful that inferior merchandise had to be produced just to satisfy the popular demand. However, *Motion Picture Herald* reported,

> While there has been no feeling that the 'G-men' cycle has been harmful, and, on the contrary, has been considered constructive in presenting a picture of the government's war on crime, at the same time, films of this type were becoming so numerous as to create some resistance on the part of the public [at the] ... box office.[45]

The new hero who appeared, to the relief of Hollywood writers, was the crusading New York District Attorney Thomas E. Dewey, whose investigations into organised crime revealed the depth of its penetration, but offered no lasting remedies, as the Kefauver Committee was to reveal fifteen years later. Still, for Hollywood, Dewey offered a new approach to the gangster film which showed how a tough law officer with the help of courageous, if frightened, victims and potential victims could outwit the deadliest criminal the story department could devise.

Among the movies which fell into this category were *Smashing the Rackets* at RKO, *I Am the Law* contributed by Columbia and *Marked Woman* and *Racket Busters*, which emerged from the seemingly indefatigable Warner Brothers. *Marked Woman* (1937), directed by Lloyd Bacon and boasting an excellent script by the young Robert Rossen and Abem Finkel, was much the best. Bette Davis, in her first part after a year's absence from the screen,[46] revels in the story about a clip joint hostess who tries to protect her younger, innocent sister (Jane Bryan) from learning how she makes her living. After Bryan discovers the truth she is too ashamed to go back to school and instead goes off to a party thrown by Davis's evil boss, where she tries to resist a man who makes advances to her only to be pushed down a staircase, dying in the process. Davis's initial reaction is to go to the police and reveal the truth, but she is dissuaded by her fellow workers and room mates who fear the revenge their boss might take. 'The law isn't for people like us,' they tell her. 'Then what is?' asks Davis, bitterly.

She reveals the circumstances of her sister's death to Police Inspector Graeme (Humphrey Bogart) and is promptly marked across the face and viciously beaten up by her boss. Despite threats and intimidation Davis and the other girls give testimony in open court that convict the racketeers, although a court reporter points the message that 'The leading citizens are either too big or too afraid. Out of the teeming millions in this city, only five girls had the courage to take the stand.' At the end of the trial the racketeers are sentenced to thirty to fifty years in the state penitentiary, and Bogart and Davis leave the court together triumphant, but destined to spend the rest of their lives in different worlds, as they fail to achieve a relationship based on common ground. This touch, which seems to have been conceived by Rossen (many of his films deal with the impossibility of relationships that in other hands would have been easily and unconvincingly worked out), adds immeasurably to the power of the film.

Dewey was, at least initially, less than delighted at Hollywood's interest in him. In March 1937 he wrote tartly to Will Hays:

> I have been greatly disturbed by the repeated use of my name by publicity agents for the motion picture companies. There is, apparently, a race going on to see which can turn out first a motion picture which the public is intended to believe is based upon my work. Naturally this is exceedingly offensive to me. Motion pictures are totally unauthorized and they will inevitably be so inaccurate as to be ingenuous. Furthermore actors will impersonate me and my assistants purporting to represent to the public the manner in which we conduct ourselves.[47]

It is not known if the pro-New-Deal Warner Brothers contributed to Dewey's next election campaign expenses but ten months later, just prior to the release of *Racket Busters*, Dewey's assistant wrote to Walter MacEwen, the Executive Assistant to Hal Wallis:

> I write to say that Mr Dewey approves the following legend.
> 'Based upon the official Court Records of the Special Rackets Prosecution of the Trucking Racket in New York City'[48]

Dewey continued to ban any mention of his own name.

Racket Busters, made in 1938 (on a budget of $417,000 which included $8,800 apportioned to Humphrey Bogart) was also directed by Lloyd Bacon. The film makes it quite clear that gangsters are involved in a wide-ranging field of industrial and commercial interests. The film concentrates on the afflictions of the trucking industry, but shows that Czar Martin of the trucking racket (Humphrey Bogart) has also infiltrated cleaning and dyeing, cafeterias, dry goods and travel agencies. In reality Lepke Buchalter and Gurral Shapiro dominated the garment trade, painting, fur dressing, flour trucking and other areas in the 1930s, so that the screen depictions of business racketeers were firmly based on historical fact.

The crusading District Attorney, given the name of Allison, issues subpoenas but can obtain no testimony capable of convicting the gangsters, because the union members live in terror of physical intimidation. In a way there was a precedent for this in contemporary events. One employer in the garment trade hired Legs Diamond and his gang of thugs to break a strike, while the Communists, key figures in the cloakmakers' union, hired a gentleman by the name of Little Orgie to protect the pickets and beat up the scabs. Both Legs Diamond and Little Orgie were working for Arnold Rothstein. In the picture the hero, Denny (George Brent), is intimidated into working for Bogart, who calls a citywide strike of truck drivers to create a dangerous food shortage and hold the city and the employers to ransom. When Denny's friend is beaten up for opposing the strike, the hero finally joins forces with the DA and gives the evidence necessary to secure the conviction of the gangsters. 'People like us', say Denny grimly, 'have only got one chance – and that's to stick together.'[49]

Most of the reviewers were quick to mention the parallel between Allison and Dewey. *The New York Times* wrote,

> Never let it be said that Warner Brothers are ones to neglect a lively social theme – particularly when it has box office potentialities. And so it is not surprising to find the enlightened frères giving enthusiastic support to a current trend which is helpfully inspired by the career of a certain prominent District Attorney.[50]

Variety noted that 'Thomas E. Dewey's name isn't mentioned, but Walter Abel who plays the fearless NY prosecutor looks and acts a good deal like Dewey.'[51]

Once Dewey faded from prominence (in his legal capacity), the gangster film had to look elsewhere for staple inspiration. It was provided by the success of the movie *Dead End* (1937), adapted by Lillian Hellman from Sidney Kingsley's Broadway play. The gangster, Baby Face Martin (Humphrey Bogart), returns to the slums of his youth and comes across Dave (Joel McCrea), who had fought in the same teenage gang as Martin but had gone on to college and is now employed by a local café owner to paint the sign over the door. The picture also deals with the social and economic undesirables known as the Dead End Kids, who run around as a violent gang because there is not much else to do.

The parallel between the apathy of society and the career of the gangster is boldly and unmistakably drawn. The film was such a success that it spawned a rash of imitators illustrating the fact that gangsters were generally good men at heart, or that they were plain unlucky to be born 'on the wrong side of the tracks'. Their final deaths were heroic in a way that the classic early gangster films would not have dared to show, but the presentation here was justified by a noble act prior to extermination.

One of the first of these was *The Last Gangster* (1937), for which MGM borrowed Edward G. Robinson from Warners. The film opens in 1927, with Joe Kovac (Robinson), at the height of his fame as a gangster. He brings back a new wife from Europe and fathers a son who is to succeed to his business. Unfortunately, Kovac is convicted on a charge of evading income tax and goes to prison for ten years. Kovac's concern is solely for this son, and he is therefore pleased that a picture of the baby holding a gun thrust into its grasp by a reporter (James Stewart) has appeared under the caption 'Public Enemy Jr'.

Mrs Kovac realises that the only way for the baby to grow up normally is to be unaware of the identity of its real father. Accordingly she marries Stewart, who emerges ten years later as the owner of a small moustache and the managing editor of a Boston newspaper. Kovac, on his release, is beaten up by his old gang, who capture his son and threaten to torture him in front of his father in order to extract the location of a one-million-dollar robbery haul known only to Kovac. To save his child Kovac reveals the appropriate information and, together, father and son make the journey back to the child's mother and stepfather.

The child, still unaware of who Kovac really is, tells the gangster of his 'father' who has taught him so many useful tricks for camping and fishing and shows his most precious possession – the Lincoln medal for outstanding achievement. Kovac, who has a fixation about Napoleon, would have preferred it to have been a Napoleon medal, says 'Now, that would be sump'n' but is impressed in spite of himself. As he returns the child to his bed, the boy makes an emotional speech of thanks to Kovac who, after much thought, decides that perhaps the boy is not cut out to be a gangster after all. Kovac makes his peace with his former wife and with the stepfather and starts out of the door, a better and nobler man, only to be fatally shot by an old enemy, who threatens to tell the boy who his father really is. Despite two bullets fired from point-blank range Kovac still manages to wrest the gun from the killer and shoot him before the boy's innocence is tainted. As the last gangster dies, he clutches the Lincoln medal with the inscription, 'For Outstanding Achievement'.

Just as Robinson tempered his image with this part and his role in *Bullets or Ballots*, so Cagney went through the same transformation in *G-Men* and *Angels With Dirty Faces* (1938). In the latter film Cagney is the product of the teeming Lower East Side of New York City. Together with his friend, Jerry Mulligan (Pat O'Brien), he steals because it is the only way for a slum kid to survive. Jerry has slight moral doubts about breaking open railway cars ("'taint like stealing coal to keep warm'), but their felony is interrupted by the police, who capture Rocky (Cagney), although Jerry is too fast for them.

Fourteen years later Rocky has been through several prisons while Jerry has become a parish priest in the old neighbourhood. The major concern of the film is the effect that Rocky has on the group of kids who worship him and want to emulate him. At the end Rocky goes to the electric chair, but, in order to impress upon the youths the undesirability of crime as a profession, he allows Jerry to persuade him to take the final walk as a snivelling coward. This finale is played out for the benefit of the reporters whose accounts of the death scene destroy the heroic stature Rocky had assumed in the eyes of the boys. Jerry's last words as he leads the gang over to the church hall are, 'Let's say a prayer for a boy who couldn't run as fast as I could.'

Cagney's pugnacity and lively wit are well represented, but the new development of the genre is illuminated in the direction of Michael Curtiz. On his first appearance in Jerry's church Cagney silently harmonises with the choir, recalling his own childhood religious experiences. His attempts to protect his girlfriend (Ann Sheridan) from witnessing his possible death in an assassination attempt, and his desire to shield Jerry from being shot while he tries to break through a police cordon, all show a more socially conscious Cagney image. The Death Row scene, with its combination of powerful acting, lighting and direction, is a fine example of how technical excellence serves to point the dramatic nature of the film.

Even taking into account the optimistic (if melodramatic) ending, there is enough realism in *Angels With Dirty Faces* to make it still powerful to contemporary audiences. Jerry complains bitterly to Rocky, 'What is the use of preaching honesty when all around us you can see dishonesty winning out?', and one of the kids, confronted with Rocky's $50 tip to them, exclaims in awe, 'My old man never made as much as that in his whole life working for the Department of Sanitation'.

The finished film was, as usual, a compromise between what the writers wanted and what the Hays Office would allow them. An internal memo from Joseph Breen stated,

> It was also agreed that there would be no definite details of crime; that the kids would be kept as far as possible from any actual scene of crime; that there would be no glorification of the killer; the gun play would be toned down to the absolute minimum; there would be no use of machine guns by criminals and the violent scene at the end would be toned down considerably.[52]

As usual Breen remained vigilant through all stages of the production. After the first screening he wrote in some agitation to Jack Warner:

Most important of all, from the standpoint of censorship, are the scenes in the death house, specifically, the march to the execution chamber. The British and Colonial censor boards will delete these scenes in toto, as they have in the past. There is also some question in our minds as to the possible acceptability to censor boards in this country of the scene in the execution chamber.[53]

In view of these strictures, *Angels With Dirty Faces* remains an impressive example of the late 1930s gangster movie, particularly in view of what the production files reveal was an inauspicious start. When the first draft of the script was completed it was offered to staff producer, Sam Bischoff. The latter wrote back to Hal Wallis:

I finished reading this and as you know I was the first here to recommend the story, as I was once told the idea of it and thought it was great. However, after reading the script, I think it's about the worst thing I ever read.[54]

Next in line was Lou Edelman, whose response to his Executive Producer was equally emphatic: 'In its present form I wouldn't touch *Angels with Dirty Faces* with a thirty foot pole.'[55] The film was a huge hit at the box office. It was budgeted at $633,000 and grossed $2,334,000. It was produced by Sam Bischoff.

Unfortunately, just as *Dead End* begat *Angels*, the latter begat a number of successors with the Dead End Kids, including *Hell's Kitchen*, *Crime School* and *Angels Wash Their Faces*, all of them made in the space of two years and each worse than the previous one. As an indication of economic performance, the last-named film was budgeted at a modest $380,000 but grossed a total of only $778,000 – a tidy profit but one indicating the public's declining interest in the genre. Trite formulaic scripts and insipid direction destroyed these films, although the Dead End Kids went on for a number of years until middle age strained credulity and the angry adolescents retired from the screen under the name of the Bowery Boys.

The temporary popularity of the Dead End Kids illustrated the way in which the gangster film developed at the end of the 1930s. In December 1938 *Variety* officially recorded the fact under the headline:

GANGSTER FILM CYCLE YEN UP AGAIN

Reason for interest being focused on the problem is that producers are aware of the public urge for more realistic treatment of films touching on current day topics and problems.[56]

It was left to Raoul Walsh to make the last two great films in this series. *The Roaring Twenties* (1939) and *High Sierra* (1941) were of sufficient all-round excellence to join the select band of seminal gangster films. Like many another classic movie, *The Roaring Twenties* had a troubled beginning. Robert Lord,

Wallis's favourite writer/producer, began work on a treatment for it in the summer of 1938. At the end of July he wrote a long-suffering memo to Wallis.

> To date my treatment of *As The World Moves On* [original working title] has met with a unanimous reaction: neither Mr [Niven] Busch [the designated screenplay writer] nor Mr [Mark] Hellinger [author of the first storyline] like it at all.
>
> If you and Mr Warner agree with them then obviously I must be taken off this story .... If the three of us ... continue working on this assignment I suspect nothing will be accomplished except the expenditure of considerable money.[57]

A week later the film was budgeted at $651,000 and Lord was given the task of producing it from Mark Hellinger's original storyline which he had already tried to rewrite. He wrote defensively to Wallis's assistant Walter MacEwen that as far as he was concerned Hellinger's story was 'simply gangster plot #3'.[58] In October 1938 MacEwen, who clearly liked Lord, wrote to Wallis excusing this negative reaction by remarking 'You know how Bob is – especially when he has three other tough assignments going'.[59] On 3 March 1939 Lord left the picture and was replaced by the genial Sam Bischoff.[60]

Eight months later Warren Duff, the writer whom Wallis now wished to assign to the project, wrote back to him in dismay after reading the latest plot summary:

> If that isn't maudlin I'm a green eyed grasshopper and if it is an exciting premise I've been playing marbles for the last fifteen years.
>
> On the other hand there may be an angle to it. Somebody may see something in it that completely escapes me. I don't know. I only know that for me to attempt to make a good script out of it would hurry my inevitable entry into the booby hatch. This is the first assignment I've fought to get out of since I've been with you. But the thought of you strolling the Paris boulevards while I tear out my few remaining hairs is too much for me.[61]

The next writer on the job was John Wexley, fresh from his triumph on *Confessions of a Nazi Spy* where he had worked successfully with the director Anatole Litvak. Together they were charged with reviving the script – from Mark Hellinger's original story. They immediately fell out. Both left the project.

In June 1939 Robert Rossen was brought in to polish the screenplay and Raoul Walsh was appointed to direct in place of Litvak. On 8 July Jack Warner circulated a memo to all departments: '*The World Moves On* will hereafter be entitled *The Roaring Nineties*.' On 9 July Jack Warner circulated another memo to all departments: 'The story heretofore known as *The World Moves On* will hereafter be entitled *The Roaring Twenties* instead of *The Roaring Nineties*.'[62]

In the final draft of the screenplay Cagney plays the role of Eddie Bartlett, whose turn to crime is once more attributed to an apathetic and ungrateful society. He returns from service in the trenches to find his former job at a garage filled, and no other employment available (a familiar enough situation to a 1930s audience). Framed by planted liquor in a police raid on a speakeasy, Eddie finally accepts employment with a gang of boot-leggers, rising through the ranks of alky-cookers to become wealthy and influential in the world of night clubs. He falls in love with a girl (Priscilla Lane) whom he presents as a singer at this club, but unfortunately she prefers the security of marriage to a young lawyer whom Eddie had met in the trenches and whom he had persuaded to perform the legal services every racketeer needs.

The film was eventually produced by Mark Hellinger himself, and one assumes it was his idea, prompted by his previous occupation as a journalist, to use the portentous 'voice-over' of 'a social historian'. The end of Prohibition is described in classic Warner Brothers New Deal style.

> Then, in the depth of the economic despair that has gripped the country, Franklin Delano Roosevelt is elected President, partially on his promise to end Prohibition . . . . Tired of years of violence, corruption and loss of personal liberty . . . an aroused public decides that law and order should once more reign.

The election of Roosevelt and the repeal of the Eighteenth Amendment spell the end for Eddie. His former employer and friend Panama[63] (modelled on Tex Guinan) tells him, 'It's all over for all of us – you, me, George. Somethin' new is happening, Eddie – something you don't understand.' Eddie is convinced and, seeing no future for himself, decides on self-sacrifice as being the only course open to him. Still in love with Prisicilla Lane, he goes to see Humphrey Bogart, who, by a necessary dramatic oversight, is still prospering illegally in the era of the New Deal. Cagney warns him not to take revenge on the lawyer who has married Miss Lane and started a family. 'There's a new kind of set-up,' intones Cagney to Bogart, in a parallel speech to Panama's. 'Guys don't go out and tear down the world 'cause it's tough, the way we did. They go out and make it better like Lloyd. It's the kind of setting you and I don't belong in any more.'

Bogart snivels as Cagney pulls a gun on him, tries sneakily to grab for his own gun and is duly shot down by Cagney. Downstairs Bogart's henchmen pronounce what they assume to be Cagney's epitaph: 'I guess Eddie must 'a talked outta turn.' As Cagney comes down the staircase, he is wounded in an exchange of fire but manages to crawl his way into the street, where he dies on the steps of a cathedral. A policeman stands over Panama, as she cradles Cagney's head. 'You know this guy?' he asks laconically. 'His name is Eddie Barlett.' 'How were you hooked up with him?' 'I could never figure it out.' 'What was his business?' asks the officer obligingly. Panama states softly and finally, 'He used to be a big shot' and thus provides cinéastes with one of the great last lines in the history of the movies.

In *High Sierra* the ending is equally apocalyptic, as if the death of Bogart, as the death of Cagney in *The Roaring Twenties*, somehow prefigured the expiry of the gangster film itself. *High Sierra*, despite the ferocity of its final scenes, allows plenty of time for a detailed analysis of the criminal psyche. Over the whole film lies the shadow of time, as if Bogart is fighting time as well as the law enforcement agencies. 'Remember what Johnny Dillinger said about guys like you and him?', Doc Barton (played by Henry Hull) asks of the Bogart character. 'He said you were just rushin' towards death. Yes, that it – rushin' towards death.'

Bogart plays Roy Earle, who is sprung from jail to plan and execute a robbery. The organiser apologises for assigning two young men to Earle and explains, 'All the A1 guys are gone – dead, or in Alcatraz.' The two young criminals' amateurism is superbly contrasted with Bogart's experienced professionalism. Less sardonic in his humour, more weary in delivery than usual, and still sporting the close-cropped hairstyle of a prisoner, Bogart exudes a Weltschmerz which is only exacerbated by the realisation that the pretty young crippled girl with whom he falls in love cares only for a boy of her own age. In the last reel Bogart is trapped by the police high in the Sierra mountains. His ensuing death after an all-night watch, instantly recorded by the hordes of radio reporters and journalists, has a tragic inevitability about it that is increased by his geographical separation from the rest of the world.

Bogart's next film of importance sealed the fate of the traditional gangster film. *The Maltese Falcon* (1941) made him the big star that everyone now knows and effectively forbade his playing of any more two-dimensional villains. His heroes thereafter, Sam Spade, Philip Marlowe (in *The Big Sleep*), the war veteran in *Key Largo*, all contain qualities of ruthlessness that recall the 1930s characters, but they are adapted to Bogart's new starring image.

The Maltese Falcon had been filmed twice before in the previous decade,[64] but with Bogart as Sam Spade and Huston in superb form as the writer and first-time director it made a larger impact on audiences in 1941 than it had done previously. It also effectively destroyed the simplicity of the classic gangster films. Urban crime melodramas abounded thereafter, but it was difficult to class them as gangster films in the accepted mould. In the late 1940s Cagney reappeared in two spectacular pictures, *White Heat* (1949) and *Kiss Tomorrow Goodbye* (1950), but his psychotic characters were a long way removed from Tom Powers in *The Public Enemy* or Rocky Sullivan in *Angels With Dirty Faces*. They owed much more to the *film noir*, the cinematic reflection of a troubled postwar era.

The development of the 1930s gangster film closely paralleled public reaction to the real article. When public sympathy in the early years of the decade was largely on the side of the energetic, enterprising, successful gangster, the climate was ripe for the mass-production of Hollywood's heroic antisocial hoodlum. The shift in the political and cultural atmosphere, during the first months of the New Deal, necessitated the switch to the government agent as the new hero. When this variation died of a surfeit of appalling scripts, the rapid advance of sociology and urbanisation had together created yet another breed of gangster. These constant mutations represented considerable softenings of the original prototype, but they corresponded directly to the current need for optimism in a country that was finally coming to grips with the ravages of the Depression. Like the Western the gangster film, in its various forms, is a revealing study of American society in transition.

8

CRY OF THE CITY

I think our governments will remain virtuous for many centuries as long as they are chiefly agricultural; and this will be as long as there shall be vacant lands in any part of America. When they sit piled upon one another in large cities, as in Europe, they will become as corrupt as Europe.[1]

Thomas Jefferson to John Jay, 20 December 1787

The last musical number of *Gold Diggers of 1935* is arguably Busby Berkeley's most original contribution to motion pictures. From the spring-board of the Dubin and Warren song 'Lullaby of Broadway' Berkeley fashioned a remarkable routine to illustrate a particular lifestyle in New York City.

A woman's face, held in miniature close up, surrounded by darkness, revolves on completion of the song, and the image fades into a surrealistic impression of Manhattan apartment blocks. A clock shows 6.45 a.m. and a milkman is on his delivery rounds. A coffee percolator bubbles fiercely. People crowd into the subways, pressing ever tighter against each other. Winifred Shaw, the Manhattan baby, arrives home, picks up the newspaper, says 'Good morning' to her neighbours on their way to work, feeds her cat and slides into bed, as Berkeley's camera follows her sensually slipping off her stockings. The clock moves round to 6.45 p.m. and New York's night life awakens. The 'Club Casino' sign starts to flash and the lights of Manhattan to blaze, producing a neon haze which hangs over the city.

Winifred Shaw and her escort, Dick Powell, are the only guests in a night club which has seemingly hundreds of dancers, all dressed in black, with the exception of one ostentatious couple in white. The camera, angled at sixty degrees to the horizontal, has an unsettling effect. Three dancers, engaged in a hard shoe shuffle, are photographed from a variety of angles, including one from under the floor, so that the stamping feet seem to be attacking the audience. Shaw is carried off by the dancing mob and Dick Powell has to fight his way through the crowd to find her. Playfully, she runs away from them all, on to a balcony and closes the french windows behind her. Laughing and singing, the crowd forces open the doors and sends the girl hurtling off the balcony to her death.

The clock moves on to 6.45 am. The morning brings its usual characters, but the Manhattan baby's cat, deprived of its mistress, miaows plaintively at the bottle of milk. The newspaper lies unopened at the door. The camera pans right, through the window and out to New York City; it pulls slowly back from the artificially created Manhattan; the city resumes its original facial features and, as the face recedes, the last words of the song are reprised: 'Listen to the lullaby of Old Broadway.'

Berkeley's reputation rests on the display of scantily clad chorus girls in a variety of geometric designs seen from unusual camera angles but he also had a dark and fevered imagination, bred by the undercurrents of contemporary urban life. Death and unpleasantness in certain areas of New York City were foreshadowed in his staging of the title number in *Forty-Second Street* (1933), which positively revels in its pimps and prostitutes and murderers. One of the last shots of this number is a steady tracking shot in on Dick Powell, dispassionately watching a girl jump out of the window, after having been beaten up by her pimp.

The projection of the American image of the city changed frequently during the 1930s. It was a decade which began with the romantic stylisation of *City Lights* (1931) and ended with the false dawn of *Angels Wash Their Faces* (1939) and the 'triumph' of urban planning. After the despair and nihilism of the 1930–2 period, the New Deal tried hard to come to terms with the depressed urban areas, but always across the Hollywood city films lay a heavy shadow of fear, which all the shrill optimism failed to dispel entirely.

This fear of the city was in no sense a phenomenon of the 1930s. The history of colonial times indicates a sharp rift in lifestyle, outlook and values between the cities, which grew rapidly on the East Coast, and the communities which established themselves inland. When the revolution broke out, it was to the British-dominated eastern cities that the Tories fled. Throughout the nine-teenth century the westward expansion of the frontier provided an experience that was uniquely American, while, it appeared, the inhabitants of the eastern cities lived their lives in the continuation of industrial expansion that had originated in Europe. As illustrated in the quotation at the head of this chapter, Thomas Jefferson had written of the dangers of urban growth as early in the life of the new republic as 1787.

The lure to the economically enslaved European tenant was the prospect of land ownership in America, and the chance to start afresh in a new environment, even if, in reality, the hopeful immigrants merely added to the growing number of city slum dwellers. The cities expanded rapidly in the late nineteenth century, profiting hugely from the exploitation of natural resources and the technological discoveries of the time. With the close of the frontier, the trade cycle depression of the 1880s and early 1890s and the increasing dependence of the formerly self-sufficient farmer on the needs of, and the services supplied by, distant cities, the rural dwellers at the turn of the century formed their most powerful and most coherent political organisation – the Populist Party.

Their Presidential candidate, William Jennings Bryan, was defeated, but their antipathy to the city, whose evils were now being exposed by a new breed of muckraking journalists and social workers, did not abate. In the twentieth century the proliferation of the automobile, the radio and the motion picture, and the expansion of consumer sales through increased credit and advertising, had the effect of drawing the rural communities ever more surely into those orbits dominated by urban values. In the interwar years, this conflict between what has been loosely termed 'the agrarian myth' and the explosion of the cities produced an uneasy truce.

What held them together, notes Richard Maltby, was a nostalgic wish among the urban upper and middle classes to pay homage to an earlier American innocence, while for the agrarian population the myth became a defensive armour with which to combat the dawning realisation that the cities were taking a political power to match their economic strength.[2]

The agrarian myth provided the archetype of the American innocent which proved particularly useful for a socially and politically conservative American cinema. Hollywood producers had less interest in exploring the realities of urban or rural life than in maintaining its profit margins. However, it soon became apparent to the sales departments of the various picture companies that a clear-cut distinction existed between the taste of a city audience and that of a country audience. One observer wrote as early as 1929,

> Perhaps it may be said that the inhabitants of large cities regard as artistically desirable what people in other types of communities call smut. The difference in the point of view doubtless lies in the fact that city life is more varied than that of rural districts and it is varied experiences, perhaps, which teaches discrimination.[3]

In 1937 approximately half the box office income in America was concentrated in ninety-three cities with populations of over a hundred thousand. The population of New York City was estimated at the time at nearly seven million. Its 617 cinemas, with a capacity of 775,393 seats, meant that there was a cinema seat for every nine citizens. In Los Angeles the ratio was seven people per seat and together the two towns provided roughly one-fifth of the gross income of the industry at the box office.[4]

The rural audiences were less economically important than those in the city, but no film released by Hollywood would return with much of a profit if it failed to do good business in the neighbourhood cinemas, and rural audiences were notorious in expressing their adverse critical judgements in violence or abuse hurled at the screen. They objected in this way to anything that they regarded as sophisticated. Into this category fell most of Hollywood's attempts to make prestige films, such as the adaptations in the mid-1930s of

Romeo and Juliet and *A Midsummer Night's Dream*, and even the Lubitsch sex comedies which relied for their effect on subtle sexual innuendo and witty verbal banter.

Rural spectators were fond of situations in which they could identify with the principal characters without undue effort. They enjoyed the easy familiarity of the serial and were the main patrons of *The Lone Ranger*, *Bulldog Drummond* and *Flash Gordon*, *The Saint*, *The Spider*, *Charlie Chan* and *Torchy Blaine* as well as the singing cowboy pictures, all of which went out as B releases. The classic series, which achieved wide popularity because of enthusiastic response from rural areas, was the Andy Hardy movies which MGM put out to glorify a totally idealised small-town America. These people, who upheld what they thought were traditional American values, discriminated against those stars whom they felt to be artificial, or whose accent they found difficult to understand.

Claudette Colbert's style of light comedy in Paramount's 'European' farces, Dietrich's appearances in von Sternberg's films and Katharine Hepburn's Bryn Mawr style of speech aroused only antipathy outside the metropolitan areas.[5] Despite Garbo's status in the American cinema, her popularity, at least her profitability, rested largely on European audiences.[6] In 1933 she ranked as the third most popular star in Great Britiain, but as low as twenty-ninth in the United States.[7] The citizens of Farmerville, Louisiana, were most disappointed to discover that *Conquest* (1938) starred Greta Garbo in a soppy historical love story, when the title had led them to expect a fierce Western. One small-town exhibitor in Pennsylvania stated wryly after showing *Anna Karenina*, 'The same Garbo draw, more chairs than patrons. Our chairs would never get dusted if we depended on the Garbo fans to do it .... Poor business.'[8]

The success in urban as well as rural cinemas of films which applied the mythology of an agrarian utopia shows that during the interwar years city audiences were happy to accept the existence of a rural idyll. Even though they lived in the cities, the anti-urban legacy of American fiction was so heavily ingrained that metropolitan movie-goers found such films comforting in their familiarity, rather than unsettling in their hostility. Fear and uncertainty seem to have been regarded as the *sine qua non* of urban life.

Two of the best films in this category were made by a German director, F. W. Murnau, who, in his first Hollywood picture, *Sunrise* (1927), captured a peculiarly American ambience. *Sunrise* concerned the tribulations of a pretty country girl (Janet Gaynor), whose husband (George O'Brien) is led astray by a smart sophisticated woman from the city. The latter is first seen revealing her legs and then taking the initiative in kissing O'Brien, in Hollywood terms a sure sign of moral laxity. After an abortive effort at drowning his wife, O'Brien reconciles himself to the continuation of their marriage, and they celebrate with a day in the big city. The set was deliberately constructed out of proportion, so that the camera would see the city as terrifyingly huge, exactly as the young couple would see it.[9]

Two years later Murnau directed *City Girl*, starring the other half of Fox's romantic partnership, Charles Farrell, who plays a farmer's son, sent into the city to sell the annual wheat crop. At a luncheon counter he meets, and is attracted by, a waitress, who lives a wretched life in a tiny bedsitter, with the company of a potted plant, which is habitually covered by the soot from the adjacent railway line. Predictably, he takes her back to the country, where the remaining drama concerns her inability to communicate with her father-in-law. The man cuffs his young daughter for having picked a grain of the precious crop, and reacts unfavourably to his daughter-in-law's accidentally placing her hat on the family bible. The finale produces a reconciliation between all parties and the rush to gather the crop before the impending storm ruins it. The country has reclaimed its own.

The converse to the romantic pastoralist was Chaplin, the romantic urban figure, whose universal tramp was essentially a product of the industrial revolution and its displacement of the individual or nonconformist. Chaplin's view of the city was strongly influenced by his own wretched childhood in Victorian London and on the circuits of music halls. The three main characters in *City Lights*, the tramp, the blind flower seller and the wealthy industrialist, owe much to nineteenth-century melodrama; the girl seems to combine the virtues of a Jane Austen heroine with the stoicism of Jo, the crossing sweeper in *Bleak House*. The sets and overall art direction suggest Dickensian England, while the plot, which demands that the girl and her poor grandmother face eviction from their tenement hovel because of their inability to pay $22 back rent, suggests more the influence of *The Drunkard* than any contemporary drama.

Mervyn LeRoy is not usually associated with such romanticism during his time at Warner Brothers in the 1930s, yet he too joined the current anti-urban bias in *Big City Blues* (1932).[10] This film again rehashes the trite tale of the young country lad, who comes to wonder at the city, only to be subjected to unspeakable horrors, for which his small town background has ill prepared him. His thousand-dollar inheritance attracts a series of disreputable characters, who help him to spend his money on a wild party at which a girl dies, and for whose death the boy finds himself pursued by the police. He returns to his home, his money spent, his pride wounded, but vowing to return to the city some day to live with a little more success.

The following year LeRoy directed another film, long since (justly) ignored by film critics, as it was by audiences at the time, which again dealt with the familiar simplifications about rural and urban life. *The World Changes* opens in the Dakota territory in the year 1856. A heavily pregnant Aline MacMahon stumbles out of her covered wagon, sinks to her knees, grasps a handful of earth and expresses her satisfaction. Her family takes root in Orinsville, the town she names after her first son. After casual visits from General Custer, who drops in to tell them that the Civil War is over (they had been entirely ignorant

145

of its existence), and from Buffalo Bill, who just happens to be passing, Orin (Paul Muni) is inspired to venture into the world of the Chicago meat factories.

He fulfils part of his ambition by rapidly becoming a millionaire, but manages to acquire on the way a neurotic wife (Mary Astor) and two worthless sons, neither of whom, to the disgust of their father, shows the slightest interest in packing meat. One of the sons becomes a banker and lives in New York with his socialite wife, while the other is a snob and a wastrel. In despair, Orin renounces the other part of his ambition (to found a meat packing dynasty), sells the firm and lives quietly in retirement from 1904 to 1929, when the Stock Market crash brings about the financial ruin of his offspring. Just before the marriage of his granddaughter, Orin dies, although not without having seen his mother, Aline MacMahon, whose sprightliness quite belies her ninety-seven years. MacMahon, her great-grandson and his girlfriend take the body back to the Mid-West for burial, and the young couple return permanently to the soil whence came their ancestors. MacMahon closes the film with the prayer she had uttered at the start, many hours before, 'Praise God, here may we live and prosper'.

This reliance on the healing powers of rural America appears time and again in the Hollywood movies of the 1930s, most of which assume that the combination of urban life and the Depression is too painful to bear. *The Life of Jimmy Dolan* (1933) illustrates this thesis, with a story of a prize fighter who declares, on winning his title, that he owes everything to his mother. At the celebration which follows the fight, Dolan (Douglas Fairbanks Jr) becomes intoxicated, smirks that his mother doesn't exist and accidentally kills a reporter who finds the revelation unamusing and threatens to expose it. Dolan's manager and girlfriend, instead of trying to help him, pocket his watch and his money and take flight, but their car is involved in an accident in which their remains are charred beyond recognition. On regaining consciousness, Dolan's well-developed cynicism is not dispelled by the situation in which he finds himself. A shyster lawyer, typical of the characters with whom he has come into contact in the city, keeps $9,500 as commission on the $10,000 Dolan has asked him to collect from his safe deposit box.

Arriving in the country, Dolan meets a young girl (Loretta Young) and her grandmother (the ubiquitous Aline MacMahon), who run a farm for deprived children. Dolan is so captivated by the honesty and simplicity of country life that he agrees to box in a local competition for the money needed to pay off the farm's mortgage, despite the fact that a public exhibition of his inimitable boxing style (he is a southpaw) would reveal his identity to Guy Kibbee, a detective who is hot on his trail for the unsolved murder. Having won the money, Dolan contentedly accepts the handcuffs, his only regret being his departure from the country and from the entrancing Loretta Young. In a touching finale the detective pronounces Dolan purged of his urban disease and mentally fit enough to return to the rural idyll.

These romanticised versions of country life proved to be acceptable to city audiences because they, too, were aware of the cultural heritage of rural America, and because such two-dimensional portraits of urban life were too divorced from reality to arouse much discussion. One film, however, got closer than any of its competitors to the central problems of city life in modern America.

The Crowd (1928), King Vidor's masterpiece, tells the story of Everyman and his struggle to survive and retain an identity in a world in which anonymity seemingly befalls all but a few. John, the protagonist, is born on 4 July 1900, believing that everything that happens happens for the best, in the best of all possible worlds. 'This young man', announces the doctor who delivers John, 'will be heard from.' A title card indicates the passage of time. 'When he was 21 John became one of the 7 million who believed that New York depends on him.' Vidor emphasises the bleak anonymity of urban life. At the mass exodus from work at 5 pm men meet their girlfriends coming out of an office building by a door which operates like a vending machine, spitting out women. On the top floor of an open bus John and his future wife, Mary, see a man walking the pavement, wearing on his back a large billboard advertising the wares of a local department store. John laughs scornfully, 'And I bet his father thought he'd be President'.

Even during this happy time in his life there are hints of the frustration that will eventually engulf John. At the birth of his son, John cannot find Mary in the overcrowded hospital. The marriage founders on the rock of John's inability to succeed in the fiercely competitive business world. Mary complains that one of John's friends has done much better from the same start in life and John realises that 'Marriage isn't a word - it's a sentence'. The series of misfortunes is made doubly effective because they are merely extensions of the calamities which befall many families. On a seaside picnic Mary becomes hysterical as the children kick her cake into the sand and knock over a pan of boiling water, while John's remedy for her ills is to play the banjo furiously.[11] When his daughter is run over by a lorry, John tries to stem the noises of the city – the crowds and the fire engines – as if they were killing the girl. 'The whole world can't stop because your baby's sick,' snaps a policeman, not unkindly.

John is reduced to juggling balls on the pavement as an advertising gimmick in order to save his rapidly deteriorating marriage, and to prevent his wife from leaving with her rich and successful brothers. The wheel has come full circle. But instead of leaving us with this and the titled moral, 'The crowd laughs with you always; but it will cry with you only for a day', Vidor plays his last scene in a crowded cinema. The marriage of the principals has been temporarily repaired and the couple are relaxing in the enjoyment of a comedy film. As they laugh and point at the screen, the camera pulls back to reveal, gradually, a gigantic cinema with everyone in the huge audience laughing and posturing in exactly the same way.

The Crowd is, by any stretch of the imagination, a remarkable film. Its visual style perhaps owes much to the German Expressionists, particularly Fritz

Lang's *Metropolis*, but thematically it anticipates the Italian neo-realists by nearly twenty years. Predictably, it fared none too well as a commercial proposition in the United States, but it made a fine showing in Europe. *Variety* called it 'a drab, actionless story of ungodly length and apparently telling nothing'.[12] But *The Crowd*, better than any previous film, dared to suggest that the American birthright of unalloyed optimism is dangerous rather than advantageous. Its statement was that good looks, talent and a desperate eagerness to please are not necessarily the factors that lead to material success. In the great American city of opportunity, of the career open to the talents, people try so hard to win that they trample on one another with impunity.

The other important body of films with a significantly dark view of the city was the action film of the early 1930s. The seminal gangster films are set in the harsh urban world, although, as Warshow points out, the gangsters inhabit a city of the dark imagination rather than the one of grim reality.[13] Nevertheless, the gangster, as a vibrant screen character that grew out of the city, left a deep impression on audiences. The relative brutality of the films, the rasping dialogue, jarring sounds and overall cynicism all lent added testimony to the current feelings about the city. The crooked lawyers and cold-blooded newspapermen, similarly in vogue in these years, were also the product and a reflection of their urban surroundings.

The heavy anti-urban legacy of history, folk-myth and fiction, joined to the despair of the first years of the Depression, seemed capable of condemning the city to a constant portrayal as the home of vice, crime or poverty. There was some hope provided, however, by the changing pattern of city growth in the 1930s, a growth that eventually necessitated official recognition of the importance of city life in the prosperity of the nation.

In the 1920s, a troubled decade for farmers who had been lured by the false boom of the war years, the inexorable drift of population from countryside to town, finally destroyed the long established rural majority. In 1910 54 per cent of the population lived in villages whose total inhabitants did not exceed 2,500. In 1920, the figure fell below 50 per cent for the first time in American history, and ten years later it was down to 44 per cent. In the 1920s over six million people migrated from the country to the cities.[14] Los Angeles increased more than threefold between 1910 and 1930. In the 1930s, despite the inability of the cities to cope with their own economic problems, New York City increased its population by 7.5 per cent, Los Angeles by 23 per cent, Detroit by 30.5 per cent and the nation's capital by an estimated 36.2 per cent.[15]

When the more affluent sections of society began to build suburban residences, they took with them their urban outlook and developed a set of values to fit their new existence. Their departure tempted more people to move into the city centre, but it also resulted in a large-scale abandonment of conditions in the sprawling ghettoes. The report of the National Resources Committee indicated the extent to which the cities were the economic basis of the country.

Urbanisation and suburbanisation have meant ... a centralisation of enterprise in the Nation's cities, metropolitan districts, urban satellites and industrial areas. Of more than 3,000 counties of the country, the 155 which contain the larger industrial cities embraced in the year 1929 – 74% of all the wages paid, 83% of all salaries paid, 65% of all the industrial establishments and 80% of the value added to the manufactured products.[16]

Politically, as well as economically, the cities in the 1930s began to discover the extent of their own power. The 1928 election, despite the defeat of Al Smith, revealed the first glimmerings of the coalition which Franklin Roosevelt was to form in succeeding campaigns. Although Hoover ran out an easy winner in the Electoral College, Smith won the popular vote in nearly all the large cities. In 1932 at least thirty-two large urban areas voted Democratic for the first time since 1916 and six others gave Roosevelt such strong support that he was able to carry the state.

Urban voters were awakening and city politicians were becoming increasingly aware that they could no longer afford to concentrate solely on the distribution of local patronage to the exclusion of a consideration of national issues. Apart from anything else, Roosevelt's immense personal popularity meant that voters would restrict their local choice to those candidates who were New Dealers.[17]

Two circumstances in particular forced city halls to take note of urban political pressure groups. The first was the effect which the Depression wrought on the brittle economic structures of the cities. Despite drastic retrenchments in salaries and services, by the end of 1931 about six hundred cities and towns had defaulted on their debts, bringing committees of bankers into control of many of them. In May 1932 sixty-seven large city mayors met to draw up a $5 billion construction programme, but, despite this and other efforts, the winter of 1932 was the worst spell of the Depression to date. In New York City a million people were unemployed, as were three-quarters of a million in Chicago. In Toledo nearly 80 per cent of the workforce was idle; in Akron the figure was 60 per cent and in Cleveland, 50 per cent. The city of Chicago owed its schoolteachers $28 million in back salaries.[18]

The relief organisations functioned in this crisis about as effectively as the Elizabethan Poor Law of 1601 would have done in its place. In New York City the Welfare department limited relief payments to $2.39 per family per week, while St Louis cut its payrolls by half in 1931 and New Orleans at this time announced that it would accept no new applicants for relief. In Detroit the Ford and Chrysler works, built just outside the city limits, remained untaxed, while their employees or, more to the point, their ex-employees suffered from malnutrition. The city government was forced to borrow from banks to meet its relief commitment. The money was loaned by the banks on the condition that relief rolls were cut by a third, even though this meant undue suffering for families who had trouble managing on the relief they were getting.

Hoover's refusal to involve the federal government in the direct provision of relief placed too large a burden on the shoulders of city administrations, which had never been known for scrupulous honesty and thrift. They were not slow to point out that they were not receiving much help from the state government, which had little time for urban problems.

The structure of the state legislatures was the other factor in promoting an urban political consciousness. As had been the case in England until the passage of the Great Reform Bill in 1832, the cities were historically under-represented in the state bodies. Philadelphia wanted to merge city and country governments for the purpose of economy, but the Pennsylvania legislature rejected the proposal. In 1930 urban pressure groups from major cities in New York, Michigan and Illinois made desperate but unavailing attempts to obtain the reapportionment of electoral districts by state legislatures. In Texas in 1937 the cities averaged one state representative for every hundred thousand citizens, while the smaller towns averaged one to 38,831.[19]

In a way the balance was redressed by the nature of the New Deal, which, for all its attempts to aid agriculture and the benefits that it was hoped TVA would disburse to the inhabitants of the Tennessee valley, was the first national adminstration to address itself directly to the plight of the cities. The relief programme which was adopted in the Hundred Days legislation was deliberately aimed at helping those people who had suffered because of the hamstrung relief policy of the Hoover administration.

Pump-priming extended its benefits far into the countryside, and the combination of AAA and the work of the Resettlement Administration and its successor, the FSA, eased somewhat the distress of the farmers, but in WPA, and to a lesser extent PWA, the New Deal gave the cities not only urgently needed funds but a sense of hope that the platitudes of the previous government ('No one has starved') had seemingly been stifled for all time.

Senator Robert F. Wagner, one of the Administration's leading spokesmen in the Senate, and the sponsor of some of the most vital pieces of New Deal legislation, constantly stressed his belief that the Depression was essentially an urban problem. He argued in the Senate that the effects of industrialisation had remade the nation, both economically and socially, and thus the task was now 'to translate the virtues, aspirations and ideals of a rural people so as to serve in the development and progress of an urban people'.

Wagner was a major supporter of the NIRA and the leading member of the successful drive to establish the rights of collective bargaining. It was Wagner who persuaded Roosevelt to see that there was a definite link between free unions and collective bargaining on the one hand, and wages, purchasing power and recovery on the other. The sudden Presidential support for the 1935 Wagner Act was almost certainly the outcome of a political manoeuvre to counteract the growing demagogic, radical threat of Huey Long, but it still represented a considerable vindication of Wagner's long-held conviction that the provisions under Section 7(a) of the NIRA were insufficient to allow labour to bargain collectively.[20]

Wagner's other pet scheme was a housing bill. Ickes and PWA had been tinkering with housing projects, but none had received official legislative backing.[21] Wagner's belief that slum housing led directly to juvenile delinquency, and his disgust at the fact that it was the unemployed who were invariably housed in the worst possible conditions, led him to introduce a new housing bill. In the Senate, during discussion of the bill, Democrats and Republicans from rural areas charged that it was designed expressly to benefit New York City and the other urban metropolises of the North-East.

The eventual Act conceded that the USHA could devote only ten per cent of its funds to any one state. For decades slums, like poverty, had been regarded by exponents of laissez faire as self-evident symbols of laziness and moral laxity. With the rural bias dominant in state legislatures, such reform legislation as was voted came principally out of an attack on the sinful city machine. The leading campaigners for better housing at the turn of the century, Jacob Riis and Laurence Veiller, emphasised restrictive control legislation, which was essentially negative in approach. Similarly flawed were the planners of the Progressive era with their fixations about zoning (an idea taken from the Germans) and the garden city (an idea which found its fullest expression in England between the wars). Until the New Deal, housing was not regarded as the concern of the federal government. Under housing programmes instigated, or at least advocated, by Wagner, a federal mortgage insurance scheme and subsidised public housing were proposed. The federal commitment to better housing, while its value proved to be limited, was of great significance to and symbolic of the New Deal's recognition of peculiarly urban problems.[22]

No better indication of the urban nature of the New Deal can be provided than a swift examination of the election results of the 1930s. In 1936 New York City turned out a sufficiently large Democratic majority to drown the anti-Roosevelt vote of upstate New York. Chicago, Boston, Detroit and Baltimore each supplied about half the Democratic pluralities in their respective states, while Los Angeles and San Francisco in California, and Philadelphia and Pittsburgh in Pennsylvania, performed a similar task.

The New Deal specifically changed the direction of the Black vote. In 1932 there were still large traces of the support that the Blacks felt they owed the Republicans for the blessings of Emancipation, but in the mid-term elections of 1934 Blacks started to vote Democratic in large numbers. In 1936 every single Black ward in Cleveland went Democratic, and Roosevelt ran twice as well among black voters in Chicago as he had done four years previously. In 1938 a *Fortune* poll revealed that 84.7 per cent of Blacks counted themselves Roosevelt admirers and supported his policies. In the 1936 election campaign John L. Lewis, a lifelong Republican who had endorsed Hoover in 1932, threw the weight of the CIO behind the President. The Organisation contributed $770,000, of which $469,000 came from Lewis's own United Mine Workers.[23] This was thought by most observers to be an excellent return on Roosevelt's investment of the Wagner Act, and, although Lewis broke with Roosevelt after what he considered to be a personal insult, organised labour was thereafter firmly wedded to the Roosevelt coalition.[24]

In fields other than politics New Dealers explored this awakening interest in the city. Intellectuals, until 1933 a body regarded with some suspicion, if not with outright hostility, by politicians, reacted to the kindly concern of the federal government, by developing in the 1930s a series of studies in urban history and urban society.[25] Roderick D. McKenzie wrote a pioneering analysis of The Metropolitan Community in the President's Commission Report on Recent Social Trends. A group at Chicago University produced *Our Cities: Their Role in the National Economy*, while Arthur Schlesinger's contribution to the History of American Life textbooks dealt with the years 1878 to 1898 and was entitled *The Rise of the City*. In 1940, in the *Mississippi Valley Historical Review*, Schlesinger published his classic article on 'The City in American History'. After the New Deal, urban history, previously regarded without interest, became a standard feature in the training of a historian.

Contemporary novelists found in urban life an explanation of character development. Budd Schulberg was a representative, rather than an outstanding, writer of the late 1930s. In *What Makes Sammy Run?*, he accounted for the unnatural aggression of the Hollywood producer Sammy Glick by exploring the poverty and the degradation of his slum childhood. Clifford Odets, and the other playwrights of the 1930s, who expanded the legitimate theatre's social horizons, went back to the slums for their inspiration. *Awake and Sing* and *Golden Boy* were Odets's contribution to this sort of drama. The WPA Federal Theater project, during its brief life, busied itself with social issues in its 'Living Newspaper' presentations. *One Third of a Nation*, which took its theme from Roosevelt's Second Inaugural Address reference 'I see one third of a nation ill-housed, ill-clad, ill-nourished', was the most famous of these dramatisations.

Only after the stage had made this new kind of urban naturalism respectable was it adopted by Hollywood, because at the start of the Depression, as we have seen, the conception of the city was strongly influenced by the agrarian myth. One of the first movies to attempt a reappraisal of city life, in the light of new political, social and cultural developments, was MGM's *The Devil Is a Sissy* (1936), for which Rowland Brown wrote the original story. Brown was also to perform the same service for *Angels with Dirty Faces*, but, whereas the Warner picture benefited from that studio's long acquaintance with some of the problems of the slums, MGM was rarely able to rid itself of the soft glow of its photography, the familiar Cedric Gibbons chic art direction and the all-pervading Louis B. Mayer philosophy.

In *The Devil Is a Sissy* Freddie Bartholomew spends half the year with his rich, socialite mother and six months with his artist father, who has separated from his wife and lives in what is supposed to be a New York tenement. At school Bartholomew suffers the barbs of MGM's slum children, one of whom reveals the grisly information that he once ate a butterfly, 'its wings tasted all dusty', and he resolves that, above all else, he will be accepted by his American colleagues, particularly Mickey Rooney and Jackie Cooper.

Rooney gives another of his astonishingly mature performances, as a prospective John Garfield, a 'punk' from the Lower East Side, who never had a chance because his father was electrocuted for murder. He takes the gang to meet his aunt, who lives a life of shame and luxury in a Park Avenue penthouse. The aunt starts to sing, Jackie Cooper begins to tap dance, the black maid joins in and the film's credibility wafts gently away in the Manhattan breeze. Although the kids steal goods to the value of $80, it is only for the purpose of acquiring a headstone for Rooney's father. Brought before the judge for their thefts (which turn out to have been Bartholomew's own property in the first place), Rooney is told that, bad as it was to steal, 'What was worse, you lied to your mother'. Rooney defends himself fiercely. 'What boy doesn't love his own mother?' he asks defiantly, affording a short preview of the Andy Hardy films, which were soon to sweep over the country. Although the film has more such danger, excitement and thrills to come, it conveniently ignores Rowland Brown's original premise of the rich child who comes to live in the slums.

By far the single most influential city film was *Dead End*, William Wyler's superb version of Sidney Kingsley's play. It had opened initially on Broadway in 1935, but it took two years to reach the screen, partly because of the play's lengthy run and partly because of the constant attempts by the Hays Office to ensure that Lillian Hellman's adaptation departed from the original in some of its inflammatory speeches. However, despite these restrictions, *Dead End* remains a compelling and, for its time, a realistic expression of life in a city slum.

Brilliantly photographed by Gregg Toland, the movie opens with a crane shot from the modern clean lines of mid-town Manhattan to the slums of the Lower East Side. The film concerns the events of a single day in a tenement district, which is thankfully devoid of jovial, colourful immigrant characters. The notorious gangster Babyface Martin, wanted by the police, returns to the scene of his childhood to visit his mother and his former girlfriend. He meets Dave, a member of Martin's youthful gang, who is now earning a precarious living, painting a shop's sign. Martin (excellently played by Humphrey Bogart) reacts with the traditional philosophy of the gangster.

Six years you work in a college and what you get now is handouts. That's a good one. Well, I'm glad I aint like you punks. Starving and freezing – for what? Peanuts. I got mine. I took it. Look silk – 20 bucks. Custom tailored – 150 bucks. And dames? – Boy!

Kay leaves the slums, not through violence but by selling her affections in return for security. She justifies her actions to Dave (Joel McCrea), who is infatuated with her, by reference to her early years of poverty. 'I'm frightened of being poor again. I hate what it does to people. I saw what it did to my family and to me.' In the end Kay, despite her love for Dave, goes off with her rich protector, rather than run the risk of renewing her first-hand acquaintance with the slums.

For those who remain there is some hope for 'decency', but little for progress. Martin's mother, ashamed of her son's exploits, slaps his face when he tries to talk to her. Francey, the ex-girlfriend (played by Claire Trevor), turns out to be a whore. Horrified, Martin asks why she didn't get a job, to which her reply is, 'They don't grow on trees, you know', and when he wants to know why she did not starve first, she retorts pointedly, 'Why didn't you?'

For the collection of adolescents who hang around the filthy river, where they go swimming, the 'gang' is the fulcrum of their lives, the only security and happiness they know in an otherwise insecure and unhappy world. Another gang sends an emissary to arrange a fight, with the deliberation of planning a visit to the circus. Martin, the gang's top graduate, offers the Dead End Kids some useful advice. 'Listen, when you fight, the idea is to win. It don't matter how. And to win in a gang fight, there's nothing like a stocking full of sand and rocks .... And if that don't work, a knife will.'

Dave assumes the role of the social commentator, pointing out that 'They start with knives and they end up with guns'; even Babyface Martin 'wasn't such a bad kid'. Dave pleads the cause of every child with a slum background.

> What chance have they got against all this? They've got to fight for a
> place to play, fight for a little extra something to eat, fight for everything.
> They get used to fighting. 'Enemies of Society' it says in the papers. Why
> not? What have they got to be so friendly about?

Dead End's originality in the mid-1930s lay in its insistence that tenements bred gangsters, nobody did anything about it and 'the vicious cycle continues with each succeeding crop of children thwarted in their growth of any sense of social responsibility by the pressure of the vicious environment'.[26] Just as the Dead End Kids are prototype Babyface Martins, so it is revealed that another bunch of youngsters, no older than ten, is already seeking to emulate them and their violent ways.

If the tenements breed filth and despair, the obvious solution is to remove them with schemes of urban renewal, a clear indication of how far *Dead End* was born of the New Deal. The passage of time has since shown that this is not the solution, but in the 1930s the New Deal's heavenly city was a greenbelt town, clean, fresh and new, with the Dead End Kids spending their surplus energy in spacious recreation parks.

The success of *Dead End* prompted Warner Brothers to lure the youngsters to make films in Burbank, so that the last three years of the decade abounded with Dead End movies. With predictable parsimony Warners dusted off a number of their old scripts and refitted them for the new stars. *The Life of Jimmy Dolan* (1933) was remade as *They Made Me a Criminal* (1939), starring John Garfield in the Douglas Fairbanks Jr role, and the Dead End Kids as the inhabitants of the farm, which serves not only to restore Dolan's faith in America but also as a rehabilitation centre for urban delinquents.

The Mayor of Hell (1933), which reappeared in 1938 as *Crime School*, was the story of a group of street urchins who are sent to a reform school. The parents, who accompany their sons to court, are a helpful cross-section of America's city ghettos – a Greek and an Italian, a Black and a comic Jew. As the sentence is passed, one hysterical mother screams, 'You sent my first boy there. He came out a murderer.' The Jewish father has other things to consider. He asks the judge how much are the fees at reform school, and is told that the state pays all costs. A broad smile crosses his face. 'Take him,' he motions with some finality.

Once at reform school, it is soon apparent that the superintendent is a crook, and that the guards are sadistic bullies. James Cagney, as a racketeer who is appointed the school's supervisor as part of a pay-off, comes under the influence of the attractive, concerned nurse (Madge Evans). He removes the superintendent and grants the boys a measure of automony, but his own nefarious activities lead him to the accidental killing of a rival, on account of which Cagney flees the state. The old superintendent resumes his place and intensifies the harshness of his rule, punishing a sick boy, whose consequent death from exposure incites a riot. Cagney returns to prevent anything more serious than the death of the superintendent, and announces that he has retired from the racketeering business to devote himself full time to the adminstration of the school, all of which takes place under the wise benevolence of a kindly federal official.

The remake five years later, *Crime School*, bears many of the influences of *Dead End*. This time in the courtroom, before the sentencing, a girl cries out, 'If you want to do something for these boys, why don't you clean up the slums? Give them a decent start in life', to which the judge responds, with no apparent relevance, 'Some of our greatest men came out of these tenements'. The Cagney hero of the earlier film is now played by Humphrey Bogart as Deputy Commissioner Braden. While in 1933 it was acceptable for a hero to be tainted with the illicit glamour of racketeering, by 1938 the rackets had lost all their appeal and Braden is purely a social worker, with an official title that sounds as though it might be related to the WPA. After he has twice risked his life to save the kids, he wins their sympathy sufficiently to impress them with the necessity, not to say the rewards, of social responsibility. At the conclusion of the film the judge announces an early parole for the Dead End Kids (immaculately attired in suits), while Braden marries the sister of one of the boys, confirming both the virtues and the existence of social mobility.

As with every formula repetition, the more pictures Warners made with the Dead End Kids, the further away they got from the original inspiration for the team's success. *Angels Wash Their Faces* (1939) concerned the participation of the youths in a Boys' Week competition at school, in which the youngster with the most civic knowledge becomes the titular mayor of the city for seven days. Spurred on by the fact that one of their friends died in a tenement house fire, deliberately started by a crooked businessman for his own fell purpose, the gang furnish the eventual winner of the contest.

By means of a laboured plot, they also take over the city's administration, expose the graft and corruption in municipal office and make a warm plea for justice, honesty, official probity and all the other things to which people are otherwise supposedly antagonistic. The final shot of the film, and of the series, is taken from the air, showing the city spread out below, clearly marked out and liberally scattered with the recreation grounds that the New Deal hoped would make responsible citizens out of potential psychopaths.

Urban renewal became something of a fad in the late 1930s, in which politicians, intellectuals and artists indulged, so long as the craze lasted, and so long as there were no other matters more pressing. By 1940 the European situation began to dominate the concern of the Left, and after the war America conducted something of a retreat from the reformist ideals of the New Deal. Film *noir* reflected current feeling in Hollywood about the state of the union, and *Scarlet Street* (1945) and *Cry of the City* (1948) evoked once more an urban world of the fevered imagination, a city lit by flashing neon signs, and comprised of seedy rooming houses and echoing comfortless churches.

At the same time, in the real city, economic and social developments proceeded at a pace that far outstrippped the zeal and ability of the urban planners to cope with them, with the result that in the 1960s the politicisation of the ghettos, combined with the degradation of their economic and social status, resulted in periodic explosions of violence. For all his lack of interest in the complexities of urban life, it would appear that Busby Berkeley, in one musical interlude in an otherwise undistinguished film, proved to be a more accurate commentator on urban history than the optimistic architects of the New Deal and Hollywood script departments.

9

GOOD CITIZENSHIP AND GOOD PICTURE-MAKING
Warner Brothers and the New Deal

MGM was a studio that spent. It was a studio of white telephones.
Warners had black telephones.

Milton Sperling, Warner Brothers executive

Of the three traditional critical approaches to Hollywood cinema in the 1930s, through genre, auteur and studio, it is the studio which offers the most insight as far as this book is concerned. Over the last twenty years the major Hollywood studios have begun to deposit production files in American university libraries, allowing a more detailed examination of the influences which shaped their films. In an industry dominated by producers, the auteur director who found it impossible to meet the rigorous demands of the commercial framework soon discovered that his services were rarely in demand. Nowhere was this harsh reality better illustrated than at Warner Brothers, where many talented directors made first-rate pictures under conditions of extreme parsimony and haste.

Of all the major studios, it was Warner Brothers who best captured the flavour of the Depression, attacking certain contemporary social and political controversies, and earning themselves the designation of an active 'social conscience'. The slogan 'Combining Good Citizenship with Good Picture-Making', was displayed prominently in the studio lobby.[1] But Warner Brothers in the 1930s were far from being the radicals that the HUAC in the 1940s loudly proclaimed them to be. The brothers and their studio were, if anything, apologists for the New Deal. Most of their 'socially conscious' films inevitably bore the marks of the confusion, compromise and general vagueness that permeated the New Deal. This chapter represents an attempt to re-examine some of the Warner films which, for all the wrong reasons, have been tarred with the radical brush.

As with most studios, however, Warners' artistic history is interwoven with their commercial record. In 1926 the studio, lacking the exhibition outlets of Fox, Paramount and Loews, was in danger of dying from economic asphyxiation. Eventually Sam Warner persuaded his less enthusiastic brothers to gamble on the adoption of the sound-on-disc process. The instant success of

Don Juan and *The Jazz Singer*, combined with the reluctance of other studios to follow suit immediately (most of them felt that sound was a temporary fad), brought huge profits to the intrepid Warners. The company balance sheet recorded a capitalisation of $100,000 at the end of 1925 but one of $50 million in January 1930. Stock dividends, split-ups of shares and cash dividends made Warner Brothers one of the alluring features of the New York Stock Exchange to which shares were transferred early in 1929. [2]

Although Warners lost money during the depths of the Depression, their recovery was strong enough to ensure an average annual net profit of $3 million in the second half of the decade [3]. When Warners bought out First National in 1929, Robert Lord, a writer at the old Warner studio in Hollywood, was sent out to become a supervisor on the Burbank lot with the specific task of speeding up the production of scripts. 'I found a country club,' he remembered forty years later. 'What we did at Warners in half a day, it took them a week to do at First National.' [4] Under the watchful eye of the executive in charge of production (Darryl Zanuck from 1927 to 1933 and Hal Wallis thereafter), neither a superfluous nail nor a superfluous writer found a welcome at the Warner Brothers studio. Warners' speed and efficiency led to a favourable relationship with voracious exhibitors, who appreciated prompt delivery of their orders.

> Warner Brothers–First National will complete its entire product of 60 pictures for 1933–4 release by May 1st. This is over an 11 month period, which is a production record for speed at the studio. [5]

When the studios demanded a fifty per cent wage cut of their employees, and took as many economising measures as possible to meet the crisis caused by dwindling box office returns, Warners were predictably in the vanguard. In the first six months of 1931 they sacked nine hundred employees. *Variety* noted: 'The example set by Paramount of economising chiefly on the payroll is being observed by the Warners. In the case of the Brothers, the economy is known to be the severest in the industry.' [6]

Parsimony at Warners stretched to the budgeting of most of their films, so that they became the masters of the cheap remake. Writers were told to concentrate on what passed in Hollywood for naturalism. 'Look out the window and describe what you see' [7] became their maxim. As John Baxter points out, 'Elegance at Warners reached its peak with Warren William in a double-breaster and snap brim hat eating lobster at the Embarcadero.' [8] Darryl Zanuck, during the six years he spent as production executive at Warners, inaugurated a tradition of translating newspaper stories into motion pictures. The key gangster films were made in Burbank, as were the main socially conscious and overtly political films of the 1930s, because Warners had more collective courage than anybody else when it came to tackling controversial subjects. They also had a sense of being outsiders. Just as the Jews were outsiders in American society, the Warner Brothers were outsiders in

158

Hollywood society. Four of Warners' male stars – Jolson, Robinson, Muni and Garfield – were Jewish, and Cagney and Bogart weren't exactly cast in the conventional mould of all-American heroes like Gable, Power, Cooper and similar stars who could be found under contract to the other studios.

Exhibitors were not slow to distinguish the Warner trademark. One showman wrote, 'I would advise any exhibitor who has not signed a Warner–First National contract to get busy and sign for they are making good b.o. pictures without spending a million to do it.[9] Another conceded, 'I must give Warner Brothers credit because there is something in their shows that appeals to the public'.[10]

The vast majority of the so-called 'program' pictures which Warners ground out used an urban locale and dealt with dramatic happenings in surroundings that were easily identified by the majority of the huge movie audience. *Three on a Match* (1932), one of Mervyn LeRoy's more unpretentious pictures, is set in the world of shop girls and hoodlums. Three girls (Ann Dvorak, Bette Davis and Joan Blondell) go their different ways after leaving school together, and chance to meet some years later, Dvorak with a rich husband (Warren William), Davis as a stenographer and Blondell having been to reform school. After lighting their cigarettes three on a match, they recall the Great War adage that three on a match meant the imminent death of one of the parties. Dvorak proves to be the unlucky one, Blondell replacing her in Warren William's affection, while Bette Davis moves up from stenographer to governess.

LeRoy made two other pictures that same year, one a dark melodrama, the other a light comedy, but both dealing with familiar Warners terrain. *Two Seconds* has already been discussed.[11] *Hard to Handle* stars James Cagney as an enterprising stunt promoter. At the end of a Marathon dance, he finds that his partner has made off with the prize money, as a result of which he himself is pursued down the pier by the outraged crowd. After toying with crooked treasure hunts and tricking society matrons into endorsing worthless weight-reducing creams, Cagney finally corners the market in grapefruit and attempts to make the whole country 'grapefruit conscious'. Robert Lord remembers writing the script in partnership with Wilson Mizner with wry affection.

> We'd sit there and we'd scream. Somehow, when it was all put together, it was funny but it wasn't nearly as funny as we thought it would be ....
> I have no idea why it was not. Bill and I rolled on the floor while we were writing it. We thought we were geniuses. It just shows you how easy it is to be wrong about your own work.[12]

Also in 1932 Cagney appeared as a belligerent cab driver in Roy Del Ruth's *Taxi*, another low-life drama, this time about the tribulations of being married to Loretta Young in a sleazy New York apartment. Even the best directors found themselves assigned to the seventy-minute urban programmer. William Dieterle, who directed the prestigious biographical pictures with Paul Muni and Edward G. Robinson, was delegated *The Great O'Malley* (1936), an unamusing, sickeningly bathetic story about an over-zealous cop (Pat O'Brien), whose attention to detail turns Humphrey Bogart to crime. As if this premise were not sufficiently discouraging, O'Brien's regeneration is brought about by Bogart's winning but crippled daughter. There were many other films of a similar nature. *Big City Blues, The Bureau of Missing Persons, The Life of Jimmy Dolan* and the countless gangster, racketeer and slum environment pictures made constant use of the same sets and, it sometimes seems, the same dialogue.

Even the spectacular musicals, which were generally the most expensive pictures produced at Warners, were tightly budgeted. The Busby Berkeley musical numbers accounted for approximately sixty per cent of the total production costs but only fifteen per cent of the playing time. The Warner showgirls, apart from their impossibly witty dialogue, at least live in a recognisably contemporary world, one that is not too far removed from the familiar low-life atmosphere of other Warner pictures.

The trend of musicals was started by the success of *Forty-Second Street*. Somehow Ruby Keeler, playing the chorus girl, Peggy Sawyer, who steps into the breach on opening night when the star (Bebe Daniels) breaks her ankle, captured the hearts of the nation in her movie début. Unfettered by the burden of talent, Miss Keeler's portrayal of the triumph of naivety and gawkiness gave more satisfaction to the paying public than the script of James Seymour and Rian James, the tortured, sick producer of Warner Baxter, the tuneful songs of Warren and Dubin and the hard-boiled dialogue tossed off by Ginger Rogers and Una Merkel.

Forty-Second Street proved to be the biggest-grossing picture in March 1933 and the fourth largest of the year. [13] It started a series of musicals starring Ruby Keeler and her leading man, Dick Powell, in which the virginal charms of the young couple were contrasted with the sexual and professional cynicism of Joan Blondell, Aline MacMahon, Clare Dodd, Ned Sparks and James Cagney. Above all, the three big musicals of 1933 (*Forty-Second Street, Gold Diggers of 1933* and *Footlight Parade*) played heavily on the convention of the game young kids trying to put on a show, in which human endurance triumphs over despair and doubt.

In *Gold Diggers of 1933* Dick Powell plays a song writer who falls in love with Ruby Keeler, again playing an unknown penniless chorus girl. After a fast-moving opening in which Ginger Rogers sings the song 'We're in the Money' at the head of a chorus line, clad only in a scanty creation made out of gold coins, the show is closed by the sheriff because of the producer's inability to pay for the scenery, ironically built out of huge dollar signs. Aline MacMahon sighs, 'That's the fourth show I've been in of and out of in two months. They close before they open', to which Joan Blondell tartly replies, 'It's the Depression, dearie.'

The two girls and Ruby Keeler share a large bed (out of economic necessity). MacMahon, musing wistfully on her trip to Bermuda the previous year, steals the neighbour's milk for breakfast. Blondell endorses the ethics of this move by remarking, 'That's all right, the dairy company stole it from the cow'. Barney Hopkins (Ned Sparks), who is the producer of a prospective show, promises all the girls jobs and tells them that the theme of the new musical is the Depression, drawing from MacMahon the dry remark, 'We won't have to rehearse that'. Inspired by a piano transcription of 'My Forgotten Man', Barney envisages, 'Men, marching, marching in the rain, jobs, jobs, the Depression, gee, don't it get yuh?' After building up everybody's hopes, Hopkins is forced to concede that the show won't open because he has not raised money. From this bright start, the movie slips into typical Hollywood fantasy. It is revealed that Dick Powell is, in fact, the black sheep of a wealthy Boston banking family. He puts up the necessary money and announces his intention of marrying Ruby Keeler, to the consternation of his elder brother (Warren William) who, eventually, marries Joan Blondell. Once more the rich have realised that true riches are only to be found with the right sort of girl, who is usually bred in the tenements of New York. Conversely, it also implies that any poor girl from a New York tenement can end as the wife of a wealthy New England banker. Social mobility triumphs again.

   Gold Diggers of 1933 was the biggest-grossing picture of June 1933 and the third largest of the whole year. [14] Exhibitors, who as a profession are easily given to pessimism, were delighted with it. One of them reported, 'Hot weather and the depression have no effect on the drawing power of this picture. Absolutely the greatest box office attraction of all time.' [15] *Footlight Parade* concerned the tribulations of James Cagney as a producer of movie theatre prologues. Once again the twin virtues of the indomitable human spirit and the indomitable Joan Blondell vanquish the underhand business methods and the machinations of Clare Dodd.

   These Warner musicals are significantly involved with economic adversity and, as such, are removed from their pale successors of 1934 and 1935 and the RKO musicals of Astaire and Rogers, the Fox musicals of Alice Faye and the MGM pictures with Jeanette MacDonald and Nelson Eddy, all of which take place in the happy Hollywood never-never land of economic security. What made them even more potent to Depression audiences was that they mixed a typical Warners naturalism with the old success formula, as seen through the triumph of the Keeler–Powell relationship. As Warner Baxter had pushed Miss Keeler on to the stage in *Forty-Second Street* with his classic exhortation, so, in *Gold Diggers of 1933*, Ned Sparks looks at her and prophesies, 'I know you; you used to be in the chorus. Someday you're coming out of the chorus.' Thus, what one obtains from the majority of the pictures turned out by Warner Brothers is a strong belief in the virtues of traditional American ideals, combined with a desire, bred partially by parsimony, to make pictures for the people and of the people. This was a major factor in their adventurous approach to serious political and social issues. It was an approach which paid off significantly in pure cash terms. *Forty-Second Street* cost $439,000 and grossed over $2,280,000; *Gold Diggers of 1933* returned gross receipts of $3,231,000 on an initial outlay of $433,000.

In 1932 Warners released *I Am a Fugitive from a Chain Gang* (discussed in detail in Chapter 2), one of the finest exposés to emerge from a major Hollywood studio. The aritistic and commercial success of the picture encouraged Zanuck, Wallis and Warner to look for equally sensational material. No other studio pursued them down this road with anything like the same conviction. *Black Legion* (1936), described on its first appearance as 'editorial cinema at its best', was a happy addition to the cinema of 'social consciousness'. [16] It is the story of Frank Taylor (played by Humphrey Bogart), who joins the local fascist Black Legion because Dumbrowski, an immigrant, is appointed to a position Taylor feels is righfully his. Taylor is portrayed as a happy, considerate husband and father, who intends to spend the raise in salary he confidently expects on presents for his wife and son.

After joining the Legion he and his hooded friends beat up Dumbrowski, who has 'stolen' Taylor's job at the factory and drive him and his father out of town. Taylor gets the job he has coveted but, in his attempts to recruit new members for the Legion, his negligence causes an accident at work, as a result of which he loses his job as foreman and is demoted to the status of a labourer once more. His successor is brutally whipped by the Legion and Taylor's wife, suspecting the 'lodge' that her husband has recently joined, leaves him. Taylor confesses his involvement with the Legion to his closest friend, but repents of the admission and murders him. In prison Taylor is warned by the Black Legion lawyer that, unless he spins a tissue of lies, accusing his wife of desertion, the Legion will destroy his family. In court Taylor is overcome by the mournful stares of his wife, and he finally tells the truth about the Legion, naming the key figures, all of whom are conveniently sitting on the front row in the courtroom. The accused are sentenced to life imprisonment, the last shot being that of Bogart disappearing from the world for ever, shooting anguished glances at his distraught wife.

Robert Lord's original story for this film was taken directly from the newspaper accounts of the activities of a Detroit fascist organisation. It aroused instant opposition from the Hays Office. Breen wrote to Jack Warner in June 1936:

> We regret to inform you that, because of certain elements in the material submitted to us, this story in its present form, is not acceptable .... [I]t has been our policy not to approve stories which raise and deal with the provocative and inflammatory subjects of racial and religious prejudice. [17]

Lord began to emphasise the economic aspect of the origins of fascism and shows how the local corner shopkeeper reacts to the price cutting of the big new supermarket by turning to violence. The oath, which Taylor is compelled to take, is administered beside an open fire, surrounded by menacing hooded figures. Its effectiveness is the result of a potent mixture of gibberish and poetry.

> Before violating a single clause of this my oath ... I will pray to an avenging devil to tear my heart out and roast it over the flames of sulphur; ... may my soul be given unto torment that my body be submerged into molten metal and stuffed into the flames of hell.

The radio speech, which originally induces Taylor to join the Legion, also pulls no punches.

> With fire and sword the Black Legion will purge the land of these traitorous aliens and throttle their every devil's scheme – until once more our beloved Stars and Stripes will wave over a united nation of free, white, 100% Americans.

Lord, who also produced the picture, reveals that there were a number of threatening letters and phone calls made against the studio and the people concerned with the production. 'The threatening letters came while the picture was being shot because there is a running line of publicity in any well-organised studio while the picture is in production. [18] So seriously did Warners take these threats that Wallis wrote to the director, Archie Mayo, as the main titles were being prepared:

> I thought I would check with you at this time to find out if you want your name on the ... picture.
> I thought that because of the nature of the subject you would prefer not to have yourself credited as the director of the picture. [19]

Mayo clearly thought it was worth the risk to keep his name on the film.

On its release the Ku Klux Klan immediately brought legal action against Warner Brothers for the use of Klan insignia copyrighted in 1925. A bitterly contested court action followed, which Warner Brothers eventually won when a judge in the Federal Court ruled that motion pictures of copyrighted articles were not a violation of United States copyright laws. [20] The publicity probably helped the box office. *Black Legion* cost $479,000 to make but grossed over $775,000.

The fictional nature of the story, however, did not fool anyone. One reviewer stated:

> Even though the Warner foreword tries to reassure us by saying that the incidents and characters depicted are fictional, we know that the story Robert Lord has written is a dramatization of the Black Legion killing of Charles Poole and the testimony of Duyton Deane, legion executioner who turned State's evidence at the trial. [21]

The only false note is the depiction of the heads of the organisation, a group of shysters, who have turned to fascism having exhausted the field of oil exploitation. Their concern is purely financial, implying a lack of fascist convictions, whereas events were just then proving that the most successful fascists were fanatics, not sharp businessmen.

For the best of reasons Lord fought hard for Humphrey Bogart to play the leading part despite pressure from Wallis to cast Edward G. Robinson. He wrote urgently to Wallis:

> There is not the slightest doubt of his [Robinson's] ability to give an outstanding performance in the part. The great trouble would be that he is decidedly not American looking. While he does not look particularly Jewish, he is distinctly a foreign type . . . . My opinion is that we must have a distinctly American looking actor. [22]

Wallis had the good grace to concede that Lord was right. Bogart got the part.

If *Black Legion* largely overcomes the compromise forced on it by official trepidation, *Cabin in the Cotton* (1932), another of the 'radical' Warner films, was fatally flawed by its ultimate indecisiveness. Richard Barthelmess, the son of an old sharecropper, is recalled from school and chosen by the chief local planter to live in his home and run the store. The dilemma in which Barthelmess finds himself is the result of his discovery that his father and the other croppers have been stealing the planter's cotton. While aware that the planter has kept the croppers persistently in debt, Barthelmess realises that he owes to the planter his education and the chance to better himself by living at the big house. The situation is complicated by the fact that the planter's daughter (Bette Davis) successfully seduces him away from his sharecropper girl (Dorothy Jordan). In one memorable scene Davis sings 'Willie the Weeper' to Barthelmess through a half-closed door, while doing an off-camera striptease. 'I'd like to kiss ya but I just washed mah hair,' she simpers and Barthelmess's dedication to his class is eroded still further. In the final reel Barthelmess makes a long-winded and boring speech, appealing to both sides for mutual co-operation. Because the landowners are the last to capitulate, it would appear that a great victory for the underprivileged, exploited share-croppers has been won. However, since the planters promise nothing more than a redress of the most rankling grievances, it is apparent that the pernicious sharecropping system is not fundamentally altered. *The New York Herald Tribune* commented on Barthelmess's great panegyric:

> There may be just a hint of social revolution in his assault on the rapacious landowners but it is not serious enough to be taken with any alarm . . . . It is his thesis that if the exploiters and the dispossessed ever get together and have a good chat, everything may be settled satisfactorily. [23]

Few of the critics took a different stance. *The New York Telegraph* felt that

> The movies should learn to take sides . . . . American film producers err

in trying to apologise every time they feel they are stepping on someone's toes .... Cabin in the Cotton could have been a strong, outstanding exposé of a vicious form of modern slavery but it is instead a weak and wishy washy straddling of an important issue. [24]

Perhaps the most damning criticism of the film was to be found in the general apathy of the audience. *Motion Picture Herald*, despite its sensitivity to anything serious which might 'damage' the industry, reviewed it quite pleasantly, [25] and the South, which might have been expected to have been incensed at the portrayal of both sides, since the South was notorious for finding objections to any film set in the South, received *Cabin in the Cotton* with hardly an excessive comment. *I Am a Fugitive from a Chain Gang*, released by the same company a few months later, aroused bitter controversy and outright banning in Georgia.

The compromise which bedevilled *Cabin in the Cotton* indicated just how limited were the possibilities that existed in Hollywood for serious discussion of important social and political problems. The demands of drama and the demands of profit, added to the cautiousness with which Hollywood approached any sort of consideration of controversial, topical issues, constantly undercut the efforts of Left-wing writers to use the screen for polemical purposes, let alone socially concerned producers who wanted to do their level best to reproduce in fiction form the traditional journalistic preserve of muckraking.

However, Warners' conscientious efforts brought them the approval of Franklin D. Roosevelt, whose generally flamboyant representation of policy-making and overall economic plans found instant approval in Hollywood. During the 1932 Presidential campaign the Warner brothers changed from confirmed Republicans to fervent Democrats. Jack Warner was summoned by his brother Harry to an urgent meeting in New York. There he was confronted by the combined exhortations of Jim Farley, Joseph P. Kennedy, Al Smith, the previous Democratic Presidential candidate, and J. J. Raskob, the current Chairman of the Democratic National Committee. 'There is revolution in the air and we need a change,' announced Harry Warner. [26]

W. R. Hearst, also a major factor in the Roosevelt campaign, jeopardised his long-standing ties with Louis B. Mayer and looked for another important film personality, who might be induced to support Roosevelt. The choice descended on Jack Warner who, assured of the future President's undying gratitude, set about organising rallies and raising money for the Democrats. One enormous gathering at the Los Angeles Coliseum, attended by nearly all the big Hollywood names, with the exception of Marie Dressler who was specifically forbidden to appear by her studio boss, Louis B. Mayer, was typical of Warner's approach. Subsequently Jack Warner was named the Los Angeles chairman of the NRA. In Santa Barbara Jack Warner joined the train carrying Roosevelt to Los Angeles. The famous Roosevelt charm was unleashed with devastating effect. 'I found him a vital and enormously magnetic man and during that twenty four hour train trip we began a friendship that endured to the day he died.' [27] Ironically, it also started a trail that led eventually via *Mission to Moscow* and other films made at the request of the President to Warner's appearance before the House Un-American Activities Committee in 1947.

Warner's veneration of the dynamic President, which grew with each highly publicised visit to the White House, was very similar to Walter Winchell's. One cannot help feeling that Roosevelt chose both these associations very carefully, as he was thereafter capable of feeding information to the public through two vital channels of mass communication. Warner recalls that Roosevelt was fond of picking his brain for information about the film industry. During one visit,

> just before I started home, the President asked me if I would like a diplomatic post overseas. 'I'm very flattered, Mr. President,' I replied, 'but I think I can do better for your foreign relations with a good picture about America now and then. And anyway I don't look so good in striped pants.'

Warner was happy to admit: 'It was no secret on the lot that I admired Franklin Delano Roosevelt, that I had a personal friendship with him that any man would envy and that I had been his guest many times at the White House.' [28]

The result of this mutual appreciation society was that for a few years Warner Brothers in the 1930s became a New Deal studio. In July 1934 Farley paid a quick visit to Hollywood.

> Jack Warner and his gang really put it on for Postmaster General Jim Farley at the Burbank studio. Everyone that is anyone in the picture biz. besides candidates for governorship internal revenue and customs collectors, other politicians et al. attended the shindig held on an Hawaian set with lakes, volcanoes and music thrown in. [29]

As previously noted in Chapter 3, Warner Brothers' press copy reflected the relationship. The picture of an exhibitor with his hand raised was covered by the words

> I SOLEMNLY SWEAR that in 1933–4 I will serve the best interests of my theatre and patrons by doing business with [Warner Brothers] .... And so I now wholeheartedly resolve to subscribe to every one of the 60 pictures of Warner Brothers RECOVERY PROGRAM for 1933–4.

As early as January 1933 Warners advertised,

> WATCH THIS COMPANY TURN OVER A NEW LEAF
> IN THE NEW YEAR
> WITH OUR NEW PRESIDENT.
> 42nd STREET AND OTHERS REPRESENT
> A NEW DEAL IN ENTERTAINMENT. [30]

The flirtation with Roosevelt and the New Deal directly affected not only the company's image but also the nature of the studio's output. At the time the romance was beginning Warners were contributing to the fashionable cycle of 'fallen women' movies with the Barbara Stanwyck vehicle *Baby Face*. Cecilia Ager pointed out the moral of these films in her review.

Baby Face appreciates how hard it is for a girl to get along in the big city. All girls need to do is to watch Barbara Stanwyck, note her resourceful-ness, heed her adaptability – and they can't lose . . . . Instinct guides a girl to the man who can do her the most good. The thing to do is to pick out a big bank building, start at the bottom and wind up with the President of the company in the penthouse. There's no such thing as unemployment – even the clerk in the outer office is a man and any man . . . can be had. See your goal clearly, keep learning on your way up, change your coiffure with the change in your standard of living . . . . Miss Stanwyck's personal sincerity makes *Baby Face* very nearly a true story. [31]

Baby Face was in production during the critical early months of 1933 when the bleak political and economic landscape encouraged sexual licence. By the time it was ready to be released, Roosevelt's Hundred Days had worked their magic. Despite the general truth of Ager's review, Stanwyck's amorality had been considerably toned down by the time the picture was released. Originally George Brent playing the part of Courtland Trentholm, the disgraced former Bank President, shoots himself in expiation of Stanwyck's guilt. A new final scene was added to the film on 12 May 1933 (possibly not seen by Ager and other early reviewers) which stood the morality propounded in the previous eighty-eight minutes of the movie on its head. The Bank's Board of Directors are now nostalgically recalling the improved fortunes of the bank:

JAMISON

Courtland Trentholm did more than his share. He and his wife sacrificed everything they had for the Bank.

GAULT

Oh yes. What became of her?

JAMISON

You'll be pleased to know that she's stuck by him. And she's proved herself a very fine woman. I had a letter from them last week. They haven't a cent. He's working as a laborer in the steel mills in Pittsburgh. And both of them are happier than they've ever been in their lives. [32]

Baby Face thus emerges as a prototype Warner Brothers New Deal morality tale.

A more explicit New Deal film would be *Wild Boys of the Road*, which since its release in 1933 has steadily acquired the reputation of 'a socialist parable'. The film begins by pointing out that many of the juvenile hoboes who are forced on to the road by the Depression come from middle-class backgrounds. The pride of the bourgeoisie is illustrated by young Tommy, who asks Eddie, his closest friend (played by Frankie Darro), not to reveal the fact that his mother is getting food from the community chest, because she has worked only four days in the past five months. Eddie himself, distressed at the sight of his father who has been laid off at the cement works, selflessly sells his old car for $22, justifying the sale to himself by asking, 'Why should I have a good time while he stands in a breadline?'

The two boys leave home and join up with Sally, a young girl (Dorothy Coonan), and the three ride on empty freight trains, battle with the police, build a sewer pipe city (very much on the lines of the one actually in existence at the time in Oakland) and meet with several hardships. Sally's kindly aunt in Chicago turns out to be the madam of a brothel, a girl in the freight train is raped by Ward Bond, the police turn water cannons on them and Eddie is framed in a hold-up by some petty thieves. In the courtroom Eddie is sentenced to the reformatory and is informed that he is 'an enemy to society and must be kept off the streets'. He responds with an impassioned speech:

> You say you've got to send us to jail to keep us off the streets. That's a lie. You're sending us to jail because you don't want to see us. Well, you can't do it. I'm not the only one. There are thousands just like me hitting the road every day. You read in the papers about giving people help. The banks get it. The soldiers get it. The breweries get it. They're always yelling about giving it to the farmers. What about us? We're just kids .... What's the use? Put me in a cell! Lock me up! I'm sick of being hungry and cold! Sick of freight trains! Jail can't be any worse than the streets!

At this promising juncture the film unexpectedly disintegrates. The presiding judge, wearing FDR spectacles and seated under the Blue Eagle, changes his mind about the sentence, and, in the soft persuasive tones of a fireside radio chat, he tells Eddie the case is dismissed.

> It's simply that things are going to be better now. Not only here in New York but all over the country. I know your father will return to work shortly. That means you can go back to school. I want you to promise me that when you've made enough money you'll buy a ticket and go back home where you belong.

Mrs William Wellman, the wife of the director, who played the part of Sally, recalled that the film originally ended with Eddie being sent to the State Reformatory until the age of twenty-one, Sally on her way for ten months to the House of Correction and the one-legged remaining member of the trio in similiar distress. Jack Warner, fearing an adverse reaction from the exhibitors and the public, dictated the rewriting to include the final scene as it now stands. [33]

During the shooting Hal Wallis was constantly warning Wellman of the film's potential dangers.

If we are to keep sympathy for these kids and show them as victims of circumstance and still withal being the average American kid, I think they [the audience] will like the characters better than if we make hoodlums out of them. [34]

The eventual result was an unhappy compromise, which pleased almost nobody except Warner, and his satisfaction must have been tempered by the feeble box office performance. Budgeted at $168,744, it eventually cost over $202,000. It grossed $103,000 abroad and $274,000 within the United States, which was a lower than average return on its investment.

One exhibitor wrote, 'No excuse in the world for making a picture like this .... People have enough hardship in the world without paying money to see it all portrayed on the screen.' [35] *Variety* complained similarly, 'Granting that boys on the road is a vital public question ... the outstanding fact is that it makes a depressing evening in the theatre'. [36] *The New York Times* seized on the film's impotence as a social statement.

the film might have been once tragic, dramatic and a stirring call for remedial action. Somehow it has missed being any of these ... by endowing it with a happy ending the producers have robbed it of its value as a social challenge. [37]

The Hays Office, though, was glad to note that its warning had been taken to heart. James Wingate, head of the New York Board of Film Censors, wrote to Albert Howson, a Warner Brothers representative in New York,

We were particularly glad to note that although certain scenes inevitably deal with the clash between the boys and the police force, yet the Police themselves have been portrayed in a sympathetic manner. Furthermore, at the end of the picture, the three leading young characters, who are taken as typical of the mob, are rescued by an understanding judge. [38]

Wingate wrote in a similar vein to Jack Warner in Hollywood. 'In view of the fine and sympathetic portrayal of the judge as the representative of law and order at the end of the picture, [it] will meet with a minimum of difficulty [as regards censorship].' [39]

If *Wild Boys of the Road* was destroyed because of its final compromise, *Heroes for Sale*, the movie directed by Wellman immediately before it, was flawed by an unhappy compromise built into the structure. The story, written by Robert Lord and Wilson Mizner, and originally called *Breadline*, concerns the efforts of Richard Barthelmess (playing a character called Tom Holmes) to find a secure life after a year in the trenches. The plot thus starts with the basic material of *I Am a Fugitive from a Chain Gang*, but it never succeeds in retaining the power to move and shock as does the original. As in *Fugitive*, the hero builds up a successful career in Chicago, this time in a laundry. In the former film one can sympathise with the hero because his is the fight of one man against a corrupt system, but in *Heroes for Sale* one can only feel irritation for the hero, because he is for ever defending a system which has conspired since the opening reel to kick him in the teeth.

The firm for which Tom works is taken over by a typical group of 1930s trouble-makers, this time known as Consolidated Industries Inc., who, as the new bosses, immediately lay off 75 per cent of the staff by installing a conveyor belt and sundry machines. The dismissed workers, understandably, have distinctly Luddite feelings about the whole business and set out to smash the machines. Tom races out to stop the riot and is hauled off by the police to serve a five-year sentence for violent conduct. His wife, played by Loretta Young, is killed trying to rescue Tom from the clutches of the mob.

One of Tom's inventions, however, accumulates over $50,000 for him, but on his return from prison he spends his money on the maintenance of a soup kitchen, abandons his son to the care of the solicitous Aline MacMahon and is thrown out of town by the police for being a 'red'; a fact which he does not seem disposed to contest, although few of his actions seem consistent with those of a dedicated revolutionary. With admirable stoicism, the hero walks across a map of America, through Harrisburg (NO HELP WANTED), St Louis (JOBLESS MEN – KEEP GOING. WE CAN'T TAKE CARE OF OUR OWN) to Nashville, where the unemployed ex-servicemen are termed hoboes and as such are driven over the state line. There, huddled in a box-car in the pouring rain, destitute and starving, Tom meets Roger, a coward introduced in the first reel, who, through a case of mistaken identity, has been awarded the war decoration that should have gone to Tom. The two chat over old times and the present political situtation.

ROGER

What do you think of all this? The country can't go on this way. It's – it's the end of America.

TOM

No. It's maybe the end of us, but it's not the end of America. In a few years it'll be bigger and stronger than ever.

ROGER

You know, you're the last guy in the world I'd ever expect to find was an optimist.

TOM

That's not optimism – just common horse sense. Did you read President Roosevelt's inaugural address?

ROGER

He's right. You know, it takes more than one sock in the jaw to lick a hundred and twenty million people.

Apart from its obvious New Deal affliliations, *Heroes for Sale* hits hard below the belt at the alternatives to the accepted political opposition. This is achieved through the character of Max, who, in addition to being a lovable Russian in the Mischa Auer tradition, is also a friendly Communist apostate. When not spouting empty slogans, Max is an inventor of such devices as a combination mangle and washing machine. He offers it to Tom and Tom's bosses to double production, whereupon Tom enquires about Max's well-known antipathy to capitalists and is told, 'I despise them, I spit on them, but I am willing to get rich with them', thereby removing Communism from the realm of serious consideration. When Tom wants to give away his share of the profits of the invention, Max exclaims indignantly,

> I make you rich and now you throw that good money away on these lazy moochers .... The poor! The needy! A cancer on civilisation! If I was running the world I would kill everybody that needed, well, anything ....
> There's only one thing important in the world and that's money. Without it you are just garbage. With it you are a king!

Pressure to emasculate *Heroes for Sale* was initially exerted by the Hays Office. On 1 March 1933 James Wingate wrote to Darryl Zanuck with reference to the first draft of the script he had been sent.

Scene 128. Some of the censor boards are becoming very strict about references to Communism etc. Therefore we think it might be wise to consider the following suggestions:
  a) Omit all references to Communism
  b) Change the questionable wording 'Red' and 'Capitalists' to something that might be less dangerous, such as, perhaps, 'Radical' and 'Employers'.[40]

As we saw in Chapter 3, *Heroes for Sale*, like *Wild Boys of the Road*, became a prime target for New Deal propaganda. This time the New Deal compromise sank the picture without critical trace. *Variety* thought that it might be sold to the public: 'were it possible for a skillful operation to be performed on parts of the yarn to make it more cohesive and less confused .... Altogether a sorry comment on what Americanism might be or isn't.'[41] *The Hollywood Reporter* was even blunter: 'Undoubtedly it is meant to be the G.A.L. for the G.A.P. (the Great American Lesson for the Great American Public) but it succeeds in arousing only a slight mental and physical discomfort.'[42]

Yet Mr Wingate was still unhappy. He wrote to Jack Warner: 'We suggest that wherever you can, you trim the scenes in which the police are shown as overly officious and unfair in carrying out their duties.'[43] Box office receipts for

171

the picture ($264,000 in North America against a negative cost of $330,000) indicated that the public agreed very largely with *The Hollywood Reporter*.

The following year (1934) Richard Barthelmess appeared in a slightly more successful piece of New Deal propaganda. It was called *Massacre* and it dealt in sympathetic terms with the plight of the American Indian. (As such, it was perhaps the only one of its kind until the revaluation of the Native American by Hollywood after the Second World War.) Barthelmess begins the film as an attraction in a Chicago Fair sideshow, performing exercises supposedly learned on the plains, but it is soon revealed that he is totally integrated into white society and cannot tell 'a medicine man from a bootlegger'.

Among his proud possessions are a black servant and a large touring car. As Joe Thunder Horse, he is summoned back to the reservation to see his dying father, the Sioux chief, Black Pony. His initial encounter with the unpleasant local official, Quissenberry (Dudley Digges), indicates that the Indians are well cared for by the white administrators, but as soon as he reaches the reservation it becomes increasingly obvious that the Indians are in dire trouble. The doctor never comes to visit Indian patients, spending his time shooting up with dope, and Barthelmess's sister is raped by a local official during the funeral of her father. Joe exacts revenge by beating up the culprit, but is sentenced to ninety days' hard labour and a $300 fine by Indian judges, who do exactly what the white officials tell them to do.

Ann Dvorak, playing an Indian with good shorthand, helps Joe to make his escape to Washington, where, as he leaps off the train, he almost falls into a Blue Eagle and NRA poster, while the Capitol rises comfortingly on the backdrop. The Commissioner for Indian Affairs supports Joe's case, but the Chairman of a Congressional Committee points out that the Indians were granted their citizenship under the Coolidge Administration, to which Joe replies:

> The Indian a citizen? He has no constitutional rights .... He's given the right to live – on waste land. He's given the right to trial – before Indian judges who are under the agent's thumb and do just what he tells 'em to do. It's a massacre any way you take it.

The man Joe had attacked dies, and Joes now faces a murder charge and, to exacerbate matters, his sister, who is the key defence witness, is kidnapped by the evil agents and severely whipped. The Indians want to burn down the courthouse, but Barthelmess, in his by now familiar conciliatory speech to the mob, convinces them that they have a duty to their good friends in Washington. At the trial the unpleasant local whites are removed, Joe is found not guilty and, hand in hand with Ann Dvorak on a misty mountain top, he decides to accept Washington's offer of the position of new local commissioner – what he terms 'a real job'.

The implications of the film are simple. The system is inherently sound. Only the individual bad eggs need to be removed. Washington is the friend of the ethnic minorities and is in favour of maintaining rule by the traditional chiefs. The picture was made coincident with the passage in Congress of the Howard–Wheeler Indian Rights Bill. The idea behind the Bill was to reconstruct the Bureau of Indian Affairs in order to develop Indian self-help. *Massacre* was based on the reports developed by Robert Gessner, which were a blistering attack on the men responsible for the plight of the modern Indian. The Bill that finally passed in Congress, like the movie that eventually came off the Burbank assembly line, was a pale imitation of the original. No self-help government was ever permitted the Native Americans under the New Deal, and Gessner's report was conveniently filed away and ignored.

From the perspective afforded by sixty years' distance it looks as though the same fate befell the film. Yet on seeing a fine cut, Wingate wrote with evident concern to Jack Warner:

> We are still concerned regarding the attitude of the Government at Washington D.C. and more particularly, the Office of the Commissioner of Indian Affairs. It is possible that the Government might take exception to the general story of *Massacre* in that it may be interpreted as reflecting unfavorably upon the Government's conduct of Indian Affairs.

A relieved note is scribbled at the bottom of the page: 'We have [Commissioner] Collier's OK on the story from Washington.' [44]

Perhaps the relief was not surprising, for also in the same production file is a review of *Massacre* by Thornton Delehanty.

> Honest, powerful and impassive ... an unsparing indictment of social injustice .... In view of what happens when Hollywood takes hold of a social theme it is almost impossible to believe that 'Massacre' could have survived in so courageous and honest a form. 'Massacre' is an appeal for a New Deal for the American Indian. [45]

Massacre, like most of the other Warner films which are generally cited as evidence of the studio's developed social conscience, was based on the fundamental belief that the social and political system of the mid-1930s was essentially sound. All the problems which arose were the result of individual wrong-doing which could and would be dealt with by the appropriate authority. Such a philosophy led directly to the making of arguably the most fraudulent picture of the decade in which, as we shall see in the next chapter, this kind of 'shysterism' alone nearly destroyed the fabric of the entire American coal industry.

10

BLACK FURY
A microhistory of compromise

The scenes which showed the more terrible conditions under which the miners lived were eliminated. The title *Black Hell*, was changed to *Black Fury*. Muni himself, with some justified bitterness, suggested *Coal Diggers of 1935* as a still better name.

C. A. Lejeune, The Observer, 6 October 1935

The Warner Brothers feature film *Black Fury*, directed by Michael Curtiz, shot in the autumn of 1934 and released in April 1935, is for the historian of the New Deal arguably the most fascinating motion picture to be made in America in the 1930s. It is the story of a young Polish immigrant miner, Joe Radek (played by Paul Muni), who inadvertently causes a split in the ranks of the Federated Mine Workers union in Coaltown, Pennsylvania. The split and the ensuing strike and lockout are followed by the introduction of blackleg labour, before single-handed action by Radek to redeem himself brings about a happy settlement.

What makes *Black Fury* particularly interesting as microhistory is that it is possible to see in its production history almost all the pressures exerted on contemporary Hollywood film-makers by external forces. The film began life as a poorly dramatised but uncompromisingly detailed narrative of the origins and course of the strike in the Pennsylvania coal fields from 1925 to 1928. The strike was the bloodiest and most desperate of all the strikes which marked the history of the labour movement in the 1920s.

At the start of the decade the outlook for the bituminous coal industry had never been healthier. Output reached an all-time high of 568 million tons and the price per ton paid by the railways touched $4.20; 640,000 men were employed earning a daily rate of $7.50. By 1930 the industry lay in ruins. New mines, particularly in the South, using predominantly Black, non-union labour, were opened up, leading to a catastrophic overproduction which caused the price of coal to drop. By 1926 the annual capacity of the industry was a billion tons compared with the demand for it which was half that amount. The price per ton dropped to $2.40 compared to $4.20 at the start of the decade.[1]

Early in 1924 the United Mine Workers of America, led by their President, John L. Lewis, negotiated a settlement with the operators in the Central Competitive Fields (Pennsylvania, Illinois, Ohio and Indiana) to preserve the $7.50 rate of pay until the end of March 1927. Yet before the end of 1924 the operators were asking the UMW to cut wages to counteract the falling price of coal and declining profits. Lewis's response was encapsulated in the union's slogan 'No Backward Step'.[2]

The union's refusal to renegotiate prompted the operators to set about its systematic destruction. The key firm was the Pittsburgh Coal Company, which had passed recently into the hands of the Mellon banking interests. In late 1924 the company shut its doors and refused to reopen until August 1925 when it agreed to hire non-union labour at a top rate of $6 a day.[3] The United Mine Workers struck to enforce the contract, but the company began its policy of evicting miners and their families from company houses and bringing in blackleg labour. It is the details of this strike which were the origin of the fictional work *Black Fury*.

The prospect of a feature film being made from such contentious material outraged the mine owners because, they felt, it would inevitably seek to lay the blame on the inhuman conditions created by them, and it alarmed the Production Code Authority simply because it dealt in the controversial issues of capital and labour. Explicit pressure was therefore exerted on the film-makers by concerned interests, and the result was a dishonest portrait of the Pennsylvania coal mines which, like the other films in this limited but fascinating genre, found only professional racketeers to be at fault.

An article by the contemporary film critic of *The Observer*, C. A. Lejeune, written at the time of *Black Fury*'s release in England, after an interview with Muni, reveals the origins of the dispute.

> This story of the Pennsylvania coal mines and their troubles was bought for the screen before the recent censorship drive in Hollywood. Paul Muni, the star, himself read it and liked it; democrat and intellectual as he is its plangent propaganda appealed to him. With the tightening of the censorship, the story had to be radically altered. The capital and labour question was neatly ducked; professional racketeers were made the villains of the piece and miners and mine-owners emerged with equal honours. As a picture of social conditions among the miners, the film that has finally emerged is plainly dishonest.[4]

The writer of the original story on which *Black Fury* is based, Michael A. Musmanno, had been at one time a judge on the Common Pleas bench in Pennsylvania. In 1928 a case was brought before him exposing the brutality of the Coal and Iron Police which had resulted in the death of a picketing miner. The behaviour of these special policemen, hired specifically by the mine owners rather than the state government, had been a scandal throughout the three-year strike. After the fateful beating of John Barcoski by these private police, Musmanno, by now representing Legislative District 12 in Western Pennsylvania, introduced a measure to repeal the Coal and Iron Police Law which had been enacted in 1866. The Musmanno Bill, as it soon became known, was opposed and finally vetoed by the Governor of the state, John S. Fisher, who, according to Musmanno, 'was beholden to the coal and steel interests in his State for his office'. In fact Fisher was himself a coal operator and was widely known within Pennsylvania to be the Mellon family's candidate.[5]

Musmanno was a resourceful individual. According to *Black Fury*'s producer, Robert Lord, Musmanno 'had kind of a flair for personal publicity' and his next step was to construct a film story. For his hero he chose the legendary mining hero Jan Volkanik, of whom he had heard tales when he worked in a coal mine himself. In 1966 Musmanno wrote:

> He was already long a legend by 1915 when a plaque of him by the noted sculptor, the late Charles Keck, was unveiled as part of the decoration of the Manchester Bridge, Pittsburgh. It is the legend of Jan Volkanik which inspired my novel *Black Fury*. I decided to take the fabulous coal miner figure and place him in the setting of the coal strike of the 1920s.[6]

This story was the one which Musmanno showed to Muni and first aroused the actor's interest. Robert Lord remembered:

> Musmanno was, I think, a friend of Muni and his wife. He was, for a judge, very liberal and far to the Left and so, if I'm not mistaken, I think Muni bought the property and gave it to me to read. I was impressed by it and they[7] said to me, 'Do you want to write a first draft?' I said 'No'. Every writer is limited .... So Abe and Carl Erickson wrote a screenplay. They were very good for this kind of heavy thing. It was what the Germans call 'schwer' and this was really 'schwer'.[8]

Musmanno's efforts were twofold. His initial story was rejected but his second attempt, a screenplay called *Jan Volkanik*, became the basis for the screenplay written by Abem Finkel and Carl Erickson. In 1950–1 Musmanno, along with many other labour sympathisers of the 1930s, turned violently anti-Communist and gave evidence against Steve Nelson and other Pennsylvania Communists.[9] However, the purpose of this microhistory is not to examine Musmanno's Left-wing credentials but to see how his experience in Hollywood reveals the pressures placed on the film-makers and the studios by vested economic interests. In 1966 Musmanno published a novel called *Black Fury*, which he claimed was the basis of his original story. The changes between Musmanno's novel and his screenplay are just as instructive to analyse as the difference between *Jan Volkanik* and the shooting script.

The novel *Black Fury* was essentially a paean of praise to the United Mine Workers of America and in particular John L. Lewis. The local union leader addresses his members in blunt terms:

176

'All this', he said with obvious deep feeling, 'was brought about by the greatest labor leader this country has ever seen – John L. Lewis . . . . John L. Lewis has been to the coal miner what Abraham Lincoln was to the slaves of his day. [10]

The hero of Musmanno's story, Jan Volkanik, tells the men during the strike of his abhorrence of Communists.

I remember what our great President, John L. Lewis said about Communists. 'If the day ever comes in the history of the UMWA when it is dominated by men who are false to the traditions of the American people and the American nation then that day I shall cease to be an officer of the United Mine Workers of America.' [11]

Hollywood's desire for political blandness plainly precluded any such treatment of the UMWA in the film version of the story. Musmanno compounded his original error by making villains out of both the mine owners and, more interestingly, the American Communist Party. The union was beset by serious factionalism and dual unionism, but Musmanno chose to concentrate on the Communists and avoid any hint of the deep disillusion with Lewis's leadership expressed by union members who were not Communists in the desperate struggles of the late 1920s. [12] There is no doubt that the virulence of his postwar anti-Communism was responsible for the tone of the novel, but it also appears to be consistent with Musmanno's union activities in the interwar years.

Although a fictional character called Roger Cadman is the man who manipulates the strike in Coaltown, Pennsylvania, he takes his orders directly from William Z. Foster. Foster is described as devious, unpleasant and anti-American.

Foster looked beyond the day when the National Miners Union [a Communist front] would supplant the UMWA and on to the day when it would eventually supplant the union of the United States itself. Democratic government was decadent and archaic; its time had come. The dictatorship of the proletariat was the inevitable government not only for America but for the world. [13]

Musmanno warns of the dire consequences of the Communist master plan.

Once established in this key spot, the movement would spread to all of Bitumina. After that, other mining areas of the country would respond, the whole trade union movement would fall in line and the dictatorship of the proletariat would be on its way with Foster as Chief Commissar in the United States. [14]

Musmanno is just as harsh on the mine owners as the Communists. They too are mostly symbols of demonology. The dominant influence in Coaltown is Eli Gord, President of Coaltown Enterprises Inc., whom we first meet as he sits in comfort in the Stowe Heights Country Club sounding off about the pernicious effect of the union.

> 'Are we going to let the United Mine Workers run the country?' he asks rhetorically. 'That United Mine Workers bunch put something over on us. Imagine a dumb uneducated hunky getting $7.50 a day.'

Since Musmanno needs to communicate Gord's view in dramatic terms he is forced to create the character of Clemenson, who sits on the board of directors of Coaltown Enterprises and is permitted to be the lone voice of reason. It is Clemenson who points out to Gord and other directors that such munificence is essentially illusory.

> The bituminous miner averages only about 175 days work a year. That means his income is around $1400 a year [but] he's got to pay for his own tools, equipment and supplies so that in the end he actually takes in about a thousand. Do you call that high pay for what is probably the dirtiest, hardest, ugliest and most dangerous work a man can find anywhere? [15]

Gord remains unimpressed and anxiously canvasses opinion as to how he might legally renege on the Jacksonville Agreement which had guaranteed miners minimum basic pay and conditions. It soon becomes apparent that his desire to create unrest in his own workforce, so that he can use the power of the courts to adjudicate that the miners have broken the agreement, is equalled by the machinations of Foster and Cadman on behalf of the Communist Party. On learning of Cadman's stated desire to form a new union:

> Gord's stern features relaxed and resolved into an expression of elation. 'That's absolutely wonderful. Is there anything we can do to help him? ... If [Cadman] can form a union to oppose the United Mine Workers, we'll be able to repudiate the Jacksonville Agreement on the basis that the UMWA, through internal dissension, has made it unenforceable'. [16]

During the ensuing strike the mine owners' behaviour (with the honourable exception of Clemenson's) is predictably punitive. No visitor could even enter Coaltown unless he promised not to talk about labour conditions. All miners living in company-owned houses were forcibly evicted.

> Several Coalandirons [Police] seized his furniture – bed, dresser, stove, chairs, tables – and threw them into the cindered street .... Two blows on the head with a blackjack dropped him senseless beside his mother. [17]

The UMWA wishes to picket peacefully, as the owners have declared their intention of bringing in blackleg labour, but Gord instructs the Coal and Iron Police to commission sufficient numbers of hoodlums to crush all resistance. Court injunctions successively prevent the union from making speeches, erecting billboards, paying for advertising, using the word 'scab' or distributing relief funds. The judge, *pace* Governor John Fisher, it transpires, owns stock in coal properties. The ultimate humiliation is reserved for the miners who wish to hold a service in a church adjacent to one of the mines working with blackleg labour. The judge decides that 'the hymnal singing is a camouflage and that the real purpose of the singing strikers is to intimidate, harass and coerce the working miners from going into the mine below'. [18]

The attorney retained by the UMWA cannot refrain from observing:

> For a mighty corporation in the United States to come into court and ask for an injunction against church services is so contrary to everything that is American, so opposed to all traditions of religious freedom, that I almost find myself speechless.

Throughout the book Musmanno takes every opportunity afforded to detail the excesses of the Coal and Iron Police, who were the subject of his earlier legislation.

> The Coal and Iron Police formed a unique organisation. They were the Siamese twins of policedom: they were state police because they received their commissions from the Governor of Pennsylvania but they were private police in that they were hired by the coal companies, paid by the companies and obeyed the orders of the companies.

When the first unrest in Coaltown is perceived, the Coal and Irons are immediately unleashed.

> This was the kind of situation in which the Coal and Iron police reveled, just as bandits of the old West enjoyed the sight of a stagecoach careening through a lonely gorge. On swift black horses the company-hired police bore down on the melee, knocking over with impartiality, men of both the old and new union.

Then the hero is set upon by anonymous hoodlums: 'Three mounted Coalandirons closed in on [Jan]. They could see the assailants running in the distance but they were interested only in Volkanik.' [19] Jan is arrested amidst much brutality, charged with inciting to riot, prison escape and battery on a police officer. He is sentenced to one and a half to three years in prison. The charges are all devoid of anything but the most spurious circumstantial evidence.

In prison Jan is transformed from an ignorant, good-humoured workhorse into a well-read, thinking, potential union leader. Musmanno ascribes this change to his reading matter, which includes *Black Beauty, Treasure Island, Little Women, Tom Sawyer*, the origins of the miners' unionisation and the details of miners' oppression in the nineteenth century: 'In a sudden flash of understanding the answer came to him – the *why*. It was the system! That was it! Nothing could be clearer or simpler. These men, the Coalandirons, were encouraged to beat people.' Thereafter Jan is at the forefront of the UMWA's attempts to end the strike without surrendering to the employers' demands that they return to work without the minimal protection offered by the previously negotiated Jacksonville Agreement. In a police-inspired brawl Jan is attacked and sustains multiple fractures. From his hospital bed Jan learns that the men have been starved into submission and intend to return to work, thus presenting Gord with a complete triumph. He discharges himself against doctor's orders, drags himself back to Coaltown and wires the whole mine with explosives, threatening to detonate it unless the employers recognise the UMWA and the Jacksonville Agreement.

Each day the newspapers carry headlines about the continuing triumph of the one-man strike. A radio station calls it 'the most unprecedented, spectacular one man show in the politico-economic history of America'. After nine days of unilateral heroics by Volkanik another member of the board of Coaltown Enterprises admits: 'the United Mine Workers, no matter what you say about them, are God-fearing men devoted to the ideals of America. Their word can be depended upon.' A few days later Clemenson starts to convince the other members of the board, one of whom remarks that, while he does not condone Jan Volkanik's illegal actions, nevertheless: 'I am indebted to him for saving us from a man who actually studied revolutionary tactics in Moscow on how to infiltrate into American industry, how to sabotage, destroy and wreck.' [20] It is this fear of the spectre of Communism as much as the increasing and unwelcome media attention that persuades Coaltown Enterprises Inc. to accept Jan's demands for union recognition.

Just as Jan's meagre store of provisions runs out completely, the mine owners capitulate and restore the Jacksonville Agreement, conferring full recognition of the UMWA. Gord resigns from Coaltown Enterprises Inc. but imposes one last humiliation on his heroic worker when he presses criminal charges against Jan for destruction of property. In court the defendant has a final speech before judgment is passed.

> Your Honor, I leave the judgment entirely in your hands. I have faith in America, I am loyal to her ideals. All that I have done was done with the belief that I was fighting for Liberty and Justice. [21]

He is sentenced to one to two years in the Allegheny County Prison. He is by no means discouraged by his incarceration. He recognises that, like John Brown, he was forced to break human law in order to obey God's.

On his return to freedom Jan is given what Musmanno clearly perceives as the supreme accolade. He is sent to Washington to help to negotiate the new code of practice for the mining industry under the recently appointed National Recovery Administration. In the capital he is attached to the staff of the national headquarters of the UMWA and asked to speak at the vital conference discussions.

> I have come here today to ask for my brothers a living wage. The operator

puts his money into the industry and we know that money is the lifeblood of a civilised community but we invest blood too, our own red blood, our limbs, our eyes, our health .... According to Department of Labor reports 79,270 miners have been killed in the last 37 years. During that same period 1,109,780 miners have been injured. [22]

Jan's arguments were duly noted.

A provision in the NRA became the Magna Charta of Labor; it was a provision straight from Lewis's brain and fist and it stated: '... employees shall have the right to organise and bargain collectively through representatives of their own choosing and shall be free from the interference, restraint or coercion of employers of labor or their agents in the designation of such representatives or in self-organisation or in other concerted activities for the purpose of collective bargaining or other mutual aid or protection.' [23]

Finally the Bituminous Coal Code was produced, approved by the President of the United States, the Administrator, the operatives and the miners. This code ushered in a new era in the coal fields of the nation. The miners hailed the document as one equivalent in importance to the Emancipation Proclamation of Abraham Lincoln. The NRA code also guaranteed national recognition for the United Mine Workers of America and the employers were made responsible for deducting union dues from pay packets and turning the revenues over directly to the union.

Musmanno is very clear about his motive for writing *Black Fury* and his own part in the story.

The sadistic and senseless killing of coal miner John Barcoski in February 1929 by the private police who adminstered the fatal beating of five hours with revolver butts, whips and brass knuckles, occurred in Imperial in West Pennsylvania, ten miles from my home in Legislative District 12 which I represented in the Pennsylvania Legislature.

He adds that his sources for his fictional accounts are

predominantly fact – the story of the coal strike 1925–1928 to gain from the coal operators recognition of the UMWA – as related in *Black Fury* with its concomitant hardships, dangers and agonies suffered by the coal miners and their families, was taken from the official records of the US Senate Committee Investigation of conditions in the coal fields of Western Pennsylvania. [24]

Musmanno's screenplay *Jan Volkanik* was submitted to Warner Brothers early in 1934. The most important fact from the studio's point of view was that Paul Muni, one of their more 'difficult' stars, was very anxious to play the part of Jan. Muni, whose real name was Muni Weisenfreund, had been an important actor in the Yiddish Theater of New York before graduating to the Broadway stage and he retained the traditional Left-wing sympathies of so many working-class intellectual Jews. Second, *Black Fury* appeared to offer further propaganda for the Warner Brothers New Deal campaign.

Nevertheless certain important changes had to be made. For a start the whole subplot about the Communists and William Z. Foster had to be excised. Cadman, the professional *agent provocateur* in the novel, becomes Cadman the professional 'trouble maker' in the script. However, Musmanno retains his realistic portrayal of miners and mining conditions and the lacerating portrait of Eli Gord. His screenplay[25] projects an opening of a series of flashes on the screen depicting the occurrence of real mining disasters from Scofield Utah on 1 May 1900 by way of eight similar tragedies to that of Harlin on 5 May 1931. No more explanation is offered than the titular indication of these events. Thereafter Musmanno wanted to show the many uses of coal for the functioning of industry and communications, hospitals and homes.

After this documentary start and the introduction of Jan Volkanik, the mine owners are seen much as they are in the novel although Musmanno's lack of ease with the craft of screenplay writing leads to an even cruder caricature than is apparent in the novel. Talking to his colleagues Gord points out:

Gentlemen, under the contract known as the Shalerville Agreement[26] we have with the miners there seems to be no way to reduce wages. Can't this contract be abrogated in some manner? Surely there must be a loophole somewhere?

Another suggests:

Can't we put someone in the miners' union to stir up trouble among them?

THERE IS MUCH RAISING OF THE EYEBROWS IN SIGNIFICANT APPRAISE-MENT . . . . ON ONE WE SEE SMUGGISH APPROVAL, ON ANOTHER APPROVAL TINGED WITH INQUIRY AS TO HOW IT CAN BE DONE.

It is at this point that the mine owners resolve to call in Cadman as a professional trouble-maker.

By forcing the strike, the mine owners legally break the Shalerville Agreement and re-open the mines, having cut wages by 35 per cent. A close shot lingers on a miner's pay slip and reveals the details exactly as in the novel:

Coal mined at 35c ton	$31.24
House rent	$ 6.00
Domestic coal	$ 1.88
Lights	$ 2.00

Store account	$ 12.65
Smithing	$ 2.00
Powder	$ 1.85
Tools	$ 4.86
Total	$ 31.24
Balance due	xxx.xx

In the novel Musmanno terms the take-home pay of $0.00 Three Pink Kisses because of the 'xxx' on the payslip.

The callous treatment of the miners and their families by the mine owners and the Coal and Iron Police is emphasised at the expense of the split in the union ranks. Jan's best friend, Joe (a character clearly based on the martyred John Barcoski), takes umbrage at the cynical shooting of a young boy's dog by a trigger-happy policeman. In the scuffle that follows the cop is slightly scratched, whereupon Joe is promptly dragged off, beaten and killed.

Soon after the strike has started, its leaders send a letter to the owners offering fair terms for a negotiated settlement. The aptly named Clemenson, whose humanity has already been noticed, wants to accept the terms, but his colleagues predictably disagree. Gord calls the strikers 'animals' and adds the observation, '85% of the human race are animals. Only 15% are decent and civilised.' As in the novel, the miners and their families march, picket and sing hymns. The Coal and Iron Police retaliate by shooting up the schoolrooms and wrecking private homes. The local minister prays for Volkanik and his men but is then served with an injunction for permitting them to sing 'Onward Christian Soldiers' at the church service.

After eight months the strike continues but the miners and their families are starving to death. The Police are depicted as delighting in taking the roofs off the houses of the strikers and wantonly destroying the clothes and food begged from neighbouring villages. A march by the men results in further tragedy, as they walk into a hail of machine-gun bullets. The tents of the shanty town that grows up on the edge of Coaltown are fired upon and children are massacred; thirty-five are announced dead, twenty hurt and scores missing. An editorial in a local newspaper cries:

No situation can justify the act of the mine authorities that compels women and children to lie in ditches and cellars for 24 hours without food and water, exposing themselves to cannon and rifle fire and lets them die like trapped animals in the flames of their camps.

The end of the strike is precipitated, as in the novel, by Jan's individual heroism and by the emergence of the Musmanno Bill which puts the Coal and Iron Police at last under state jurisdiction. This time Musmanno adds a final twist to the tale by depicting an explosion down the mine which causes a number of fatalities. The widows and potential widows crowd the pithead, but once again it is Jan and the unsung ordinary miners who limit the damage rather than any measures the owners should have provided.

Musmanno's second attempt at the story places all the blame on the shoulders of the mine owners and their hired *agents provocateurs*. They manipulate the miners for self-interested financial reasons and then take an antagonistic attitude to the well-meaning advice from Washington. Plainly, Musmanno was preaching class war, and the depiction of policemen firing on helpless women and children, while a fair representation of what was actually to happen on Memorial Day in 1937 outside the Republic Steel Plant in South Chicago when police killed ten strikers, [27] was obviously too inflammatory for the Warner Brothers executives in 1934.

Documents in the files of the Hays Office substantiate this theory. After much censorship of the first draft of *Black Hell* as it was then called, Joseph Breen wrote to Will Hays in New York on 20 September 1934.

> The story of *Black Hell* is the story of a group of dishonest racketeering men who fatten on industrial strife and disorder. The heavies in the story are these men, who operate a kind of fake employment bureau in Chicago ... and *not* the employing company. It will be clearly established in the story that the companies are really being victimized by the dishonest Croner [the new name for the Cadman character], just as are the workmen. Organized labor is constructively pointed up. The several speeches of the organized labor men are are on the right side of decency, and law and order. The employing company also is made to appear as reluctant to employ the strike-breakers and the special policemen but are compelled to do so because of contractual obligations. No serious damage is done to any property of the company. Most important of all, the employing companies and the coal industry, generally, are not playing as heavies. They are, rather, the victims, as are the men, of the dishonest intrigue of the racketeers. [28]

Breen's report to Hays was the result of a letter written to the latter the previous month by J. D. Battle, Executive Secretary of the National Coal Association.

> On behalf of those who have a heavy investment in coal mines and the several hundred thousands of employees engaged in mining directly and the millions indirectly employed, may I not suggest that careful consideration be given to this matter and if possible the picture be shown to a group of practical coal men in New York before released. I believe if this method is followed all of us may be saved considerable embarrassment. [29]

Within the week Hays had written to Harry Warner asking him to make sure that nothing 'offensive' crept into the picture. 'I will be glad if you will check up on the matter as, of course, particular care is necessary in the treatment of this type of subject matter, especially at this time.'[30]

The final script was a perfect example of harmonious compromise between Hollywood's self-censorship body and the studio executives and their joint deference to big business. It might have left the writers, producer, star and director all fuming at the process of emasculation but it left nothing but warm feelings between the Warner Brothers and Joseph Breen. On 8 October 1934 the *Black Hell* script was stamped 'Final'. The following day Breen wrote to Jack Warner:

> It is very encouraging for us to note ... that without exception Mr Wallis has done exactly as we suggested. This we feel will materially help the script from the viewpoint of the bituminous coal operators who have already intruded themselves into the undertaking .... The censor boards throughout the country are particularly critical of all scenes showing any serious conflict between employer and employee and, with startling frequency in recent months have gone so far as to delete photographs in newsreels of such conflict.[31]

The Production Code Authority had examined the script at every stage from treatment to shooting script precisely to be able to defend the studio and the industry against just such an attack as the one mounted by the appropriately named Executive Secretary of the National Coal Association. As early as 7 May 1934 Breen had written to Jack Warner to commend him for the treatment of *Black Hell* but counsel still further caution in the writing of the script: 'strengthen and play up even more so the fact that Croner is promoting strife among the miners as the agent of a firm of professional strike-breakers masquerading as coal and iron police'.[32]

On 12 September Breen wrote to Warner with his detailed comments on the draft of the script dated 4 September:

> Beginning with Scene 219 up to and including scene 232, great care will have to be exercised to play down 'the confusion and vicious brutality' of the Coal and Iron Policemen. The confusion will be all right but the vicious brutality will have to be handled with great care.
> There should be no such action as that suggested at the end of scene 22 wherein the mounted policeman 'clubs down' the miner 'mercilessly' ....
> In scene 260, page 121, you should eliminate, from the standpoint of political censorship, the brass knuckles used by McGee [the leading villainous Coal and Iron Policeman].[33]

After further detailed requests for changes in the traditional censorship areas of the screen portrayal of violence, all of which were incorporated into the final shooting script, Breen adds a further ominous warning on the more complex issue of industrial policy.

With a view to protecting ourselves against any valid criticism on the part of the organized forces of the bituminous coal industry, we respectfully suggest that in scene 61 on pages 26 and 27, you might insert a line, spoken by Mike to the effect that while miners may not have ideal working conditions, nevertheless, working conditions of the coal industry have vastly improved and are getting better all the time. The point here is to get a line or two that may establish the fact that the miners have little to complain against, and that Croner is unjust in his criticism of the employing company. [34]

In the final shooting script Scene 61 becomes Scene 63 but the confrontation between Croner and Mike includes Mike's speech:

MIKE

(struggling to control his temper)

That's big talk, Croner – but things ain't as bad as they used to be, and they're getting better all the time. So maybe us miners would sooner be a little empty in the head than in the belly!

Breen seized every opportunity afforded by the 4 September draft of the script to emphasise the legitimacy of the miners' union (herein termed the Federated Mine Workers of America rather than the United Mine Workers).

On this same angle of industry policy, we also suggest that in Farrell's speech in scene 129 on page 62, you also include a line to the effect that working conditions in the bituminous coal fields have greatly improved, and, that while these may not be all that the miners would want them to be, they are, nevertheless, reasonable working conditions and acceptable to organized labor. In scene 132 on page 65, we suggest a strengthening of Farrell's speech by a line having him state plainly that, if the miners go back on their word, and go on strike, the company would be *justified* in invalidating the Shalerville Agreement *and employing other workers to do the work*. [35]

In Scene 132 (the revised 129) Farrell's speech appears to have been written by Breen.

It took years of struggle to make the bosses recognize the Federated Mine Workers of America. Then, two years ago, we talked things over with them and got them to sign the Shalerville Agreement. Naturally we didn't get everything we wanted but it was a good start.

In return for higher wages and better working conditions we promised that they'd have no labor trouble for the period of that agreement .... And if we go back on our word they'll throw us all out! And they'll be right. They'll go into the law courts and say, 'We got millions sunk in our mines and we can't operate them 'cause those

Union guys are too busy fighting among themselves.' And the Judge'll say, 'O.K. Tear up the Shalerville Agreement. Those guys broke their word.' And he'll be right. THEN they'll lock us out and run the mines without us – until we come crawling back, begging for anything they can pay us.

Breen's even-handedness extended to the sympathetic portrayal of the mine owners. Musmanno's sadistic Eli Gord has already become the harassed, essentially honourable Hendricks before Breen pointed out to Warner:

In scene 198, page 95, we recommend – again, under the general head of industry policy – that you have Hendricks, the President of the Company, say quite frankly to Jenkins, that he is proceeding to employ strike-breakers very *much against his will*, and have him insist with Jenkins that the police so conduct themselves as to take every possible precaution *against the abuse or mistreatment of the miners*. Again from a general policy standpoint, it will be a serious lack of judgment, if we deliberately show the employing company as condoning or approving the brutal treatment by McGee and the others. It should be established that even though this treatment follows, the responsibilty for it rests squarely upon Jenkins and McGee and *not* the employing company. Hendricks' several speeches should be carefully re-written with this point in mind. [36]

Responding to their anxieties the final shooting script contains the following speech by the Vice-President of the Coal Associates Inc.

HENDRICKS

Well, I am worried. I don't like this business of hiring outside men – it only leads to trouble. But we've got to protect our interests. For the first time in five years we have a chance to get out of the red and pay some dividends and we're not going to let them stop us. We tried to play ball with our men by granting them everything we reasonably could, but when they double cross us we're through! If they think they have a right to strike let them! (FIRMLY) We're going to open our mines and keep them open no matter what it costs!

Hendricks then worries that this might be seen as an open invitation to the police to create mayhem so he warns sternly:

Now wait a minute. Please understand that we are retaining your organization solely for the purpose of protecting our properties and keeping them in operation. (EMPHATICALLY) We will not countenance any violence on your part and will hold you strictly accountable for any abuse of your authority.

Nevertheless the very next scene shows the nature of the recruitment of the special policemen:

CAMERA PANS ALONG THE TABLE covered in Hickory maces, black-jacks, handcuffs and enormous black leather holsters.

BIG RECRUIT

This is the first time I was ever on the right side of a copper's badge!

Breen was anxious that the villains as previously circumscribed be shown to be entirely responsible for any breaches of the law.

Wherever possible, you should strive to keep away from showing either Joe, or any other of the employees, doing any very great damage to the property of the employing company. This is particularly important at the present time, with so much industrial unrest prevalent throughout the country. If you will throw the emphasis, wherever you can, on the activities of Croner, McGee, Jenkins, et al. who are the crooked agitators, and definitely away from the legitimate labor leaders, as well as the employers, it will, we think, help the story very much, and, at the same time, keep it free from any reasonable criticism in this regard.

Care was thus taken in the script to portray the apolitical racketeers in the classic manner of Hollywood villains. Croner's boss Jenkins, who has much the same relationship to Croner as had Cadman to Foster in Musmanno's original story, is first described sitting in his office at night:

C.U. FRENCH TELEPHONE ON A DESK

148 MED SHOT. INT. JENKINS OFFICE NIGHT

It is an impressively furnished walnut-paneled room .... At one end of the desk is Jenkins' right hand man, McGee. He is heavy set and powerfully built. He wears rather flashy clothes and has his hat pushed back off his low forehead. He is studying a large mounted map. It is a U.S. Geological Survey map showing several counties in an unnamed state. On the top of it has been printed in ink PROPERTIES OF COAL ASSOCIATES INC.

Perhaps the most emotional scene excised by Breen was Musmanno's original, factual account of the sadistic eviction of the miners from their company houses.

It might be as well, also, if you do not actually need it, to delete entirely scene 226 on page 108, in which the company carpenters deliberately hack away at the roof of Mike's house solely for the purpose of getting Mike out of the place. This is a very serious reflection on the employing company, which it might be well for you to pass up .... We would be glad to read the final script before you go into production. [37]

Breen's advice was duly heeded.

At the climax of the film the action moves to Washington as a newspaper headline proclaims 'Government Steps In To Settle Coal Strike'. This is in marked contrast to Musmanno's original story in which the government assumed a less active role. The government's stated resolve to 'prosecute such criminal parasites' is sufficient to induce Muni to leave the mine with the villainous McGee whom he has already captured in single combat. McGee is hauled off to stand trial for the murder of the John Barcoski character and Muni is chaired in triumph by the united band of celebrating miners as his girlfriend watches in admiration. This contrasts with the original Musmanno version in which the hero is immediately prosecuted for destroying private property and sent to prison. Since Warner Brothers had already taken pains to avoid any such destruction, they could justifiably present the audience with the traditional happy ending.

It might be reasonably supposed that Musmanno would have divorced himself entirely from the finished film since it was so far removed from his original aims. Instead he positively embraced it, travelling with it as it was shown throughout Pennsylvania with the specific intention of overturning the Governor's veto of his bill. The audiences were shown the film, heard Musmanno speak and were then urged to write to their Congressmen indicating their support for the Musmanno Bill which was to abolish the Coal and Iron Police. [38]

The climate for such legislation was very different in 1935 than it had been when the Bill had originally been introduced during the time of the Hoover Administration. *Black Fury*'s cautious endorsement of the company union was in step with the general current policy of the Roosevelt Administration. Not until June 1935, three months after the release of *Black Fury*, did the National Labor Relations Act become law and Roosevelt's personal support of Senator Wagner, the Bill's chief sponsor, was a belated tactical move. The Musmanno Bill eventually passed both Houses of the Pennsylvania Legislature for the second time and was signed into law by Governor George H. Earle. [39]

Pressure on Warner Brothers not to deviate from their stated policy was maintained even while the picture was still shooting. On 2 November Hays wrote to Myron C. Taylor of the United States Steel Corporation:

> Copy of the memorandum to you of the 31st ultimo in regard to the proposed picture *Black Hell* is just now received.
>
> The possibility of worry in connection with this picture has not been without thought. Messrs. Warner Brothers have it definitely in mind, both as to the picture itself and the publicity, and our own office in Hollywood is in touch with it.
>
> Both Harry M. Warner, President of the company who is here, and Mr Jack L. Warner, vice president in charge of production on the Coast, have assured me that they will exercise the greatest care in production.

I am enclosing original correspondence which you might note with interest and then kindly return.[40]

Hays sent Taylor copies of letters between Breen and himself, Breen and Jack Warner, Harry Warner and himself, Battle and himself as well as the initial letter from Battle which had started the correspondence.

On 6 February 1935 as the film was being edited, scored and dubbed ready for its release the following month, R. H. Sherwood of the Central Indiana Coal Company wrote to Hays indicating further anxiety on behalf of the coal operators. Hays replied five days later:

> I am sure the company is earnestly endeavouring to have the picture free from objectionable matter.
>
> I have had a number of talks myself with Mr Warner, President of the Company, and with our Production Code Administration on the Coast, and the Production Code Administration has had many conversations with the studio personnel in charge of the undertaking, has read the various scripts, and a few days ago saw the completed picture, and advise that in their opinion it is free from any reasonable objection.
>
> I am sure all interested parties have undertaken to make certain not only of the authenticity of any presentations, but that there shall be nothing in the picture to which proper objection can be taken.[41]

Even during its previews the picture was bedevilled by unwelcome controversy. On 26 March, days before it was due to open in New York, the State Censorship Board was threatening to ban the film because of the persistent fear of encouraging disorder in the ranks of organised labour. Breen wrote to his opposite number in New York, Dr James J. Wingate, attaching copies of good reviews for the film which had appeared that day in the trade papers, *Variety* and *The Hollywood Reporter*.

> I direct your attention to the unwonted enthusiasm with which the local critics have greeted this fine picture. I send these along because I think the New York Board ought to take these comments into consideration in forming their judgment on this picture. These comments are so strikingly similar in estimating the importance of the picture and so unusually intelligent, that they cannot be dismissed lightly.
>
> How a picture, so thoroughly acceptable as this, can be in danger to the extent which you suggested over the telephone yesterday, is simply incredible. It is my personal thought that if this kind of picture cannot be shown on the screen, the industry might as well fold up.
>
> This is no cheap, trite story, but a dignified document dealing with a legitimate subject that is certain to be of great interest to everybody. To suggest that we must continue to follow a set formula, arbitrarily established, to tell a story of this kind is, in my judgment, stretching things pretty far.

.... True it is that the brutalizing racketeers are deputy sheriffs or 'peace officers'. But, despite this, they are still racketeers – definite criminals, if you please – who come to be 'peace officers' by dishonest and fraudulent methods. Those who are responsible for the presence of these 'peace officers' are the very men who have instigated and fomented all the disorder and strife.

Maybe there is some misgiving about the labor disorder which is shown in the picture. But here, again, you have disorder brought about by criminal racketeers – and not by labor men. The labor fellows are represented as thoroughly sound and sensible, and on the side of peace, law and order. It is the criminals who are the fomenters of all the trouble.

I certainly hope that the censor board in New York will not involve itself in the rejection of this picture. The picture is not only a good picture – it is a *great* picture. We shall hear much more about it, I am sure, and the whole cause of political censorship is certain to be materially injured by any such rejection. [42]

Breen clearly was fighting other battles than those of *Black Fury* alone, and he could see that, if the New York Board was going to reject a picture whose teeth his office had laboured mightily to extract, it would inevitably make his task more difficult when a genuinely 'subversive' picture came his way.

It appears that Wingate must have been unable to persuade the New York Censorship Board of Breen's views since three days later on 29 March Breen wrote again to him, relating the genesis of the project and the detail of his unstinting efforts to remove all traces of Musmanno's original conception from the shooting script.

The story is a very honest story – in fact, too honest, if one were to become analytical, because, in actual life, from what experience I have had, the miners would have done much more to the mines than they do in this picture .... In ordinary life there would be a thousand miners doing what Joe does, in order to protect themselves from the brutalizing force of the special police ....

I am fearful that if the New York Board seriously interferes with this picture, there is certain to follow a very definite unfavorable reaction to that act. I talked with Hal Wallis about the thing, and he is infuriated. He tells me, also, that a number of the boards to which the picture has been submitted have passed it, and he is at a loss to understand the possible unfavorable reaction of the New York Board.

I think you ought to see the picture again if you can and study it. It is an important picture and you are going to hear much about it. It is just possible that the trouble the company is having with the New York Board may be the spark which will ignite a terrific row, and we ought to be thoroughly alive to the situation. [43]

Eventually the lobbying by the Hays Office proved effective enough to ensure that the picture opened at the Strand Theater two weeks later than planned but uncut. Like New York, film censorship boards in Alberta, Ontario, Maryland and Ohio demanded the elimination of scenes depicting police brutality, although Pennsylvania censors, who might have been supposed to have been the readiest to take offence, passed it without a single cut.

The same pattern was discernible overseas where various censorship bodies found *Black Fury*, even in its diluted condition, to be too inflammatory for public consumption. In Peru the film was banned because of its mob scenes. Other countries demanded the excision of what they regarded as statements of radical propaganda and the British Board of Film Censors insisted on the removal of a speech by Croner in which he makes explicit reference to the unfair relationship between the men and their exploitative union leaders. [44]

Although *Black Fury* looks like a fraud of a picture to a sophisticated audience of the 1990s, especially when contrasted with plays that could be seen in New York in the mid-1930s like Clifford Odets's *Waiting for Lefty* or *Black Pit* by Albert Maltz, it clearly retained enough of its original radicalism to disturb authorities all over the world. In this light it is perhaps understandable that many critics accepted the illusory radicalism. The *New York Evening Journal* declared: 'The Warner Brothers studios, which, more than any other are alive to topical subjects, have made of it an important and courageous document.' [45] Even the normally perceptive critic of *New Republic*, Otis Ferguson, reported that *Black Fury* was more powerful than Pudovkin's classic struggle of the committed revolutionary, *Mother* (1926), because it had

> direct and hard hitting action where action is needed. *Black Fury* has this motion and sway of life whatever we may think of its social content (and from the row being kicked up on several sides we may think some very thoughtful things indeed) .... If we must talk of greatness, it is about time the men responsible for this picture were given the inside rail. [46]

To Andre Sennwald in the *New York Times* the film's power was undiminished by any of the compromises that had been forced on it.

> Some of us cannot help regretting the film's insistent use of the whitewash brush, which enables it to be in several editorial places at the same time. But when we realize that *Black Fury* was regarded by the State Censor Board as an inflammatory social document and that it has been banned in several sectors we ought to understand that Warner Brothers exhibited almost a reckless air of courage in producing the picture at all .... Both in Michael Curtiz's direction and in the screen play by Abem Finkel and Carl Erickson, the photoplay achieves a melodramatic vigor and an air of cumulative power which is rare in the Hollywood cinema. By all odds, *Black Fury* is the most notable American experiment in social drama since *Our Daily Bread*. [47]

Exhibitors, while differing in their reports of the amount of business done by the movie, held very much the same opinions as to its melodramatic power. One of them wrote:

> Here is a production that will cause talk and give satisfaction, but it is of such a nature that properly to advertise it would be dynamite. We are in the midst of strike trouble here and under such conditions had to soft pedal ad. copy. [48]

Generally the picture attracted substantial audiences in the industrial East but fared poorly west of the Alleghenies. It was considered too depressing, too realistic to be a huge commercial success. The picture's negative cost was assessed at $479,000 and its gross revenues at $802,000. Once the costs of distribution and exhibition were deducted it would have left a bare profit. Muni's acting, commented on everywhere with favour, gained an Academy Award nomination. [49]

The conservative undercurrents of the film were initially noted by two diverse sections of the press. On the one hand, the trade papers, as usual, reviewed the film perceptively, attuned no doubt to the changes made to Musmanno's original story by rumours of problems in the writing and production stages. On the other hand the Left-wing press, with the exception of *New Republic*, subjected it to the kind of scrutiny its staple readership of intellectual Socialists would expect should be applied to any Hollywood film which aspired to examine the worlds of capital and labour.

One of the reviews which Breen had sent to Wingate in New York included this extract from *The Hollywood Reporter*:

> The writers of the screenplay have been most circumspect in avoiding any major issues between labor and capital, and have blamed all the trouble on out-and-out racketeering. In this way Finkel and Erickson take off the odious 'propaganda' label and without resorting to too much flag waving, have written an intelligent and interesting story of a 'hunkie'. [50]

The Nation, on the other hand, bitterly resented the propaganda for conservative unionism.

> Unlike the more easily satisfied workers in this story, the intellectually alert spectator will find himself unable to content himself with the half loaf of truth which the producers throw out to him. Despite the clamor and violence and bloodshed, despite the vigorous and well-sustained movement, despite Paul Muni, he will probably conclude that such a picture is really worse than no loaf at all.

The organ of the Communist Party, *New Masses*, predictably called *Black Fury*

> a calculated attack on the rank and file movement; it portrays radicals [Communists] as *agents provocateurs* in the employ of strike-breaking

detective agencies; in addition, it is so constructed as to further confuse the millions of workers and middle class people who are already confused about the real social and political issues of today .... *Black Fury* is demagogic, untrue and malicious about the working class. [51]

Black Fury is an excellent example of the inevitably doomed attempts of film-makers in Hollywood in the 1930s who occasionally tried to use contemporary social, economic or political issues as the basis for a commercial motion picture. Let the final word on its troubled production rest with its producer, Robert Lord.

I remember that was a terribly stormy picture. Mike [Curtiz] was not 100% solid on certain scenes. He would rehearse and then he'd say, 'Get Bob'. I'd look and it wouldn't work. The actors would read *Variety* and ... we'd reschedule. The only simile I can give you is like if you're doing an appendectomy and the patient starts to die on the table .... We re-shot for six days ... and while we were editing [the co-screenwriter] poor Carl Erickson blew his brains out. I would say on the whole the picture was just about 50% as effective as it should have been .... When *Black Fury* was over I was awfully happy. [52]

11

FOREIGN AFFAIRS

Censor hit a new all-time high in his banning of My Weakness (Fox).
Flicker was tabooed because 'the lace panties on the girls would
contaminate the morals of the New Germany'.

Variety, 30 October 1934

Levels of unemployment in the United States remained high throughout the
1930s but the volume, rather than the efficacy, of government activity in
Washington helped to dispel much of the violent anger which had greeted
Roosevelt when he initially took office. The period of Roosevelt's first
administration was dominated entirely by domestic events. It was only after
his huge electoral victory over Alf Landon in 1936 that the President felt strong
enough to interest himself and his country in circumstances in Europe which
were demanding his attention.

In 1933 Ramsay MacDonald tried to get Roosevelt to commit America to a
multilateral disarmament treaty, but the President refused to jeopardise
America's right to neutrality. Davis, the Chairman of the US delegation to
the Geneva Disarmament conference in May 1933, believed that Hitler was the
'best' of all the European leaders. At the World Economic Conference in
London a few months later Roosevelt destroyed the possibility of world
monetary stability by his insistence on economic nationalism and a managed
economy – a view supported by Keynes.[1]

In 1935 the Senate rejected the proposal that America should join the World
Court and passed Pittman's Neutrality Resolution which prohibited the
export of munitions from the United States. This determined isolationism
was partly the logical continuation of the refusal to join the League of Nations
in 1920 and partly a response to the findings of the Nye Committee's
investigations into the munitions industry which had started in 1934. The
risk of the United States becoming embroiled in an international war was thus
greatly reduced but by the same token it could be argued that such a policy
encouraged the aggressor nations to be more aggressive.

The rise of Fascism and Nazism in Europe was an obvious testing ground
for conflict between the producers and their radical employees in Hollywood.

The first major confrontation came with the Spanish Civil War. A documentary compilation of its horrors, *Spain in Flames* (1937), quickly ran into trouble with the authorities. It was banned by the Ohio and Pennsylvania state censorship boards as 'pure Communistic propaganda, dressed up as a plea for democracy'. *Variety* was also disgusted by the war but for its own idiosyncratic reasons. 'With war in Spain having butchered a million people in the past year, it is becoming increasingly difficult to get romance into musicals with a war setting.'[2]

In the ranks of the feature film the Spanish Civil War was notable for its almost complete absence. Even in the two movies which were made at the time the war itself kept a low profile for perfectly sound practical reasons. Paramount made *The Last Train from Madrid* (1937) only after much interference from the Hays Office. *The New York Times* advised that the film should not be taken 'too literally or too seriously. True, it treats of the Spanish revolution, but merely as Hollywood has in the past regarded the turmoils of Ruritania and Zenda.'[3]

Universal's projected (and appropriately titled) *Delay in the Sun* and Twentieth Century Fox's *Alcazar* both died a quiet death, having been refused permission to live on their knees.[4] Walter Wanger's *Blockade* (1938) was the only other contemporary Hollywood film to deal with the Spanish Civil War. The movie had a predictably troubled prehistory which fatally compromised the finished product. Initially the Dartmouth-educated Wanger, known as a maverick producer with a political if not radical interest, had asked Clifford Odets and the director Lewis Milestone to work on an updated version of Ilya Ehrenburg's book *The Loves of Jeanne Ney*.

The new film version was to be known as *The River Is Blue* and followed the fortunes of expatriate Spaniards who return to their country in its time of trouble. When the script got bogged down, Wanger, on the advice of Harold Clurman, a director of the Group Theater and at that time working as an assistant to the Hollywood producer, called out John Howard Lawson from New York. Lawson immediately dispensed with the Milestone and Odets treatment and began afresh, inventing the idea of a blockade of a Spanish port. To make it palatable he included the story of the conversion to the cause of committed humanitariansim by a beautiful female spy.[5]

From the outset *Blockade* never stood a chance of becoming the outspoken and courageous document that Wanger had hoped to oversee. In February 1937, while the script was being prepared, Joseph Breen, the Production Code Administrator, advised Wanger solemnly that

> It might be as well for you in shooting this picture not to definitely identify any of the combatants with either faction of the Spanish Civil war. This means that you ought not to definitely identify by means of uniform or otherwise, the soldiers actively participating in the fracas.[6]

Six days later Breen reported with evident satisfaction to Hays that the picture 'is the first to use the Spanish revolution as a background. The studio [*sic*] has taken great pains not to take sides in the matter.'[7] Breen also warned Wanger that

> any material involved with or played against the background of the present civil war in Spain is, in our opinion, highly dangerous from a practical standpoint as well as distribution in Europe ... this picture ... may be pretty generally booted about in Europe by those governments which may be 'for' or 'against' the parties engaged in the war.[8]

Breen persistently stressed that the film must be completely fictional, so that 'none of the *incidents* or *locations* in your story could possibly be tied in with the actual events that have occurred or are occurring in Spain'.[9] At this point the film was known as *Castles in Spain*. It was subsequently known as *The Rising Tide, The Adventuress, The River Is Blue* as well as the initial *The Loves of Jeanne Ney* and the final *Blockade*.[10] The occasional change of title is frequently the result of interference from the Sales Department. In this case it appears symbolic of the film's inability to focus on anything specific for any period of time.

The final shooting script already contained those compromises which destroyed the honesty of its original conception. Wanger was possibly the most adventurous independent producer in Hollywood at the time; Lawson was the key mover in the Screen Writers' Guild and the Hollywood Communist Party in the late 1930s. Together they made a film which contained no verbal or visual clues that gave the prospective audience the slightest idea about what was happening in the Spanish Civil War.

Breen kept up a barrage of correspondence to Wanger so that the producer was never at any time under any misapprehension about the policy of the Hays Office.

> You will of course be careful not to identify at any time the uniforms of the soldiers shown throughout the story. You will have in mind that your picture is certain to run into considerable difficulty in Europe and South America, if there is any indication in the telling of your story that you are 'taking sides' in the present unfortunate Spanish Civil War. It is imperative that you do not, at any time, identify any of the warring factions.[11]

It is, in this light, understandable that *Blockade* is a predictable mess of missed opportunities whose basic message is that the land belongs to the peasants. Henry Fonda plays Marco, a peasant in a land one assumes is not too far distant from Spain, when the valley in which he lives is attacked, for no very apparent reason, by nameless invaders, who one can only assume are the troops of General Franco. Marco meets and is captivated by a beautiful woman (played by Madeleine Carroll) who is working for her father as a commercial spy. Marco pierces the father's disguise, follows him home and in a struggle kills him. At the time he is unaware of the relationship between this man and the woman who bitterly castigates the hero on discovering the body of her murdered father. In his defence he pulls out a snapshot of the countryside. 'That's why I'm fighting,' he explains.

Understandably the Madeleine Carroll character no longer wishes to pursue her inherited career but before she can leave the profession she is commanded to deliver a message to the blockaded port of Castelmar which will help to destroy the province. However, a haunting encounter with the starving population makes her regret having passed on the message which will enable a submarine of an unknown power, but whose crew probably speaks German, to emerge and sink a vital supply ship in sight of the port.

In the most moving scene in the film the old peasants and other workers gather on the shore to watch what they assume is the supply ship sinking, taking with it their hopes of survival. Miss Carroll, appalled by the monstrosity of her crime, cries out, 'I'm a traitor. Not to my country, because I have no country, but to the people here.' Marco and she then discover that the villains of the piece are double agents working (presumably) for the Fascists, while serving as top officials (presumably) for the Loyalists. Fortunately it transpires that the supposed supply ship was an empty decoy and the real supply ship is now steaming into harbour to lift the blockade.

As Carroll and Fonda prepare to die the (presumably) Loyalist Commander arrives, saves the couple, orders the arrest of the traitors and offers Fonda a month's leave in recognition of his sterling service. The hero replies as the camera tracks into a big close up.

> Leave? You go on leave to find peace – away from the front – but where would you find it? the front is everywhere – They've turned our country into a battlefield. There's no safety for old people and children ... the churches, schools and hospitals are targets. It's not war – war is between soldiers – this is murder ... we've got to stop it. Stop the murder of innocent people. The world can stop it. Where is the conscience of the world?

Thirty-five years later Fonda recalled the speech as

> the only thing left that was controversial – and you couldn't complain about it .... The Legion of Decency, the Catholic Church, everybody you could think of was putting pressure on [Wanger]. Before we went into it anything that might have been controversial was eliminated from the story. There wasn't any suggestion that they were Loyalists. They were just Spaniards .... It was not the picture that Walter Wanger had thought of making. It was taken away from him.[12]

Nevertheless, when the film was released in June 1938, eighteen months after the first script had been shown to the Hays Office, it still aroused fierce hostility. One trade paper found it

> a frank, direct and somewhat courageous indictment of war in the name of entertainment, done with a candor which is surprising when considering a world film market become exceedingly sensitive to the screen's political influence.

The reviewer added that he wondered 'how much of Walter Wanger and how much of the Hays Office the final result represents'. [13]

The nervousness of the Hays Office can be understood in the light of a letter it received from Joseph H. Lamb, the New York state Deputy of the Knights of Columbus, soon after the opening of *Blockade*.

> The picture is historically false and intellectually dishonest. It is a polemic for the Marxist controlled cause in Spain, which would ruthlessly destroy Christian civilisation. Particularly in view of the well known sympathies of some of those associated with the picture and of the fact that a definite phase of Marxist strategy is to acquire a controlling influence over the cinema, this red trial balloon should be punctured. [14]

Hays's attempts to reason with the Knights of Columbus were given short shrift. The agency ensured that it was banned in various cities in Nebraska, Louisiana and Ohio, and further complained to the Hays Office that

> when a government such as that in Spain today, consisting of real Communists, Anarchists and even Atheists, is held up as a champion of democracy through such a picture as *Blockade*, it becomes an insult to the intelligence of democratic peoples. [15]

Even the opening of the film was controversial. According to Lawson it was scheduled to be premiered at one of the big Hollywood cinemas

> but at the last minute, the opening was stopped by political pressure. Copies of the script and the film itself were being sent to Paris and to London for consultation with important political figures there .... The picture had not been substantially changed. Only minor cuts and re-arrangements had been made. The film was not slashed and it was not censored heavily but it was changed to please the reactionary political elements in Paris and London. [16]

Although this sounds like conventional Left-wing demonology and/or an attempt to justify a fatally flawed script thirty-five years after it had been written, the recollection ought to be taken in the context of the correspondence surrounding the making of this film which lies in the files of the Hays Office and has been previously quoted at length.

Blockade eventually opened in a small theatre in Westwood village, while the

Fox West Coast theatre chain, after urgent demands from Catholic pressure groups, declined to screen it at all.[17] The Catholics, because of their identification with anyone fighting the despised atheistic Loyalists, were the most bitter opponents of the film. *The Catholic News* accused the film of being 'subtle foreign political propaganda', *The Catholic Worker* called for a boycott, if not actual picketing, of the film wherever it was shown and in Flint, Michigan, the hostility of the local Catholic priest caused the film to be withdrawn after just two days. The priest later admitted that he had not actually seen the film.[18]

Despite the furore, however, the majority of people who did see the film crushed it in quite the most effective way. One exhibitor wrote, 'This was the controversial picture that was supposed to reek of Communism. Naturally I watched it closely and for the life of me I can't see where the shots of Communism crept in.'[19] One happy manager in North Dakota reported that his patrons made no effort to rip up the seats, while an exhibitor in Ozark, Alabama, wrote in evident confusion: 'Who was who? What was what? And why was why?'[20]

In England *The Daily Telegraph* called the plot 'just situation C3 in Hollywood's card index' and C. A. Lejeune, the noted critic of *The Observer*, equally damned its radical pretensions.

> The film is careful to identify no party in the conflict but is full of broadly humane theories that will get a round of applause .... The heroine gives up spying when she learns that she is part of Something Bigger Than We Are. The villain's gilded temptations confine themselves to offers of tea, cigarettes and biscuits.[21]

Blockade should be regarded as being in the mainstream of Hollywood's radical pictures, flawed by a compromise written into its structure. It suffers from Lawson's ponderous attempts to write what he called a 'humanistic'[22] rather than an overtly political picture. Unfortunately, neither the script nor the acting of Madeleine Carroll carry too much conviction, and Fonda and Dieterle, despite some neat touches, are no way near their best form. Andre Sennwald in *The New York Times* summed up the affair, when he concluded his report on what he also felt was an unsatisfactory picture by pointing out:

> If it expresses an honest hatred of war, if it deplores the bombing of civilian populations, and if it closes with an appeal to the conscience of the world, it is doing the most we can expect an American picture to do .... Mr. Wanger has displayed rare courage in going even so far ... he will probaby be punished for his temerity.[23]

Sennwald was right. Wanger had expected to run into difficulty in some foreign markets, but he was shaken by the reception *Blockade* was accorded in the United States.[24] During the shooting he had engaged Lawson and Dieterle to collaborate on a story about a Jewish doctor and his flight from persecution in Nazi Germany. It was to be an adaptation of Vincent Sheean's *Personal History*. Lawson has rueful memories of it.

> Just before it was to go into production, the sets were built and the actors were all engaged, Wanger called us in … and he was really deeply troubled. He said, 'The whole thing is off. I have to get my money from banks and I'm told I'll never get another penny if this anti-Nazi film goes into production'. [25]

The banks had clearly been alarmed by the reception given to *Blockade* and decided that they could not risk a further loss on another political picture. *Personal History* resurfaced two years later, heavily rewritten, as Hitchcock's *Foreign Correspondent*.

As late as 1943 RKO were forced to change the background setting of *The Fallen Sparrow* from the Spanish Civil War in 1938 to the safer territory of Nazi Occupied France in 1940. Robert Fellows, the producer of the film, was informed by the studio executive, William Gordon, that the State Department still desired friendly relations with the Spanish government as there was a remote possibility that Spain might be induced to join the Allies in the war against Germany. In any case the picture with a Spanish setting might be offensive to the Latin American market which had emerged with renewed importance after the closure of the European sales outlets. Joseph Breen was also at the heart of these urgings and although Fellows did his best to resist such blandishments he also agreed to shoot protective cover in the scenes where reference was made to the Spanish Civil War. [26]

The interest taken in foreign affairs by the major studios before 1939 was largely restricted to what they considered to be the capricious and indiscriminate banning of their pictures. In May 1936 Hitler banned the films of the following stars because of their non-Aryan lineage: Fred Astaire, Ginger Rogers, Mae West, George Arliss, Johnny Weissmuller and Warner Oland. Arliss had notably played the roles of the famous Jews Disraeli, Shylock and Rothschild. Oland had been the star of the *Charlie Chan* series and Weissmuller, despite his cavortings in the jungle as Tarzan, was obviously of Jewish descent. Mae West was once heard saying 'Ish Kabibble', but the links of Astaire and Rogers with anything remotely Jewish were never discovered. [27]

Fox glumly accepted the banning in Germany of their film My Weakness, because of the corrupting effect of its displayed lingerie, but they retaliated to the dismissal of *Country Doctor* by digging through the records to prove that Jean Hersholt, whose appearance in the movie was apparently at the root of the prohibition, was untainted by Jewish ancestry. [28] The Germans were unconvinced and the ban remained in force. Buried in the correspondence between the Hays Office and Warner Brothers on the subject of the script for *Angels With Dirty Faces* is a recommendation from Breen to Jack Warner suggesting that Warners cut the line 'I'm boycotting Germany'. [29] It was one of the few

Hays Office recommendations that Warners as a matter of studio policy did not contest.

If the Spanish Civil War was a somewhat abstract, moral issue (there were few Spanish refugees in Hollywood or producers with Spanish relatives), the question of anti-Nazism seriously engaged the attentions of many people in Hollywood. The large Jewish community in Hollywood joined with the Gentiles, who were also outraged at reports of what the Nazis were doing, to form the Anti-Nazi League. Paul Muni, Lewis Milestone, Donald Ogden Stewart, Fredric March and Florence Eldridge, who had been among those donating money for ambulances to Spain, were again among the activists, but this time they were joined by Ernst Lubitsch, Eddie Cantor and Sylvia Sidney, among others. Up to the signing of the Nazi–Soviet Pact, the Anti-Nazi League drew its power from the fact that it coalesced the Communists, the Liberals and the concerned Jews, but after the Pact the unity was dispelled and the League changed its name to the League For Democracy. [30]

When Hitler marched into Prague in March 1939 *Variety* saw in it only

an additional blow to the American companies' foreign film income . . . .
For these major companies [Paramount, MGM and Fox], the German
sweep through Central Europe this month represents a loss of 2.5% to 3%
of the total foreign business. [31]

As late as July 1940, with German troops in control of much of the continent, Paramount was reluctant to abandon the lucrative markets of Occupied Europe. Mitchell Leisen, the director, was told to shoot two versions of *Arise, My Love*, one for release in countries sympathetic to Nazi Germany and one for release elsewhere. In the original script by Charles Brackett and Billy Wilder, the process of dictatorship was treated with the writers' particular brand of cynicism which was then toned down in the revised version to a level presumed to be acceptable to the Nazis. [32]

The most successful, in both artistic and financial terms, of the pictures which in some measure dealt with issues of foreign policy at this time were the Warner Brothers' series of biographies of great nineteenth-century figures of progress. After a year of playing 'humble' men (*Bordertown*, *Black Fury* and *Dr Socrates*), Paul Muni returned to his larger-than-life characterisations. In *The Story of Louis Pasteur* (1936) he portrayed the great scientist, battling against disease, ignorance and obstinacy and championing the cure for anthrax in livestock by inoculation and experimenting to find the cure for hydrophobia. The film balances its ringing declarations of the relationship between science and the future of humanity, with scenes of Pasteur's solicitous wife refusing to let business interfere with his digestion, clucking round him as he prepares to head back to the laboratory with the admonition, 'Louis, really, you know you haven't closed your eyes in forty eight hours'. The film proved to be a sound commercial proposition, although one reviewer, while appreciating that the anthrax and rabies cures were historically important, bewailed the fact that Warners had missed a golden opportunity to exploit 'the childbirth angle'. [33]

The Life of Emile Zola (1937), with much the same production team, approached the question of relating the theme of the picture to contemporary circumstances with a little more courage. Its original title was *Truth is on the March*, and a treatment was written as early as July 1936 by Geza Herczeg and Heinz Herald. Sending it to Wallis and Warner they added a note of explanation.

> This film is not an ordinary biography, it contains far more: the eternal, ceaseless fight for freedom and right. The right, basis of all human society, represents the equilibrium of the world. If this equilibrium is ever put out of balance it shakes the entire world. It is immaterial whether it happens in Germany or Turkey. It is the proclamation of an eternal hope, an eternal faith, which is classically expressed in his [Zola's] own words: LA VERITEE EN MARCHE .... 'The truth is on the march and nothing can stop it!' We think that it had [sic] never been more timely than today to know this, see it and hear it. [34]

Although the film starts with the successful rise of Zola as a novelist, its main body is devoted to Zola's defence of Dreyfus, who is languishing in prison on Devil's Island after being framed by the army establishment. The key scene is Zola's trial for having accused the Esterhazy court martial of acquitting the man responsible for the crime for which Dreyfus has been sentenced. The judges in their ceremonial robes, seated on a raised platform, look more like avenging furies than impartial dispensers of justice. Their refusal to admit the Dreyfus case as evidence and the conspiracy of the army high command are obviously meant to parallel some of the actions of the Nazis.

Zola's speech to the jury is a magnificent piece of acting, showing Paul Muni at his very best. Dropping his voice to a whisper, raising it tremulously to declare his belief in Dreyfus's innocence, he concludes: 'By all that I have written to spread the spirit of France, I swear that Dreyfus is innocent. May all that melt away – may my name perish – if Dreyfus be not innocent. He is innocent.' When Dreyfus (played by Joseph Schildkraut) is eventually released from prison, he walks through the door and out into the sunlight, and then repeats the process twice, to assure himself that he is really free, a sequence which does not appear in the shooting script. The film ends with Zola's funeral at which Anatole France (Morris Carnovsky) delivers the oration.

> You, who are enjoying today's freedom, take to your hearts the words of Zola. Do not forget those who fought the battles for you and bought your liberty with their genius and their blood. Do not forget them and applaud the lies of fanatical intolerance .... He [Zola] knew that there is no serenity save in justice. No repose save in truth.

The reaction from reviewers and exhibitors was one of high praise for the film's dignity and solemnity of purpose. Even Joseph Breen, after warning that no reference should be made in the script to *Madame Bovary* and *The Confessions of Claude* because they were 'looked upon by many people as pornographic',[35] wrote to Jack Warner after seeing the finished film: 'This is a magnificent picture and quite outstanding. Not in a long while have we seen anything which is so profoundly impressive and interesting. Congratulations!'[36] *The New York Times* proclaimed it

> at once the finest historical film ever made and the greatest screen biography ... it has achieved this brilliant end without self-consciousness, without strutting glorification, without throwing history out of focus.[37]

An English critic pointed to the fact that 'Like so many of the Warner Brothers' productions it has its message, the necessity of upholding individual liberty and inevitable triumph of democratic justice'.[38] An exhibitor in Pierre, South Dakota, reported happily:

> Was afraid of this for my small town situation. Didn't need to be as I found that even the lower classes enjoyed it. The picture is well deserving of its rating as the Best Picture of 1937.[39]

The film was a financial as well as an artistic triumph. Budgeted at $700,000, it ran over by $130,000 but grossed more than $2 million. By comparison, *Pasteur* had cost less than $400,000 but grossed only $1,187,000. *Zola* clearly sold well all round the world although Hays Office files observe that it frequently ran into difficulties. At the end of August 1938 it was noted that although Peru had previously banned the film the country's censors had been persuaded to pass the film with all the cuts restored but only on condition that it was exhibited in a maximum of five cinemas in Lima and at a 25 per cent increase in admission price in an attempt to discourage the attendance of the diasffected masses.[40]

This would appear to protect the film against the criticism that, worthy as *The Life of Emile Zola* undoubtedly is, it was conceived as a modern statement, yet felt the need to disguise itself as historical romance. More to the point, as Frank Nugent wrote: 'The picture skirts the real issues behind the Dreyfus case (the word "Jew" is never uttered) and skips recklessly over the political, racial background of the plot.'[41] By ignoring the anti-Semitism of the Dreyfus case, the film automatically renounces the right to make an effective statement on current anti-Semitism in Nazi Germany and has to resort to the noble but somewhat abstract funeral oration. Once more the Hollywood desire to avoid offence turned what might have been a forthright radical expression into a muddled compromise, albeit a compromise which in no way diminished the film's artistic stature. Predictably, at the annual Academy Awards the picture won three Oscars, which somehow managed to elevate its importance as a document of courageous honesty.

For the next Muni saga, *Juarez* (1939), the story of the struggle between

Maximilian Hapsburg and Benito Juarez, President of Mexico, the Warner Brothers' press release showed no reluctance to reveal the analogies of nineteenth-century Mexico with twentieth-century history.

> In the year 1939, there are leaders whose principles are those of authority, whose selfish interests demand conquests, opposing heroes whose love of liberty demands equal rights for all .... Like Benito Juarez, the lives of Jan Masaryk and Eduard Benes [leaders of the recently Nazi Occupied Czechoslovakia] are dominated by the principles of democracy .... The theme of the picture, that democracy can make no condescensions to the most benevolent authoritarianism is significant to the present day world. [42]

The movie opens with Napoleon III (Claude Rains) predicting the success of the Confederacy at the impending Battle of Gettysburg, thereby instantly proclaiming his stupidity. Juarez, in retreat before the French army, receives a letter of support from Lincoln, when news of the President's assassination is brought to him. Juarez stands silently on a hill, communing with Nature. The United States emerges as the only country to refuse to recognise Maximilian's *de facto* regime, and sends no representative to the Emperor's coronation.

Maximilian is shown to be serious, well-intentioned and entirely above playing the role of puppet king for the benefit of the vested interests of the large landowners. He tries hard to bridge the gap betwen himself and Juarez by offering the latter the position of Prime Minister and then freeing Juarez's captured lieutenant, Diaz (John Garfield). Diaz reports that 'only a word – democracy' stands between the two men's ideas of how to rule Mexico justly and fairly. Muni echoes the phrase softly. 'Only a word ... but it is an unbridgeable gulf – irreconcilable principles. When a monarch misrules, he changes the people. When a President misrules, the people change him.' In the end Maximilian is captured by Juarez and shot, but before he dies he explains to an aide that, by executing him, Juarez has proved that his desire is for the peace of Mexico not for the plaudits of the world.

In financial terms *Juarez* proved to be much less successful than its two predecessors. It cost nearly $1,500,000 to produce and took only $1,169,000 in North America and a poor $463,000 in overseas rentals. Once the distribution costs are added *Juarez* would appear to have lost money. However, *Variety* reported that the film played to packed houses in Bombay, where the Indians no doubt appreciated the homilies on the importance of home rule and national sovereignty. More significantly, the trade paper also reported that Warners were now more likely to make pictures of this type rather than utilising the style they had employed in *Confessions of a Nazi Spy*, which was a sensational semi-documentary exposé of the German–American Bund. [43]

Although Warners were fond of defending their biographical series as bold stands of anti-Fascism, the lesson to be drawn from *Juarez* and the others was that the basic reference for American foreign policy was still the Monroe Doctrine. The significant inference to be drawn from the picture which was relevant to the world situation in 1939 was that America was prepared to fight only to defend its immediate interests.

To a large extent Hollywood's pusillanimous approach to foreign affairs in these years was in keeping with the pusillanimous foreign policy of the United States and the Great Powers of Europe. In 1935 the US Congress passed the Neutrality Laws and the League of Nations failed to prevent the Italian invasion of Abyssinia. In 1936 Hitler re-occupied the Rhineland. In 1937 German bombs obliterated Guernica and Congress passed its Third Neutrality Act.

On 5 October 1937 Roosevelt was finally stirred to a response. Disturbed by the Japanese assault on Shanghai and increasing evidence of the dangers posed by the growing Rome–Berlin *rapprochement*, the President made his most outspoken speech to date in Chicago, the capital of the isolationist heartland. He warned that if aggression triumphed elsewhere in the world America would inevitably be drawn into the conflict and in one of the phrases which would now be referred to as a 'soundbite' he called for the aggressor nations to be 'quarantined'. Isolationist Senators and the powerful Hearst press called for the President's impeachment and almost immediately Roosevelt began to falter. Within days he told journalists, 'Look, "sanctions" is a terrible word to use. They are out of the window.' [44]

The most consistently anti-Nazi studio and therefore the one most confused by the vagaries of the President's foreign policy was Warner Brothers. In the mid-1930s the chief salesman of Warner Brothers in Germany was murdered by Nazi thugs in a Berlin backstreet. Jack Warner wrote: 'Like many an outnumbered Jew he was trapped in an alley. They hit him with fists and clubs and then kicked the life out of him with their boots and left him lying there.' [45] It is a reasonable starting point as an explanation for the studio's fervent anti-Nazi behaviour, although a recent doctoral dissertation and Doherty's book *Projections of War* have both complained that they have uncovered no evidence that any such murder ever took place. [46] However, an alternative explanation for Warners' political stance has not emerged, not is it clear why Jack Warner would choose to invent such a fantasy.

Whatever the real reason, Warners' sales office in Germany was closed down as early as July 1934, although Paramount, Fox and MGM were still operating there in 1939. When the *March of Time* episode called *Nazi Conquest No. 1* was offered for sale, Warners refused to buy it. [47] Harry Warner took a grim pleasure in putting out a series of unprofitable patriotic shorts dealing with great moments in American history. The fact that Warners willingly sacrificed money for prestige was genuine proof of the sincerity of their patriotism. When the war was going badly for the Allies, after the fall of France in 1940, Jack Warner issued a fascinating order forbidding any employee to speak German for the duration of the war. 'At least one producer and a few department heads', reported Variety, 'have gone back to the old practise of counting ten before they burst into speech.'[48]

Harry and Jack Warner disliked each other intensely but on the issue of raising money to save Jews from Nazism they appeared equally committed. The writer Alvah Bessie in his autobiography recalls a private fund-raising rally for the United Jewish Appeal in the studio boardroom compulsorily attended by every Jewish producer, writer, actor and director on the lot. Jack Warner stood behind the table brandishing a rubber truncheon which he periodically smashed on to the table in front of him.

> 'I've been looking at the results of the Jewish Appeal drive and believe you me, they ain't good .... Everybody's gonna double his contribution here and now – or else!' The rubber truncheon crashed on the table again as everyone present reached for their checkbook.[49]

At a similar occasion Hal Wallis, the non-Jewish Executive Producer, rose to make a magnanimous pledge. The next day he called one of the functionaries and asked to reduce the amount. According to Bill Schaefer, Jack Warner's executive secretary, when Warner got to hear of this the ensuing disagreement became as important in Wallis's eventual acrimonious departure from the studio as the more notorious public row over the credit for the success of *Casablanca*.[50]

On the other hand the brothers were also capable of their own magnanimous gestures. Rudi Fehr, a film editor, started work for Warner Brothers in 1936 and recalled that the studio

> had this strong anti-Nazi drive. I was from Berlin. I had very strong feelings about that, so I gave a week's salary, a big $60. About ten days after I sent the check in, I got a note from Harry Warner. 'Rudi, I just looked up the payroll. I'm hereby returning your check. Please tear the check up and give me a check for $10.' That was unheard of for the head of a company.[51]

It is therefore no coincidence that much the most impressive anti-Nazi document to be made in Hollywood before America's entry into the war was Warners' *Confessions of a Nazi Spy* (1939), which was adapted from the published experiences of a former FBI agent, Leon G. Turrou, who had resigned from the Bureau and sold the story of how he had cracked a Nazi spy ring hidden inside the ranks of one of the German–American Bunds. Robert Lord, the producer of the film, recalled that the director, Anatole Litvak, contrary to his usual practice, came to the studio half an hour before the first shot of the day was to be made; Edward G. Robinson, the star of the picture, was 'immensely co-operative' and John Wexley and Milton Krims, the writers and part of the radical fringe, behaved with admirable consideration. 'Everyone on the picture was just extremely helpful,' he concluded. 'We all wanted to make it.'[52]

According to a letter to Joseph Breen from Luigi Luraschi who worked in the foreign sales department at Paramount's New York office, such a project was dangerous in the extreme.

> I feel sure if the picture is made and is in any way uncomplimentary to Germany, as it must be if it is to be sincerely produced, then Warners will have on their hands the blood of a great many Jews in Germany. If they are willing to call this smart showmanship then I imagine they must know what they are about. [53]

Predictably, such a response found an immediate echo in the Hays Office. Its initial comments on the first draft of the script sent to it by Warner Brothers were circulated as an internal memo which noted:

> Hitler and his government are unfairly represented in this story in violation of the Code .... To represent Hitler *ONLY* as a screaming madman and a bloodthirsty persecutor and *nothing else* is manifestly unfair .... Are we ready to depart from the pleasant and profitable course of entertainment to engage in propaganda, to produce screen portrayals arousing controversy, conflict racial, religious and nationalistic antagonism? ... Where's the line to be drawn? Why not make the Stalin purges, the Japanese rape of China, the Terror of Spain etc. [54]

Joseph Breen restricted his comments to a letter dated 30 December 1938 to Jack Warner in which he raised

> for your serious consideration the question as to whether or not your studio, and the industry as a whole should sponsor a motion picture dealing with so highly controversial a subject. [55]

Lord sent the Hays Office a copy of the second draft with the warning:

> It goes without saying that this script must be kept under lock and key when you are not actually reading it, because the German American Bund, the German consul and all such forces are desperately trying to get a copy of it. [56]

Lord was not exaggerating. On 23 November Dr Georg Gyssling, the German Consul in Los Angeles, had written to Breen enclosing a clipping from *The Hollywood Reporter* which had announced work on the start of the script. He wanted to know if Breen would 'kindly see to it that the matter will not result in difficulties such as we have unfortunately experienced before?'. [57] On New Year's Day 1939 Jack Warner received an anonymous letter referring to plans announced in the press to make *Confessions*.

> I would suggest that after you finish the picture it would be suitable to follow with I AM A COMMUNIST starring Eddie Cantor and a few other

Communist Jews .... Mr Warner, please don't think the American people are as dumb as you think they are.

It was signed AN AMERICAN BORN. [58] Warner held out against all pressure. As the film went into production, Lord wrote Breen a letter quoting a list of twelve impeccable research sources for the script. [59]

In the film Paul Lukas plays Dr Kassel, the head of a German-American Bund which is serving as a cover for Nazi activities in America. One critic of the party at a meeting is dragged off and beaten, while another is forcibly taken back to Germany by the Gestapo, who are operating openly in New York. Litvak and Lord made judicious use of genuine newsreel inserts of the notorious German-American Bund rally in Madison Square Gardens on Washington's Birthday, 22 February 1938, during which opponents who made themselves heard were unceremoniously removed and beaten up by the Bund's uniformed hoodlums.

Goebbels appears in one scene in which he directs the dissemination of propaganda destined for major American cities. The pipe-smoking FBI agent (played by Robinson) flatters information out of an inefficient spy (Francis Lederer) and cracks the ring. Eighteen spies are tried, caught and convicted. Robinson wonders aloud, 'Are the Nazis insane? We know what they're trying to do. It's absurd but its potential power is terrifying.'

The New York Times thought that 'the picture has cheapened its cause and sacrificed much of its dignity by making its villains twirl their long black mustaches. (A short black one can be villainous enough)' [60] but elsewhere the reaction was extreme. On 27 April Warner Brothers held a private screening for their own employees. The next day Robert Rossen, who was shortly to start work on the script of *The Roaring Twenties*, wrote a short formal note to Hal Wallis. 'I am indeed proud this morning to be able to say that I work in a studio that has the courage and ability to make *Confessions of A Nazi Spy*.' Staff producer Lou Edelman sent a fawning memo to Jack Warner echoing the sentiments but without Rossen's style. 'Last night the motion picture had a Bar Mitzbah [sic.] It came of age. It said "Today I am a Man".' [61] Jack Warner confessed that 'no picture ever aroused so much bigotry and hate as this one. We were bowled over by vicious letters, most of them unsigned and there were dozens of phone calls in similar vein.' One of them warned that if the picture opened as planned the whole Warner family would be wiped out and the theatre destroyed. On the eve of the official premiere his wife, Ann Warner, received a letter containing a detailed floor plan of their house on Angelo Drive in Beverly Hills. Not surprisingly, the opening audience was composed of almost as many policemen and special agents as paying customers. [62]

A cinema showing the film in the German-populated area of Milwaukee was burned to the ground by an outraged band of pro-Nazi sympathisers. Just to put the *New York Times* review into perspective, in April 1940 the news filtered back to Hollywood that several Polish exhibitors who had dared to screen *Confessions of a Nazi Spy* had been hanged in the lobbies of their own cinemas. [63] In the circumstances gross receipts of $1,531,000 against a negative cost of $681,000 represented a healthy financial performance.

The release of the picture provoked the German Chargé d'affaires, Hans Thomsen, into writing angrily to Cordell Hull, the Secretary of State, denouncing the film as an example of the pernicious propaganda that was 'poisoning' German–American relations. [64] German influence prevented the picture's exhibition in Italy, Japan and most of the Danubian, Baltic and Scandinavian countries, but within the British Empire it was shown, unusually for a controversial film, without a single cut. [65] Germany's positive reaction was to inform the State Department that the German film industry was engaged on a series of documentary films dealing with American unemployment, gangsterism and judicial corruption.

To the isolationists before Pearl Harbor, and to the HUAC in the late 1940s, any foreign policy statement from Hollywood during the late 1930s was tantamount to a declaration of 'premature anti-Fascism'. After all, despite the 'quarantine the aggressor' speech that Roosevelt made in Chicago in 1937, there had been little in the way of official support for intervention in European affairs. In that same year a Gallup poll discovered that 70 per cent of those questioned thought that America's entry into the First World War had been a mistake. [66] The investigations of the Senate Committee chaired by Senator Gerald P. Nye into the profits and influence of the munitions industry concluded that the munitions makers, along with international bankers and businessmen, had been responsible for dragging the United States into the Great War.

Not surprisingly, the majority of the Cabinet was opposed to intervention and Roosevelt, in the last two years of his second Administration, had to cope with a resolutely isolationist Senate. Most of the key Senatorial committees were headed by senior Southern senators, whose antipathy to Roosevelt's policies had been well demonstrated in the Neutrality Laws and their fight against the spread of more New Deal measures. Roosevelt himself, facing the prospect of a third term, could ill afford to take a militant stand on foreign policy, and he contented himself with increasing aid to Britain which eventually became the Lend-Lease Bill. At the time that Hollywood radicals were hoping to make a stand against Fascism, the Federal Theater was being wound up, because of its supposed Communist domination.

Ironically, the one avenue open to those who passed for militants in Hollywood was to make pictures calling for a strong national defence. Hearst's Cosmopolitan company, coincidentally releasing through Warner Brothers, made a string of films in the 1930s, including *Devil Dogs of the Air, Here Comes the Navy, Submarine D1* and *Wings of the Navy*, all of them directed by Lloyd Bacon, who was himself a naval officer in the Reserves. Another section of these recruiting pictures featured Dick Powell and Ruby Keeler (*Shipmates Forever* and *Flirtation Walk*) and Glenda Farrell and Joan Blondell in *Miss*

Pacific Fleet. These films were fully and enthusiastically reviewed by the Hearst press and even by less partial sources. *Variety* wrote of *Wings of the Navy* that it was 'Timely and topical, it is a convincer to mould public opinion and support in favour of current government plans for wide expansion of American air defence forces'.[67] Politics sometimes makes strange bedfellows.

Confessions of a Nazi Spy proved to be unique in its explicit denunciation of Nazi practices, and the storm it aroused in official circles made Warners wary of openly attacking foreign governments while America was still officially at peace. Jack Warner tried hard to follow the Administration's line in foreign policy, but until the Japanese attack on Pearl Harbor it was particularly hard to do so. Roosevelt's personal anti-Fascist feelings were largely echoed by Ickes, Hopkins, Perkins, Corcoran, Morgenthau and Wallace, but they were hamstrung by the impossibility and undesirability of leading America into another war. After six weeks of hard bargaining Roosevelt managed to force through an amendment of the 1939 Neutality Laws, but his internationalist foreign policy caused tremendous concern to many of his supporters on the eve of an election year. In the last weeks of the campaign the President even declared in a speech at Buffalo that 'This country is not going to war', and he told a crowd in Boston, 'I shall say it again and again: your boys are not going to be sent into any foreign wars'.[68]

The attack on Pearl Harbor left no room for further discussion on the question of entering the war. It relieved the President from, as he put it, 'walking on eggs', and unleashed a torrent of anti-Nazi pictures, which Hollywood had been storing up for some months. The unity engendered by the Second World War produced such extravagant productions as Warners' *Mission to Moscow* and MGM's *Song of Russia*, both of which caused serious embarrassment to their respective producers in the postwar anti-Soviet backlash.

The 1930s, in comparison, were a time of confusion for those in Hollywood who were interested in foreign affairs. It seemed at one point that Jack and Harry Warner were the most dedicated anti-Nazis in town. The hard core of Communists toed the party line on the Stalin purges, the Nazi–Soviet Pact and the invasion of Finland, although not always without a tinge of anxiety at such moral contortions. However, the rise of Fascism and the formation of the Popular Front by all anti-Fascists mixed so many liberal Left-wing elements as to make sustained coherent strategy impossible.

Radicals in Hollywood faced not only ideological incoherence but also the idiosyncratic workings of the motion picture industry and its unique mixture of art and commerce. The studios were in business to make money, and politics were thought to be an obstacle to the pursuit of profits. The reluctance of the American Senate to endanger the country's neutral status, combined with the President's personal but sporadic desire for a firmer anti-Fascist commitment, made for a cautious and confusing foreign policy in the years immediately preceding Pearl Harbor.

12

SNAPSHOT
Hollywood and the nation, September 1939

Entertainment is the commodity for which the public pays at the box office. Propaganda disguised as entertainment would be neither honest salesmanship nor honest showmanship.

Hays Office Annual Report, March 1938

The increasing number of pictures produced by the industry that treat honestly and dramatically many current themes proves there is nothing incompatible between the best interests of the box office and the kind of entertainment that raises the level of audience appreciation whatever the subject touched.

Hays Office Annual Report, March 1939

The two contrasting statements from the Hays Office would suggest that the year 1939 marked a significant stage in Hollywood's slow growth to political maturity. John Mosher in his review of *Juarez* in *The New Yorker* pointed out that had the picture been released in 1929 'it would have been called *Maximilian & Carlotta* or just *Carlotta*. In 1939 it was good business to put the emphasis on the power of democracy.'[1] In March 1939 Robert E. Sherwood announced that he had decided to permit the release of the film version of his play *Abe Lincoln in Illinois* because he believed that the international situation was too serious for Lincoln's sentiments about democracy to be withheld from the world's audiences.[2] The sentiments cost RKO, who won a bidding war with Samuel Goldwyn, $225,000 to secure the play's film rights. At Twentieth Century Fox Darryl Zanuck commissioned Lamar Trotti to write *Young Mr Lincoln* for his favourite contract star, Tyrone Power. Owing to the vagaries of the studio system Power went into *The Rains Came* and Henry Fonda was signed to play Lincoln.

We have already seen that Warner Brothers had to be forcibly restrained from releasing a torrent of anti-Nazi films. In May 1939, at the time of the release of *Confessions of a Nazi Spy*, Warner Brothers had three scripts, *Concentration Camp*, *Boycott* and *Underground Road*, all of an anti-Nazi nature, ready for filming, but postponed production owing to the nature of

American foreign policy at that time. *Variety* reported: 'Studio story editors are jittery over the current deluge of spy, refugee and anti-Nazi stories .... Sudden declaration of war or conclusion of peace treaty would ruin their market value.'[3]

Instead Warner Brothers mixed their aggressive foreign policy with their traditional shrewd parsimony. Hal Wallis wrote to Jack Warner, having heard the news that England was about to reissue the hit 1930 picture *The Dawn Patrol* which had been part of the anti-war cycle of films initiated by the success of Universal's *All Quiet on the Western Front*. Wallis suggested that they should re-make the Howard Hawks version as a vehicle for Errol Flynn and their own British stock company. 'I think it would bring us a fortune now when the whole world is talking and thinking war and re-armament.'[4] However this time the tone was subtly altered. Blue pages were inserted into the old script with the revised dialogue. In the new edition Courtney praises Scott for his patriotism: 'All through the centuries, the instant old Britain's in any kind of trouble every kid, every lad, is up and at 'em just like you – ready to give it to 'em.' Scott's farewell to his commanding officer who has had to send him up in 'a crate like that' is resigned rather than bitter, a foretaste, perhaps, of the deaths the audience were soon to experience for themselves. 'A gallant gentleman died this afternoon. So many fine chaps who have died and are going to die in this and future wars .... Goodbye, old son.'

In September 1939 the Hollywood studio system was more secure and confident than at any time in the previous ten years. There were 17,000 cinemas in more than 9,000 towns across the United States. There were more cinemas than banks, twice as many cinemas as hotels with fifty or more rooms. On average there was one cinema seat for every twelve Americans; the proportion rose to one in eight in New England but dropped to 1:21 in the East South Central states. Admission prices ranged from 10 cents to $2.20 but averaged between 25 cents and 35 cents. An estimated ninety million Americans went to the movies each week.[5] An annual average of $25 was spent by each family on going to the movies.

In 1939 the domestic box office produced receipts of $673 million, or 67.4 per cent of the total earned by all the entertainment business in the country. The American film industry was worth over $2 billion; $1.8 billion was invested in the theatres, $112 million in the production studios and $20 million in distribution. Hollywood employed around thirty thousand people and the studios' combined payroll was between $133 million and $145 million.[6]

Studio finances had been restored to comforting health. The year 1939 was the first since 1931 in which all the studios recorded a trading profit. Between 1932 and 1938 Universal enjoyed only one year in which it did not make a loss. In 1939 it made a substantial profit of $1.2 million and doubled it the following year. It was, however, now under the 'protection' of the Wall Street firm of Standard Capital Corporation, which had controlled 80 per cent of its common stock since 1936.[7]

Loews Inc. survived the Depression better than any other studio because of its limited numbers of movie theatres, although it consequently saw its profits rise more slowly than its major competitors in the boom years of the Second World War. In 1939 Loews owned 66 acres of Culver City and dubbing studios in Paris, Barcelona and Rome in which it could create soundtracks for the foreign versions of its films. In 1937 it had bought Gaumont-British to circumvent the British quota laws which limited the number of non-British made films which could be imported. [8]

In 1939 Loews held 125 listed subsidiary companies; Paramount, after its traumas of the Depression, owned 194 subsidiaries. Apart from its 26-acre studio site in Hollywood and the old Astoria site on Long Island it owned cinemas, film exchanges, processing laboratories and location facilities which were worth $109 million. Paramount paid its contract star Mae West $222,000 in 1933 when the success of *I'm No Angel* and *She Done Him Wrong* virtually saved the studio but $480,000 in 1938 when she was reduced to appearing in such unsuitable vehicles as *Every Day's a Holiday.* [9]

Robert Lord at Warner Brothers earned $134,000 in 1939 and established writers could certainly earn in excess of $100,000 at many studios. The number of directors in Hollywood during the 1930s remained virtually constant at around 240 but the number of producers throughout the decade leaped from thirty-four in 1927 to 220 ten years later. [10]

During the 1930s Los Angeles itself continued to grow, though not at the boom-town rates of the previous decade. Between 1929 and 1939 official statistics showed a rise of a quarter of a million people to a figure just short of one and a half million. [11] Of them 395 were accredited permanent Hollywood correspondents for newspapers and magazines all over the world. In 1939 they registered 15,709 publicity stories and 109,083 still photographs with the Advertising Advisory Council to feed the world's insatiable appetite for Hollywood. [12] The American industry's domination of world film markets amounted to cultural imperialism.

Throughout the 1930s the press stories which emanated from Hollywood were different in kind from those which had emerged before the Depression. In the 1920s the archetypal stars were Rudolph Valentino and Pola Negri who lived fabled romantic lives in Moorish palaces in the Hollywood Hills. They were remote, ethereal beings who lived lives completely removed from the experiences of their fans. The Depression reversed the tide of exotic extravagance. Publicity chiefs at the studios were now expected to protect (within reason) their stars' privacy and facilitate a carefully arranged elopement to Santa Barbara or San Diego rather than a huge Beverly Hills wedding. [13]

The stars of the 1930s were the girl or boy 'next door' types like Ginger Rogers or James Stewart. Female stars emphasised the importance of diets and beauty-building exercises which every woman could do, rather than the value of expensive cosmetics. Male stars shyly confided that their favourite foods were Mom's deep-dish apple pie or her corned beef and cabbage. According to the fan magazines Warner Baxter had to nerve himself to go through with a formal dress-up party and Gary Cooper's favourite article of clothing was a cheap pair of seersucker pants. William Powell sold his $250,000 home because he found its Georgian opulence too intimidating and Deanna Durbin's parents were so unpretentious that it was solemnly reported that they answered their own doorbell. [14]

In the 1920s no star willingly confessed to having a family because such an admission was feared to diminish his or her exotic charms. In the 1930s Irene Dunne, Miriam Hopkins, Constance Bennett and Joan Crawford, who for one reason or another couldn't have their own children, made sure a press photographer was present to record the happy event of their adoption of young children. Fans were impressed too by the revelation that Ronald Colman had his own library; Ray Milland, somewhat puzzlingly, was reportedly wading through the *Encyclopaedia Britannica* and Barbara Stanwyck 'enjoys serious things – a lake by Corot, a book by Thackeray'. The rise of the child star was another predictable phenomenon of the domesticated 1930s in Hollywood. Shirley Temple sold mud pies to passing motorists because her parents allowed her only a dollar a week pocket money in an attempt to make sure she remained unspoiled. [15] To be a star in Hollywood in the 1930s was to feel the comforting protection of a studio contract, the studio police and the studio publicity machine. From the outside it looked like a fair exchange for growing up inside a powerful, demanding family whose business was dominating the images and dreams of the world.

In September 1939 *Gone With the Wind* was in post-production. Although it came from Selznick International Pictures rather than one of the Big Five studios, it was distributed by MGM and its profits were to swell the coffers of Loews Inc. On its first release in 1939 MGM files indicate that it gathered domestic receipts of $30 million, foreign sales (already restricted by the outbreak of war in Europe) of $19 million and produced a book profit of $16,222,000 after the division of the spoils with Selznick. By 1970 the film had taken over $200 million. [16]

Gone With the Wind was the most profitable film ever made by Hollywood for over thirty years until inflation caused it to be overtaken by its competitors in terms of gross receipts if not in the number of paid admissions. Perhaps also because every frame betrays the obsessive hand of its producer, David Selznick, the film can stand as the apogee of the films which emerged from Hollywood's producer-dominated studio era. It won eight Oscars and the Irving Thalberg Award for Selznick. It certainly destroyed Frank Capra's hopes of a fourth Oscar for *Mr Smith Goes to Washington* to follow the triumphs of *It Happened One Night*, *Mr Deeds Goes to Town* and *You Can't Take It With You*. As he commented wryly afterwards, 'Moral: Don't make the best picture you ever made in the year that someone makes Gone With The Wind.' [17]

The year 1939 was an exceptional one even in a decade which produced a great many outstanding films. It wasn't just that *Mr Smith* was Capra's best picture to date but it appeared as if all Hollywood's top directors found their form at the same time. As well as the films already discussed, Ernst Lubitsch made *Ninotchka*, George Cukor *The Women*, William Dieterle *The Hunchback of Notre Dame*, Mitchell Leisen *Midnight*, Victor Fleming *The Wizard of Oz* and John Ford directed *Drums Along the Mohawk*, *Young Mr Lincoln* and *Stagecoach*, all released in 1939.

The Hays Office's *Annual Report* for 1939 recalled the nascent film industry's constant recourse to the chase and the custard pie and trumpeted its newly acquired trappings of maturity. Certainly in 1939 it appeared as if the American film industry, along with the country at large, had climbed out of the pit of the Depression and was ready to ingest the intoxicating air of economic and social contentment. It was therefore a major inconvenience to Hollywood when Germany invaded Poland on 1 September 1939, started a conflagration in Europe and caused further political tremors to resonate through an industry which always prized political stability.

On the same day in America, General George C. Marshall was sworn in as Chief of Staff. He soon discovered that, although the American army was 227,000 strong, only 75,000 of them had the right equipment. Lieutenant General Hugh Drum assembled his First Army for manoeuvres and announced that he was short of combat strength by 246,000 men, 3,063 machine guns, 348 howitzers and 180 field guns. Between September 1939 and June 1940 the Senate continued to cut down appropriations for the armed forces. A Gallup poll taken at this time revealed that 65 per cent of the Americans who responded favoured boycotting Germany but 90 per cent of them would fight only if America itself were invaded; 96.5 per cent felt that the United States should stay out of the European war at all costs but 84 per cent of them wanted an Allied victory. [18] There was a clear mandate for the President to sit on the fence. If its political leaders and its audiences didn't want to get involved, why should Hollywood?

The answer to the question was that some of the men who controlled the film industry felt strongly about the need to fight the Nazis. One was Charlie Chaplin, who had been in charge of his own artistic destiny for twenty years. *The Great Dictator* (1940) had been in preparation since before the Munich agreement was signed in September 1938. The German Consul, Dr Georg Gyssling, wrote to Joseph Breen at the Hays Office in October 1938 quoting from the synopses of Chaplin's projected movie which had appeared in various newspapers. He went on to warn Breen that he had better put a stop to all this nonsense immediately or it would 'naturally lead to serious troubles and complications'. [19]

In February 1939 Senator Robert Reynolds of New Jersey wrote to Breen enclosing a letter from one of his constituents which warned of the dire consequences of producing *The Great Dictator*. The letter betrayed much the same tone as that adopted by Dr Gyssling.

Chaplin is a native of Great Britain and for a quarter of a century has accepted as his special privilege the generous bounty and protection of a complacent government to which of course he is most reluctant to pledge his allegiance.

Regardless of how much we deplore the inhuman persecution of a minority race in a foreign land, this man should not be permitted to use the United States as a background and sounding board with the avowed purpose of stirring up further strife between Germany and the United States government. [20]

Although the letter was essentially an *ad hominem* attack on Chaplin it was representative of the strength of feeling among those isolationists who wished America to remain wedded to the principles of foreign policy laid down by its first President, George Washington. In his farewell address in 1796 Washington had indicated his intention not to run for a third term as President and had counselled his countrymen to 'steer clear of permanent alliances with any portion of the foreign world'. In fact Washington was merely referring to the difficulties caused by the French treaty of 1778 but it had, as with the Constitution and the Bill of Rights, been subsequently regarded as a mandatory article of faith. [21]

It was certainly enough to scupper Wilson's plan for America to join the League of Nations and Roosevelt, coincidentally now intending himself to run for President for an unprecedented third term, was wary enough of the isolationist lobby not to force the issue on a reluctant Congress. Instead he opted to press the House for a clause in the Neutrality Laws which permitted foreign powers to buy arms from the United States provided they were paid for in cash and transported in foreign vessels. It wasn't a lot of help to cash-starved Great Britain, particularly since loans to belligerent countries were explicitly forbidden.

In the circumstances *The Great Dictator* was a brave film for Chaplin to make. The universal Little Tramp is transmuted into a specifically Jewish barber whose country is about to be absorbed into the totalitarian empire of Adenoid Hynkel – the Tramp's *doppelgänger*. Ironically, the film works best in its moments of pure Chaplin comic genius and least successfully when it is taking a moral stand. The closing six-minute speech to camera delivered by the barber, who has been mistaken for the dictator, is an unobjectionable but unpersuasive series of platitudes. The message of the film is not so much timely as timeless. Its politics are clouded by religious sentiment. The Jewish barber cries:

In the seventeenth chapter of St. Luke it is written, 'The kingdom of God is within man'. Not in one man or a group of men but in all men. In you! You, the people, have the power to make this life free and beautiful!

The Great Dictator was at root a moral tale and, despite its predictable blacklisting by countries sympathetic to Nazi Germany, it lacked the immediate overt political passion of *Confessions of a Nazi Spy.*

Warner Brothers, like Roosevelt, were aware of the current feelings in the country at large about the desirability of being caught up in events in Europe. Jack and Harry Warner wired the President that they would

> like to do all in our power within the motion picture industry ... to show the American people the worthiness of the cause for which the free peoples of Europe are making such tremendous sacrifices. [22]

They decided to soften their *Confessions* stance and reverted to historical dress treatment of the contemporary world situation. In *The Private Lives of Elizabeth and Essex* (1939) the isolationist Elizabeth tries to calm the interventionist Essex who wants to invade Ireland.

> I've kept the peace and given my people happiness, relieved the poor and restored our coinage .... It takes more courage not to fight when one is surrounded by foolish hotheads urging wars in all directions. [23]

The following year Warners started to inch their way back into the fight for intervention. Howard Koch was given Seton I. Miller's script of *The Sea Hawk*, which had been originally developed for Errol Flynn and Olivia de Havilland following their triumph in *The Charge of the Light Brigade* (1936) but it was then decided that not enough time had elapsed since *Captain Blood* (1935), to which it was too similar. [24] Koch wrote to Walter McEwen of his plans to rewrite Miller's draft of the ending.

> Upon the information in the documents which Thorpe brings, Elizabeth abandons the policy of 'appeasement' towards Spain .... The unifying theme ... is that the gods favor those that sail by the wind (the free) against those propelled by the galley oar (a symbol of enslavement). [25]

The final draft leaves nobody in any doubt that *The Sea Hawk* was Warner Brothers' latest contribution to the cause of interventionism. In the opening scene a black-garbed Philip II of Spain sits in front of a map of the world, gloating:

> With our ships carrying our flag to the seven seas, with our arms sweeping over Africa, the Near East and the Far West ... we are invincible everywhere but on our own doorstep .... We will never keep Northern Europe in submission until we have a reckoning with England.

Pointing to the map behind him, Philip continues, 'With England conquered nothing can stand in our way. One day, before my death, we shall sit here and gaze upon this wall. It will have ceased to be a map of the world; it will be Spain.' Elizabeth (Flora Robson) resists the demands for an attack on Spain and tells the hero, Geoffrey Thorpe (Errol Flynn), that 'A large fleet is a luxury that England cannot afford .... Our safety lies in diplomacy, not force.'

In this policy she is supported by the traitor Lord Wolfingham (played by Henry Daniell) who rehearses the classic argument with the interventionist Frobisher (Donald Crisp), telling him that England cannot afford an open break with Spain.

WOLFINGHAM

We need defense only if we are attacked. To disregard Philip's warning is to invite an immediate war.

FROBISHER

While to heed it is to throw ourselves at his mercy. I believe Philip's thirst for power can only be quenched in the English Channel. If Philip is bold enough to make demands now what will he do when the Armada is built?

Following Koch's rewrite, Thorpe executes a daring escape from enforced servitude in the Spanish galleon that is fortuitously carrying dispatches from Philip to his admirals informing them of the impending sailing of the Armada. He can then present incontrovertible evidence of Spain's intention to attack England. The Queen renounces her appeasement policy and prepares for war.

> We have no quarrel with the people of Spain or of any other country; but when the ruthless ambitions of a man threaten to engulf the world, it becomes the solemn obligation of free men, wherever they may be, to affirm that the earth belongs not to any man but to all men and that freedom is the deed and title to the soil on which we exist. [26]

It was America's eventual entry into the Second World War which solved the unemployment problems of the Great Depression. The enormous demands of the American war machine gave real jobs to all those who had been marginalised by the fragile nature of the American economy in the 1930s. At the time of Pearl Harbor there were still nine million men unemployed and three million on relief rolls. Roosevelt's New Deal and his myriad work-creating agencies ultimately were less effective than Hitler's Wehrmacht and Luftwaffe. The New Deal's major contribution, like Hollywood's, was more spiritual than temporal. Will Hays, writing in *The Nation*, overstated his case but attempted to sum up the importance of Hollywood to the country in the 1930s.

> No medium has contributed more than the films to the maintenance of the national morale during a period featured by revolutions, riot and political turmoil in other countries. It has been the mission of the screen ... to reflect aspiration, achievement, optimism and kindly humor in its entertainment. Historians of the future will not ignore the interesting and significant fact that the movies literally laughed the big bad wolf of the Depression out of the public. [27]

The purpose of this book has been to examine the relationship between the social and political climate of the 1930s in America and the Hollywood film industry. It seems clear that the relationship was one of close mutual dependency, the consequence of the industry's proximity to the needs and aspirations of the American people. Although Hollywood films in the 1930s were shown all over the world, they were conceived as and remained uniquely American in character.

One of the reasons for the keen appreciation of the tastes of the domestic audience lay in the characters of the movie moguls. The four Warner brothers, Louis B. Mayer, Marcus Loew, Carl Laemmle (of Universal), Adolph Zukor (of Paramount) and William Fox had all been exhibitors at early points in their careers, and hence all had first-hand experience of the tastes of audiences. This indeed proved to be crucial in the fight of Zukor, Laemmle and Fox to destroy the monopoly of film production enjoyed by the Motion Picture Patents Company in the first years of the century. It was their perception of what the public wanted that led to their creation of the star system, and it was their perception of the film industry's potential that accounted for their tenacity in defying the legal controls of the Patents Company. When they moved into production they preserved that healthy respect for the audience.

The audience was, of course, to a large degree white, Anglo-Saxon Protestant and native-born. It is ironic that the men who mediated between them and the hordes of recently arrived urban immigrants were almost exclusively working-class Jews born in Central Europe. Gabler writes of Louis B. Mayer that he was uniquely situated because of his deep yearnings to join the establishment to provide reassurance for all Americans against the anxieties and disruptions of the time. He did this by producing movies which trumpeted the values of family, loyalty, virtue, tradition and patriotism. [28]

The other studios largely shared these general beliefs but MGM pursued them with a fervour that bordered on the religious. It is well known that Mayer's own favourite production was the *Andy Hardy* series starring Mickey Rooney as an all-American boy, Lewis Stone as the Judge, his stern but loving father, and Fay Bainter as his saintly mother. Mayer's interest extended to acting out scenarios for the embarrassed writers, demonstrating precisely how Andy would say his prayers.

It wasn't just that the films' chances for financial success would be enhanced if they were liked by Middle America. It was that many of the Jewish-born moguls, none more so than Mayer, believed passionately in the fantasy of goodwill to be found behind the white picket fences of well-mannered, well-spoken, small-town America.

Even the moguls' own lives appeared to follow this pattern. They nearly all married young to Jewish girls who kept the faith of their fathers. Once they became successful in Hollywood they shunted off their wives along with the religious and social traditions they had inherited. They were reluctant to promote the cause of Jewish actors and more particularly Jewish actresses, and they pursued non-Jewish girlfriends with a tenacity that frequently led to remarriage. One thinks of David Selznick writing the scene for Robert Walker and Jennifer to sit on the ubiquitous chair on the front porch in *Since You Went Away* knowing not only that the audience would enjoy the sight but that he was personally in the process of divorcing Louis B. Mayer's daughter, Irene, to marry Jennifer Jones. Mayer himself, Harry Cohn and Jack Warner as well as Selznick all followed this pattern.

What distinguishes Charles Laughton reciting the Gettysburg Address in *Ruggles of Red Gap*, a little boy doing the same thing to his blind grandfather at the Lincoln Memorial in *Mr Smith* or Gary Cooper mumbling about Ulysses S. Grant outside Grant's Tomb in *Mr Deeds Goes to Town* is a sensation of credibility. The patriotism and the reverence sound and feel real and they stem not just from the ragamuffin immigrant kid Capra but from the semi-literate loudmouth Cohn. Certainly the moguls wanted power and wealth, as do those who run the studios today, but the Jews who invented Hollywood felt they owed the country a favour and they repaid it the best way they knew how – by making movies which celebrated the country which took them in and permitted them the luxury of earning wealth beyond their dreams of avarice.

The closeness of the relationship between Hollywood and its domestic audience was nowhere better illustrated than by their reaction to the sharp swing in the national mood between the last depressing months of the Hoover administration and the boisterous optimism of the First New Deal. The reaction of the economy to the injections of federal money was seen in the sharp rise in the industrial production index. President Roosevelt's inspiring First Inaugural Address, the instant creation of new government agencies, the provision for direct relief, all helped to regenerate a sense of national buoyancy. The well-documented sudden twist by the film industry was purely an instinctive response to the new social and political climate of the country.

Given what we know about the moguls and their studios, it is perhaps not surprising that the underlying socially conservative nature of the New Deal, its attempts to restore a respect for national institutions, which had been seen to be ineffective during the early years of the Depression, appealed enormously to Hollywood. Maltby writes that Hollywood's portrait of society, at least as seen in certain key films, was an idealistic vision of an essentially unified community devoted to the pursuit of spiritual peace through material acquisition and good neighbourliness. [29]

He points out that the value-judgements to be gained from a study of Hollywood films of the 1930s could be enumerated in four ways: a successful romance will solve all the problems of the hero and the heroine; the wider crime problem can be solved by the capture of the individual criminal; war and the preparation for war are thrilling, heroic and glamorous; the good life is still essentially an acquisitive life. [30] It is possible in all sections to point to movies which do not follow such rules, but overall it would be unwise to deny the essential truth of such a list. It was never articulated or discussed as such but

221

the drive to make commercially successful pictures along industrial lines of production inevitably gave rise to various unwritten rules and the four listed above are applicable to a large percentage of the output from Hollywood during the period under discussion. The underlying philosophy of what pleased the public in large numbers was fortunately shared by the movie moguls and the Roosevelt administration.

The keynote of the New Deal, as it was of Hollywood, was irrepressible optimism, and, ironically, just as Hollywood's optimism was largely illusory, so the New Deal's legislation came to an end in 1938 with ten million men unemployed, relief payments difficult to obtain and insufficient in quantity, sharecroppers driven off the land and a host of associated problems still unsolved.

Hollywood's devotion to the pursuit of its profits made the American film industry a logical colleague of the coal, steel and other long-established large-scale industries with a similarly conservative social and political outlook. Its instinctive suspicion of any federal interference paralleled precisely the reaction of many of the heavy industries when faced with the prospect of drawing up an NRA code, granting labour the powers of collective bargaining or even investing in research and development before changing economic circumstances forced them to experiment. Technological caution meant that Hollywood fought the introduction of sound, of colour, of television and of the wide screen before it bowed to demand which originated elsewhere.

The film industry's desperate desire not to offend the powerful Catholic Church over the sexual content of the films of the early 1930s was matched by an equally spineless display when confronted with the wrath of the bituminous coal industry. The fate that befell *Black Fury* at Warner Brothers is particularly significant when one considers that, in relation to the other studios, Warner Brothers in the 1930s were the fiercest of fighters for the freedom of artistic expression in order to deal with topics of social relevance. The Hollywood film industry during that decade threw its considerable weight firmly behind the figures of the establishment.

The tribulations of *Black Fury*, of *Gabriel over the White House*, of *Dead End* and *Blockade*, are clear indications of the political bias and crucial deployment of power of the Hays Office. It is easy to condemn the Hays Office as a crude, right-wing organisation, dedicated to the stifling of healthy, liberal sentiments. In reality, of course, it performed a defensive function, planned largely by the heads of the studios. That defence had the effect of helping to distance American films from political and social reality. The movies of the early 1930s, for all their technical cumbersomeness, reflected their immediate society in the clearest possible image. The foundation of the Legion of Decency and the reconstitution of the Production Code Authority resulted in the imposition of such rigid requirements on film-makers that they were effectively debarred from dealing with the realities of the national experience. The mirror was still there after 1934, but its image was cloudy and slightly distorted. Stories that threatened to deal with controversial political issues were fatally compromised. More and more the inclination was to fall back on the inoffensive light-hearted musicals, comedies and romances.

Obviously there were excellent film-makers working successfully and relatively happily on certain political topics in the Hollywood of the late 1930s. In particular, one thinks immediately of Frank Capra, whose most prolific period this was. Yet the Capra films were so enormously popular simply because his slightly Right-wing, populist, traditionalist philosophy was perfectly attuned to the sentiments of the time, portraying as it did the essence of that unified, benevolent community referred to already. It does not help to categorise Capra purely as an anti-New-Dealer, because the vast majority of his audiences must surely have voted for Franklin Roosevelt. It was simply that his incurable belief in the ultimate triumph of the individual, the much vaunted 'John Does', was complemetary to the new-found hope induced by the New Deal. Irrepressible optimism was one of Roosevelt's most attractive characteristics, just as it was part of the message of *Mr Deeds Goes to Town* and *You Can't Take It With You*.

Along with the Capra movies, the Errol Flynn–Olivia De Havilland epics, the screwball comedies and the Astaire–Rogers musicals were all celebrations of the new assurance that Americans had rediscovered in their daily lives. Hollywood under the New Deal retreated into its factory and manufactured the images that shaped the dreams of America, if not of the world.

FILMOGRAPHY

PRIMARY FILMS

Title	Director	Year	Production company
Sunrise	F. W. Murnau	1927	FOX
The Crowd	K. Vidor	1928	MGM
City Girl	F. W. Murnau	1929	FOX
The Coconuts	R. Florey & J. Santley	1929	PAR
Animal Crackers	V. Heerman	1930	PAR
Cimarron	W. Ruggles	1930	RKO
Little Caesar	M. LeRoy	1930	WB
City Lights	C. Chaplin	1931	UA
Five Star Final	M. LeRoy	1931	WB
Monkey Business	N. McLeod	1931	PAR
Platinum Blonde	F. Capra	1931	COL
The Public Enemy	W. Wellman	1931	WB
Quick Millions	R. Brown	1931	FOX
Susan Lenox	R. Z. Leonard	1931	MGM
American Madness	F. Capra	1932	COL
Big City Blues	M. LeRoy	1932	WB
Blonde Venus	J. von Sternberg	1932	PAR
Cabin in the Cotton	M. Curtiz	1932	WB
The Dark Horse	A. E. Green	1932	WB
Horse Feathers	N. McLeod	1932	PAR
I Am a Fugitive From a Chain Gang	M. LeRoy	1932	WB
If I Had a Million	various	1932	PAR
Lawyer Man	W. Dieterle	1932	WB
Million Dollar Legs	E. Cline	1932	PAR
The Mouthpiece	E. Nugent & J. Flood	1932	WB
One Hour With You	E. Lubitsch	1932	PAR
Scarface	H. Hawks	1932	UA
Two Seconds	M. LeRoy	1932	WB
Washington Masquerade	C. Brabin	1932	MGM
Baby Face	A. E. Green	1933	WB
Duck Soup	L. McCarey	1933	PAR
Forty-Second Street	L. Bacon	1933	WB

224

Gabriel over the White House	G. La Cava	1933	MGM
Gold Diggers of 1933	M. LeRoy	1933	WB
Hallelujah I'm a Bum	L. Milestone	1933	UA
Heroes for Sale	W. Wellman	1933	WB
I'm No Angel	W. Ruggles	1933	PAR
Lady for a Day	F. Capra	1933	COL
The Life of Jimmy Dolan	A. Mayo	1933	WB
Man's Castle	F. Borzage	1933	COL
Mayor of Hell	A. Mayo	1933	WB
Roman Scandals	F. Tuttle	1933	UA
She Done Him Wrong	L. Sherman	1933	PAR
State Fair	H. King	1933	FOX
Wild Boys of the Road	W. Wellman	1933	WB
The World Changes	M. LeRoy	1933	WB
The Gay Divorcee	M. Sandrich	1934	RKO
Broadway Bill	F. Capra	1934	COL
It Happened One Night	F. Capra	1934	COL
Massacre	A. Crosland	1934	WB
Our Daily Bread	K. Vidor	1934	UA
Stand Up and Cheer	H. MacFadden	1934	FOX
Black Fury	M. Curtiz	1935	WB
G-Men	W. Keighley	1935	WB
Gold Diggers of 1935	B. Berkeley	1935	WB
A Night at the Opera	S. Wood	1935	MGM
One More Spring	H. King	1935	FOX
The President Vanishes	W. Wellman	1935	PAR
Roberta	W. A. Seiter	1935	RKO
Top Hat	M. Sandrich	1935	RKO
Black Legion	A. Mayo	1936	WB
Bullets or Ballots	W. Keighley	1936	WB
The Devil is a Sissy	W. S. Van Dyke	1936	MGM
Follow the Fleet	M. Sandrich	1936	RKO
Fury	F. Lang	1936	MGM
Modern Times	C. Chaplin	1936	UA
Mr Deeds Goes to Town	F. Capra	1936	COL
My Man Godfrey	G. La Cava	1936	UNIV
The Plainsman	C. B. DeMille	1936	PAR
The Plow that Broke the Plains	P. Lorentz	1936	
Swing Time	G. Stevens	1936	RKO
Ali Baba Goes to Town	D. Butler	1937	FOX
The Awful Truth	L. McCarey	1937	COL
A Day at the Races	S. Wood	1937	MGM
Dead End	W. Wyler	1937	UA
Easy Living	M. Leisen	1937	PAR
The Last Gangster	E. Ludwig	1937	MGM
The Life of Emile Zola	W. Dieterle	1937	WB
Lost Horizon	F. Capra	1937	COL
Marked Woman	L. Bacon	1937	WB
They Won't Forget	M. LeRoy	1937	WB
You Only Live Once	F. Lang	1937	UA
Angels with Dirty Faces	M. Curtiz	1938	WB
Blockade	W. Dieterle	1938	UA

Bringing Up Baby	H. Hawks	1938	RKO
Crime School	L. Seiler	1938	WB
Dodge City	M. Curtiz	1938	WB
Racket Busters	L. Bacon	1938	WB
The River	P. Lorentz	1938	
You Can't Take It With You	F. Capra	1938	COL
Angels Wash Their Faces	R. Enright	1939	WB
Confessions of a Nazi Spy	A. Litvak	1939	WB
Jesse James	H. King	1939	FOX
Juarez	W. Dieterle	1939	WB
The Roaring Twenties	R. Walsh	1939	WB
Stagecoach	J. Ford	1939	UA
Young Mr Lincoln	J. Ford	1939	FOX
The Grapes of Wrath	J. Ford	1940	FOX
The Great Dictator	C. Chaplin	1940	UA
High Sierra	R. Walsh	1941	WB
Meet John Doe	F. Capra	1941	WB
The Sea Hawk	M. Curtiz	1940	WB
Sullivan's Travels	P. Sturges	1941	FAR
The Westerner	W. Wyler	1940	UA
It's a Wonderful Life	F. Capra	1946	RKO

SECONDARY FILMS

The Covered Wagon	J. Cruze	1923	PAR
The Iron Horse	J. Ford	1924	FOX
Three Bad Men	J. Ford	1926	FOX
Underworld	J. von Sternberg	1927	PAR
Showgirl in Hollywood	M. LeRoy	1928	WB
The Love Parade	E. Lubitsch	1929	PAR
The Virginian	V. Fleming	1929	PAR
All Quiet on the Western Front	L. Milestone	1930	UNIV
The Big House	G. Hill	1930	MGM
Divorcee	R. Z. Leonard	1930	MGM
The Doorway to Hell	A. Mayo	1930	WB
For the Defense	J. Cromwell	1930	PAR
City Streets	R. Mamoulian	1931	PAR
The Easiest Way	J. Conway	1931	MGM
A Free Soul	C. Brown	1931	MGM
The Front Page	L. Milestone	1931	UA
His Woman	E. Sloman	1931	PAR
Possessed	C. Brown	1931	MGM
Public Defender	J. W. Ruben	1931	RKO
Scandal Sheet	J. Cromwell	1931	PAR
The Secret Six	G. Hill	1931	MGM
Strangers May Kiss	G. Fitzmaurice	1931	MGM
Tarnished Lady	G. Cukor	1931	PAR
Unfaithful	J. Cromwell	1931	PAR
Attorney for the Defense	I. Cummings	1932	COL
The Conquerors	W. Wellman	1932	RKO
The Crash	W. Dieterle	1932	WB

The Crowd Roars	H. Hawks	1932	WB
Faithless	H. Beaumont	1932	MGM
Final Edition	H. Higgins	1932	COL
Hard to Handle	M. LeRoy	1932	WB
Hell's Highway	R. Brown	1932	RKO
Love is a Racket	W. Wellman	1932	WB
The Phantom President	N. Taurog	1932	PAR
Red Dust	V. Fleming	1932	MGM
Red Headed Woman	J. Conway	1932	MGM
Scandal for Sale	R. Mack	1932	UNIV
State's Attorney	G. Archainbaud	1932	RKO
Taxi	R. Del Ruth	1932	WB
Three on a Match	M. LeRoy	1932	WB
Trouble in Paradise	E. Lubitsch	1932	PAR
Washington Merry Go Round	J. Cruze	1932	COL
Blonde Bombshell	V. Fleming	1933	MGM
Bureau of Missing Persons	L. Bacon	1933	WB
Clear All Wires	G. Hill	1933	MGM
Counsellor-at-Law	W. Wyler	1933	UNIV
Dark Hazard	A. E. Green	1933	WB
Design for Living	E. Lubitsch	1933	PAR
Flying Down to Rio	T. Freeland	1933	RKO
Footlight Parade	L. Bacon	1933	WB
This Day and Age	C. B. DeMille	1933	PAR
Three Little Pigs	W. Disney	1933	PKO
20,000 Years in Sing Sing	M. Curtiz	1933	WB
As the Earth Turns	A. E. Green	1934	WB
Belle of the Nineties	L. McCarey	1934	PAR
Flirtation Walk	F. Borzage	1934	WB
Here Comes the Navy	L. Bacon	1934	WB
Hi Nellie	M. LeRoy	1934	WB
Little Man, What Now?	F. Borzage	1934	UNIV
Little Miss Marker	A. Hall	1934	PAR
The Merry Widow	E. Lubitsch	1934	MGM
Barbary Coast	H. Hawks	1935	UA
Captain Blood	M. Curtiz	1935	WB
Devil Dogs of the Air	L. Bacon	1935	WB
The Frisco Kid	L. Bacon	1935	WB
Miss Pacific Fleet	R. Enright	1935	WB
Oil for the Lamps of China	M. LeRoy	1935	WB
Public Hero No. 1	J. W. Ruben	1935	MGM
Shipmates Forever	F. Borzage	1935	WB
The General Died at Dawn	L. Milestone	1936	PAR
The Petrified Forest	A. Mayo	1936	WB
Public Enemy's Wife	N. Grinde	1936	WB
Story of Louis Pasteur	W. Dieterle	1936	WB
The Texas Rangers	K. Vidor	1936	PAR
Back in Circulation	R. Enright	1937	WB
Gold Diggers of 1937	L. Bacon	1937	WB
The Good Earth	S. Franklin	1937	MGM
The Great O'Malley	W. Dieterle	1937	WB
Last Train from Madrid	G. M. Arthur	1937	PAR

Make Way for Tomorrow	L. McCarey	1937	PAR
Nothing Sacred	W. Wellman	1937	UA
On the Avenue	R. Del Ruth	1937	RKO
Shall We Dance?	M. Sandrich	1937	RKO
Spain in Flames		1937	
The Spanish Earth	J. Ivens	1937	
A Star Is Born	W. Wellman	1937	UA
Submarine D-1	L. Bacon	1937	WB
The Adventures of Robin Hood	M. Curtiz	1938	WB
Carefree	M. Sandrich	1938	RKO
The Dawn Patrol	E. Goulding	1938	WB
Gold Diggers in Paris	R. Enright	1938	WB
I Am the Law	A. Hall	1938	COL
Smashing the Rackets	L. Landers	1938	RKO
Destry Rides Again	G. Marshall	1939	UNIV
Drums Along the Mohawk	J. Ford	1939	FOX
Dust Be My Destiny	L. Seiler	1939	WB
Each Dawn I Die	W. Keighley	1939	WB
Golden Boy	R. Mamoulian	1939	COL
Gone With the Wind	V. Fleming	1939	SI/MGM
Hell's Kitchen	L. Seiler	1939	WB
Idiot's Delight	C. Brown	1939	MGM
Midnight	M. Leisen	1939	PAR
Ninotchka	E. Lubitsch	1939	MGM
One Third of a Nation	D. Murphy	1939	PAR
Story of Vernon and Irene Castle	H. C. Potter	1939	RKO
Wings of the Navy	L. Bacon	1939	WB
Abe Lincoln in Illinois	J. Cromwell	1940	RKO

NOTES

1 SNAPSHOT: HOLLYWOOD AND THE NATION, SEPTEMBER 1929

1 John Baxter: *Sixty Years of Hollywood* (London, 1973), p. 13; A. Scott Berg: *Goldwyn* (London, 1989), p. 56.
2 Robert Lord, interviewed by the author, April 1972, Hollywood.
3 Scott Berg: *Goldwyn*, p. 39.
4 Robert Sklar: *Movie-Made America* (London, 1975), p. 68.
5 Neal Gabler: *An Empire of Their Own: How the Jews Invented Hollywood* (New York, 1989), p. 270.
6 Christopher Finch and Linda Rosenkrantz: *Gone Hollywood* (London, 1979), p. 140; p. 4.
7 Finch and Rosenkrantz: *Gone Hollywood*, pp. 153–4.
8 John Russell Taylor: *Strangers in Paradise* (London, 1983), pp. 37–9.
9 Robert Sklar: *City Boys* (Princeton, 1992), pp. 22–3.
10 Gavin Lambert: *Norma Shearer: A Life* (London, 1990), p. 122.
11 Ronald Brownstein: *The Power and The Glitter* (New York, 1992), p. 20.
12 Richard Maltby: 'The political economy of Hollywood: the studio system', in Philip Davies and Brian Neve (eds), *Cinema, Politics and Society in America* (Manchester, 1981).
13 Douglas Gomery: *The Hollywood Studio System* (Basingstoke, 1986), p. 2.
14 Gomery: *Hollywood Studio System*, p. 16.
15 Brownstein: *The Power and the Glitter*, p. 20.
16 Gomery: *Hollywood Studio System*, p. 124.
17 Tino Balio: *United Artists: The Company Built by the Stars* (Madison, Wis., 1976), pp. 72–3.
18 Gomery: *Hollywood Studio System*, p. 55.
19 Gomery: *Hollywood Studio System*, p. 52.
20 W. E. Leuchtenburg: *The Perils of Prosperity* (Chicago, 1958), pp. 178–9; G. E. Mowry: *The Urban Nation* (New York, 1968), pp. 16–17.
21 Leuchtenburg: *Perils of Prosperity*, p. 186.
22 Leuchtenburg: *Perils of Prosperity*, p. 188.
23 Leuchtenburg: *Perils of Prosperity*, p. 202.
24 John A. Garraty: *The Great Depression* (New York, 1987), p. 29; Leuchtenburg: *Perils of Prosperity*, p. 202; Mowry: *Urban Nation*, p. 17.

2 TROUBLE IN PARADISE

1 Morrie Ryskind, interviewed by the author, 23 February 1972, Beverly Hills.
2 F. L. Allen: *Only Yesterday* (New York, 1959), p. 245; Hearings before Subcommittee on Labor, House of Representatives, 72nd Congress, First Session on HR206, HR6011, HR8088, pp. 98–9. Quoted in D. Shannon (ed.): *The Great Depression* (Englewood Cliffs, N.J., 1960), pp. 26–8.
3 Arthur M. Schlesinger Jr: *The Crisis of the Old Order* (London, 1958), p. 176; A. Fried (ed.): *The Jeffersonian and Hamiltonian Traditions in American Politics* (New York, 1968), p. 396; noticeably, Hoover vetoed the Wagner–Garner Relief Bill which would have extended Reconstruction Finance Corporation loans to small businesses and industries. See B. Rauch: *The History of the New Deal* (New York, 1963), p. 20.
4 Irving Bernstein: *The Lean Years* (Baltimore, 1966), p. 311.
5 W. E. Leuchtenburg: *Franklin D. Roosevelt and the New Deal* (New York, 1963), p. 19; J. R. Commons: *History of Labor in the United States 1896–1932*, quoted in Shannon: *Great Depression*, pp. 7–10.
6 *Papers and Proceedings of the American Economic Association*, no. XXX (February 1941), pp. 250–1, quoted in Shannon: *Great Depression,* p. 6.
7 Frances Perkins: *The Roosevelt I Knew* (Edinburgh, 1947), p. 79.
8 Bernstein: *Lean Years*, p. 293; p. 298; p. 326.
9 Murray Kempton: *Part of Our Time* (New York, 1967), p. 5.
10 Schlesinger: *Crisis*, p. 178.
11 Subcommittee on Labor quoted above, quoted in Shannon: *Great Depression*, p. 122; 'And if the Revolution Comes . . .', *Harpers*, CLXIV (March 1932).
12 Schlesinger: *Crisis*, p. 228.
13 Schlesinger: *Crisis*, p. 217; p. 451; p.22.
14 Colonel J. Joy to Will H. Hays, letter dated 26 February 1932. Documents in the *I Am a Fugitive from a Chain Gang* file in the collection of papers of the Association of Motion Picture Producers and Distributors now housed in the Library of the Motion Picture Arts and Sciences, Los Angeles, California.
15 Darryl F. Zanuck to Joy. Documents in the *I am a Fugitive from a Chain Gang* file.
16 Grosses for all Warner Brothers films abstracted from Warners Special Collection (hereinafter WSC) in the Doheny Library, University of Southern California.
17 *Motion Picture Herald*, 18 July 1931.
18 *Motion Picture Herald*, 24 October 1931.
19 *Variety*, 29 December 1931.
20 *Variety*, 26 July 1932.
21 *Variety*, 23 February 1932.
22 *Variety*, 6 September 1932; 25 October 1932.
23 A film adaptation of the stage play written by Elmer Rice which had starred Paul Muni on Broadway.
24 The movie, which cost only $284,000 to make, still made a small profit despite the antagonism of the Hearst Press, which took it as a personal affront to the noble Fourth Estate and refused to carry reviews or advertising for it.
25 It might have been Zanuck talking to his writers at the Warner Brothers studio.
26 *Variety*, 3 December 1930.
27 *Variety*, 23 June 1931.
28 Gertrude Jobes: *Motion Picture Empire* (Hamden, Conn., 1966), p. 305; D. Gomery: *The Hollywood Studio System*, p. 20.
29 *Variety*, 22 December 1931.
30 Gomery: *Hollywood Studio System*, p. 31; pp. 28–9.

31 Gomery: *Hollywood Studio System*, pp. 125–7.
32 Gomery: *Hollywood Studio System*, p. 148; p. 162; p. 175; p. 52.
33 *The Hollywood Reporter*, 23 June 1933; 1 August 1933.
34 Quoted in W. E. Leuchtenburg: *The Perils of Prosperity* (Chicago, 1958), p. 266.
35 W. Lippmann: *Interpretations, 1931–1932*, quoted in A. B. Rollins (ed.): *Franklin D. Roosevelt and the Age of Action* (New York, 1960), p. 29.
36 Schlesinger: *Crisis*, p. 493; Schlesinger: *The Coming of the New Deal* (London, 1960), p. 9; John A. Garraty: *The Great Depression* (New York, 1987), p. 16.
37 Garraty: *The Great Depression*, p. 17.

3 THE BLUE EAGLE

1 Arthur M. Schlesinger Jr: *The Crisis of the Old Order* (London, 1958), p. 498.
2 Joseph P. Lash: *Eleanor & Franklin* (New York, 1973), p. 477.
3 *Variety*, 7 March 1933.
4 Ezra Goodman: *The Fifty Year Decline and Fall of Hollywood* (New York, 1961), p. 172.
5 Arthur M. Schlesinger Jr: *The Coming of the New Deal* (London, 1960), p. 13.
6 Schlesinger: *Coming*, p. 173; W. E. Leuchtenburg: *Franklin D. Roosevelt and the New Deal* (New York, 1963), p. 45; Raymond Moley: *After Seven Years* (New York, 1939), pp. 369–70.
7 Ellis W. Hawley: *The New Deal and the Problem of Monopoly* (Princeton, N.J., 1966), p. 390.
8 Schlesinger: *Coming*, p. 110.
9 Frances Perkins: *The Roosevelt I Knew* (Edinburgh, 1947), p. 162; Schlesinger: *Coming*, p. 393; p. 371.
10 Perkins: *Roosevelt*, p. 181.
11 Hillman's testimony before the Senate Finance Committee on the minimum wage and the impact of the NRA is quoted in Frank Friedel: *The New Deal and the American People* (Englewood Cliffs, N.J., 1964), p. 37.
12 Friedel: *New Deal*, p. 41.
13 Schlesinger: *Coming*, p. 112; Perkins, *Roosevelt*, p. 172.
14 *Variety*, 8 May 1933.
15 Darryl F. Zanuck to Robert Lord, 27 January 1933; Zanuck to William Wellman, 8 March 1933; Zanuck to Wellman, 18 March 1933, memoranda in *Heroes For Sale* file, WSC.
16 Gertrude Jobes: *Motion Picture Empire* (Hamden, Conn., 1966), p. 329.
17 *The Hollywood Reporter*, 26 August 1933; *Variety*, 29 August 1933.
18 Aljean Harmetz: *Round Up the Usual Suspects* (London, 1993), p. 78.
19 *Motion Picture Herald*, 30 November 1935; *Business Week*, 9 November 1935.
20 Arthur M. Schlesinger Jr: *The Politics of Upheaval* (London, 1961), p. 571; *The Hollywood Reporter*, 19 September 1936.
21 *The Hollywood Reporter*, 8 October 1936.
22 *Variety*, 11 November 1936.
23 Perkins: *Roosevelt*, p. 193.
24 *The New Republic*, 20 May 1940.
25 J. M. Burns: *Roosevelt – The Lion and the Fox* (New York, 1956), p. 241; 'Soak the Rich' became 'Soak the Successful' and NRA stood, according to Hearst, for 'No Recovery Allowed'.
26 Schlesinger: *Crisis*, p. 442.
27 B. Rauch: *The History of the New Deal* (New York, 1963), pp. 206–7.
28 *The New Republic*, 5 December 1934; *American Mercury*, July 1934.

29 Raymond S. Franklin: 'The Paradox of the New Deal' in Herbert D. Rosenbaum and Elizabeth Batelme (eds), *FDR: The Man, The Myth, The Era 1882–1945* (Westport, Conn., 1987), pp. 119–20.
30 W. E. Leuchtenburg: 'The Achievement of the New Deal' in Howard Sitkoff (ed.): *Fifty Years After: The New Deal Evaluated* (Philadelphia, 1985), p. 211.
31 William Troy, review of *Duck Soup* in *The Nation*, vol. 137 (13 December 1933), p. 688.
32 *Motion Picture Herald*, 3 February 34; Rauch: *History*, p. 93; *Motion Picture Herald*, 10 June 1933.
33 *The Hollywood Reporter*, 4 January 1933; see also *The Hollywood Reporter*, 12 May 1933 and *Variety*, 11 July 1933.
34 *The Hollywood Reporter*, 12 May 1933.
35 *The Hollywood Reporter*, 26 August 1933.
36 *Scribners*, January 1939.
37 *New Theatre*, July 1936; *Variety*, 27 May 1936; 19 August 1936.
38 *Motion Picture Herald*, 4 July 1936; 12 December 1936.

4 THE SWIMMING POOL REDS

1 Christopher Finch and Linda Rosenkrantz: *Gone Hollywood* (London, 1980), p .262.
2 Robert Warshow: *The Immediate Experience* (New York, 1970), p. 33.
3 Alfred Kazin: *Starting Out in the Thirties* (London, 1966), p. 4.
4 Quoted in Neal Gabler: *An Empire of their Own* (New York, 1988), p. 323.
5 Murray Kempton: *Part of our Time* (New York, 1967), p. 8; pp.3–4.
6 Kazin: *Starting Out*, p. 83.
7 See S. J. Perelman's humorous essay: *And Did You Once See Irving Plain?*.
8 Gabler: *An Empire*, p. 325.
9 Merle Miller and Evan Rhodes: *Only You Dick Daring* (New York, 1964), p. 181.
10 Gabler: *An Empire*, p. 330.
11 *The Hollywood Reporter*, 30 June 1933.
12 *The Hollywood Reporter*, 4 May 1936.
13 Bob Thomas: *Thalberg* (New York, 1970), pp. 250–1.
14 *Variety*, 6 May 1936; *The Hollywood Reporter*, 9 October 1937; *Motion Picture Herald*, 2 July 1938.
15 Leo Rosten: *Hollywood: The Movie Colony, the Movie Makers* (New York, 1941), p. 318.
16 *Variety*, 15 June 1938; *The Hollywood Reporter*, 7 May 1937.
17 *New York Times*, 2 April 1939; Frank Capra: *The Name Above the Title* (New York, 1971), pp. 267–71.
18 Pandro S. Berman, interviewed by the author, 19 March 1972, Beverly Hills.
19 Kempton: *Part of Our Time*, pp. 181–210. This is a fascinating, but very bitter, account of the fate of the Workers Theater in Hollywood. Kempton admits that he had not been to Hollywood before writing the essay, and one gathers from his writing that he dislikes or is at the very least indifferent to films. Nevertheless, it remains a perceptive analysis of the Hollywood Communists.
20 Gabler: *An Empire*, pp. 336–8.
21 S. J. Perelman: *My Life in Scotland Yard*; Philip French: *The Movie Moguls* (London, 1969), pp. 23–4; p. 2.
22 Adolph Zukor: *The Public Is Never Wrong* (London, 1954), p. 21.
23 French: *Movie Moguls*, p. 34.
24 Budd Schulberg: *Moving Pictures* (London, 1982), p. 191.

25 R. Brownstein: *The Power and the Glitter*, p. 21.
26 *Fortune*, December 1931, vol. 6, pp. 51–8. The article is reproduced in full in Tino Balio (ed.): *The American Film Industry* (Madison, Wisc., 1976), pp. 256–70.
27 *New York Times*, 12 January 1920. Quoted in Lewis Jacobs: *The Rise of the American Film* (New York, 1939), p. 398.
28 Abel Green and Joe Laurie Jr: *Showbiz: From Vaude to Video* (Garden City, N.Y., 1952), p. 205.
29 Quoted in French: *Movie Moguls*, p. 73.
30 Anon.: *The Sins of Hollywood*, p. 77. Quoted in Robert Sklar: *Movie-Made America* (New York, 1975), p. 76.
31 Lester Roth, quoted in Gabler: *An Empire*, p. 367.
32 Upton Sinclair: *Upton Sinclair Presents William Fox* (Los Angeles, 1933), p. 10.
33 Quoted in Gabler: *An Empire*, p. 277.
34 Gabler: *An Empire*, p. 256.
35 Bob Thomas: *King Cohn* (London, 1967), p. 60; Mel Gussow: *Don't Say Yes Until I Finish Talking* (New York, 1972), p. 107.
36 *The Hollywood Reporter*, 8 September 1934.
37 *The Hollywood Reporter*, 13 September 1934; 18 September 1934.
38 *The Hollywood Reporter*, 15 October 1934; 3 October 1934.
39 Rosten: *Hollywood*, p. 136.
40 Rosten: *Hollywood*, p. 136; *Variety*, 11 September 1934; 25 September 1934.
41 *Variety*, 25 September 1934.
42 Bosley Crowther: *Hollywood Rajah* (New York, 1961), pp. 226–7; the information about *Wild Boys of the Road* appeared in *Variety* (issue of 30 October 1934) a week before the election.
43 *The Hollywood Reporter*, 5 November 1934; 7 November 1934.
44 Rosten: *Hollywood*, p. 134.
45 Rosten: *Hollywood*, p. 145.
46 *The Hollywood Reporter*, 31 August 1935.
47 *Variety*, 14 October 1936.
48 Lester Cole, interviewed by the author, 23 April 1972, San Francisco.
49 Donald Ogden Stewart, interviewed by the author, May 1971, Hampstead, London.
50 *New Theatre*, November 1934, p. 22.
51 Raymond Durgnat and Scott Simmon: *King Vidor, American* (Berkeley and Los Angeles, 1988), p. 152.
52 King Vidor: *A Tree is a Tree* (Hollywood, 1989), pp. 222–7; Lewis Jacobs: *The Rise of the American Film* p. 459; *New York Times*, 7 October 1934.
53 William Troy, *The Nation*, 24 October 1934.
54 *Motion Picture Herald*, 7 December 1934.
55 Otis Ferguson, review of *Modern Times* in Alistair Cooke (ed.): *Garbo and the Nightwatchmen* (London, 1937), p. 342.
56 *Variety*, 1 March 1939; 6 November 1935.
57 *The Hollywood Reporter*, 14 November 1935.
58 *The Hollywood Reporter*, 15 February 1936.

5 FANFARE FOR THE COMMON MAN

1 Warner Brothers' contribution to the genre is discussed in detail in Chapter 9.
2 *The Hollywood Reporter*, 31 January 1935.
3 *Variety*, 27 February 1935.
4 Mel Gussow: *Don't Say Yes Until I Finish Talking* (New York, 1972), pp. 82–4.

5 *Los Angeles Citizen*, 28 August 1939; *The Hollywood Reporter*, 1 September 1939.
6 *Variety*, 31 January 1940.
7 *Motion Picture Herald*, 10 February 1940. The italics are in the original article. Quigley was a conservative Catholic, who left most of the leader writing to his Editor, Terry Ramsaye (author of the classic book on silent movies, *A Million and One Nights*). It needed a major issue like this or *Blockade* (see Chapter 11) to induce him to write his own editorial.
8 Ford won his second Oscar as Best Director (the first had been for *The Informer*, 1935). Jane Darwell won the award for Best Supporting Actress for her portrayal of Ma Joad.
9 Ford and Capra were both raised as Catholics but showed more evidence of the fact in their movies than in their private lives.
10 Gussow, *Don't Say Yes*, p. 86.
11 *Los Angeles Evening Herald*, 23 January 1940.
12 From the many anecdotes told about Ford it seems that the man positively enjoyed tormenting his actors. Henry Fonda was not surprised at the number of actors who pointedly refused to work with him twice. Interview with the author, 3 May 1972, Bel Air.
13 John Baxter: *The Cinema of John Ford* (London, 1972), p. 45.
14 This speech appears in the published script (J. Gassner and D. Nichols (eds): *Twenty Best Film Plays* (New York, 1943) but not in most prints of the film in circulation.
15 Fonda reveals that he was persuaded to take the role only on Ford's assurance that he would be playing the part of the young man and not the Great Emancipator. Interview with the author, 3 May 1972, Bel Air.
16 Baxter: *John Ford*, p. 34.
17 F. J. Turner: *The Frontier in American History* (New York, 1945), p. 1; p. 30.
18 *The Hollywood Reporter*, 12 December 1933.
19 Robert Lord, interview with the author, 12 May 1972, Hollywood; William Wellman, interview with the author, 14 February 1972, Brentwood, Los Angeles.
20 *Motion Picture Herald*, 27 February 1937; *Monthly Film Bulletin*, vol. 4, no. 38, p. 37; G. Greene, *The Spectator*, 12 February 1937.
21 Bean was a historical figure. Walter Brennan won an Oscar as Best Supporting Actor for his portrayal of Bean. John Huston's *The Life and Times of Judge Roy Bean* starring Paul Newman was made in 1972.
22 *Variety*, 1 September 1937.
23 These figures are, of course, the classic Populist bogeymen.
24 Final sceen credit is shared with Paul Green.
25 *Variety*, 31 January 1933.
26 *Motion Picture Herald*, 13 May 1933; *Variety*, 6 June 1933.
27 Dwight Macdonald: *On Movies* (New York, 1971), p. 114.
28 *Variety*, 31 July 1935.
29 Frank Capra, interviewed by the author, 10 February 1972, La Quinta, California.
30 *Frank Capra: One Man – One Film*, pamphlet published by the American Film Institute (Washington, 1971), pp. 18–19.
31 Richard Griffith: *Frank Capra*, pamphlet published by the British Film Institute (London, 1948), p. 7.
32 *Variety*, 2 February 1932.
33 Frank Capra: *The Name Above the Title* (New York, 1971), p. 240.
34 Capra: *The Name*, p. 183.
35 The Homestead Act of 1862 tried to legislate the Jeffersonian ideal of a nation of self-sufficient farmers.Longfellow Deeds also recognises that working the land is the only true currency in paying for it.

36 Capra: *The Name*, p. 241.
37 As John Doe leaves the platform, after having been framed and publicly humiliated by Norton, he is scorned and reviled and pelted with rolled up newspapers, soggy from the teeming rain. The scene conveys the impression of a modern progress to Calvary.
38 Jeffrey Richards: 'Frank Capra and the Populist Cinema', in *Cinema* no. 5, Cambridge, February 1970.
39 Joseph McBride: *Frank Capra – The Catastrophe of Success* (London, 1992).
40 McBride: *Frank Capra*, pp. 53–4.
41 Capra: *The Name*, p. 240.

6 THE HAYS OFFICE

1 Terry Ramsaye: *A Million and One Nights* (London, 1964), pp. 810 21.
2 The 'Don'ts' and 'Be Carefuls' were a list of eleven things to be avoided in pictures and of twenty-five subjects which were to be treated with special care. They were included as Rule 21 of the Code of the Motion Picture Industry, adopted at a trade practices conference conducted by the Federal Trade Commission in New York City in October 1927.
3 W. E. Leuchtenburg: *The Perils of Prosperity* (Chicago, 1958), pp. 159–61.
4 L. J. Leff and J.Simmons: *The Dame in the Kimono* (London, 1990), p. 8.
5 Richard Maltby: *Harmless Entertainment* (Metuchen, N.J. and London, 1983), p. 104.
6 Margaret Thorp: *America at the Movies* (London, 1946), p. 113; Maltby: *Harmless Entertainment*, p. 101.
7 *Motion Picture Herald*, 18 July 1931.
8 John Baxter: *The Cinema of Josef von Sternberg* (London, 1971), p. 100.
9 Lamar Trotti to Will Hays, letter dated 22 April 1932 in the *Blonde Venus* file amongst documents of the Hays Office now deposited in the Library of the Academy of Motion Picture Arts and Sciences, Los Angeles, California.
10 Trotti to Hays, letter dated 30 April 1932, *Blonde Venus* file.
11 *Motion Picture Herald*, 21 March 1931.
12 *Variety*, 20 June 1933.
13 Colonel Joy to B. P. Schulberg, letter dated 17 April 1931 in the *One Hour With You* file, Hays Office documents.
14 *Motion Picture Herald*, 3 February 1934.
15 *Motion Picture Herald*, 17 December 1933. *The Cradle Song* (directed by Mitchell Leisen) starred Evelyn Venables and Sir Guy Standing and concerned endearing events in a convent.
16 *Variety*, 15 June 1934; see also Maltby: *Harmless Entertainment*, p. 104.
17 For the *Blockade* boycott see below, Chapter 11.
18 Will Hays to James Wingate, letter dated 14 February 1933 in the *Gabriel Over the White House* file, Hays Office documents.
19 Block booking was the system whereby companies sold their films in blocks to independent distributors and exhibitors For every good film in a block there might be ten poor ones which the exhibitors had to buy if they wanted the one commercial picture. It is a system that still operates in television distribution.
20 *Variety*, 19 June 1934.
21 *The Hollywood Reporter*, 29 June 1937.
22 Quoted in Thorp: *America at the Movies*, p. 76.
23 'Motherhood: What it means to Helen Twelvetrees' in M. Levin (ed.): *Hollywood*

and the Great Fan Magazines (New York, 1970), p. 37; 'Ginger Rogers: Did I Get What I Wanted Out of Life?', *ibid.*, p. 130, 205–6.

24 The title was changed in response to a Hays Office ruling which decreed that a divorced woman could be gay (original meaning) in certain situations but the institution never could.

25 All financial statements abstracted from the RKO files deposited in the Special Collections of the Library of the University of California, Los Angeles.

26 *Motion Picture Herald*, 16 January 1937; *The Hollywood Reporter*, 27 July 1936.

27 *Motion Picture Herald*, 21 December 1935; *Variety*, 8 September 1935.

28 *Motion Picture Herald*, 1 September 1934; 8 September 1934.

29 *New York Times*, 26 March 1938.

30 *Variety*, 7 August 1935.

31 Joseph Breen to Samuel Goldwyn, in the *Dead End* file, Hays Office documents.

32 Breen to Goldwyn, *Dead End* file.

33 The one invariably induces the other; compare the sightseeing sequence in Capra's *Mr Smith Goes To Washington* and the end of Ford's *Young Mr Lincoln*.

34 James Wingate to Will Hays, memorandum dated 28 January 1933, in the *Gabriel Over the White House* file, Hays Office Documents.

35 Wingate to Irving G. Thalberg, letter dated 28 January 1933, in the *Gabriel Over the White House* file, Hays Office documents.

36 Wingate to Louis B. Mayer, letter dated 2 February 1933, in the *Gabriel Over the White House* file, Hays Office documents; the Jolson picture referred to is *Hallelujah, I'm a Bum*.

37 Wingate to Thalberg, letter dated 6 February 1933, in the *Gabriel Over the White House* file, Hays Office documents..

38 Wingate to Thalberg, letter dated 8 February 1933, in the *Gabriel Over the White House* file, Hays Office documents.

39 Wingate to Will Hays, letter dated 11 February 1933, in the *Gabriel Over the White House* file, Hays Office documents.

40 Wingate to Hays, memorandum dated 16 February 1933, in the *Gabriel Over the White House* file, Hays Office documents.

41 Wingate to Mayer, letter dated 16 February 1933, in the *Gabriel Over the White House* file, Hays Office documents.

42 Wingate to Hays, memorandum dated 7 February 1933, in the *Gabriel Over the White House* file, Hays Office documents.

43 Wingate to Hays, memorandum dated 8 February 1933, in the *Gabriel Over the White House* file, Hays Office documents.

44 Colonel Herron to James Wingate, letter dated 28 February, in the *Gabriel Over the White House* file, Hays Office documents.

45 Wingate to Hays, memorandum dated 23 February 1933, in the *Gabriel Over the White House* file, Hays Office documents.

46 Wingate to Hays, letter dated 1 March 1933, in the *Gabriel Over the White House* file, Hays Office documents.

47 Geoffrey Shurlock, memorandum dated 2 March 1933, in the *Gabriel Over the White House* file, Hays Office documents.

48 Wingate to Hays, telegram dated 3 March 1933, in the *Gabriel Over the White House* file, Hays Office documents: 3 March was the climactic day of bank failures. The following day was Roosevelt's inauguration.

49 Will Hays, internal memorandum dated 7 March 1933, in the *Gabriel Over the White House* file, Hays Office docments.

50 *New York Times*, 8 March 1933.

51 Wingate to Thalberg, letter dated 30 March 1933, in the *Gabriel Over the White House* file, Hays Office documents.
52 Hearst, controlling the California delegation to the 1932 Democratic Convention, made the decision to switch from Garner to Roosevelt (to avoid the nomination of the conservative Newton D. Baker) and thus started the triumphant roll of the Roosevelt bandwagon.
53 *The American*, quoted in *The Hollywood Reporter*, 5 April 1933.
54 William Troy, *The Nation*, 26 April 1933.
55 *Variety*, 4 April 1933.
56 *Literary Digest*, 22 April 1933.
57 Directed by William Wellman for Paramount.
58 Joseph Breen to Walter Wanger, letter dated 19 September 1934, in *The President Vanishes* file, Hays Office documents.
59 Breen to Wanger, letter dated 20 September 1934, in *The President Vanishes* file, Hays Office documents.
60 Hays to Adolph Zukor, letter dated 22 November 1934, in *The President Vanishes* file, Hays Office documents.
61 Hays to Zukor, letter dated 23 November 1934, in *The President Vanishes* file, Hays Office documents.
62 *The Hollywood Reporter*, 22 November 1934; 23 November 1934.
63 Hays to Breen, memorandum dated 29 March 1935, in *The President Vanishes* file, Hays Office documents.

7 THE LEFT-HANDED ENDEAVOUR

1 Walter B. Pitkin, *The Outlook*, 29 July 1931.
2 R. Warshow: *The Immediate Experience* (New York, 1970), p. 130.
3 Kenneth Allsop: *The Bootleggers* (London, 1970), p. 410.
4 Allsop: *The Bootleggers*, pp. 343–4; *Variety*, 25 October 1939.
5 Daniel Bell: *The End of Ideology* (Glencoe, Ill., 1960), p. 115.
6 Allsop: *The Bootleggers*, p. 292.
7 Allsop: *The Bootleggers*, p. 110.
8 From the film *20,000 Years in Sing Sing* directed by Michael Curtiz, 1933, Warner Brothers.
9 Pasley continued, 'It is a curious fact that Capone is the object of a sort of hero worship. People go out of their way to shake hands with him' (F. D. Pasley: *Al Capone* (London, 1931), p. 74.
10 John Kobler: *Al Capone* (Greenwich, Conn., 1972), p. 298.
11 Allsop: *The Bootleggers*, p. 384.
12 *Variety*, 13 October 1931; 30 June 1931.
13 Allsop: *The Bootleggers*, p. 342.
14 Allsop: *The Bootleggers*, p. 244.
15 Kobler: *Al Capone*, p. 313.
16 Bell: *The End of Ideology*, p. 121.
17 Allsop: *The Bootleggers*, p. 326.
18 W. E. Leuchtenburg: *The Perils of Prosperity* (Chicago, 1958), p. 216.
19 *New York Times*, 10 January 1931.
20 *New York Times*, 18 April 1931.
21 *Variety*, 14 January 1931.
22 Pat McGilligan (ed.): *Backstory: Interviews with Screenwriters of Hollywood's Golden Years*, (Berkeley, 1986), p. 57.
23 John Webster, *The Duchess of Malfi*, Act III scene ii.

24 John Webster, *The White Devil*, Act V scene vi.
25 Colonel S. Joy to E. B. Derr of United Artists, letter dated 4 June 1931 in the *Scarface* file, Hays Office documents.
26 Memorandum written by Colonel S. Joy dated 22 September 1931, in the *Scarface* file, Hays Office documents.
27 *Hollywood Citizen News*, 20 March 1935.
28 *Motion Picture Herald*, 17 December 1932.
29 *Sight and Sound*, winter 1967–8, pp. 3–8.
30 *Variety*, 20 February 1935.
31 *Variety*, 8 May 1935.
32 Will H. Hays to Harry M. Warner, letter dated 1 March 1935 in the *G-Men* file, Hays Office documents.
33 Joseph Breen to Jack L. Warner, letter dated 1 March 1935, in the *G-Men* file, Hays Office documents. Original underlining.
34 Breen to Warner, letter dated 6 March 1935, in the *G-Men* file, Hays Office documents. Original underlining.
35 Harry Warner to William Keghley, memorandum in the *G-Men* file, Hays Office documents.
36 *The New Republic*, 16 May 1935.
37 Joseph Breen to James Wingate, letter dated 6 April 1935, in the *G-Men* file, Hays Office documents.
38 *Motion Picture Herald*, 29 June 1935.
39 Jack Moffitt to Jack Warner, telegram in *G-Men* file, WSC.
40 Breen to Hays, memorandum dated 10 April 1935, in The *G-Men* file, Hays Office documents.
41 *The Hollywood Reporter*, 30 July 1935.
42 *Motion Picture Herald*, 3 December 1936.
43 *New York Times*, 27 May 1936.
44 *Variety*, 3 June 1936.
45 *Motion Picture Herald*, 2 November 1935.
46 In 1936 Davis had fled to England in an unsuccessful legal attempt to break her contract with Warners.
47 Thomas Dewey to Will H. Hays, letter dated 16 March 1937 in the *Racket Busters* file, Hays Office documents.
48 Letter to Walter MacEwen dated 18 January 1938, in the *Racket Busters* file, WSC.
49 This is a good example of the sort of line which Left-wing writers (Rossen was for a time a member of the Hollywood Communist Party) would try to slip past vigilant producers. See Chapter 4.
50 *New York Times*, 11 August 1938.
51 *Variety*, 17 August 1938.
52 Joseph Breen, memorandum dated 6 April 1938, in the *Angels With Dirty Faces* file, Hays Office documents.
53 Breen to Jack L. Warner, 14 April 1938.
54 Sam Bischoff to Hal B. Wallis, memorandum dated 14 January 1938, WSC.
55 Lou Edelman to Hal Wallis, memorandum dated 18 January 1938, WSC.
56 *Variety*, 14 December 1938.
57 Robert Lord to Hal Wallis, memorandum dated 25 July 1938, in *The Roaring Twenties* file, WSC.
58 Lord to McEwen, memorandum dated 1 August 1938.
59 McEwen to Wallis, memorandum dated 19 October 1938 in *The Roaring Twenties* file, WSC.
60 Memorandum dated 3 March 1939, in *The Roaring Twenties* file, WSC.

61 Warren Duff to Hal Wallis, memorandum dated 7 March 1939, in *The Roaring Twenties* file, WSC.
62 Jack L. Warner, memoranda to all departments dated 8 July 1939, 9 July 1939.
63 The original name in the script is Kansas. It was changed to Panama presumably because Kansas patrons might take offence at the portrayal of the speakeasy owner. Panama was less commercially important to Warners and it was just hard luck if anyone living in Panama objected.
64 It first appeared as *The Maltese Falcon* (directed by Roy Del Ruth for Warners) in 1931, starring Ricardo Cortez and Bebe Daniels; in 1936 it reappeared as *Satan Met a Lady*, directed by William Dieterle and starring Warren William and Bette Davis.

8 CRY OF THE CITY

1 Quoted in Richard Maltby: *Harmless Entertainment*, p. 155.
2 Maltby, *Harmless Entertainment*, p. 154.
3 *Exhibitors Herald World*, 27 July 1929.
4 *Motion Picture Herald*, 8 May 1937; *Variety*, 12 May 1937. The approximate figure is the result of the differing statistics printed by the two journals.
5 Examples include Colbert in Lubitsch's *The Smiling Lieutenant* (1931, Paramount) and *Midnight* (directed by Mitchell Leisen, 1939, Paramount); Dietrich in von Sternberg's *The Scarlet Empress* (1934) and *The Devil Is a Woman* (1935, both Paramount); Hepburn in Cukor's *Sylvia Scarlett* (1935, RKO) and *Quality Street* (1937, RKO).
6 Margaret Thorp: *America at the Movies* (New Haven, 1939), pp. 19–21.
7 *Motion Picture Herald*, 15 December 1934.
8 *Motion Picture Herald*, 9 November 1935.
9 Kevin Brownlow: *The Parade's Gone By* (New York, 1969), p. 261.
10 The film was completed and forgotten by both the director and the producer. Mervyn LeRoy interviewed by the author, 2 March 1972, Bel Air, and Robert Lord, interviewed by the author, 19 March 1972, Hollywood. Neither could remember anything about it.
11 When the characters are carried over to Vidor's next film about Everyman (*Our Daily Bread*, see Chapter 4) the banjo reappears to be pawned by the hungry couple as payment for a scrawny chicken.
12 *Variety*, 22 February 1928.
13 R. Warshow: *The Immediate Experience* (New York, 1970), p. 130.
14 W. E. Leuchtenburg: *The Perils of Prosperity* (Chicago, 1958), p. 225.
15 Constance M. Green: *The Rise of Urban America* (New York, 1967), p. 165.
16 Quoted in Green: *The Rise*, p. 158.
17 B. McKelvey: *The Emergence of Metropolitan America 1915–66* (New Brunswick, N.J., 1966), p. 83.
18 Green *The Rise*, p. 153; McKelvey: *The Emergence*, p. 81.
19 Green: *The Rise*, p. 154; McKelvey: *The Emergence*, p. 103.
20 J. J. Hutmacher: *Senator Robert F. Wagner and the Rise of Urban Liberalism* (New York, 1968), p. 116; p.205.
21 Hutmacher: *Wagner*, p. 206.
22 P. S. Broughton in his introduction to R. S. Lubove: *The Progressive and the Slums* (Pittsburgh, 1962), p. xv; p. 237.
23 McKelvey: *The Emergence*, p. 95. W. E. Leuchtenburg: *Franklin D. Roosevelt and the New Deal* (New York, 1963), pp. 187–8; A. Schlesinger Jr: *The Politics of Upheaval* (London, 1961), p. 428; G. E. Mowry: *The Urban Nation* (New York, 1968), p. 90; S. Lubell: *The Future of American Politics* (New York, 1956), pp. 29–60.

24 F. Perkins: *The Roosevelt I Knew* (Edinburgh, 1947), pp. 102–3; pp. 128–31.
25 McKelvey: *The Emergence*, p. 109.
26 *Variety*, 4 August 1937.

9 GOOD CITIZENSHIP AND GOOD PICTURE-MAKING

1 Alvah Bessie: *Inquisition in Eden* (East Berlin, 1967), p. 218. Julius Epstein remarked on watching studio policemen shooting at Warner Brothers' striking employees in 1946 that the sign should have been amended to read 'Combining Good Citizenship with Good Marksmanship'.
2 Benjamin B. Hampton: *A History of the American Film Industry* (New York, 1970), p. 380–4; *Variety*, 9 October 1929; 27 October 1929.
3 *Variety*, 22 January 1941.
4 Robert Lord, interviewed by the author, 1 April 1972, Hollywood.
5 *Variety*, 27 March 1934.
6 *Variety*, 27 May 1931.
7 Robert Lord, letter to the author, dated 28 June 1972.
8 John Baxter: *Hollywood in the Thirties* (London, 1968), p. 50.
9 *Motion Picture Herald*, 11 March 1933.
10 *Motion Picture Herald*, 14 October 1933.
11 See Chapter 2, pp. 20–1.
12 Robert Lord, interviewed by the author, 13 May 1972, Hollywood.
13 *Motion Picture Herald*, 11 March 1933.
14 *Motion Picture Herald*, 3 February 1934.
15 *Motion Picture Herald*, 5 August 1933.
16 *New York Times*, 18 January 1937; *Variety*, 20 January 1937.
17 Joseph I. Breen to Jack L. Warner, letter dated 18 June 1936, in the *Black Legion* file, Hays Office documents.
18 Robert Lord, interviewed by the author, 29 April 1972, Hollywood.
19 Hal Wallis to Archie Mayo, memorandum dated 24 September 1936, in the *Black Legion* file, WSC.
20 *Motion Picture Herald*, 9 April 1938.
21 *New York Times*, 18 January 1937.
22 Lord to Wallis, memorandum dated 16 July 1936, in the *Black Legion* file, WSC.
23 *New York Herald Tribune,* 30 September 1932
24 *New York Telegraph*, 3 October 1932.
25 *Motion Picture Herald*, 10 September 1932.
26 Jack L. Warner (with Dean Jennings): *My First Hundred Years in Hollywood* (New York, 1964), pp. 215–16.
27 Warner: *My First Hundred Years*, p. 208: Bob Thomas: *Clown Prince of Hollywood* (New York, 1990), p. 93.
28 Warner: *My First Hundred Years*, pp. 224, 285.
29 *Variety*, 24 July 1934.
30 *Variety*, 10 January 1933.
31 *Variety*, 11 June 1933.
32 See *Baby Face* file, WSC.
33 Mr and Mrs William Wellman, interviewed by the author, 14 February 1972, Brentwood, Los Angeles.
34 Wallis to Wellman, memorandum dated 29 June 1933, in the *Wild Boys of the Road* file, WSC.
35 *Motion Picture Herald*, 4 November 1933.
36 *Variety*, 26 September 1933.

37 *New York Times*, 23 September 1933.
38 James Wingate to Albert Howson, letter dated 10 August 1933, in the *Wild Boys of the Road* file, Hays Office documents.
39 Wingate to Jack L. Warner, letter dated 9 August 1933, in the *Wild Boys of the Road* file, Hays Office documents..
40 Wingate to Zanuck, letter dated 1 March 1933, in the *Heroes for Sale* file, Hays Office documents.
41 *Variety*, 25 July 1933.
42 *The Hollywood Reporter*, 17 July 1933.
43 Wingate to Jack L. Warner, letter dated 20 March 1933, in the *Heroes for Sale* file, Hays Office documents..
44 Wingate to Jack Warner, letter dated 9 December 1933, in the *Massacre* file, Hays Office documents.
45 *Massacre* file in the WSC.

10 BLACK FURY

1 I. Bernstein: *The Lean Years 1920–32* (Baltimore, 1966), p. 127; H. Pelling: *American Labor* (Chicago, 1960), p. 153.
2 Joseph G. Raybeck: *A History of American Labor* (New York, 1959), pp. 307–9; Bernstein: *The Lean Years*, p. 130. The wording of Lewis's response was echoed two years later in 1926 in Britain by A. J. Cook, the Secretary of the National Union of Mineworkers, when he answered a similar demand for a cut in wages or longer hours of work with the words, 'Not a penny off the pay, not a minute on the day'.
3 Bernstein: *The Lean Years*, p. 130.
4 *The Observer*, London, 6 October 1935.
5 Michael A. Musmanno: *Black Fury* (New York, 1966), pp. 301–2.
6 *Musmanno: Black Fury,* p. 317.
7 The executives in charge of the production were Jack L. Warner and Hal B. Wallis.
8 Abe Finkel (who also shared the screenplay credit on *Black Legion*) was Muni's brother-in-law and, according to Lord, the only man at the studio permitted to argue with the temperamental star. From an interview conducted by the author with Robert Lord in Hollywood, 29 April 1935.
9 Musmanno belonged to a vigilante organisation called Americans Battling Communism and by all accounts behaved in his judicial capacity with precisely the same bias that he castigates in *Black Fury*. David Caute, *The Great Fear* (London, 1978), pp. 218–21.
10 Musmanno: *Black Fury*, p. 69.
11 Musmanno: *Black Fury*, p. 246.
12 Philip Taft: *Organized Labor in American History* (New York, 1964) pp. 395–9; S. Perlman and P. Taft: *History of Labor in the United States 1896–1932* (New York, 1935), vol. IV, p. 567.
13 Musmanno: *Black Fury*, p. 168.
14 Musmanno: *Black Fury*, p. 99.
15 Musmanno: *Black Fury*, pp. 16–17.
16 Musmanno: *Black Fury*, p. 51.
17 Musmanno: *Black Fury*, pp. 117–19.
18 Musmanno: *Black Fury*, p. 187.
19 Musmanno: *Black Fury*, p. 54; p. 95; p. 97.
20 Musmanno: *Black Fury*, p. 271; p. 272.
21 Musmanno: *Black Fury*, p. 282.
22 Musmanno: *Black Fury*, p. 292–3.

23 Musmanno: *Black Fury*, p. 291.
24 Musmanno: *Black Fury*, p. 301.
25 Quotations from the *Jan Volkanik* script are taken from what appears to be the only remaining copy in the files of the Story Department in the Warner Brothers studio, Burbank, California now located in the WSC.
26 The Jacksonville Agreement signed in Jacksonville, Florida in 1924 has now been changed in the script to the fictional 'Shalerville' Agreement.
27 An editorial in the magazine *New Masses* indicates that Paramount News suppressed its newsreel of the Chicago Memorial Day massacre. The *St Louis Post Dispatch* was the first newspaper to reveal this information but the newspaper owners closed ranks behind the steel magnates and insisted that there could be no compromise with 'labor violence'. See *New Masses*, 29 June 1937, and Howard Fast: 'An Occurrence at Republic Steel', in I. Leighton (ed.): *The Aspirin Age* (London, 1964), p. 406.
28 Joseph Breen to Will H. Hays, report dated 20 September 1934, in the *Black Fury* file, Hays Office documents.
29 J. D. Battle to J. Breen, letter dated 29 August 1934, in the *Black Fury* file, Hays Office documents.
30 Hays to Harry M. Warner, letter dated 4 September 1934, in the *Black Fury* file, Hays Office documents.
31 Breen to Jack Warner, letter dated 9 October 1934, in the *Black Fury* file, Hays Office documents.
32 Breen to Jack Warner, letter dated 7 May 1934, in the *Black Fury* file, Hays Office documents.
33 Breen to Jack Warner, letter dated 12 September 1934, in the *Black Fury* file, Hays Office documents.
34 Breen to Jack Warner, letter dated 12 September 1934, in the *Black Fury* file, Hays Office documents.
35 Breen to Jack Warner, letter dated 12 September 1934, in the *Black Fury* file, Hays Office documents.
36 Breen to Jack Warner, letter dated 12 September 1934, in the *Black Fury* file, Hays Office documents.
37 Breen to Jack Warner, letter dated 12 September 1934, in the *Black Fury* file, Hays Office documents.
38 Musmanno: *Black Fury*, pp. 302–3.
39 Musmanno: *Black Fury*, p. 303.
40 Hays to Myron C. Taylor, letter dated 2 November 1934, in the *Black Fury* file, Hays Office documents.
41 Hays to R. H. Sherwood, letter dated 11 February 1935, in the *Black Fury* file, Hays Office documents.
42 Breen to Dr James J. Wingate, letter dated 26 March 1935, in the *Black Fury* file, Hays Office documents.
43 Breen to Wingate, letter dated 29 March 1935, in the *Black Fury* file, Hays Office documents.
44 Entries dated 10 May 1935, 27 April 1935, 26 March 1935, 31 March 1935, 11 April 1935, all in the *Black Fury* file, Hays Office documents; *Variety*, 9 February 1938; *Motion Picture Herald*, 27 April 1935; *The Hollywood Reporter*, 27 March 1935; 17 April 1935.
45 Quoted in *Variety*, 17 April 1935.
46 *The New Republic*, 24 April 1935.
47 *New York Times*, 11 April 1935.
48 *Motion Picture Herald*, 27 June 1935; 3 August 1935; 14 September 1935.

49 The Best Actor award that year went to Victor McLaglen for his performance in *The Informer* (RKO).
50 *The Hollywood Reporter*, 26 March 1935.
51 *The Nation*, 24 April 1935; *New Masses*, 23 April 1935.
52 Robert Lord interviewed by the author, 29 April 1972, Hollywood.

11 FOREIGN AFFAIRS

1 W. E. Leuchtenburg: *Franklin D. Roosevelt and the New Deal* (New York, 1963), pp. 197–204.
2 *Variety*, 17 March 1937; 29 July 1937.
3 *New York Times*, 19 June 1937.
4 *The Hollywood Reporter*, 22 March 1937.
5 John Howard Lawson: *Film The Creative Process* (New York, 1963), pp. 124–7.
6 Joseph Breen to Walter Wanger, letter dated 22 February 1937, in the *Blockade* file, Hays Office documents.
7 Breen to Hays, Progress Report on *Blockade* dated 28 February 1937, Hays Office documents.
8 Breen to Wanger, letter dated 3 February 1937, in the *Blockade* file, Hays Office documents.
9 Breen to Wanger, letter dated 7 February 1937, in the *Blockade* file, Hays Office documents.
10 Memorandum dated 10 May 1938, in the *Blockade* file, Hays Office documents.
11 Breen to Wanger, letter dated 4 January 1938, in the *Blockade* file, Hays Office documents.
12 Henry Fonda, interviewed by the author, 3 May 1972, Bel Air.
13 *Variety Preview*, 3 June 1938.
14 Letter from Joseph F. Lamb to Will H. Hays. Quoted in *New York Times*, 26 June 1938.
15 *Motion Picture Herald*, 9 July 1938.
16 John Howard Lawson, interviewed by the author, 12 May 1972, Van Nuys, California.
17 M. Thorp: *America at the Movies*, pp. 212–13.
18 *New York Times*, 7 July 1938; *Life* magazine, 18 July 1938.
19 *Motion Picture Herald*, 19 November 1938.
20 *Motion Picture Herald*, 22 October 1938; 24 December 1938.
21 *Daily Telegraph*, 6 June 1938; *The Observer*, 12 June 1938.
22 Lawson: *Film*, p. 127.
23 *New York Times*, 17 June 1938.
24 *Life*, 18 July 1938.
25 Lawson, interviewed by the author, 12 May 1972.
26 R. Sklar: *City Boys*, pp. 146–7.
27 *The Hollywood Reporter*, 10 June 1936.
28 *Variety, 25 November 1936.*
29 Joseph Breen to Jack Warner, letter dated 19 January 1938, in the *Angels with Dirty Faces* file, WSC.
30 *New York Daily News*, 17 August 1938; *Variety*, 29 December 1937, lists the names of all those who contributed towards buying ambulances for Spain.
31 *Variety*, 29 March 1939.
32 *Variety*, 24 July 1940.
33 *Variety*, 12 February 1936.
34 Memo dated 15 July 1936, in the *Life of Emile Zola* file, WSC.

35 Joseph Breen to Jack Warner, letter dated 12 February 1937, in the *Life of Emile Zola* file, Hays Office documents.
36 Breen to Warner, letter dated 17 May 1937, in the *Life of Emile Zola* file, Hays Office documents.
37 *New York Times*, 12 August 1937.
38 *Monthly Film Bulletin*, vol. 4, no. 45, p. 197.
39 *Motion Picture Herald*, 9 April 1938.
40 Memorandum dated 31 August 1938, in the *Life of Emile Zola* file, Hays Office documents.
41 *New York Times*, 12 August 1937.
42 Press release in the *Juarez* file, WSC.
43 *Variety*, 27 December 1939.
44 Leuchtenburg: *Roosevelt*, pp. 226–7.
45 Jack Warner (with Dean Jennings): *My First Hundred Years in Hollywood* (New York, 1964), p. 249.
46 Thomas Doherty: *Projections of War* (New York, 1993), p. 311n; Aljean Harmetz: *Round Up the Usual Suspects* (London, 1993), p. 53.
47 *Variety*, 20 April 1938.
48 *Variety*, 29 May 1940.
49 A. Bessie: *Inquisition in Eden* (East Berlin, 1967), p. 78.
50 Neal Gabler: *An Empire of Their Own*, pp. 289–90.
51 Harmetz: *Round Up*, p. 67.
52 Robert Lord, interviewed by the author, 15 May 1972, Hollywood.
53 L. Luraschi to J. Breen, letter dated 10 December 1938, in the *Confessions of a Nazi Spy* file, Hays Office documents.
54 Memorandum in the *Confessions of a Nazi Spy* file, Hays Office documents.
55 Breen to Warner, letter dated 30 December 1938, in the *Confessions of a Nazi Spy* file, Hays Office documents.
56 Robert Lord to Joseph Breen, letter dated 24 December 1938, in the *Confessions of a Nazi Spy* file, Hays Office documents.
57 George Gyssling to Joseph Breen, letter dated 27 October 1938, in the *Confessions of a Nazi Spy* file, Hays Office documents.
58 *Confessions of a Nazi Spy* file, WSC.
59 Robert Lord to Joseph Breen, letter dated 25 January 1939, in the *Confessions of a Nazi Spy* file, Hays Office documents.
60 *New York Times*, 29 April 1939.
61 Memoranda dated 28 April 1939, in the *Confessions of a Nazi Spy* file, WSC.
62 Warner: *My First Hundred Years*, pp. 262–3.
63 *Variety*, 24 April 1940.
64 *Los Angeles Examiner*, 6 June 1939.
65 *Variety*, 31 May 1939.
66 George E. Mowry: *The Urban Nation* (New York, 1968), pp. 130–6.
67 *Variety*, 18 January 1939.
68 Leuchtenburg: *Roosevelt*, pp. 320–1.

12 SNAPSHOT: HOLLYWOOD AND THE NATION, SEPTEMBER 1939

1 Quoted in M. Thorp: *America at the Movies* (London, 1946), p. 174.
2 *Variety*, 1 March 1939.
3 *Variety*, 10 May 1939.
4 Quoted in Rudi Behlmer: *Inside Warner Bros.* (New York, 1985), p. 73.

5 Thorp: *America*, p. 19.
6 L. Rosten: *Hollywood: The Movie Colony*, p. 3.
7 D. Gomery: *The Hollywood Studio System*, p. 152.
8 Gomery: *The Hollywood Studio System*, pp. 60–2.
9 Gomery: *The Hollywood Studio System*, p. 41.
10 Thorp: *America*, p. 91.
11 J. R. Taylor: *Strangers in Paradise* (London, 1983), p. 16.
12 Christopher Finch and Linda Rosenkrantz (eds): *Gone Hollywood* (London, 1980), p. xi.
13 Finch and Rosenkrantz: *Gone Hollywood*, pp. 171–2.
14 Thorp: *America*, p. 62: p. 54.
15 Thorp: *America*, pp. 55–8.
16 Thomas Schatz: *The Genius of the System* (London, 1989), p. 292; John Baxter: *Sixty Years of Hollywood*, (London, 1973), p. 125.
17 F. Capra: *The Name Above the Title*, p. 298.
18 William Manchester: *The Glory and the Dream* (Boston, 1974), pp. 201–2.
19 Dr Georg Gyssling to Joseph Breen, letter dated 31 October 1938, in *The Great Dictator* file, Hays Office documents.
20 *The Great Dictator* file, Hays Office documents.
21 Richard Hofstadter: *Great Issues in American History Volume 1* (New York, 1958), pp. 214–15.
22 Collection OF73, 'Motion Pictures 1945', Franklin D. Roosevelt Library, Hyde Park, New York. Quoted in Neal Gabler: *An Empire of Their Own* (New York, 1988), p. 343.
23 John Davis: 'Notes on Warner Brothers Foreign Policy', in *The Velvet Light Trap*, no. 4 (Madison, Wisc., 1972), p. 27.
24 *The Sea Hawk* file, WSC.
25 Koch to McEwen, memorandum dated 20 March 1940, in *The Sea Hawk* file, WSC.
26 Ironically, this final speech was frequently cut from prints on its first release in the United States but retained for foreign distribution. Happily it has been restored to all prints on release today.
27 *The Nation*, 4 April 1934.
28 Gabler: *An Empire*, p. 119.
29 Richard Maltby: *Harmless Entertainment* (Metuchen, N.J. and London, 1983), p. 152.
30 Maltby: *Harmless Entertainment*, pp. 55–6.

BIBLIOGRAPHY

UNPUBLISHED SOURCES

Warner Brothers Collection, Department of Special Collections, Doheny Library, University of Southern California, Los Angeles (WSC)

MGM Special Collection, Doheny Library, University of Southern California, Los Angeles

RKO Special Collection, University Library, University of California, Los Angeles

Correspondence files of the Hays Office, now called the Association of Motion Picture and Television Producers Inc., deposited in the Library of the Academy of Motion Picture Arts and Sciences, Los Angeles, California (Hays Office documents)

The clippings files of the Academy of Motion Picture Arts and Sciences, deposited in the Library of the Academy of Motion Picture Arts and Sciences, Los Angeles, California

The clippings files of the British Film Institute, London W1

MAGAZINES AND PERIODICALS

The Hollywood Reporter
Daily Variety
Variety
New York Times
Motion Picture Herald
New Republic
The Nation
Photoplay
The Velvet Light Trap

BOOKS AND ARTICLES

Abbot, Edith. *The Tenements of Chicago* (Chicago, 1936).
Allen, Frederick Lewis. *Only Yesterday* (New York, 1959).
Allen, Frederick Lewis. *Since Yesterday* (New York, 1965).
Allsop, Kenneth. *The Bootleggers* (London, 1970).
Anger, Kenneth. *Hollywood Babylon* (Phoenix, Arizona, 1965).
Bainbridge, John. *Garbo* (New York, 1955).
Balio, Tino (ed.) *The American Film Industry* (Madison, Wisc., 1975).
Balio, Tino. *United Artists: The Company Built by the Stars* (Madison, Wisc.,1976).

Baxter, John. *Hollywood in the Thirties* (London, 1968).
Baxter, John. *The Gangster Film* (London, 1970).
Baxter, John. *The Cinema of Josef von Sternberg* (London, 1971).
Baxter, John. *The Cinema of John Ford* (London, 1972).
Baxter, John. *The Hollywood Exiles* (London, 1976).
Baxter, John. *Sixty Years of Hollywood* (London, 1973).
Behlmer, Rudy (compiler, editor and annotator). *Inside Warner Brothers* (New York, 1985).
Behlmer, Rudy. *Memo from David O. Selznick* (New York, 1973).
Bell, Daniel. *The End of Ideology* (Glencoe, Ill., 1960).
Berg, A. Scott. *Goldwyn* (London, 1989).
Bergman, Andrew. *We're in the Money* (New York, 1970).
Bernstein, Irving. *The Lean Years* (Baltimore, 1966).
Bessie, Alvah. *Inquisition in Eden* (East Berlin, 1967).
Brownlow, Kevin. *The Parade's Gone By* (New York, 1969).
Brownstein, Robert. *The Power and The Glitter* (New York, 1992).
Burns, James MacGregor. *Roosevelt: The Lion and the Fox* (New York, 1956).
Capra, Frank. 'Sacred Cows to the Slaughter', *Stage*, July 1936.
Capra, Frank. *The Name Above the Title* (New York, 1971).
Capra, Frank. *One Man – One Film*, American Film Institute pamphlet (Washington, 1971).
Caute, David. *The Great Fear* (London, 1978).
Ceplair, Larry and Englund, Steven. *The Inquisition in Hollywood: Politics in the Film Community, 1920–1960* (Garden City, N.Y., 1980).
Chaplin, Charles. *My Autobiography* (London, 1966).
Clurman, Harold. *The Fervent Years* (New York, 1957).
Coffee, Lenore. *Storyline* (London, 1973).
Cogley, John. *Report on Blacklisting I. Movies* (New York, 1956).
Cooke, Alistair (ed.). *Garbo and the Nightwatchmen* (London, 1937).
Corey, Lewis. *The Decline of American Capitalism* (New York, 1934).
Corliss, Richard. *The Hollywood Screenwriter* (New York, 1972).
Corliss, Richard. *Talking Pictures* (Woodstock, N.Y., 1974).
Crosby, P. *Three Cheers for the Red, Red and Red* (McLean, Va., 1936).
Crowther, Bosley. *The Lion's Share* (New York, 1957).
Crowther, Bosley. *Hollywood Rajah* (New York, 1961).
Dale, Edgar. *The Content of Motion Pictures* (New York, 1935).
Davis, Bette. *The Lonely Life* (New York, 1962).
Davis, John. 'Notes on Warner Brothers Foreign Policy', *The Velvet Light Trap*, no. 4, Madison, Wisc.
DeMille, Cecil B. *Autobiography* (London, 1969).
Doherty, Thomas. *Projections of War* (New York, 1993).
Dunne, Philip. *Take Two: A Life in Movies and Politics* (New York, 1980).
Durgnat,Raymond and Simmon, Scott. *King Vidor, American* (Berkeley and Los Angeles, 1988).
Eyles, Allen. *The Marx Brothers: Their World of Comedy* (London, 1966).
Filler, Louis (ed.), *The Anxious Years* (New York, 1963).
Finch, Christopher and Rosenkrantz, Linda (eds). *Gone Hollywood* (London, 1980).
Flynn, Errol. *My Wicked, Wicked Ways* (London, 1960).
Freedland, Michael. *The Warner Brothers* (London, 1983).
French, Philip. *The Movie Moguls* (London, 1969).
French, Philip. 'Incitements against Violence', *Sight and Sound* (winter 1967/8).

Fried, Albert (ed.). *The Jeffersonian and Hamiltonian Traditions in American Politics* (New York, 1968).
Fridel, Frank. *The New Deal and the American People* (Englewood Cliffs, N.J., 1964).
Gabler, Neal. *An Empire of their Own: How the Jews Invented Hollywood* (New York, 1989).
Galbraith, John Kenneth. *The Great Crash* (London, 1955).
Garraty, John A. *The Great Depression* (New York, 1987).
Gassner, J. and Nichols, D. (eds). *Twenty Best Film Plays* (New York, 1943).
Goldman, Eric F. *Rendezvous With Destiny* (New York, 1961).
Gomery, Douglas. *The Hollywood Studio System* (Basingstoke, 1986).
Gomery, Douglas. 'Warner Bros and Sound', *Screen* (Spring 1976).
Goodman, Ezra. *The Fifty Year Decline and Fall of Hollywood* (New York, 1961).
Green, Abel and Laurie, Joe Jr. *Showbiz: From Vaude to Video* (Garden City, N.Y., 1952).
Green, Constance. *The Rise of Urban America* (New York, 1967).
Griffith, Richard. *Frank Capra*, British Film Institute pamphlet (London, 1948).
Griffith, Richard and Mayer, Arthur. *The Movies* (London, 1948).
Gussow, Mel. *Don't Say Yes Until I Finish Talking* (New York, 1972).
Haider, C. *Do We Want Fascism?* (New York, 1955).
Hampton, Benjamin B. *A History of the American Film Industry* (New York, 1970).
Harmetz, Aljean. *Round Up The Usual Suspects* (London, 1993).
Hawley, Ellis W. *The New Deal and the Problem of Monopoly* (Princeton, N.J., 1966).
Hecht, Ben. *A Child of the Century* (New York, 1934).
Hecht, Ben. *Gaily, Gaily* (New York, 1963).
Higham, Charles and Greenberg, Joel. *The Celluloid Muse* (New York, 1969).
Higham. John. *Strangers in the Land* (New York, 1967).
Hofstadter, Richard. *The Age of Reform* (New York, 1955).
Hofstadter, Richard. *Great Issues in American History Vol. 1* (New York, 1958).
Hofstadter, Richard. *The Paranoid Style in American Politics* (London, 1966).
Hofstadter, Richard. *The American Political Tradition* (London, 1967).
Howe, Irving. *The Immigrant Jews of New York* (London, 1976).
Hutmacher, J. J. *Senator Robert F. Wagner and the Rise of Urban Liberalism* (New York, 1968).
Ickes, H. L. *The Secret Diaries of Harold L. Ickes* (New York, 1954).
Inglis, Ruth. *Freedom of the Movies* (Chicago, 1947).
Izod, John. *Hollywood and the Box Office 1895–1988* (London, 1988).
Jacobs, Lewis. *The Rise of the American Film* (New York, 1939).
Jarvie, I. C. *Towards a Sociology of Cinema* (London, 1970).
Jobes, Gertrude. *Motion Picture Empire* (Hamden, Conn., 1966).
Jowett, Garth. *Film: The Democratic Art* (Boston, 1976).
Kael, Pauline. *I Lost It at the Movies* (New York, 1969).
Kael, Pauline. *Kiss Kiss Bang Bang* (New York, 1969).
Kahn, Gordon. *Hollywood on Trial* (New York, 1948).
Kazin, Alfred. *Starting Out in the Thirties* (Boston, 1966).
Keats, John. *Howard Hughes* (New York, 1970).
Kempton, Murray. *Part of Our Time* (New York, 1967).
Kerstein, Lincoln. 'James Cagney and the American Hero', *Hound and Horn* (April/ June 1932).
Klingender, F. D. and Legg, S. *Money Behind the Screen* (London, 1937).
Kobler, John. *Al Capone* (Greenwich, Conn., 1972).
Kracauer, Siegfried. *From Caligari to Hitler* (Princeton, 1947).
Lambert, Gavin. *Norma Shearer: A Life* (London, 1990).

Lash, Joseph P. *Eleanor and Franklin* (New York, 1973).
Lasky, Jesse. *I Blow My Own Horn* (New York, 1957).
Latham, Aaron. *Crazy Sundays* (New York, 1970).
Lawrence, Jerome. *Actor: The Life and Times of Paul Muni* (New York, 1974).
Lawson, John Howard. *Film: The Creative Process* (New York, 1963).
Lee, Alva. *America Swings to the Left* (New York, 1933).
Leff, Leonard J. and Simmons, J. *The Dame in the Kimono* (London, 1990).
Leighton, Isabel (ed.). *The Aspirin Age* (London, 1964).
LeRoy, Mervyn. *Take One* (London, 1974).
Leuchtenburg, W. E. *The Perils of Prosperity* (Chicago, 1958).
Leuchtenburg, W. E. *Franklin D. Roosevelt and the New Deal* (New York, 1963).
Levin, M. (ed.). *Hollywood and the Great Fan Magazines* (New York, 1970).
Lubell, Samuel. *The Future of American Politics* (New York, 1956).
Lubove, R. S. *The Progressives and the Slums* (Pittsburgh, 1962).
Lynd, H. S. and H. M. *Middletown in Transition* (New York, 1937).
McArthur, Colin. *Underworld USA* (London, 1972).
McArthur, Colin. 'The Roots of the Western', *Cinema*, no. 4 (1969).
McBride, Joseph. *Frank Capra: The Catastrophe of Success* (London, 1992).
Macdonald, Dwight. *Against the American Grain* (New York, 1962).
Macdonald, Dwight. *On Movies* (New York, 1971).
McGilligan, Pat (ed.). *Backstory: Interviews with Screenwriters of Hollywood's Golden Years* (Berkeley, 1986).
McKelvey, B. *The Emergence of Metropolitan America 1915–66* (New Brunswick, N.J., 1966).
Maltby, Richard. 'The Political Economy of Hollywood: The Studio System' in Philip Davies and Brian Neve (eds), *Cinema, Politics and Society in America* (Manchester, 1981).
Maltby, Richard. *Harmless Entertainment* (Metuchen, N.J. and London, 1983).
Manchester, William. *The Glory and the Dream* (Boston, 1974).
Marx, Samuel. *Mayer and Thalberg: The Make Believe Saints* (New York, 1980).
May, Henry F. *The End of American Innocence* (London, 1946).
Miller, Merle and Rhodes, Evan. *Only You Dick Daring*(New York, 1964).
Mitchell, B. *Depression Decade* (New York, 1947).
Moley, Raymond. *After Seven Years* (New York, 1939).
Morin, Edgar. *The Stars* (London, 1960).
Mosley, Leonard. *Zanuck: The Rise and Fall of Hollywood's Last Tycoon* (Boston, 1984).
Mowry, G. E. *The Urban Nation* (New York, 1968).
Pasley, F. D. *Al Capone* (London, 1931).
Pelling, H. *American Labor* (Chicago, 1960).
Penguin Film Review, Nos 2, 5, 6, 7 (London, 1947–8).
Perkins, Frances. *The Roosevelt I Knew* (Edinburgh, 1947).
Perlman, S. and Taft, P. *History of Labor in the United States 1896–1932* (New York, 1935).
Perlman, W. J. (ed.). *Movies on Trial* (New York, 1971).
Pickford, Mary. *Sunshine and Shadow* (New York, 1955).
President's Commission on *Recent Social Trends, vol. I* (New York, 1933).
Ramsaye, Terry. *A Millon and One Nights* (London, 1964).
Rauch, Basil. *A History of the New Deal* (New York, 1963).
Richards, Jeffrey. 'Frank Capra and the Populist Cinema', *Cinema*. no. 5 (February 1970).
Richards, Jeffrey. *Visions of Yesterday* (London, 1973).

Robey, R. *Roosevelt versus Recovery* (New York, 1934).
Roddick, Nick. *A New Deal in Entertainment: Warner Brothers in the 1930s* (London, 1983).
Roffman, Peter and Purdy, Jim. *The Hollywood Social Problem Film* (Bloomington, 1981).
Rogers, J. H. *Capitlalism in Crisis* (New Haven, 1938).
Rollins, A. B. (ed.). *Franklin D. Roosevelt and the Age of Action* (New York, 1960).
Roosevelt, Eleanor. *This Is My Story* (New York, 1937).
Roosevelt, Eleanor. *This I Remember* (New York, 1949).
Rosenbaum, Herbert D. and Batelme, Elizabeth (eds). *FDR: The Man, The Myth, The Era 1882–1945* (Westport, Conn., 1987).
Rossiter, A. P. *Angel With Horns* (London, 1960).
Rosten, Leo C. *Hollywood: The Movie Colony, The Movie Makers* (New York, 1941).
Schatz, Thomas. *The Genius of the System: Hollywood Filmmaking in the Studio Era* (New York, 1988).
Schlesinger, Arthur M. Jr. *The Crisis of the Old Order* (London, 1958).
Schlesinger, Arthur M. Jr. *The Coming of the New Deal* (London, 1960).
Schlesinger, Arthur M. Jr. *The Politics of Upheaval* (London, 1961).
Schlesinger, Arthur M. Jr. 'When the Movies Really Counted', *Show* (April 1965).
Schulberg, Budd. *Moving Pictures* (London, 1982).
Schwartz, Nancy Lynn. *The Hollywood Writers' Wars* (New York, 1982).
Seldes, Gilbert. *Movies for the Millions* (London, 1937).
Shannon, David A. (ed.). *The Great Depression* (Englewood Cliffs, N.J., 1960).
Sherwood, Robert E. *Roosevelt and Hopkins* (New York, 1948).
Shindler, Colin. *Hollywood Goes To War: Films & American Society 1939–1952* (London, 1979).
Shipman, David. *The Great Movie Stars – The Golden Years* (New York, 1970).
Short, Kenneth (ed.). *Feature Films as History* (Knoxville, Tenn., 1983).
Shulman, Irving. *Harlow* (London, 1964).
Sinclair, Andrew. *The Age of Excess* (London, 1962).
Sinclair, Upton. *Upton Sinclair Presents William Fox* (Los Angeles, 1933).
Sitkoff, Howard (ed.). *Fifty Years After: The New Deal Evaluated* (Philadelphia, 1985).
Sklar, Robert. *Movie-Made America* (New York, 1975).
Sklar, Robert. *City Boys* (Princeton, 1992).
Smith, H. N. *Virgin Land* (New York, 1950).
Sokolsky, G. 'America Drifts to Fascism', *American Mercury* (July 1934).
Spatz, Jonas. *Hollywood in Fiction* (The Hague, 1969).
Spivak, J. L. *America Faces the Barricades* (New York, 1935).
Stebbins, R. 'Mr Capra Goes To Town', *New Theatre* (May 1936).
Swanberg, W. A. *Citizen Hearst* (New York, 1963).
Taft, Philip. *Organized Labor in American History* (New York, 1964).
Taylor, John Russell. *Strangers in Paradise: The Hollywood Emigres 1933–1950* (London, 1983).
Taylor, Robert Lewis. *W. C. Fields – His Follies and Fortunes* (New York, 1968).
Terkel, Studs. *Hard Times* (New York, 1971).
Thomas, Bob. *Clown Prince of Hollywood* (New York, 1990).
Thomas, Bob. *King Cohn* (London, 1967).
Thomas, Bob. *Thalberg* (New York, 1970).
Thomas, Bob. *Selznick* (London, 1972).
Thorp, Margaret F. *America at the Movies* (New Haven, 1939 and London, 1946).
Turner, F. J. *The Frontier in American History* (New York, 1945).
Trumbo, Dalton. *Additional Dialogue* (New York, 1972).

Twelve Southerners. *I'll Take My Stand* (New York, 1972).
Vidor, King. *A Tree is a Tree* (New York, 1953).
Viertel, Salka. *The Kindness of Strangers* (New York, 1969).
Walker, Alexander. *The Celluloid Sacrifice* (London, 1966).
Walker, Alexander. *Stardom* (London, 1970).
Walker, Alexander. *The Shattered Silents* (London, 1986).
Wallis, Hal B. with Higham, Charles. *Starmaker: The Autobiography of Hal Wallis* (New York, 1980).
Warner, Jack L. with Jennings, Dean. *My First Hundred Years in Hollywood* (New York, 1964).
Warshow, Robert. *The Immediate Experience* (New York, 1970).
White, W. L. 'Pare Lorentz', *Scribners* (January 1939).
Williams, T. Harry. *Huey Long* (New York, 1969).
Zukor, Adolph. *The Public Is Never Wrong* (London, 1954).

ORAL EVIDENCE

Interviews conducted with:
Donald Ogden Stewart, London, May, June 1971
William Wellman, Los Angeles, 14 February 1972
Frank Capra, La Qunita, 18 February 1972
Morrie Ryskind, Beverly Hills, 23 February 1972
Mervyn LeRoy, Bel Air, 2 March 1972
Pandro S. Berman, Beverly Hills, 10 March 1972
Robert Lord, Hollywood, March, April, May, June 1972
Lester Cole, San Francisco, 23 April 1972
Henry Fonda, Bel Air, 3 May 1972
John Howard Lawson, Van Nuys, 12 May 1972

INDEX

Page numbers in bold denote a major section/chapter devoted to subject